To Cami,
Xmas 2009
READ & REJOICE
in your TALENT

Dick + Deine

Dai Vernon: A Biography

Dai Vernon: A Biography
Artist • Magician • Muse | 1894-1941

David Ben

SQUASH PUBLISHING

Library and Archives Canada Cataloguing in Publication
Ben, David
Dai Vernon : a biography : artist, magician, muse, 1894-1941 / David Ben.
Includes bibliographical references and index.
ISBN 0-9780675-0-9

1. Vernon, Dai, 1894-1941. 2. Magicians--Canada--Biography. 3. Magic--History--20th century. I. Title.

GV1545.V47B45 2006   793.8092   C2006-902473-1

Cover design by Kevin McGroarty

Book layout and design by Gabe Fajuri

Copyright © 2006 by David Ben.

All rights reserved. No part of this publication may be reproduced or transmitted in any form or by any means, electronic or mechanical, including photocopy, recording or any information storage and retrieval system now known or to be invented, without permission in writing from the publisher.

Squash Publishing
Chicago, IL 60618
www.squashpublishing.com

Magicana
15 Madison Ave.
Toronto, Ontario
M5R 2S2
www.magicana.com

ISBN 0-9744681-5-0

First Edition
10 9 8 7 6 5 4 3 2 1

For the children of magicians: may you grow up and continue to believe in miracles.

"You are all a bunch of pessimists. The chap with the goods will make good."

—David Verner
New York, 1916

Contents

1. Railroads and Steamboats / 1
2. Artifice, Ruse and Subterfuge / 31
3. The Man Who Fooled Houdini / 64
4. Inner Circles / 99
5. Shadows With Shears / 131
6. Phantoms of the Card Table / 161
7. Centers and Secrets / 196
8. Midway To Manhattan / 230
9. Over The Rainbow / 263
10. Mercury Falling / 299

End Notes / 334
Sources / 339
Bibliography / 342
Acknowledgements / 356
Index / 358

Chapter One
Railroads and Steamboats

Dazed and confused, arms bandaged and in slings, propped up in a hospital bed like a paperclip that had been bent out of shape, the patient was surrounded by men in long white coats holding clipboards. He finally realized that they were addressing him.

"What do you mean, 'Can I hold the pen?'"

"We are very concerned about gangrene, Mr. Verner, and I am sorry to say, we may have to amputate your right arm. We require your authorization."

"What? My arm? I am not going to sign anything. Where is Dr. Daley? I need to see Dr. Daley."

In November 1941, at the age of 47, David Verner, the greatest sleight-of-hand artist of the twentieth century, a man described by his peers as the James Joyce of magic—someone who comes along once a century and changes everything—was being asked to sanction the end of his career. The staff at Bellevue Hospital had no notion of Verner's life, work and passion, nor that his arms were the instrument of his art.

Weighted down by a pail of mercury on a Robert Moses construction project on East River Drive, Verner, known publicly as Dai Vernon, had fallen six stories into the East River, one of the tributaries that separates Manhattan from the mainland. Seeing a worker struggling to carry a load over a wooden plank and up a steel girder, Vernon had offered to help. He underestimated both the weight of the pail and the strength of the board; the board snapped. Vernon fell, bouncing off wood and steel like a rag doll and tumbling into the icy, oily water below. He struggled for air, his arms broken in the fall. Yanked from the water by co-workers whose only knowledge of first aid involved a full bottle of whiskey to numb the pain, Vernon was bundled up and carted to the hospital. Things couldn't have been worse. Or so he thought.

Now they wanted to cut off his arm.

For Dai Vernon, a man who had dedicated his life to magic, being a one-armed magician embodied the unthinkable, a life not worth living. Houdini may have proclaimed that his mind was the key that set him free, but, without his hands, escaping from a paper bag would have been impossible. Vernon was an innovator, someone who went to great lengths to ensure that the art progressed, that it did not stagnate or wither away under the weight of mediocrity. His specialty was sleight-of-hand, the fuel that stoked the fire of magic.

But why was the world's greatest sleight-of-hand magician working on an East River construction project? It seems an odd and unlikely place to find a magician, particularly one of Vernon's stature.

Vernon was working on the project because he was an artist more than a magician. Yes, he did tricks and he performed them with grace, elegance and an economy of motion like no one before him, but, like many artists, he was more interested in perfecting his craft than in presenting it to the public. His obsession came at a cost. He had two sons, fifteen-year-old Edward and nine-year-old Derek, and a wife, Jeanne, who reminded him constantly of the difficulty they had making ends meet. He needed *some* money to survive and had been presented with three opportunities to bring in money for his family's expenses.

Before turning to the construction job, however, Vernon was offered an engagement performing an act he created featuring a Chinese character, Dr. Chung, at the Majestic Theatre in Paterson, New Jersey. Although he did not perform often, when he did, he was well paid. Another opportunity, one which would entail travel out of New York, was to cut silhouettes at a function run by the Junior League in Asheville, North Carolina. Vernon was an expert at cutting silhouettes, the New York *Daily News* having described him as *the* master of this once popular art. Vernon had often fallen back on this trade to make ends meet. His third choice was the chance to earn a steady income as a project manager on a construction site on the East River.

Railroads and Steamboats

Vernon had met the main contractor for the construction project at the apartment of an amateur magician named Sam Margules. The contractor was looking for people who could read blueprints. He was willing to pay them $37.50 to $50 per day. Vernon was told that it would be an easy job. He had to be on site at 7:30 am and remain there until 3:00 p.m., walk around and look busy. Vernon had studied Engineering at the Royal Military College in Kingston, Ontario, so he knew blueprints. Vernon saw the job as an opportunity to earn a decent salary while still being able to perform his magic at night. His wife, Jeanne, was much more succinct: "You have never worked a day in your life. It's time you did some honest work."

Now, two weeks later, doctors wanted to amputate.

Vernon had always loved magic.

Most magicians remember the first trick that drew them to the craft. It leaves an indelible mark. It was Vernon's father who showed him his first trick, at least the one that made a lasting impression. The exact date was June 11, 1899—Vernon's fifth birthday.

His father, James Verner, was a tall and handsome man with a handlebar moustache and a quiet Victorian disposition. He looked at Vernon and said, "I'm going to show you something you will really like." James then asked his son to bring a box of colored chalk and an eggcup to the table. The chalk was easy to find, as David was always coloring things, inspired by his uncle, Frederick Verner, a painter and member of the Royal Academy in London. Next, he went to the kitchen and picked up a wooden eggcup from the cupboard. When he returned to the dining room, his father whisked away the tablecloth and invited the birthday boy to join him at the oak table. His father removed three pieces of chalk from the box—red, green and yellow—and drew three "X's" on the bare wood.

"Choose any of the three colors," he said.

Vernon pointed to the red mark. His father took the eggcup, showed its interior to his son, and placed it mouth down over the red mark.

"Watch," he said.

His father slowly and deliberately placed the palm of his left hand beneath the table, centering it below the position of the red X, the mark now concealed by the eggcup. After a short dramatic pause, his father whacked his hand down, creating a loud bang, onto the cup. James withdrew his hand from beneath the table. There was

David Frederick Wingfield Verner—Dai Vernon, ca. 1897.

now a faint trace of colored chalk—a red X—on the palm of his hand.

Vernon was stunned.

"Can you do it again, father?" he asked. "Can you do it with the green this time?" Vernon's father repeated the trick over and over again, always with the same results.

Vernon asked his father how he had learned to do that and the reply was, "I learned a few tricks from my father; I was a boy once, you know."

James' own father, Arthur Cole Verner, had indeed taught him how to perform a few simple magic tricks. Arthur Cole Verner was born on March 28, 1811, the second son of David Verner, in County Armagh, Ireland. Although he came from an impoverished family of Anglo-Irish stock, his family held upper class associations. Arthur Cole Verner's uncle was William Verner, a Lt-Col who would serve at Corunna, Orthes and Toulouse, and whose gallant performance at the Battle of Waterloo would earn him a Baronetage.

When James Verner showed his son his first magic trick in 1899, magic was in the midst of a Golden Age. Larger than life personalities performed supernatural feats on stages throughout the world, all under the guise of theatrical entertainment. When Arthur Cole Verner first witnessed a performance of magic, it was an art still shrouded in superstition. Those who were not frightened by the

Railroads and Steamboats

performances of wandering entertainers would often seek their counsel to cure ailments or cast a magic spell. Signor Blitz of Moravia, a rather grandiose stage name for an Englishman named Antoni van Zandt, arrived in Dublin in 1832. In his memoir, *Fifty Years In The Magic Circle*, Blitz wrote,

> *Immediately after reaching Dublin, I commenced my entertainments, remaining nearly six months, amusing the citizens in public and private, and as few persons of my profession had ever visited that city, the impression I produced on the minds of many was extraordinary. Numbers consulted me respecting diseases and complaints, seeking advice and medicine, supposing I possessed the power to relieve pain, and suffering, and all the ills life is subjected to.*

> *When I justly remonstrated with these people, assuring them of my want of knowledge and inability to render them the necessary relief, their sad expression of countenance and disappointment frequently gave way to tears. Such scenes were frequent as they were lamentable and trying.*

It is not surprising that people would turn to magicians for counsel. Magic was often performed in taverns and on fairgrounds, by what we would describe today as "buskers" or street performers. These performers would attract a crowd to a table or booth, often assembling the mob to hear a sales pitch for a product or service such as a magical elixir that would cure all aliments. Occasionally the crowd would be assembled so that confederates could pick a pocket or two.

Arthur Cole Verner, however, was a learned man, having graduated from Trinity College, Dublin in 1828. He was reared on the classics and recognized these performances for what they were: entertainment designed to relieve the burdens of daily life. Life in Ireland was hard. Arthur Cole Verner attempted to follow the example of his uncle by joining the military but was rejected because of a deformed right arm. So in 1835, like many others, he decided to embark on a new life and immigrated to Upper Canada, now Ontario.

Initially, he attempted farming the fields of Southern Ontario, rich with soil deposited by the glacial retreat thousands of years earlier. He soon returned, however, to his natural calling, education, and obtained his first position as the principal of Hammondsville Grammar School, some six miles northeast of Oakville, Ontario. A natural leader, Verner became actively involved with the community and was a participant in the Rebellion of 1837 in which William Lyon Mackenzie marched into the city of York, now Toronto, to break apart the Family Compact, the collection of families that controlled the political and economic life of the city.

It was around 1842 when the Verner family moved from Hammondsville to Guelph. There, Verner started the Guelph (or Wellington District) Grammar School, initially in his home and then in a new facility. Dai Vernon's own father, James William David Verner was born on March 14, 1843, in this town, a middle child, one of nine, two of whom died in infancy. The Verner family returned to Hammondsville in 1847 when Arthur was hired as master of Oakville Common School.

Described by his students as an inspiration, he was considered the best Greek and Hebrew scholar in his part of the country. Although he was a religious man—Verner belonged to a sect known as the Holy Catholic Apostolic Church—he was not opposed to performing a little magic in the classroom to illustrate how the senses could be deceived.

Arthur Cole Verner was appointed the head of Halton County Grammar School in 1854. He harbored, however, greater ambition and resigned from that post the same year to found and develop a village south of his home. He called it Vernerville. Verner believed there would be high demand for produce due to the outbreak of teh Crimean War, and he wanted to profit from it. Verner was, in essence, a pioneer and brought his family up in the wilderness. Although a number of artisans moved to Vernerville, the town did not prosper and the Verners later moved to Sandwich, a town of five hundred people near Windsor, Ontario and Detroit, Michigan on the U.S.-Canadian border.

While Arthur Cole Verner was cutting a path in the woods of a fledgling country, magic was shedding the skin of superstition, at least in the larger centers of Europe, primarily through the work and influence of two magicians, Jean Eugène Robert-Houdin and Johann Nepomuk Hofzinser.

On July 3, 1845, after years of apprenticeship as both a watchmaker and a mechanic of fine automata, Robert-Houdin opened his *Soirées Fantastiques* at the Palais-Royal, 164 Galerie de Valois in Paris.

Railroads and Steamboats

Magicians who had been regarded with suspicion either because of superstition or social standing now had a champion in Robert-Houdin. His manner was cultured and his magic was rooted in science, not specters. He combined mechanical apparatus, some based on scientific discoveries and others on faux-science, with sleight-of-hand and created a balanced program that his audience knew was based on ingenuity rather than witchcraft.

Hofzinser was born on June 19, 1806 and, like Robert-Houdin, opened in 1857 his own parlor, his Salon Hofzinser, where on three evenings a week in he presented "An Hour of Deception" for intimate gatherings of patrons. Hofzinser, too, was considered by the public and by his peers to be a great artist. A gifted originator of card tricks with poetic plots and devices, he also created many novel effects that relied more on sleight-of-hand than mechanical ingenuity.

Secrets were the lifeblood of the mystery merchant. Magicians kept their secrets not only from the public, but also from each other. In the 1840s, few books disclosed the inner machinations of the magician's craft. The psychological and technical minutia that performers use to ignite each individual audience member's imagination remained hidden. These secrets were passed on person to person. This is why, in that era, most professional magicians began their careers as a sorcerer's apprentice, first witnessing the performance of an itinerant conjuror and then pleading with him to take them on as an assistant, committing industrial espionage to pilfer the secrets. Many still do.

As magic shows gained in popularity, amateurs—and even celebrities—became attracted to the fold. Charles Dickens, entranced by the performances of Robert-Houdin at St. James Theatre, London, soon developed enough proficiency in the craft to enable him to perform his magic under various pseudonyms including "The Unparalleled Necromancer Rhia Rhama Rhoos, educated cabalistically in the Orange Groves of Salamanca and the Ocean Caves of Alum Bay." W. & F. Hamley, Ltd., the large and world-famous toyshop founded in 1760, introduced a magic department around 1876, eventually adding to its magical wares in 1899 when it absorbed Joseph Bland's Magical & Conjuring Repository. Most significantly, an English barrister and amateur magician named Angelo Lewis began to write a serial column on conjuring for *Every Boy's Magazine* in 1871 under the pen name of Professor Hoffmann.

He continued this column for five years before releasing it in book form in 1876 under the title *Modern Magic*.

Heavily criticized at the time by conjurors of the period as a scandalous exposé of the craft, *Modern Magic* introduced the secret art to aspiring young magicians everywhere and ushered in a true amateur class of practitioners. The book provided modern descriptions of the best tricks from pivotal works in French as well as proper technique in sleight-of-hand, and it detailed the secrets of mechanical apparatus used by professional magicians then appearing on the London stage. Although magicians cried, "Exposure!" and predicted the demise of their profession as every aspiring amateur magician now had unfettered access to their stock and trade, other books followed in its wake.

Although the center of the magic world was London, it did not take long for the craft to take root in America. Magic tricks were advertised and sold in America as early as 1749. By 1885, the premier magic depot in America was Martinka & Co., established by Francis and Antonio Martinka in what is now referred to as Chelsea, the flower district on New York's Lower West Side. Martinka supplied the great European magicians with much of their apparatus. The brothers employed seven or eight employees, some of them mechanics, some craftsmen, some clerks, all managed under the watchful eye of stern Mrs. Martinka. The business even had a small theatre, the Palace of Mystery, complete with small stage in the rear of the building that became the testing ground for the wonders produced. To gain access to Martinka's, however, you had to be a professional magician and professional magicians were few and far between. In addition, customers had to know what they wanted and were expected to place an order and then depart, this being no place for idle chitchat unless, of course, the customer was a professional of some standing in the field. Such professionals might be invited into the back room, and a sign of the quality of their professional work would be the quiet advice to which you now had open access. Martinka & Co. had a professional interest in guarding the secrets of the magic trade lest their commercial value diminish if information were revealed or passed on indiscriminately.

Back in Canada, Arthur Cole Verner had become a community leader. He was the warden of St. John's Church and was elected the mayor of Sandwich in 1878, 1884 and 1885. However, his wife, Harriet Ayre—who came from Jersey in the Channel Islands—died

Railroads and Steamboats

William J. Hilliar manipulates cards on the stage in Martinka's Magical Palace.

in October of 1888. Arthur himself was ill at the time, and after his wife's passing he moved from Sandwich to Ottawa to be with his son, James. James had just moved across the river from Hull to Ottawa to take a position as a clerk in the Patent and Copyright Branch of the Canadian Government, then part of the Department of Agriculture. James Verner lived on Metcalfe Street, a short walk to the Parliament Buildings where the Ministry and his office were located.

In March 1890, having recovered from his wife's passing, a robust Arthur Cole Verner had a fall that caused internal hemorrhaging. He died on April 2, 1890. He was in his eightieth year. His obituary described him thus: "Socially, he was a most genial, considerate and entertaining gentleman. His charitableness was a proverb among all who knew him, and as a matter of course he was the victim of many impostors." One can only speculate as to the identity and practices of the many imposters, the very type of people that his grandson would find so intriguing in years to come.

In 1893, James Verner courted and married Helen E. Erskine, a Presbyterian twenty years his junior. She joined the Church of England to marry the Anglican James. The wedding ceremony took

James, Helen, David (Dai) and infant Charles Napier. The Verner family, ca. 1899.

place in Galt, Ontario, the hometown of the bride and a short distance from Guelph, Ontario, where James Verner himself had been born. The couple returned to Ottawa and James Verner continued his employment as a clerk at the Department of Agriculture.

Their son, David Verner, was born on June 11, 1894 in Ottawa, Canada, the capital city of a fledgling country. He was christened David Frederick Wingfield Verner. Both parents agreed that David had to be in the boy's name. Helen's father was named David, and James Verner had David as one of his own given names, taken from his paternal grandfather. So David was decided upon without any argument. Frederick was given to the child in honor of James Verner's brother, Frederick, the artist who was a member of the Royal Academy in London. The new couple placed nine other names for the child in a hat, one of which was "Wingfield" from the father's side and another "Erskine" from the mother's side. "Wingfield" was drawn.

By now, North America was a full participant in magic's Golden Age. America always embraced one master of magic at a time, and the man for that time was Alexander Herrmann, who traveled from town to town on the new railroads that were spreading exponentially across America. Herrmann was the veritable personification

Railroads and Steamboats

of a magician. Whereas the old school cloaked each performance in a mysterious manner, Herrmann made his performances joyous occasions, preferring to end each trick in a manner that filled the theatre with laughter. The public considered him superior to any other wizard they had witnessed. He became known as Herrmann the Great.

In March 1895, Martinka & Co. published *Mahatma*, "the only paper in the United States devoted to the interests of magicians, spiritualists, mesmerists, etc." Single copies sold for ten cents and Vol. 1, No. 1 featured Robert-Houdin, "Father of Modern Magic" on the cover. Herrmann the Great died of heart failure in his private railway coach at Ellicottville, New York on December 17, 1896, en route to a scheduled performance in Bradford, Pennsylvania. Although the New York *World* proclaimed that magic itself had died with Herrmann, magic survived, and once the air had cleared, Herrmann's chief rival, Harry Kellar, occupied the highest place among magicians in America.

Like those before him, Kellar learned from his employers and then departed, exploiting the novelties and the mysteries he had learned, adding additional miracles he had witnessed traveling in England, South America, and on the Continent. Eventually he settled in the United States. He never toured his show beyond the United States, Canada and Mexico after 1884. Although Kellar became America's preeminent magician only after the passing of Alexander Herrmann, by 1898 he had earned the love and respect of the American public in his own right, having traveled extensively and completed repeat performances in the principal cities of the United States.

In the late 1890s another American magician would also alter the course of magic history. His name was Dr. J. William Elliott, born in the state of Maine on April 27th, 1874. He attended Harvard Medical College and graduated from Bellevue Medical School in New York. His obsession, however, was not medicine, but magic. In order to practice sophisticated sleight-of-hand with playing cards for hours without being disturbed, he was known to rent a small room or closet in each hotel wherever he traveled. In 1899, the year in which Dai Vernon was discovering his first magic trick, Dr. Elliott was advertised as "The Champion Card Manipulator of the World." He had a major impact on sleight-of-hand, demonstrating the impressive achievements that could be won only through fastidious and diligent practice. Elliott developed a technique in which he could secretly transfer the concealed card from the back of his hand to the front and then back again—invisibly—with a turn of his wrist and, equally important, a technique for apparently plucking the cards from thin air. He taught this secret technique to several confidants, one of whom peddled it to Harry Houdini.

Houdini, born Ehrich Weiss, adopted the name Houdini in homage to Jean Eugène Robert-Houdin. Houdini was playing dime museums when he met Elliott. Dime museums were buildings divided into two parts, the first for curios, freaks or an exhibition, and the second for a variety show that featured performers with little or no special staging requirements. The magician who could manipulate playing cards was a natural fit and would be expected to perform from five to fourteen shows per day. Dr. Elliott also taught the technique to another young magician who would soon gain international fame as a card manipulator. His name was Howard Thurston. The era of manipulation—particularly card manipulation, the act of magicians plucking playing cards from thin air, making them vanish and then reappear—was born. Houdini billed himself as the "King of Cards" and Howard Thurston borrowed the moniker of his teacher, without permission, and portrayed himself as "The World Champion of Card Manipulation."

During this time, the gulf between professionals and amateurs grew. The amateur class, inspired by the books of Robert-Houdin, Professor Hoffmann, and Edwin Sachs, developed an insatiable appetite for more secrets. Their appetite was further whetted by the performances of touring professionals. Professionals, on the other hand, sought tricks and techniques that would persuade the vaudeville circuit operators and managers such as Edward Albee, B. F. Keith and Martin Beck to put them on stage.

Of course, Dai Vernon was oblivious to these developments. He wanted to discover how his father could knock a chalk mark—any mark—through the family table and onto his hand. One day, when he was five or six, he took apart the tongue and groove leaves of the table and made a slide from the leaves, one on which he could drive his toy trains. It was at that moment that he saw the marks under the table exactly where his father had been doing the trick. The chalk marks were drawn quite heavily beneath the table. He reasoned that his father had secretly placed the marks—one for each color—beneath the table before the performance. As such, it

Railroads and Steamboats

would not matter what color he selected; his father could make any color appear to pass through the table and onto his hand by striking his palm on the appropriate mark beneath the table. His father had recourse to multiple options, each of which would achieve the desired result.

Many people who discover the modus operandi behind a magic trick are often disappointed by its inherent simplicity. Secrets are perceived as valuable as long as they remain hidden. Vernon, however, was elated by his discovery. He had figured out not only how his father had performed the trick, but also how he was able to immediately repeat the performance regardless of which color chalk had been named. He had to tell his father that he had figured out how the trick had been performed.

"Father, could you please do that trick again? The one with the chalk."

James Verner told his son to bring the chalk and the eggcup to the table and he would do his best. Unaware that his son had discovered his secret, James chalked three marks on the oak table—red, yellow and green—and asked his son which of the three should be covered with the eggcup. Red. Again, with the dramatic flair that had become routine, James displayed the palm of his left hand and then placed it beneath the table. He brought his right hand down with force on the base of the eggcup and then withdrew the hand from beneath the table, the faint outline of chalk scored onto its palm. This time, the response from his child was muted.

"Father, would you mind if I looked under the table?"

Before James Verner could articulate a response, his son dived beneath the table. He knew the exact location of the treasure buried deep in the lagoon and he wasn't going to wait a moment more to retrieve it.

"Aha!"

James Verner had to confess that his son had discovered the secret to the cornerstone of his magical repertoire. Perhaps it was time to teach his son the one or two magic tricks that he had learned from his own father—a card trick in which the ace of hearts would rise magically to the top of the pack and a string game known as the Cat's Cradle.

Vernon had a voracious appetite for information and, as both tricks appealed to his imagination, he soon needed more. First, he collected string tricks. He collected them like other children collect baseball cards. He carried links of string in his pocket with which to practice and, any time he found a boy, girl or friend of the family who could do a string trick, he would ask for the secret. He also scoured magazines, in particular *The Boys Own Paper*, an English periodical targeted for young boys, and *Chums*, its American counterpart, for additional tricks. Soon he had forty of them. He wanted, however, fifty-two, one for each card represented in the pack of Little Lord Fauntleroy cards he also carried with him. It took a while—an eternity for a young boy—but by the time he was six, he had completed his task.

Vernon exhibited this trait, the quest for information and the obsession to master new skills in areas of interest, throughout his formative years. Soon after Guiglielmo Marconi invented wireless communication, the youngster, following instructions in *The Boys Own Paper*, erected his own system of wireless communication that spanned the length of his bedroom. He converted his mother's manual sewing machine into an electric one and then fabricated baseball pennants of his favorite teams, Harvard, Yale and Princeton, in order to experiment with the different stitches that were illustrated in the handbook that accompanied the machine. It wasn't enough to know that baseball bats were made of wood. He needed to know the type of wood that was used. He constructed toy submarines, powered by tin propellers and rubber bands, in a makeshift woodworking shop in the basement. He then unleashed the vessels in the family bathtub and watched them circumnavigate the basin.

He was interested in anything that could be considered out of the ordinary. Feats that required physical dexterity or coordination were attacked with equal vengeance. If it looked hard or sensational, Vernon had to try to emulate it. While simple things that could be learned in five minutes left him cold, tasks that took three or four months—even years—to master left him elated. When he finally had it, he felt pleased with himself that he had conquered something substantial.

The Boys Own Paper and *Chums* also carried advertisements. Vernon spied several for magic depots that offered secrets for sale: A. W. Gamage Ltd., a major English department store with a magic section; Davenports, another English emporium founded by Lewis Davenport in 1898; and Roterberg's, founded by August Roterberg, originally from Hamburg, Germany, but now of 145 Illinois Street,

Railroads and Steamboats

Chicago. All three offered magic tricks by mail. Vernon wrote for their catalogues as soon as he saw their advertisements. He waited feverishly each day—an eternity—for the postman. When the catalogues finally did arrive, he was not disappointed. The A.W. Gamage Ltd. catalogue was particularly impressive, thick as a telephone book, and widely illustrated with all sorts of arcane accoutrements—at least to a young boy—such as magic props, carnival goods, ventriloquist figures and even Punch and Judy puppet outfits. Vernon would scheme and save to get the money to place an order and then wait—impatiently—for the postman to deliver each parcel.

While the catalogues were impressive, the wares he received were not. The quality never seemed to match the images which the written descriptions conjured in his vivid imagination. This was a boy who, at age two, broke his arm jumping from a tree with the mistaken belief that he could fly. When he read about a Fairy Prince and Princess, he conjured up his own image of what these people looked like and was always disappointed when the illustrations of the palaces, groves and woods that accompanied the story were different from what he himself had imagined. It is not surprising, therefore, that he was disappointed in the "stage-sized" prop that he received in the mail, the one that would allow him to catch coins from the air. It had cost him a great deal of money and had arrived in an old dilapidated carton, the box having been used two or three times before. The prop was nothing more than a large glass jar, just like the ones frequently found at his local chemist.

Not all magical apparatus was slipshod, however. Warren Soper, a wealthy industrialist responsible for setting up the first electric streetcars in the city of Ottawa, was an amateur magician who often provided free entertainment at children's parties. Soper had spectacular apparatus, including a shining star that could catch a playing card on each point as well as a crystal casket that could produce copious quantities of balls and other objects. Soper had purchased these props from established European magic depots. Apparatus from France or Germany were beautifully made, but Vernon never managed to get ahold of these treasures. He could not afford them. Eventually he tried to make his own apparatus, going so far as to fabricate a set of linking rings, unbroken hoops of metal that link and unlink in a magical fashion, by soldering crude iron in circles.

One thing sold by magic depots that never seemed to disappoint

Vernon were books.

Books were a familiar sight in the Verner household. After all, James Verner's occupation was to receive and record, in fine penmanship in the official registry of the Canadian government, the pertinent details of each work submitted for copyright. Hundreds of books came across his desk in any given year. The first book Vernon discovered was a compendium of articles from a larger encyclopedia, about the size of two telephone books, with a green baize cover. It contained short descriptions of a broad range of topics, including Legerdemain, a perennial entry in encyclopedias since the ten-volume 1792 second edition of *Encyclopaedia Britannica*. The secrets on display in this compendium, however, were taken largely from a mid-nineteenth popular press publication, *The Secret Out*. Its pedagogical starting point was "The Pass."

> *To perform Card tricks with neatness and dexterity, it is indispensable to know how to "Make the Pass." "Making the Pass, or Shifting the Cards," is the technical term for shifting a card from the middle to the top or bottom of the pack, or vice versa. This only to be acquired by practice, as it is purely a mechanical operation.*

The text described the rudimentary technical details of the sleight and five variants. As a young boy, Vernon wondered why it was so important to put a finger in a specific place and why it said that much practice was required to perfect the sleight. Why couldn't the person holding the cards just cut the desired card to the top or bottom? Vernon failed to realize that the action had to be performed secretly! Now, thanks to the catalogues of A.W. Gamage Ltd. and Davenports and Roterberg, Vernon discovered a world of books that were devoted exclusively to magic. He ordered *Modern Magic* and a new work, *New Era Card Tricks*.

Vernon also discovered that the public libraries in Ottawa held a few books and magazines related to magic. He read each and every one of them, including *Magic*, a new publication from England published by Ellis Stanyon, and *Mahatma*, published by Martinka & Co. in New York City. Vernon's greatest ambition as a boy was to live in New York City, the place where magicians met. He wanted to see, first hand, the magical palace that Martinkas must have been.

In January of 1901, Vernon's father brought home a small, black and red-decorated gray cloth book with a magician performing a

Railroads and Steamboats

card trick embossed on the cover. The book had been submitted to his office for copyright registration. It was called *Howard Thurston's Card Tricks*.

Thurston had gained press attention as the "The Man That Mystified Herrmann," the public and press believing that a magician's rank was somewhat dependent on how well he could fool his peers. If Thurston could fool Herrmann, he had to be good. Unfortunately the "Herrmann" that Thurston fooled—and even then there is some debate—was actually Leon Herrmann, the nephew of the great Alexander, one who himself had tried to profit from his uncle's good name and reputation after his untimely demise. Thurston parlayed the headline into a series of bookings, including Tony Pastor's theatre in New York City (at fifty dollars per week), a contract with William Morris as "The Man That Mystified Herrmann," and an extended run in the fall of 1900 as the *King of Cards* at the Palace Theatre in London, the finest vaudeville theatre in the world. Thurston then signed a publishing deal with L. Upcott Gill in England to write a book that revealed some of the staples of his card work, including the technique for concealing a card behind his hand and its production at the fingertips, the very technique that had been taught to him by Dr. William Elliott. It was advanced technique. Vernon was in seventh heaven and attacked the contents with full force.

Vernon was fascinated by magic because the goal—that perfection towards which he was always striving—was somehow less important than the process, the striving itself. Once he undertook a task, he would promise himself, almost to the point of being sick, to follow through on that task. He became obsessed with the process.

In 1902 Howard Thurston—the King of Cards—was engaged to perform his act at the Russell Theatre, Ottawa. Even better, J.R. Booth, a neighborhood friend who shared Vernon's interest in magic, informed Vernon that his father, a wealthy industrialist, had invited Howard Thurston home for dinner. Vernon could not believe his good fortune. Here was the opportunity to meet a great magician, someone he idolized. Thurston accepted the invitation, but the range of conversation was limited. Thurston, then thirty-two years of age, was only interested in business, asking for advice from an obviously successful entrepreneur on where he should invest his money. The two boys hung on to every word, hoping and praying that Thurston would talk magic. Not once did Thurston

The King of Cards, Howard Thurston.

mention the word or offer to show the two youngsters a trick.

Mr. Booth was mildly surprised himself and, sensing the boys' disappointment, encouraged the boys to perform a trick for Thurston. Vernon performed a card trick, one taken from Thurston's very own book and which incorporated the pass. Vernon fooled him badly. Thurston confessed that he had no idea how the youngster had accomplished the feat. At first Vernon thought that Thurston was teasing him. How could the King of Cards not be familiar with this, a trick and technique he learned from the master's own text? As soon as Thurston reciprocated by performing his own card trick, making a card vanish behind one knee and reappear behind the other, using the back and front palm described in his book, Vernon realized that Thurston wasn't teasing him. His technique was sloppy. Vernon knew that he could have performed it better himself. So it was true; Thurston had no idea how to perform the pass. Vernon was greatly disappointed. He thought Thurston would say, "Here, son, let me show you how to do that properly." Instead, Thurston asked Vernon to show him how he did *his* tricks. Vernon now realized that there was little correlation between *reputation* and actual *skill*.

In August of 1902, the Verners attended the Canadian National Exhibition, the finest exhibition and agricultural fair in North

Railroads and Steamboats

America. Although James Verner would not let his son roam the fair unattended in the evening, he was allowed to prowl its grounds during the day. An English magician, William J. Hilliar, was appearing at the fair, performing a version of The Miser's Dream, a feat in which the magician plucks an endless supply of silver coins from the air, a trick that dates back to Robert-Houdin but one which had experienced a revival in the hands of the "King of Koins," T. Nelson Downs, at the Palace Theatre in London. Although Hilliar had just ghost written a book on the subject, *Modern Coin Manipulation*, Vernon had not read it. It was the first time he had seen anyone actually perform the feat. Vernon watched three shows, reconstructed the method, returned home, and experimented with the technique. He didn't need the 'stage-sized' glass jar after all.

While James Verner loved magic and was pleased by the boy's skill, he was worried about his son's mania and would often reprimand him, particularly when he caught Vernon practicing magic before a mirror after the lights in his room were to be extinguished at 9:00 p.m. He thought that his son's obsessive devotion to detail and to practice was unhealthy. He advised Vernon that there is moderation in all things, and that his son should try to strike a happy balance between theory and practice.

Much to the consternation of his parents, Vernon continued to study magic and to purchase its secrets and practice. At school, Vernon would erect an atlas on his desk like it was a Chinese folding screen and practice his magic behind it. On more than one occasion the teacher intervened, asking him what he had or was doing behind the book, and then confiscating his prop. The cards and other small gimmicks that were confiscated during these sorties would be returned to him at the end of each term. Vernon took comfort in the fact that, when they were returned, the objects still looked new, as if he had just received them in the mail.

The Verners lived at that time in a large, old-fashioned three-story home on Waverly Street. The house had a fully furnished maid's quarters on the top floor—really the attic—of the house. Vernon built a mysterious cabinet in the space, a trunk into which he could crawl and then disappear through a secret compartment both in the trunk and adjoining wall. Vernon also held his own spirit séances in the attic, making a small casket answer questions by having his younger brother, Charles Napier (known as "Napier"), operate a secret thread to animate the box. Vernon had bored a hole through the tar and pebble roof of the house and extended the thread to the cabinet below. Vernon established the *mis-en-scene* with burning candles and drawn drapes. The six or seven children—neighborhood friends and acquaintances—who paid a penny or two for admission, looked on with awe. So did James Verner when he discovered the puddle on his dining room table, a body of water that had been created by the drops of rain that trickled through the hole in the roof to the floor below.

Vernon's mother was equally annoyed, she being the model of Victorian propriety with definite ideas about how children should be raised, how they should behave, and with whom they should be associated. Vernon was all too happy to meet anyone and everyone, and invite them to his home. Mrs. Verner, however, believed that the only playmates her son should have should be the sons or daughters of people that she knew. Anyone else was likely to be a hoodlum. Mrs. Verner was also shocked to learn, for example, that her son would praise or befriend someone of a different color or creed. She held her Christian beliefs dear and believed, like many Victorians, in the superiority of her race and social standing. Vernon, however, was interested in anyone who excelled or did things out of the ordinary, regardless of their background, race, color, creed or formal training.

His mother also took issue with the quality of his performances. At a school festival at which children recited verse, played an instrument, or sang a song, Vernon gave a magic show complete with a blunderbuss, a gun with a funnel-shaped barrel. In his act, Vernon borrowed a watch, pulverized it, loaded the pieces into the gun and shot the pieces—restoring the watch in the process—into a borrowed hat. This was a novel effect for most in the audience, although Harry Kellar had been performing a more sophisticated version for many years, as had Robert-Houdin before him.

Vernon made his first mistake when he borrowed the hat. The Derby was well worn and when he took it in his hands from the gentleman who provided it, he turned up the sweatband and proclaimed, "I *think* it is empty." His mother could not believe her ears. She thought it in very bad taste for her son to say he 'thought' the hat was empty, as if to imply that small vermin might be crawling beneath the sweatband. She left the performance early. When Vernon returned home, he found his mother crying. Vernon could not understand why. He knew he had put on a good show and was

Railroads and Steamboats

proud of it. She said, however, that she was ashamed of him. The incident with the sweatband was apparently not his only *faux pas*.

She explained, "I was also so ashamed at how beastly professional you were. All the other children did their things so politely and sweetly, they were all so diffident and natural as children; people would think I adopted you from a circus."

Vernon began to think that she was right, and that perhaps he was like a clown in the circus. He didn't want to be a clown. He wanted a little dignity. Perhaps there was no need to be a *professional* magician. His father asked him what he wanted to become. His father was hoping he would say 'engineer,' given his predilection for constructing things. Vernon wanted to travel. He wanted to live in New York. He wanted to be a magician, not a professional magician, but a magician like l'Homme Masqué or Cagliostro, magicians with exotic names who lived lives full of adventure. He was interested in the prestige and romance, not the profession.

With vaudeville in full swing, Vernon continued his education into the higher branches of conjuring. Few performers had enough star power to carry an entire evening of entertainment; most shared the bill with other specialty acts that toured the circuit.

Vernon studied them, how they walked on, how they interacted with the audience, and how they left the stage. He became a connoisseur, not just of conjuring, but of variety entertainment in general, always trying to understand how a performer developed presence or authority on the stage. Vernon would occasionally have the opportunity to speak with them.

These performers were remarkably accessible, agreeing to meet the young enthusiast at the stage door. He was never presumptuous or forward as a child. He used to sit patiently waiting and, when the opportunity arose, would say, "I'd love to talk to you about magic." He never said, "How do you do this or that?" having refined his interrogatory technique from asking for string tricks long before. No, Vernon would compliment them on the show, and they were pleased by the way that he approached them. He would show them a few things that he did and they realized that he was a serious student. At that point, they would open up and show him a trick or two, often offering some advice as to what books to read and how to approach magic both from an amateur and a professional point of view. The encounters were brief. He'd see them for a short time, as they were only there for a few days—perhaps a week at most—before moving on to perform in another town or city, and they had other things to do besides conversing with a budding magician.

At dinner one evening, Vernon heard his father describing to his mother the diverse nature of the objects that were submitted to his office for copyright registration. Recent submissions included a book that explained how to cheat at cards. Vernon pricked up his ears. He asked his father if he could see the book. His father's response was disappointing. James said that Vernon was far too young to read about gambling. Vernon pressed his father and asked whether or not the book was illustrated. Perhaps he could look at the illustrations? James Verner replied that the book had photographs, not illustrations, as was the custom. Few books at the time—*The Modern Conjurer* and *Modern Coin Manipulation* being exceptions—used photographs to illustrate sleight-of-hand. James Verner held his ground and refused to bring the book home.

Gambling held a prominent place in North American culture in the late nineteenth century. Then, as today, gambling had both its proponents and its opponents. One major difference, however, was regulation. There were not the gaming authorities—at least not honest ones—that licensed operations and controlled, or at least tried to, the integrity of the game and its players. Cheating was rampant.

Unbeknownst to Vernon, the book that his father had described at the dinner table was entitled *Combined Treatise on Advantage Card Playing and Draw Poker* by F.R. Ritter, and it did have photographs that illustrated the gamblers' stock and trade. Vernon was not permitted to see the book. Six weeks later, however, Vernon was walking along Bank Street in Ottawa, one of two main thoroughfares, when he wandered into a stationery store to look at the books. This store was his favorite because the proprietors didn't mind if the customers perused the publications for extended periods of time. Vernon noticed a small book with the King of Hearts brightly displayed on its cardboard cover. Assuming that this was the book that his father had been discussing, Vernon mustered the money to purchase a copy. It cost 25 cents, a small fortune for an eleven-year old boy in 1905. Vernon brought the book home and showed it to his father. Although not pleased with the purchase, James Verner permitted his son to keep the book because it had been bought with his own money.

Railroads and Steamboats

The book that Vernon purchased was not, however, the one by Ritter. It was *The Expert At The Card Table*, a discounted trade edition of a book published in 1902 subtitled, *Artifice, Ruse and Subterfuge At The Card Table*, originally published "By the Author," one S.W. Erdnase, as a small, green cloth bound book.

The Expert At The Card Table became Vernon's life map.

The book was divided into two parts: Card Table Artifice and Legerdemain. It set out the "Primary Accomplishments" of the advantage player and then provided a glossary of technical terms that would enable the practitioner to make more rapid progress in mastering the techniques that followed. Vernon recognized, even at the age of eleven, that reading a technical treatise was very different from reading a novel. It was important to develop a thorough understanding of the fundamentals before trying to practice or master more advanced technique. Vernon then attacked the rest of the book with relish. Here, before his eyes, were the secrets to the most sophisticated sleight-of-hand the world had ever seen. The descriptions of each technique were terse, but upon close analysis,

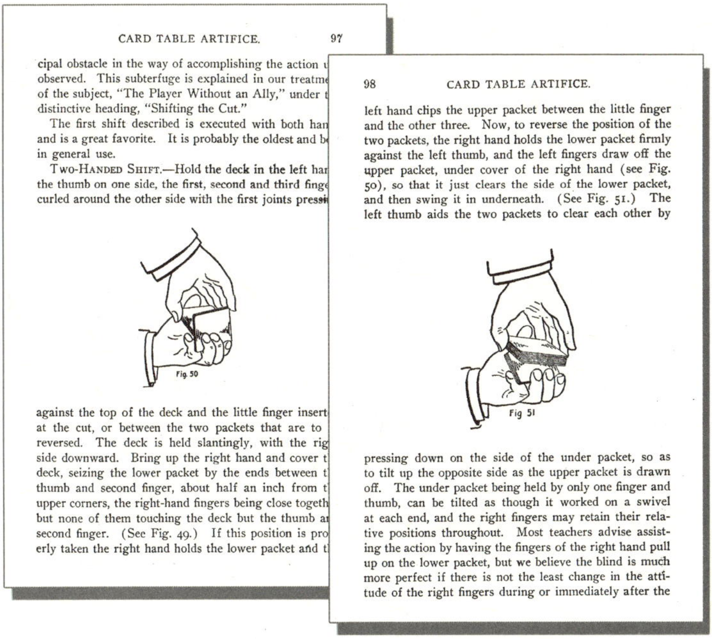

Erdnase's book The Expert at the Card Table *taught Vernon the fundamentals of the pass.*

contained nuance and detail like no other work published before. Gamblers and magicians had exposed the principles behind the secret machinations and manipulation of playing cards; none, however, had ever done so with such organization, detail or eloquence.

The book also offered extensive notes and technical analysis on "The Pass," the rudiments he had learned (or thought he had learned) from the compendium with the chapter on Legerdemain, from the books by Professor Hoffmann and, of course, from Howard Thurston. The purpose of the pass, however, now became clear. "Put your faith in Providence but always cut the cards!" The cut is the *bête noir* of the advantage player. All effort—collecting cards, running them up into a secret sequence for the deal and retaining that order—is for naught if the cards are cut before the deal. A simple cut of the cards changes everything. In every country, wherever people play cards for money, effort has been made to secretly circumnavigate the cut. S.W. Erdnase upped the ante by saying that there had yet to be "a pass" invented that could "be executed by a movement appearing as coincident card table routine." If a mathematical "proof" for the pass existed, Vernon wanted to be the one who found it.

Vernon took the book to school, hiding it under his textbooks so that he could study it further. He also practiced religiously at church, sitting with his family like a good little boy in a pew second from the front, having placed his father's silk hat on his lap in order to conceal his hands as he practiced various sleights with the deck of Little Lord Fauntleroy cards he always carried. One day the minister, Reverend Gorman, looked down and stared at him, knowing full well that the boy was hiding something beneath the hat. The minister kept staring. Vernon felt guilty but did not alter his practice regimen.

When Vernon read, "The only trouble with this trick is the extreme difficulty to master it, but the tyro will not be satisfied until he masters every sleight in the calendar," Vernon said to himself, "I *must* master every sleight in the calendar." When he read the secret to the Cards Up the Sleeve and it said, "Sleights required. Masterly feats of palming, and unflinching audacity," he vowed to cultivate said audacity.

Even though the book was the first technical work to make sleight-of-hand an exact science, articulating the most minute details of finger position and whether the deck was to be held firmly or lightly, Vernon mastered most of the contents by the age of twelve. It was then that he received some unexpected hands-on advice from a stranger in the Carnegie Library in Ottawa.

So at the library I noticed a fellow—probably in his 30's—he kept looking at me. Then I began to be a little ashamed, perhaps I thought, he was a schoolteacher and wondered why I was looking up these articles on magic. One day, he followed me and said, "Come here, Sonny; I see you are much interested in the article you are reading." I said, "Yes, that's my hobby."

He said, "Do you do any tricks?" I always carried this little deck of cards, and he said, "Show me a trick." I had been practicing the pass so I took the cards and did it. In those days magicians never carried a full pack of cards—all the old books said, "a magician never works with a full pack, he works with a Pique pack of 32 cards—a full pack is too bulky." That time I was practicing with the bigger cards and I had 20 of them. I did the pass for him. He said, "You have to do it this way." I may have been very bad at the time. This opened my eyes; he said, "You square up the pack." He was very nice about showing me... That's when I really learned the pass. I came away with the feeling how well some of these things could be done.

The first full evening of magic that Vernon witnessed, magic that was performed in a theatre that ordinarily staged theatrical presentations rather than variety acts, was by Harry Kellar. Kellar, who had made several forays into Canada in previous years, appeared in Ottawa for the first time from September 9-15, 1906 at the Russell Theatre.

Two posters that advertised Kellar's performances, both produced by the Strobridge Litho. Company of Cincinnati, the world's best theatrical lithographers, caught Vernon's eye. These posters were designed to lure people to the theatre to see the wonders and mysteries Kellar would present. In many ways they were as enchanting as the performance itself.

The first poster was a portrait of Kellar, his pale face surrounded by a sea of ghostly green and blue, contemplating the secrets that two bright, cardinal red imps perched on his shoulders whispered into his ears. The second, in lighter shades, announced that Paul

Valadon, "The Greatest Sleight-Of-Hand Expert Of The Century Direct From England's Home Of Mystery The Egyptian Hall, London" would be a special feature of "Kellar's Wonders."

Although Vernon did not have any ambition to become a professional magician with a stage act of boxes, barrels, levitations and the like, he went six times to see Kellar perform, even sneaking off from school to attend a mid-week matinee. The original draw for Vernon had been the presence of Paul Valadon. Vernon had to see "The Greatest Sleight-Of-Hand Expert Of The Century." He was not disappointed. Valadon was excellent. Vernon was even more impressed, however, by Kellar—not so much by the fact that he had these boxes and illusions, but by the way he presented them. His *pièce de résistance* was the Levitation of Princess Karnac.

Several years earlier at Egyptian Hall, London, John Nevil Maskelyne created a sensation by levitating his assistant in the air and keeping him there with no visible means of support. Maskelyne would then pass a hoop around the man to demonstrate the absence of all trickery. The effect on Maskelyne's audiences was nothing short of sensational, and for years, Kellar coveted the levitation for his own show. Maskelyne, however, was not interested in parting with it. So, resorting to industrial espionage to unearth the trick's modus operandi, Kellar hired Paul Valadon.

Valadon had been a feature artist at Egyptian Hall for over five years and was familiar with all aspects of Maskelyne's work. Kellar promised Valadon not only a part in his show if he provided him with the secret to the levitation but also the place as his anointed successor once he himself retired. Valadon joined Kellar in America, and Kellar inserted the piece, now performed with a woman, into his program. He called it The Levitation of Princess Karnac. The audience was just as entranced as the woman floating in air—actually more so. It was a great illusion, perhaps the greatest special effect ever performed on the stage at a time when audiences were used to the fantastic being performed live, not on film. Vernon realized for the first time that for something to be truly magical—really magical—it had to be mysterious.

Grand touring shows such as Kellar's appeared infrequently in Ottawa. The cost of constructing illusions, transporting the show from city to city, promoting it in each local and then staging it, was great. Few embarked on such an enterprise. Vernon had to be content with variety artists who continued to appear at the Ben-

Railroads and Steamboats

nett Theatre. Fortunately, as the Bennett was part of the B.F. Keith circuit, the caliber of these artists was quite high. One magician who appeared on that stage and who would have great impact on Vernon's attitude towards magic, its performance, and even its essential difference from other arts at this time was J. Warren Keane.

J. Warren Keane and Co. was considered one of the cleverest and most novel magic acts on the vaudeville stage. When the curtain rose, the audience was treated to a beautiful woman, Keane's wife, playing a grand piano. Keane entered, and played the character of a dashing, debonair man, wooing his sweetheart with magic. He performed magic with silk handkerchiefs, cigarettes and playing cards, all in song or rhyme, for and with the woman playing the piano. Vernon was impressed and asked Keane, when he met the artist backstage, where he got his ideas. Keane said that many came from the pages of a book that was completely unrelated to magic. The title was *Why People Think Certain Things at Certain Times*. Keane explained to Vernon the concept of thought association, how one word or image in one field can ignite or produce ideas in another. Keane also told Vernon that he should not worry about how each trick or effect was accomplished. There were always many ways to achieve each effect.

Keane then cautioned Vernon to never, under any circumstances, show anyone how a trick worked simply to satisfy their curiosity.

Vaudeville conjurer J. Warren Keane

Not even his mother! The person might seem genuine and interested when asking how the trick is done, and he might say that he'll never tell anyone else, but he'll probably tell someone the first chance he gets. Better to keep them curious. Magic, according to Keane, would be much better served this way.

This was the most time a professional magician had spent with Vernon. He absorbed each and every word. Keane then performed a card trick for Vernon, one that fooled him *very* badly. Keane spread out the pack of cards and removed one without revealing its identity to Vernon. He then asked Vernon to name any card in the pack.

Vernon asked, "Any card?"

"Yes, any card in the pack, there are fifty-two."

Vernon said, "The ace of clubs."

Keane slowly turned the card over in his hand. It was the ace of clubs.

Vernon was stunned. A chill went up his spine. It was the creepiest feeling he had ever experienced.

Keane said, "I know that this trick interests you immensely."

Vernon replied, "Why, I don't know why it shouldn't; it's the greatest thing I've ever seen."

Keane explained how he had engaged Vernon's undivided attention, had made Vernon concentrate on one vein of thought and then let Vernon see the face of one card in the pack—the ace of clubs—while he was handling the cards. The image of the card registered in Vernon's subconscious mind. By holding Vernon's attention and then suddenly asking him to name a card, Keane was betting that Vernon would name the one card that had registered in his mind, the one card that Keane had just removed from the pack and held in his hand.

The budding magician couldn't believe it.

Vernon became fascinated by these psychological gambits. He started to read books by William James and anything else that pertained to psychology. He was fascinated with how one could play with a person's mind, lead him up the garden path and divert him in some way. He regarded being able to sway people in the wrong direction as the highest form of deception, something that could not be carved in stone, something without hard and fast rules that would apply to all people, all of the time. Vernon would explore these concepts and ideas, without limit, his entire life.

Railroads and Steamboats

Even though Vernon had been exposed to world-class magicians and the new science of psychology, he was still very interested in the world of gambling and advantage play. *The Expert At The Card Table* had taught him the superiority of gambling sleights. He had met magicians but where could one—particularly a teenager—meet a professional cheat? How could he see one *in action*? They did not perform on the vaudeville stage, and they did not fraternize with magicians.

Vernon did not have to wait very long to meet his first gambler, someone who could show him things that were not generally known to magicians. The encounter took place in the summer of 1909. Vernon was fifteen years old and on a fishing expedition with his father, learning to fly cast and catch rainbow trout on Lake Muskoka in central Ontario. Vernon met the man on the veranda of the lodge where he was staying, after a long day on the lake. The man was staying at the lodge, too, but fishing on a neighboring lake. Vernon was practicing with a pack of cards.

The man asked, "Sonny, what are you doing?" Before Vernon could respond, the man said that he would show Vernon something. He took the cards and said, "Shuffle them, square them up and put them on the table."

Vernon did as he was asked. The man then reached over and cut to an ace. He said, "Now you see, when I cut, I always cut a high card."

Vernon asked if the man would mind doing that again.

The man said, "Well, I'll tell you, you take out a card." Vernon selected a card from the pack, noted its identity and then shuffled it back into the deck. The man reached over and cut at the card that Vernon had selected and shuffled back into the deck!

Vernon thought he would happily trade in all the tricks in his growing repertoire to learn that one trick as neatly and as cleanly as the man did it. Why? Because Vernon could not detect a false move of any kind in the man's actions. It was as if nothing out of the ordinary had happened. The man then showed Vernon how he put a very mild crimp or crease in a card so it could be cut to after shuffling the deck.

Vernon was impressed by the man's ability and extremely grateful to him for sharing his technique. Vernon's imagination had been ignited. He thought that this gambler could certainly do card tricks if he wanted to. Vernon vowed from that point on, any time he heard about a professional gambler, to find out if that gambler knew anything in the way of what they called "advantage play."

As it turned out, Ottawa and the Ottawa Valley had more than its fair share of professional gamblers. The booming pulp and paper industry attracted a large number of men, prospectors and laborers just like those who jumped to San Francisco or the Yukon in search of gold nuggets; these men, however, sought their fortune in lumber and electricity. Rail was the predominant form of travel, moving vast numbers of people and goods from one economic zone to another. Vernon used to walk the tracks, maintaining his balance without falling off, counting each section of the iron rail, trying to surpass his best each and every time.

On many occasions, always in different places, he would see playing cards—checkered-backed Steamboats—strewn along the side of the tracks. If was as if someone had thrown a whole deck of cards out the window like seeds scattered by the wind. What could they mean? Had someone been playing cards? Did they win or lose? Where were they going? Where did they end up? What world did they come from?

Vernon thought it had to be an exotic world, one full of excitement and danger.

Chapter Two
Artifice, Ruse and Subterfuge

"Verner," a young man cried out, "Tell me the name of *that* card."

The young man was a classmate of Vernon's, and the two were walking home from school when the companion noticed a half dozen cards scattered several feet apart along the side of the road, some lying face down and others face up, abandoned by their mates in the pack.

Vernon muttered that it would be impossible to identify the cards. His friend chided him. "I thought you were supposed to be a magician."

"Alright, I'll try," said Vernon. "Which one do you want me to name?"

"That one," the boy said, pointing to one dog-eared card stranded several yards away from the rest.

"Right."

Vernon touched his fingertips to the side of his head and rubbed his temples slowly.

"I sense...the card must be...the...three...of...hearts!"

Slowly, it dawned on the boy that Vernon wasn't joking. The challenger bent down and picked up the card. It *was* the three of hearts.

The boy stood in disbelief. Vernon resumed the walk home confident that the story of his feat of divination would spread through the corridors of the school like wildfire.

Vernon was not the only one performing miracles. It was 1907 when Harry Kellar announced that he would be retiring the following year and, to everyone's surprise, that he would pass the mantle of magic to Howard Thurston, not Paul Valadon. Kellar agreed to tour with Thurston for one year, presenting a joint program and introducing Thurston to North American audiences as his anointed successor. Kellar performed his last formal stage show on Saturday, May 9, 1908 at Ford's Theatre in Baltimore. (Paul Valadon died of tuberculosis in Phoenix, Arizona in 1912, a broken man who had lost his wife, his props and his health.)

Harry Houdini, on the other hand, had graduated from dime museums, and was moving up the ranks of show business with a new act. While performing in 1899 in the Palm-Garden, a beer hall in St. Paul, Minnesota, Martin Beck, an ambitious vaudeville impresario, challenged Houdini to escape from a set of handcuffs. Houdini escaped and assured Beck that he could do so from any restraint. Under Beck's stewardship, Houdini was transformed from the King of Cards to the man no restraint could hold. By 1909 Houdini was, to paraphrase George Bernard Shaw, standing with Sherlock Holmes and Jesus Christ as one of the three most famous men the world had ever known.

While Houdini and Thurston inspired a new generation of magicians, Vernon sought inspiration from other sources: books that detailed the secrets of magic, sleight-of-hand performers who displayed great artistic skill, and professional gamblers.

In January 1909, The Downs-Edwards Company, a U.S. subsidiary of a Canadian magic dealer located in Bridgeburg, Ontario, published *The Art of Magic* by T. Nelson Downs, ghost written by John Northern Hilliard. The book was beautifully written and garnered the sort of reviews that had greeted Hoffmann's *Modern Magic* decades earlier. Professional magicians were appalled that their confidence had been betrayed and their cherished secrets exposed for all to see. Amateur magicians were thrilled to learn inner secrets of the craft, secrets that were not the product of a bygone era but rooted firmly in the twentieth century.

The book resonated with Vernon. The secrets it disclosed were primarily concerned with sleight-of-hand, not mechanical apparatus. Much of the material was taken directly from the repertoire of the performers whom he had met and admired, performers like J. Warren Keane, Emil Jarrow, and Nate Leipzig. It was also the first magic book to suggest that magicians should study the techniques of professional gamblers and, in particular, the work of S. W. Erdnase.

Vernon's understanding of magic received another boost with the appearance of Max Malini on his personal horizon. Born Max Katz, Malini had started performing while tending bar in New York. He later went on the road to earn enough wealth and respect to win the hand of the woman he loved, changed his name to Malini, and by the time he returned to New York years later, had not only perfected a great repertoire but also built a small fortune in the process. Over the course of his long career, Malini appeared before countless celebrities and heads of state, including President Harding, John D. Rockefeller, John Jacob Astor, King Edward VII, Baron de Rothschild, the King of Siam and the President of China.

One night Vernon's father came home with the evening newspaper in hand to show his son an advertisement he thought the boy would find interesting. It featured a man with a felt hat turned up on one side accompanied by the caption "Famous Magician, Malini will appear tonight at the Rideau Club." Vernon implored his father to take him to the club. Despite his father protesting that children were not admitted, Vernon persuaded his father to allow him to watch the first half of the show. A club attendant showed Vernon where he could stand to best advantage: in the hall, peeking through the curtain. Although Vernon saw only the first part of the show before his father chased him home to bed, the boy was awestruck.

Malini was the first performer that Vernon saw who could mesmerize an entire room of extremely sophisticated people with little or no visible apparatus. Although he was a stout man with a guttural accent, and his manner and vocabulary appeared unsophisticated, Vernon recognized that magic, in Malini's hands, was poetry. Everything appeared effortless and completely natural. More importantly, Malini had *presence*, that intangible ingredient that allows some people to dominate and light up a room.

Vernon also continued to keep his eyes open for anyone who gambled, in hopes of learning if they knew anything about advantage play. He met his second gambler, a man named Nightingale, who demonstrated that it was possible to invisibly deal the second card from the deck while appearing to deal the first. Numerous writers had described Second Dealing, but Vernon had never actually seen it performed. Nightingale proved that, if one understood the proper technique and put in the requisite time to master it, it was possible to perform the deal flawlessly. This was no easy task. S. W. Erdnase wrote, "To become an adept at second dealing is as difficult a task as can be given in card handling."

Vernon also learned why those playing cards had been scattered along the tracks. The cards were remnants of a deck that been used in a poker game, one that had been switched out for a "cooler," a deck stacked so that the dealer—really the victim—would receive a wonderful hand but also so that one of the other players would receive an even better hand. The cheats operated as a team, choreographing the game and the switch for the big score in the smoking car of the train as it neared the station.

Cheating at cards required precision planning and nerves of steel. Vernon appreciated the sophistication of the con and the importance of detail. He started applying these principles of deception to his own work. He could divine the name of cards scattered on the route home from school because he had taken the time to mark them so that he could easily determine the identity of each at a later time. He also disfigured the cards so that they appeared well worn. He waited for his friend to discover the cards and issue the challenge. He then confidently yet theatrically identified the card and continued on his journey. It was the stuff that miracles were made of.

Upon graduating from the Ottawa Model School in 1907, Vernon entered Ashbury College, the pre-eminent school for young men in the Ottawa region. Founded in 1891 by Mr. George Woolcombe, the object of the school was to develop not only a high standard of scholarship, but also an upright, manly and Christian character in the boys entrusted to its care. It was a school for children of wealth. Vernon's father, however, was decidedly middle-class.

James Verner was a career civil servant. He had started his employment with the Department of Agriculture in 1889 as a clerk, third class, at an annual salary of $100.00. By 1907, James Verner had been promoted to clerk, second-class, with an annual salary of $500.00. The fees for Day Boys at Ashbury College were $120.00 per annum. Fortunately, Vernon had a friend who became his patron, or sponsor, into Ashbury College. The friend was the wealthy industrialist, founding governor of Ashbury College, and prominent amateur magician, Warren Soper.

Vernon was a mediocre student, placing habitually in the bottom third of his class of 15 students. He excelled in sports, however, primarily in football, ice hockey and track and field. Vernon was a prominent player on the Ashbury Football team. *The Ashburian* described him as, "a beautiful tackle and a very steady man, who helps greatly (when he doesn't miss the train). He is a good runner and is the hardest man to tackle on the team." Vernon was also an excellent hockey player and the captain of the team for the 1912 season. His summer sport was track and field. When the college held its annual sports field day on June 11, 1912, coincidentally Vernon's eighteenth

Artifice, Ruse and Subterfuge

Ashbury College hockey team. David Verner (Vernon) is at the center, seated.

birthday, Vernon won the inaugural Fleming Cup for amassing the highest number of points in the events of the day. S.H. Fleming, the wife of the remarkable railway engineer and Ashbury College member of the board, Sir Sanford Fleming, the man who gave the world Standard Time, presented the trophy to Vernon.

Vernon enjoyed traveling with the teams as much as the games themselves. When the hockey team was in Brockville, and returned to the hotel after roaming the town, Vernon and his fellow teammate Hughson, held a reception in the bridal suite. *The Ashburian* reported, "Verner endeavored to play "Alexander's Ragtime Band" on a piano which hadn't been tuned for, at least, twenty years. Dear reader, you can imagine the result." Vernon had been studying piano for many years under the stern eye of his mother, and the not-so-stern eye of fellow student, friend, and ragtime pianist, Keller Gamble. Vernon loved to party, stay up late, and wake up even later. He was often late for team practices and even games. Vernon was stripped of his captaincy in his senior year because of his tardiness, despite being described by *The Ashburian* as the best all-around player on the team.

Vernon augmented his formal education with field trips of his own design. Not one to let his schooling interfere with his education, he continued to seek out the odd or the unusual. He would ride a motorcycle, for example, to a remote logging site if he heard that an inhabitant had some experience as an advantage player. When the reformed gambler John Phillip Quinn, the author of *Fools of Fortune*, appeared at the Y.M.C.A. to lecture on the dangers of gambling, Vernon made sure he was in attendance. Vernon was surprised to learn after the lecture, however, when he had confided to Quinn his interest in the techniques of advantage play, that Quinn was not so reformed after all. Quinn asked Vernon if his father could give him an entrée to a poker game at the Rideau Club. Quinn had heard that the stakes were sizable and offered Vernon a percentage of his winnings for the opportunity to play.

Vernon would also skip classes to visit the cinema, meeting Gamble who often provided the musical accompaniment to the motion picture. Vernon would practice a sleight with cards or coins while watching the picture, occasionally dropping to his hands and knees to locate a card or coin that accidentally tumbled to the floor of the darkened cinema. Gamble taught Vernon how to practice, not just music but also his magic. The magic that Vernon was interested in performing required a great deal of practice.

Gamble unlocked the mystery. He said, "You have to use your head when you do anything. Most people don't. They practice aimlessly. You must use your head to continually analyze what you are doing. Ask yourself why this finger doesn't move in just the way you want or why this wrist turns in such a way. You have to continually think about whatever it is you're practicing." Vernon renewed his attack on his favorite techniques to see not only how they were executed but also why. When he discovered deficiencies, he tried to correct or improve them, adding a touch or nuance of his own design.

Vernon also learned the value of secrets. For someone so young, he had been granted extraordinary access to magicians and their secrets. It took another Canadian magician named Allan Shaw to teach him their real value and power. Vernon approached Shaw after one of his performances and inquired about a private lesson. He assured Shaw that he was willing to pay for it. Vernon wanted to learn how Shaw was able to produce cards at his fingertips, not from the backhand palm as performed by Howard Thurston. Shaw said, "I have never divulged anything I do in my act. If you want that one little move, I'll charge you $20." At the time, twenty dollars was a significant sum of money, particularly for a card trick. Vernon was obsessed, however,

Artifice, Ruse and Subterfuge

with learning the secret.

Vernon scrambled to gather the money. He emptied his bank account, borrowed change from his younger brother, and asked his father for the rest. James Verner refused. He said, "You are not paying any money to these professional performers; they just milk you out of money." Still, Vernon desperately wanted to learn the technique. His most valuable personal possession was a set of Keuffel and Esser drawing instruments given to him by his father. James Verner had paid fifty dollars for the set, hoping that it would perhaps spark his son's interest in a more productive pursuit. But Vernon just had to learn the secret of Shaw's technique. He took the set of drawing instruments to a hockshop and pawned them for ten dollars.

Vernon met Shaw and handed him the twenty dollars. Within two minutes, Shaw had taught Vernon everything he needed to know about the technique; Vernon was bitterly disappointed. Shaw maintained its value was commensurate with his initial perception of its worth. It took Vernon months to reclaim the drafting set from the pawnshop.

Not only were Vernon's parents concerned about his development and career path, they also had concerns about his odd hours and strange friends.

> *When I got older and would go to play pool, the pool hall closed at 11 o'clock in those days. My mother would say, "Where would any respectable boy be at this time; you are probably prowling the streets." I used to tell her I was playing billiards (pool had a certain stigma attached to it because of the people who used to hang around there). It's a wonderful scientific game. She would get terribly annoyed; I would get a severe lecture. I said, "Would you rather I told you a lie and make you happy or tell you the truth and make you unhappy?"*

On one outing Vernon decided to have his shoes shined at the Russell Hotel. As soon as he put his foot up for the shine, he noticed a pack of cards lying at the side. He picked up the cards and said to the attendant, "Think of a card." The boy named a card. Vernon palmed it out of the pack, hesitated for dramatic effect, and then reached behind the boy and produced the card from his ear. The boy was flabbergasted.

The boy said, "That's wonderful, I've only seen one other fellow do something with a pack of cards. He comes in here every Sunday to have his shoes shined. He just takes a pack and tears them in half."

"Do you know his name?" Vernon asked.

"Cliff Green," the boy replied.

Imagine, another boy in town who was interested in sleight-of-hand! Vernon came across others interested in magic, but primarily in mechanical apparatus, and their enthusiasm generally wavered as soon as they realized that practice was required to further their development. Vernon made an appointment through the shoeshine boy to meet Cliff Green at the Russell Hotel.

As soon as Green entered the hotel, Vernon sighed. Green was a flamboyant young man, dressed in effete fabric, wearing fine wools that were clearly exquisitely tailored. Vernon learned that Green's father was a woman's tailor and made all of his son's clothes. That, Vernon thought, explains it.

The boys chatted briefly and Green gave a brief demonstration of card fanning and manipulation. Vernon wasn't particularly impressed, but acknowledged that Green was attempting difficult work and had obviously put a great deal of time into practicing the material. Vernon asked Green where he had learned his tricks. Green replied that he had picked them up while attending a magic society meeting in Detroit. The idea that magicians formed societies where they performed magic and exchanged secrets with each other on a regular basis took Vernon by surprise. Up to that point, he'd had to hunt for information.

Green then asked Vernon what kind of work he performed. In reply, Vernon took the cards and gave them a slow and deliberate shuffle, his right hand holding the deck from above, his left fingers stripping clumps of cards from the pack into the cradle of his waiting palm. It was an unusual shuffle; one that Vernon had seen Leipzig demonstrate. During the course of the shuffle, Vernon noticed that the bottom card of the pack was the three of diamonds. Extending the deck towards Green, Vernon said, "Here, cut the cards."

Green reached over, cut the cards and then carried the cut. Vernon maintained a slight step where the deck had been reassembled. Then Vernon asked Green to name a card. By sheer coincidence Green said, "The three of diamonds." Not one to let a tremendous opportunity pass him by, Vernon instantly cut to the named card.

Green staggered, completely flummoxed by the impossible feat. Vernon's retort was quick: "That's what I do. And now, what type of *mysterious* tricks do you do?"

At the end of their session, Vernon and Green exchanged information. Vernon borrowed Edwin Sachs' *Sleight Of Hand* from his new friend and, after a thorough reading, discovered that it was quite different from Hoffmann's classic, *Modern Magic.* Even more interesting to Vernon was the fact that much of the material in Sachs' book worked its way into the repertoire of Max Malini.

Occasionally Vernon and Green would venture off together to see a professional magician appearing at the Russell Theatre. One such performer was William Louis McCord, a gifted sleight-of-hand magician who toured vaudeville in the guise of Silent Mora, a Chinese character who performed magic in pantomime. McCord taught Vernon how to spin a wand at his fingertips and make a small ball or other object, as large as an orange, disappear. Vernon and Green visited McCord at his hotel after his performances and stayed with him until after midnight, discussing magic and listening to his stories. McCord was an idealist and much more bitter than most performers Vernon had encountered. In professional show business, McCord warned them, the quality of the act had little bearing on its commercial success. Fortunately, Vernon had no intention of being a professional magician.

If Vernon had an ambition, it was to become a visual artist. He was listed on the masthead of *The Ashburian* as one of two "Artists" on staff. He worked on the design and layout of the magazine and contributed the occasional illustration to its pages. Pen and ink was his favorite medium. Vernon graduated from Ashbury College in June of 1913 without the financial safety net that secured the future of his fellow classmates. Most Ashbury students headed to either McGill University in Montreal or Royal Military College in Kingston upon graduation. Vernon was accepted into the engineering program at McGill University. Montreal was the economic epicenter of Canada and had a thriving cultural scene. Vernon had visited the city on several occasions, both with his parents and as a member of the Ashbury football, hockey and track and field squads. Classes at McGill commenced in September 1913. Unfortunately, at age nineteen, the transition to university life was more challenging than anticipated. Vernon was not a stellar student and had poor academic habits. He demonstrated little motivation to follow prescribed procedures or programs. His stay at McGill was short, and he returned home before the end of the year, just in time to work out with the Ashbury College hockey team at the Gladstone Avenue Rink.

James Verner continued to steer his son towards a career in engineering or architecture. Tom Keefer, a distant relation of Mrs. Verner, had designed a number of bridges in Canada, and his son, Allan

Keefer, was an architect with numerous commissions to his name, including the expansion of Ashbury College. James Verner arranged for his son to visit Allan Keefer at his office to learn what it was like to be an architect. The plan, however, backfired. Vernon saw the rolls and rolls of profiles, front and side elevations, and beautiful buildings rendered in watercolor and asked Keefer where these structures were located. Keefer responded that none of them had been built. They were just renderings, submissions for projects, all of which had been rejected. Vernon was disgusted that so much hard work provided such little return. Architecture was not for him. In April 1914, at his father's request, Vernon, along with eighty-eight others, wrote the entrance exam for the Royal Military College of Canada. Unfortunately, Vernon did not fare well in the exams and was not offered a position at the college.

On June 28, 1914, the Archduke Franz Ferdinand of Austria was assassinated in Sarajevo, Bosnia. By August 1, 1914, after a series of diplomatic crises, Germany declared war on France. Soon thereafter, Britain and her Commonwealth Allies, including Canada, were drawn into the conflict. Thousands of young Canadian men volunteered to fight on behalf of Britain. Vernon, however, ignored the call of the "mother" country.

Of the eighty-eight candidates who had written the Royal Military College entrance exam with Vernon in the spring of 1914, fifty-six had qualified, and fifty-four of those reported to the college soon after the war was declared and asked to be commissioned, hoping to join the Canadian Expeditionary Forces to be sent overseas. They wanted to see action before the war was over; most thought that the conflict would end by Christmas. Ordinarily, students at the college would embark on a three-year program. Canada's involvement in the war, however, altered that timetable.

In December 1914, the British army offered twenty extra commissions to Royal Military College cadets, accepting only cadets who had completed at least one year of training at the college. Once these twenty commissions had been fulfilled, twenty-eight new recruits were admitted to the school, some from matriculants and some from among those candidates who had failed to qualify for a place previously. Vernon entered Royal Military College of Canada on January 4, 1915 as Cadet #1109.

On February 9, 1915, Vernon wrote home, asking his mother to send him his set of drafting instruments and some props. He also described the program.

Artifice, Ruse and Subterfuge

Dearest Mother,

I received the pajamas, pads, and candy to-day, many thanks. I am going to ask you to send one more parcel if it isn't too much trouble – my case of instruments, and my red trick balls. Also my wig, and a couple of packs of my blue back cards. I want, if I possibly can to get a stripe on my uniform before Easter. When you gain a stripe it entitles you to several priveledges [sic], and gives you authority over the rest of the class. As the shows count more than anything else I may have a chance for one. We give our big show in March. The one the Recruits before us put on cost them about two hundred dollars. I am at the head of the Theatrical Committee and am held responsible.

Still further,

When you see me next I will probably have a flowing mustache. I hope I won't frighten you. The time seems to be slipping by pretty quickly. I suppose it is because we work so hard. Nearly every night after Tattoo we have a rink fatigue for about an hour.

We always have to sleep with our windows wide open and get soaked drills if we are caught with them shut. I suppose you know that everything is run entirely by the seniors, except every morning from 9 o'clock until one o'clock when we have classes. Outside of these hours we never see the professors as they all live in the city. At night there is never any master around, just the seniors. They look after us. No sooner are we in bed than someone comes along the hall shouting "Turnout on the Second Flat for Artillery practice." We have to buckle on our belts and bayonets over our pajamas and turnout. They may keep us any place from five minutes to two hours. I am sorry I can't write more but I have to stop now.

As a postscript scrawled along the upper left corner of the first page, Vernon wrote,

Put in the parcel. Book. The "Art of Magic" Nelson Downs.

Royal Military College was certainly no place for fun and games. The seniors, in particular, would often haze the raw recruits, "putting them through hell." The goal was to prepare them mentally

Dai Vernon: A Biography

Cadet David Verner.

and physically for extraordinary situations. In one winter ritual, the seniors cut a ten-foot long opening through the ice of frozen Lake Ontario. They marched the recruits to the opening and commanded each recruit, when called, to jump and swim to the other side. Those who didn't jump were pushed. Vernon thought nothing of it. He just dove in and swam across to the other side. On May 5, 1915, Vernon wrote to his sixteen-year old brother Napier:

I suppose you are worrying yourself sick wondering why I do not drop my handsome kid brother a line once in a while. You wrote us a nice long card and I neglected to answer it. Cheer up and I'll tell you a few things we do around this cemetery. To tell the truth there is more about what we don't do. You can't imagine what it is like to be told in "gentle words", whenever you do anything in any but the orthodox and regulation manner. They won't even let you tie your bootlaces as you wish, and as for the way we have to wear our tin-can bonnets like the Hon. Mr. Hooligan, well they have to be at the exact angle, if not it would be a sage and timely precautionary measure to don our thickest and heaviest underwear before the sun goes down. Poor Kenny had his little behind severely spanked last night, just because the yelling of the time, was not quite as audible as the six-o'clock whistles. You know he is senior in the new dormitory and is held responsible.

Next week will be pretty well taken up with route marches. We will probably walk about thirty miles and go several by boat. The session

Artifice, Ruse and Subterfuge

N.C.O's are provided with horse and will enjoy seeing us wearily trudging along. I will write to you later and tell you all about our sleep in the open.

I don't think there will be much swimming here before I leave as the water doesn't get bearable until well on in the summer. The Commandant has forbidden anyone going in until further orders, so the seniors can't force us to take any icy baths in the cold gray morn.

To-day the seniors had machine gun practice across the foot-ball field at some targets placed against the Old Fort. These guns fire 400 rounds per minute so you can imagine the noise they make. One continual bu-rr.

On June 23, 1915, Vernon and six others in the batch of twenty-eight cadets who had joined the college in January, left "at parents request," a term used to describe all departures from the program apart from graduation or expulsion. Vernon returned to Ottawa to live with his parents and his two younger siblings, Napier and Arthur, at 88 MacLaren Street. He had just turned twenty-one. James Verner used whatever political connections he had mustered in his twenty-six years as a civil servant to obtain a position for his son. Vernon became a draftsman in a government architect's office. It was not the career or the life that Vernon had envisioned for himself. He still dreamed of living in America. Later in life, he commented,

I always longed to live in New York; this was my one ambition. And I wanted to go to art school. I decided that I was going to be an artist. I wanted to get some real training and I heard about the Art Students League.

James Verner eventually relented and gave his son permission to study art in New York City. Perhaps it was meant to be. If his son was going to be an artist, there was nothing he could do to stop it.

Vernon arrived in New York in the fall of 1915 and took up residence at the Commodore Hotel on 42nd Street. Upon arriving, he sauntered down to Broadway, eager to drink in the lights and glamour he had so often dreamed about. Broadway during the day, however, looked like any other main street. It was not at all what he had expected. He then set out for Martinka's Magical Palace, the magic emporium he had read so much about and that was considered the epicenter of the craft. He couldn't find it. He walked back and forth along Sixth Avenue, full well expecting to spot a façade outfitted like a castle. He eventually stopped before a dingy little store, number 493, and double-checked the street address he had scrawled on a piece of paper. This *was* it. A bell rang when he entered the shop and an elderly woman, Mrs. Martinka, emerged into the showroom and stood behind the counter.

"What do you want?" She asked him in a rather curt manner.

Vernon wasn't sure. She handed him a catalogue and told him to call her if he wanted anything, and walked to the back of the store. It was not the kind of reception he had expected. Vernon left as quickly as he came.

He headed off towards 215 West Fifty-Seventh Street, the home of the Art Students League, and was relieved to discover an impressive building. Vernon preferred the cavalier approach to education espoused by the Art Students League. Unlike McGill University or the Royal Military College, the League did not award diplomas or degrees and there was no set curriculum. Instructors such as John Sloan and Robert Henri were there to teach, offer criticism, and debate the meaning of art and the role of the artist in society. The League offered a broad range of artistic study, favoring no particular school or specific approach to painting, allowing its students to choose their own courses of study.

The most attractive aspect of the school, at least as far as Vernon was concerned, were the Friday soirees where staff, students, writers, cartoonists and the occasional social dilettante or patron would congregate to drink, discuss art, and socialize. Vernon attended these gatherings on a regular basis. One evening, another regular advised Vernon to avoid the school. "Art school," the man said, "will ruin you. The great artists never go to art school. Once you learn something about perspective, something about foreshortening, a few little rules, art school can do only one thing—dwarf you and kill your style, your originality. You'll be copying another person's format." That was all it took. Vernon's attendance at the League became more sporadic, while his passion for magic continued unabated.

One day, while walking uptown from another pilgrimage to Martinka's, Vernon noticed another magic store, Clyde W. Powers, at 231 West 42nd Street. It was much more modern in appearance than the Magical Palace on Sixth Avenue. Vernon entered the shop and Paul Carlton, a young man with red hair, emerged from a back room. He

Artifice, Ruse and Subterfuge

Clyde W. Powers (second from right) holds court at his magic emporium in Manhattan on 42nd Street.

said, "Are you interested in handkerchief tricks, coin tricks, apparatus? What would you like to see?"

Vernon said, "Primarily cards. If there is any trick with cards I don't know that fools me, I'd be willing to buy it for $20."

Carlton looked at Vernon as if he was either a farm boy or a wealthy kid who thought he knew a thing or two. As such, Carlton thought he was going to set Vernon back on his feet. He took a pack of cards, fanned them out and asked Vernon to select one. Vernon recognized immediately that it was a trick deck by the way Carlton handled the cards. He didn't like Carlton's attitude and decided to intentionally mess up the trick. Carlton had to repeat the trick several times before he succeeded. Vernon said, "I think I know that trick. They're Strippers."

Carlton reached below the counter and took out another pack and then another. Vernon was conversant with both of them. Frustrated, Carlton asked Vernon where he was from and how he had come to be familiar with so many secrets. Vernon answered that he was from Canada, and then quickly turned the tables on the other young man. "Can you do any tricks with an ordinary pack, not trick cards?"

Carlton did some, though not very well, certainly not up to Vernon's standards. Carlton then asked Vernon what he did. It was the Cliff Green meeting all over again.

Vernon picked up the deck and immediately placed it back on the counter. He said, "I've been around all day, and my hands are a little bit dry and dirty. Is there any place I could wash my hands. Then I'll show you a couple of things."

Carlton pointed Vernon towards the lavatory. In the simple action of picking up and replacing the pack, Vernon had palmed out one of the cards from Carlton's deck. Once in the washroom, he removed a set of special eye scissors that he carried with him and cut a microscopic, elliptical piece off each end of the card. He then rubbed his hand on some dust and soiled the edge of the doctored card so that it would conform with the others once it had been secretly added to the pack. Vernon returned to the showroom and secretly replaced the short card on the pack as he picked it up from the counter. He then performed three or four tricks for Carlton, tricks that he had developed during his time with Cliff Green.

Carlton, nearly slack-jawed, yelled to the back of the store for the proprietor: "Clyde, come out here!"

Carlton explained to Clyde Powers that Vernon was willing to pay twenty dollars for any trick he didn't understand. Powers said, "I've got a trick we sell for $20. It's not in the catalogue and we don't show it to the average customer, only people very advanced in magic. I'll do it for you; I'm sure you haven't seen it before."

Powers performed the effect. It was a complicated trick, one involving three selected cards, a secret stack and much spelling. Powers asked, "Did that fool you?"

Politely, Vernon answered, "No."

Powers was not convinced.

Vernon continued, "You betrayed yourself. You were careful the way you divided the cards and I thought you would have an exact number in each pile, but when you spelled them out, the whole thing cleared up in my mind that you took 12 cards that spelled with 12 letters and 11 with 11 letters and so. When I returned the cards, I noticed that you put them right at the bottom of these groups that you shuffled."

Powers, now completely taken aback, said, "My God, you mean to say you just analyzed that right now?"

He then asked Vernon to show some of the tricks that he himself performed. Powers looked on with approval, and then asked Vernon

Artifice, Ruse and Subterfuge

where he learned to do these tricks. Vernon's reply was innocent: *"The Expert At The Card Table."*

Powers shook his head. "Nobody understands that book. It's like geometry." Vernon assured Powers that the explanations were perfectly clear to him.

Powers said, "Young man, make this place your home. We have a back room; when Kellar or Ching Ling Foo, or Houdini, Dr. Elliott or any of these well-known magicians are in New York, they don't stay out in front here, they walk in the back room. This is the inner sanctum. We don't invite our customers back there, only professional magicians. You can go back there whenever you like."

Vernon was thrilled. It had been his ambition before he came to New York to meet these famous magicians. He had read about them and knew their stories. Now he was confident that he could hold his own if he ever had the opportunity to speak with them. More importantly, now he had the chance.

As Vernon floated out of the store, Powers added, "Don't forget! Every Friday night we hold a séance." Vernon didn't need a second invitation. He visited Powers' shop practically every day, arriving in the afternoon when most of the other magicians made their entrances. He also stayed late on occasion for the séances that Powers staged for Park Avenue socialites. Spiritualism had resurfaced sixty years after the first families of spiritualism—the Fox Sisters and the Davenport Brothers—fueled the public's interest in the spirit world. Now, in the twentieth century, the manifestations were more sophisticated. The centerpiece of Powers' séance was a teakettle that emitted an audible human voice. For twenty dollars, the voice inside the kettle whispered answers to questions posed to it by those who put the spout to their ears. Was it a genuine example of communication with the afterlife? No. It was a magic prop belonging to Harry Kellar.

Even though Kellar had retired from the stage in 1908, he never lost his love for magic. He visited Powers' magic shop frequently, haunting the backroom with stories of his exploits and his opinion on the state of the art. Vernon listened to Kellar, the man who inspired him as a boy, the one who taught him by example that without mystery, there is no such thing as magic. Kellar was disturbed that Thurston discarded most of the illusions that had been purchased from him. Furthermore, Kellar was particularly livid that Thurston could be so cavalier with the secrets of the craft. When Thurston performed The Levitation of Princess Karnac, an illusion in which Kellar had invested significant resources, Thurston invited members of the audience on to the stage, knowing full well that they too would become privy to the secret. Thurston was not concerned. He believed that the presence of an onstage committee enhanced the effect—creating the perception of an illusion so perfect that even those on stage could not fathom how it was performed. If it enhanced the experience for the thousand people seated in the theatre, Thurston saw no harm in exposing the secret behind the magic to those called on stage. Not surprisingly, Vernon disagreed, siding with Kellar.

Vernon believed in the strict rule of secrecy. He had worked hard to amass a body of technique from gamblers and develop his own extensions of that work to fool other magicians. That was Vernon's goal in 1916: to perform magic that fooled those well versed in the craft.

Vernon could fool other magicians because his approach was novel. New York magicians, for example, were unfamiliar with his notion of "think of a card." Instead of asking a person to remove a playing card physically from the pack, note and then return it, Vernon developed a variety of techniques whereby the participant made a *mental* rather than *physical* selection of a card, and still he would be able to locate or divine its identity. Inspired by J. Warren Keane, Vernon conducted his own experiments into the cards that people were most likely to name. Vernon was able to marry the principles of deception with his interest in psychology and the public's fascination in mental telepathy.

Further, Vernon's technique was extemporized. He understood that that the proper technique would vary in each particular circumstance. The first magic secret he ever learned, the one that his father performed with chalk marks at the dinning room table, set the precedent. Advantage players reinforced it. The task for the performer was to perfect a wide body of technique and then improvise. Vernon had an agile mind, one that could make adjustments on the fly, and a supreme self-confidence in his own abilities. This brashness reflected both his youth and his training.

Not all magicians embraced the cocky Canadian. Some were affronted by his bravado. *The Sphinx*, which by 1916 was ensconced as the magic industry's premier publication, published this derisive snippet in the April 1916 issue.

Broadway Chatter
By One of the Boys

Fred Griffith – "I've cut out all magic except the billiard balls."

Artifice, Ruse and Subterfuge

Al Anderson – "Magic isn't my vocation, it's my vacation."
Poole – "Oh, yes, I work now and then." Ad lib, "Mostly then."
Ziska – "One more whack and then I'm through."
Green – "It's all a matter of luck."
Verner (fresh from Canada) – "You're all a bunch of pessimists. The chap with the goods will make good."

It helped, of course, that Vernon was interested primarily in card tricks. He could focus on card tricks because they were his hobby. He was not interested in earning a living as a magician and did not require large props that could be seen by thousands in a theatre. Besides, traditional apparatus, the types of props available to magicians at Powers' shop or in the Martinka catalogue, offered little room for extemporization. In Vernon's hands, a deck of cards became a musical instrument capable of infinite variety.

One magician who openly attempted to duplicate Vernon's feats was Joseph Dunninger. Two years Vernon's senior, Dunninger shared two of Vernon's attributes—a quick mind and unbridled self-confidence. His own magic was just as bold and often just as extemporized. Dunninger, however, was particularly interested in mentalism, the purported act of reading someone's mind in the guise of entertainment. Vernon's "Think-A-Card" tricks were right up his alley. Dunninger's reconstructions were on track, and Vernon admired him, somewhat reluctantly, for both using his head to figure out methods and for having the nerve to perform them.

Before long, Dr. James William Elliott, the Undisputed Card Champion of the World, teacher of Thurston and many other card manipulators, paid a visit to Powers' emporium. Vernon approached Elliott to express his admiration for his contributions to card magic. He was surprised to learn that Elliott had very little regard for *The Expert At The Card Table*. Elliott thought that much of the material was ridiculous, as described by Erdnase. Vernon begged to differ and told Elliott that, for him, the book was like the Bible. As if a gauntlet had been thrown down, Elliott then asked Vernon to fool him.

Vernon removed a deck of cards from its case and asked Elliott to select one. He instructed Elliott to place the deck behind his back and insert the card into it. It was the only way, Vernon explained, that Elliott could be sure that Vernon had no idea of the location of the card. Elliott did as asked and handed the pack back to Vernon. Amazingly, Vernon divined the identity of Elliott's selection. Elliott confessed that he was completely bamboozled.

Nate Leipzig, James W. Elliott and Adrian Plate at the entrance to Powers' shop.

    Vernon explained the secret to Elliott. Vernon had fooled him with a simple dodge. Elliott had heard of Vernon's reputation for subtle work and thought he had taken away all possible avenues. "I congratulate you," Elliott said. "You used one of my own weapons."

    Vernon and Elliott would meet on several occasions and sit in Elliott's hotel until the wee hours discussing magic. They were a pair of kindred spirits, both in love with magic and content to be students of the craft. During one of their sessions, Elliott reiterated the *real* secret of magic to his young apprentice. It was simple: be natural.

    The concept of naturalism was a recent phenomenon. Actors, for example, were adopting a more 'natural' approach to their craft, one that relied less on histrionics and more on natural mannerisms, emotional integrity, and truth. But how was a magician supposed to perform the supernatural, naturally? It was a challenging task. Elliott believed that the presentation and sleights had to be consistent with the character, motivation, and context of the performance. Inconsistent or unnatural actions puncture illusion the same way that wrong notes destroy a melody. Robert-Houdin advised magicians to be actors; Dr. Elliott told them to act naturally. "Be Natural" became Vernon's mantra in magic.

Artifice, Ruse and Subterfuge

With his confidence brimming, Vernon felt more at home in New York. The lights in Times Square *were* very bright, and the city was truly the epicenter of the magic world. Vernon returned to Martinkas, this time with more bravado, and befriended Henry Christ and Sam Horowitz, two young magicians employed as stock boys in the back room. Vernon and Horowitz had one special thing in common. Both had been fooled backstage by J. Warren Keane and his psychological card trick—Vernon in Ottawa and Horowitz in Paterson, New Jersey.

Vernon also met another young magic aficionado, Sam Margules, two years his junior. The son of Russian and Romanian Jews, Margules became Vernon's closest friend in New York and sponsored both Vernon and Cliff Green, who had recently immigrated to the city to try his hand at vaudeville, into the Magicians Club of New York. The May 1916 issue of *The Sphinx*, which reported the minutes of the club meeting, recorded that "Greene [sic] manipulates cards to perfection and Verner [Vernon] does second sight and mind reading with cards...several which are wonders."

James Verner sensed, at least from his perspective, that his son was adrift. It was time he came home. James sent his son enough funds to purchase a train ticket to Ottawa. Vernon ignored the request and spent the money. His father wrote a second time and this time, included a train ticket with the missive. Vernon discovered that he could return the ticket at the station for its face value and did so. His father wrote a third time, offering to send him another ticket, this time with the caveat that it would be the last. Vernon told his father to save his money. He was staying in New York.

It was all well and good to have magic as a hobby and to loiter in the backroom of magic shops, but Vernon needed money to survive. Fortunately, the Margules family embraced him as one of their own. Theirs was the first Jewish home Vernon had been in. The warmth that permeated the household was anything but Victorian. Vernon informed Sam of his predicament—he wanted to stay in New York but did not have a job. "Come with me to Coney Island," Sam suggested, "there are lots of jobs down there."

Coney Island was America's gift of leisure to the middle class. It reached its pinnacle as a resort community in 1910, when the crowds that flocked there exceeded those that attended any other sport or pastime in America. Visitors spent $45 million and devoured over ten million hot dogs that year. Coney Island was decidedly less grandiose when Vernon arrived in the summer of 1916. Its premier attraction, Dreamland, had been destroyed by fire on May 27, 1911 and had been replaced by the Dreamland Circus Sideshow—a large tent that housed the Congress of the World's Greatest Living Curiosities—the first permanent freak show in America. Featured on the bill was Albert Levinson, a magician who played as Al Flosso, The Coney Island Fakir. The sideshow attracted as many as thirty thousand visitors a day and led to a proliferation of similar attractions.

Coney Island also had roller coasters, carousels, and log rides down perilous drops that offered visitors a cacophony of sounds and experiences. Its greatest attraction, however, was its natural playground of sand and surf, one that could accommodate one million people at any given time. As soon as he saw it, Vernon knew that he had to spend a season on the beach.

Margules had started working weekends at Coney Island while he was still in school, bringing home eighty dollars each week to his family, ever the dutiful son. He worked for a glassblower, Bill Hart, who made ships in bottles, as well as larger, more elaborate pieces out of glass. Hart's booth had an open flame where people could watch him work. The glassware, however, was not for sale. The only way to obtain his handcrafts was to play a game. The player would pay a quarter or more in order to draw three cards—each one written with the name of one of the objects—from a box. The player then had his or her pick of the one of the objects listed on the cards.

Vernon soon noticed that each player would walk away with only a glass pin, a pair of glass cufflinks, or a marble, each of which was worth about a half a cent. No one ever won any of the valuable prizes. The game was crooked. It was Sam Margules' job to persuade the crowd that everything was on the up and up. Sam showed the players that the cards listed all types of prizes—large and small. As he pointed to a large glass clock on the wall for emphasis, Sam switched out the cards listing valuable prizes for ones that listed glass trinkets. He then placed the cards into the box. Unbeknownst to the crowd, the only prizes available were worthless ones.

Sam was sure that he could arrange for Vernon to work one of the other games. Vernon thought it would be fun, and he was willing try anything at least once. Sam escorted him from one dingy booth to the next, to meet the various proprietors. One questioned him, "Do you know the gimmick on this joint?" Vernon knew what the word 'joint' meant but was unfamiliar with 'gimmick.' He asked, "You mean the trick to it?" The operator looked at him as if he were some kind of half-wit and then glared at Sam. Vernon vowed to learn the jargon of

Artifice, Ruse and Subterfuge

Vernon's confidant, Sam Margules.

the trade as if they were the technical terms set out in the prologue of *The Expert At The Card Table*.

Fortunately Sam was well liked. One operator, Goldie, acquiesced to Sam's request and told an underling to put Vernon to work. He said, "Now listen, we pay $40 a week salary and all you can steal." Vernon was thrilled to make forty dollars a week. He didn't quite understand, however, the phrase "all you can steal." It meant, of course, that he could steal from the till provided he wasn't too greedy and didn't get caught.

Vernon was assigned the dart game. Players tossed darts at little round cardboard tags pinned to a board. Each tag had a number on it. The player won the prize that corresponded with the number on the tag. Vernon's job was to make it appear as though valuable numbers were pegged to the board when really there were none. The gimmick was to misrepresent the identity of the numbers on the tags. This fraudulent action transformed winners into losers. Soon after he started, a little girl came up, handed him a quarter and asked for three darts. It was against Vernon's nature to deceive her. He let the girl win—and more than his fair share of others. Goldie fired Vernon within the week. Unfortunately, it was not soon enough.

One afternoon, a friend of Goldie's approached Vernon and asked to borrow his raincoat. It had started to rain and the stranger wanted to buy some cigarettes, but didn't have an umbrella. Vernon handed the man his raincoat, an expensive one, imported from England. Vernon had purchased it in Canada for sixty dollars.

Neither the man nor the coat returned. When asked, Goldie admitted that he'd never heard of the man. How could Vernon have been so gullible? The experience hardened him. Trust no one. Still, he had to earn a living. Suddenly it dawned on him.

As a boy, Vernon and his family had vacationed on Old Orchard Beach, Maine. There he recalled seeing a man on the pier cutting silhouettes, small profiles of people cut from black paper mounted on card stock and sold as souvenirs. At the time, Vernon had been so impressed that he returned to the hotel, took some paper from the writing bureau and inked it black. He then borrowed a pair of scissors from his mother's sewing basket and tried to mimic the actions of the artist. His attempt was a complete success, which pleased James immensely. It was one of the few times his father praised his artistic endeavors. The other memory from that vacation which stuck with Vernon was one of brushing against a long black umbrella bag fastened to the side of the artist's display as he moved in to get a closer look. The bag had been packed with quarters.

Vernon asked around Coney Island to find out if anyone in the area cut silhouettes. It turned out that one fellow in Luna Park did, but that was it, and Luna Park had not yet opened for the season. The artist was cutting silhouettes in the interim on the Hudson Day Line, one of the shipping lines that transported people to Coney Island from the city. According to Vernon's sources, the artist made a lot of money. Vernon's thought, naturally, was, "Why can't I?"

Strolling down Kensington Walk towards Steeplechase Pier, Vernon came across a man on his hands and knees, trying to tack some black fabric onto a frame. A sign beside him said, "Learn To Entertain." Vernon asked the man what the sign meant. The man responded that he was going to sell card tricks and things like that. Vernon confessed that he was interested in magic. The man got up from his hands and knees, brushed off the dirt, and ushered Vernon into the little store that he was framing.

Vernon knew this diminutive Englishman could handle a pack of cards as soon as he fanned them. Extending a hand, he introduced himself as Dai Vernon. He had adopted the name Vernon because New Yorkers had a difficult time pronouncing the two "ers" in Verner. With a thick accent, it often came out as "Voinoi." It was easier to change the name, inspired by the popular dance team of Vernon and Irene Castle, than fight for corrections. He had shortened his first name to Dai—pronounced "Day," Welsh for David—several years earlier.

As they passed the deck back and forth, each performing a trick or two for the other, Vernon learned that this man, Larry Gray, was a recent immigrant from London, first to Toronto, where he worked as a waiter and studied art, and then to New York. He had taken a job as a waiter so that he wouldn't starve to death. A fellow waiter, an Irishman named Donahue, had seen him perform some tricks at the restaurant and suggested they set up a store at Coney Island and sell magic to make some extra money. Donahue knew nothing about magic but had squirreled away enough money to rent a space for a season. Gray accepted his proposal to demonstrate and sell the magic—a packet of tricks for fifty cents—in return for fifty percent of the profits.

There is a vast difference between a magician and a pitchman, a person able to attract a crowd and peddle pocket tricks as if they were worth all the tea in China. Gray could attract crowds easily, but did not know how to close the sales. People just walked away without opening their wallets. Vernon offered to give it a whirl. He knew instinctively that to be successful at Coney Island, you had to be loud and blatant. He had also seen one or two other pitchmen in his travels and remembered their opening remarks:

Now at this performance we only have one, two…how many we got? We only have six to pass out. If you want one after these six are gone, I'm sorry, you'll have to wait until the next performance. We're only allowed to pass six out at this performance.

Vernon's approach—fabricating a sense of immediacy—worked well, and though he could have sold eight or ten packets of magic to each crowd, he was a stickler for his word and only parted with six. He added, however, that another performance would start shortly. Donahue was impressed and offered to usher Gray out of the equation. He had prepaid $700, half the rent for the season, to secure the location. The balance was due in July. Vernon was the one who could help him recoup his investment. Vernon was surprised, however, that Donahue could be such a fickle friend. Vernon declined the offer, stating that he would never take away another person's job, and then tabled the idea of cutting silhouettes. He could attract some additional traffic to the booth and was willing to split some of his profits with Donahue for use of the space. An agreement was reached.

Vernon returned to New York, purchased a large piece of cardboard for ten cents, obtained a remnant of wallpaper, one that could be pasted to the board as a background, and then put a frame around it. He purchased a supply of the black paper, flag paper put in prayer books and Bibles, and laboriously cut out knights with armor, a horse, and several portraits. He purchased a jar of Carter's paste and mounted his creations to the board. The next day he was open for business.

Early into the season, a man came by, studied the silhouettes and asked who cut them. Vernon said that they were his. "You must have drawn them first," the man said. Vernon assured him the silhouettes were cut freehand. The man said, "Here, let me show you something." He picked up Vernon's paper and scissors, put two pieces together and cut a double silhouette, two profiles at once, made to appear as though one person was standing behind the other. The technique was brand new to Vernon. The man introduced himself as Perry, Luna Park's resident silhouette artist. "When you get a bank roll," he said, "come around and see me. I will give you a few lessons." Vernon was content to continue on his own, working and basking in the unconventional lifestyle of a Coney Island regular.

> *State's bank used to play "The Star Spangled Banner" at one o'clock; that was our alarm clock. We'd hear this and we'd just hop out of bed like soldiers. There was nothing in the morning at Coney Island; it was an evening or late afternoon spot. We'd go down to the ocean, put on our bathing suits and have a dip until sundown, then come and open the store.*

Vernon also spent a great deal of time playing poker. He was still passionately interested in card cheats and knew by now how to find them. He had to sit in games. It was in this way that Vernon learned that Poker was not always America's favorite pastime. That position was reserved for Faro. Faro was a game for aristocrats, played in a dignified manner for large stakes. The game achieved widespread popularity because it was the fairest banking game ever devised. The house advantage against the player was very small. The game eventually fell out of favor because the only way the house could win consistently was to cheat. Vernon also learned that other cheats held Faro dealers in great esteem. The Faro dealer had to be as sophisticated as the players and capable of manipulating cards with grace and precision. "Dealing the bank," as it was known, was a badge of

Artifice, Ruse and Subterfuge

honor and the pinnacle of the professional's career.

As the game had been out of favor for nearly two decades, Vernon recognized that its dealers were virtually extinct. Still, he vowed to find them and learn the secrets of their craft. He knew it would not be easy. He was informed that Faro dealers belonged to a closed-society, one that did not share secrets readily, even with other advantage players. He would have to find them before they, and their knowledge, vanished forever.

As for cutting silhouettes, sales were not as vibrant as originally projected. Not enough traffic passed by the store. Donahue had been misled as to the value of the location. The site was humming when he first scouted it. All other streets—including Surf Avenue—were deserted in comparison. Donahue paid the advance because the broker timed it perfectly, showing the property just when the crowd assembled to board the steamship that left Steeplechase Pier for New York. Most of the time, though, the place was deserted. Vernon swallowed his pride and visited Perry in Luna Park. He studied the way Perry attracted customers and managed the crowd. Eventually, Perry offered Vernon the opportunity to work with him on a percentage basis. Vernon accepted the offer.

After the season came to a close in September, Vernon plied his new trade at one-day bazaars and fairs around New York, New Jersey, and Pennsylvania. He also continued to seek the new and unusual. He was particularly interested in carnivals and the characters that worked there. When he heard, for example, that a carnival featured a magician, Vernon set out to meet him. Vernon was also on the lookout for gamblers to see if they had any techniques that he could apply to magic. So, while waiting for a carnival show to open in Orange, New Jersey, Vernon struck up a conversation with the man, he was surprised to learn, who was responsible for the "privilege car," a car where they have the "privilege" of gambling.

Carnivals often had a large railroad car outfitted for dice and card games. People would play craps or poker to while away the time it took to travel from one stop to another. Once the man realized that Vernon wasn't a "square," he was invited to join the "privilege" car. Enchanted by Vernon's technique, the players on board asked him why he even bothered to fool around with magic. He should be an advantage player, they said. Vernon, however, didn't have heart, the larcenous spirit required to take someone's money under false pretenses. He told them he just couldn't do it. The hustlers were puzzled. "What do you mean?" they asked. "Anybody else would take it from you if they could, so why don't you take it from them?" Vernon was content to remain a student of the craft. Fortunately, he had made enough money at Coney Island to sustain himself during the fall and winter.

Vernon continued to cut silhouettes in and around New York. A society woman, however, suggested Vernon venture farther afield and contact the organizer of the Boston Allied Bazaar and rent a booth. Vernon made the necessary arrangements. One day, while cutting the silhouette of an irritable, uncooperative child, Vernon heard a woman remark, "I think you are getting that very well, the proportion is very good, why don't you dip his head?" He wondered who was telling him how to do his work. He finished the silhouette and then cut a few others. The woman, an elderly lady in widow's weeds, said, "I hope you weren't annoyed, but I had a little boy that used to do this work very well."

Vernon continued, "I don't doubt it at all, Madam. But this is quite a different thing. If your little boy was ever up against what I am up against right now, you'd find it wouldn't be so easy."

The woman replied, "My little boy, in fact, is grown up now and is quite a well known artist."

Vernon intimated that he knew most of the well-known artists around New York, and he asked her for the name of her son. She replied, "Charles Dana Gibson."

Vernon was dumbfounded. Gibson was a cultural icon, famous for the Gibson Girls, pen-and-ink drawings that defined the look and character of the modern American woman. His work was featured prominently in a host of magazines, including *The Century, Harper's Monthly,* and *Bazaar*. Gibson also contributed a weekly drawing to *Life*. Vernon idolized Gibson and often tried to copy his drawings. Mrs. Gibson offered to introduce Vernon to her son. She went off into a back room and returned with an unsealed letter addressed to her son. It said, "This letter will introduce a very interesting young man I met. He cuts the silhouettes that you did when you were a little boy."

Charles Dana Gibson was born in Roxbury, Massachusetts in 1867. It was his silhouettes that first gained him recognition as an artist. He left Massachusetts to study at the Art Students League but left after two years to go to work to help pay his parents back for their generous support. He soon gained prominence as *the* pen and ink artist of his time.

Vernon contacted Gibson as soon as he returned to New York. Ver-

Artifice, Ruse and Subterfuge

non told Gibson that his ultimate ambition was to become a portrait artist. Much to his surprise, Gibson advised Vernon to forsake the idea. The life of an artist, Gibson maintained, was one of disappointment and broken hearts. Gibson told Vernon the fable of the crow and the canary:

One day a crow met a canary and they argued about who had the best voice.

The canary said, "Why, you know you can't sing like I can," and the canary sang his beautiful tones.

The crow said, "That's not singing, listen to this. 'Craw, craw.' That's quality."

So they said, "Let somebody judge; let's have a referee."

Just then a big, fat pig came waddling along the road and they said, "Listen, will you judge a contest? We've had an argument. We want to know who sings best."

First the canary sang. He sang beautifully. The old crow followed and went, "Craw, craw."

The pig said, "Well, black face, you have a real voice, you can sing. The little yellow fellow, he can't sing."

The little canary started crying. Just then, a very kindly man came along and said, "Hello little bird, what are you crying about?"

"Well, I'm crying because I had a contest with a crow and I lost."

"You are a good sport; a good sport doesn't cry when he loses."

The canary said, "I am a good sport. I'm not crying because I lost. I'm crying because the judge was a pig."

Gibson continued, "In art, all forms of art, unfortunately the judges are pigs. If you want your heart broken, go in for art."

First Vernon had been told to avoid art school because it crippled an artist's individual style. Now he was told to forsake a professional career by a man he admired greatly. In March 1917, Vernon sent a postcard to his father from the Zoo Garden in Philadelphia, wishing him and Napier a happy birthday and updating his father on the state of his affairs. James Verner, resigned to the fact that his son was staying in New York, replied on March 19, 1917 and advised his son to continue his studies.

On May 17, 1917, as Vernon was preparing to return to Coney Island for a second summer season, his eighteen-year-old brother Napier enlisted in the 72nd Queens Battery of the Canadian Expeditionary Force. The war in Europe had raged on longer than anyone had anticipated, and there was a shortage of troops. The year before, Canadian Prime Minister Robert Borden had pledged that Canada would send 500,000 men overseas for the cause. The population of the country at that time was barely eight million. Whether it was by accident or design, Vernon had managed to avoid military service since the outbreak of hostilities in August 1914. Most of his time had been spent studying art, practicing magic, cutting silhouettes, and bathing in the ocean while his classmates from Ashbury College, McGill University and Royal Military College, and now his brother set out to fight the Huns in the fields of Belgium and France.

Vernon invited his parents to visit him at Coney Island for a summer holiday. On July 25th, James wrote to his son, c/o The Saltaire, a hotel located at 2 - 19th Street, Brighton Beach, Coney Island and said he was considering the possibility but then wrote again on August 13th to decline the invitation. As a result of high casualties and dwindling enlistments, the government enacted *The Military Service Act* in August 1917. Canada would meet its commitments overseas by conscription. Able-bodied men were now required by law to register for the armed forces. On October 3, 1917, James again wrote to his son and enclosed a few newspaper clippings. The clippings spoke of a new opportunity.

Canadians Are Wanted For Royal Flying Corps

It is announced by the Royal Flying Corps Committee of the Aero Club of Canada which has offices at 99 Sun Life Building, Toronto, that the Imperial Royal Flying Corps is now ready to receive 600 cadets for training as flying officers.

The corps has established five great aerodromes, one at Camp Borden, two at Deserento, and two at Armour Heights, adjacent to Toronto.

Artifice, Ruse and Subterfuge

One of the Toronto University buildings has been turned over to the chief instructor of the corps and his staff, for lectures and technical educational purposes, while at the aerodromes, the most complete aeronautical equipment has been installed.

It takes five months to complete the course.

A second clipping read:

May Become Flying Officer

The Royal Flying Corps committee, of the Aero Club of Canada, having headquarters in the Sun Life Building, Toronto, is organizing a committee of local citizens with a view of giving the young men of this locality more information relating to the opportunity now offered by the Imperial Royal Flying Corps in Canada, for those desiring commissions at once, or in future, as flying officers. This, it is stated, is now the senior and best paid branch of the service, and the education derived will doubtless be of the greatest advantage after the war. It is now possible for any deserving young man possessing the right qualifications to go through without expense to himself.

On November 6, 1917, Vernon received Postmaster Certificate No. 583977 ordering him to register for military service. It was time to return home and visit old haunts while waiting to be called for active duty. Although Ottawa looked much the same, times had changed. Passing the Russell Theatre, he noticed a sign that advertised Lincoln, the International Card Expert, on the bill. Vernon was incensed that an imitator was using the moniker associated with Nate Leipzig, the great New York card magician. Going backstage later that evening, Vernon discovered, much to his surprise, Leipzig himself. Leipzig was Lincoln. Leipzig informed Vernon that his agent had advised him to change his name. The name Leipzig, during those troubled times, was bad for business.

Vernon was called in for his military medical examination on April 12, 1918. His medical record indicated that he had a slight deformity in his "left elbow joint due to fracture of upper end of radius extending into joint." The deformity was created when, at age two, Vernon fabricated paper wings and jumped out of a tree in the mistaken belief that he could fly. The break was not set properly. The doctors noted, "rotation & supination normal," but added that he had, "slightly limited extension." Doctors also diagnosed that he had enlarged thyroid glands but indicated, "Not sufficient to interfere with service." Vernon listed his occupation as "artist."

Vernon was assigned on April 16, 1918 to the 2nd Depot Battalion, East Ontario Regiment, of the Canadian Contingent Expeditionary Force, a reserve force for the Canadian Expeditionary Force sent overseas. He immediately sought a discharge so that he could enlist in the Imperial Flying Corps. On April 17, 1918, the Secretary of the Canadian Division of the Aerial League of the British Empire wrote to Captain G.R. Drummond, Officer in charge of the Mobilization Centre, requesting that Vernon be examined as a potential candidate. The examination was held in Montreal, and Vernon received his discharge on June 21, 1918, having served a total of 65 days in "His Majesty's Service." Vernon reported to the Chief Recruiting Officer, Royal Air Force, King Street, Toronto, on June 25, 1918 to train as a pilot. He was assigned a desk job and instructed to learn everything he could about airplane engines. He told his Commanding Officer, however, that the only engine he cared for was the one that powered the train back to New York. He persuaded his Commanding Officer to grant him leave. Vernon returned to New York.

With the sinking of the Lusitania, America joined the war effort and once committed, the American people embraced the call to arms with vigor. Everyone pitched in to do his or her part. Entertainers were no exception. Vernon cut silhouettes for the cause, giving fifty percent of the proceeds to the war effort while keeping fifty percent for himself. Despite his protestations, organizers preferred Vernon to wear his uniform when he cut the silhouettes, as it attracted larger crowds to his stand. Vernon met many great entertainers and public figures during these drives. At the Italian Bazaar held at Grand Central Palace, the great Italian operatic singer Enrico Caruso circulated with the crowd. Vernon approached the great tenor.

> *I asked him if he'd mind getting up on the little bandstand and saying a few words to the crowd. So he got up and gave a little talk about the opera, about Italy and different singers and somebody said, "Why don't you sing?" And this was the thrill of my life when he sang, he was really great, that voice was absolutely glorious.*

Whereas Vernon spent sixty-five days in a reserve force located in Ontario and then extended a six-week leave from the air force to a six-month stay in New York, his brother was not so lucky. Napier served twenty-one months, six months of which were as a 'gravel cruncher' in the trenches of France, operating a machine gun. He was hospitalized several times, first with German measles, then with Rubella, and finally with Impetigo. S.W. Erdnase wrote, "Advantages that are bound to ultimately give a percentage in favor of the professional are absolutely essential to his existence." Somehow, Vernon had endeared himself to his Commanding Officer and had his assistance in covering up or explaining his extended leave to superiors.

Although Vernon managed to avoid active service overseas for the duration of the war, he did not emerge unscathed. James Verner died of a heart attack in August 1918. Armistice was declared on November 11, 1918. Napier was discharged, shell shocked, from the Canadian Expeditionary Forces on April 5, 1919, unaware that his father had passed away. When he walked through the door of his parents' home, his father was the first person he called for.

Vernon had the task of telling his brother, tears welling in his eyes, that his father was no more. It was a role he did not relish and one that he would not forget.

Chapter Three
The Man Who Fooled Houdini

His business card may have described his profession as "Silhouettest" and listed his address as 88 MacLaren Street, Ottawa, but Vernon's heart was in the United States, the country where, in his mind, fortunes could be made or lost based on ability, not social standing. His brother Napier, now home from the war, could attend to their mother and younger brother. It was time to return to America and assert his independence just as Canada had asserted its own administrative independence from Great Britain during the course of the war.

Vernon headed for Chicago, home to several magic shops, including Roterberg's, whose catalogue he had ordered as a youth. Chicago was also a hotbed of illicit gambling and had two major supply houses that outfitted professionals with marked cards, loaded dice, and machines—secret apparatus designed to switch cards into and out of play—as well as furniture, tables, and playing surfaces designed to provide the owner with an operational advantage. In addition, the city was the home of Frederick J. Drake & Co., the publishing house responsible for distributing *The Expert At The Card Table*, and the last known address of its author. Vernon recalled the hunt for Erdnase,

> Of course, I was curious to know who Erdnase was, and years later when I went to Chicago, there was a fellow named Myers (he used the name John C. Sprong) who worked in the Post Office having a job where he used to check when the trucks come in or something. He sat in a little cubicle and he had plenty of time to practice cards. He

became an expert card manipulator. Naturally, he was a student of Erdnase, which was the best textbook on cards written up to that date. He said he found out from Drake, who was one of the later publishers of Erdnase that Erdnase is Andrews spelled all mixed up. His real name was Andrews. "I [Sprong] asked Mr. Drake who this fellow Andrews was, and he said he was sorry, he couldn't tell me. So I went back there religiously for months and kept badgering the old man to tell me something about this Andrews. He said he couldn't betray a confidence and couldn't tell anything about Andrews."

Although he was unable to learn more about Andrews, Vernon still had extraordinary luck for someone so obsessed with manipulating it. While he was sitting at a checkerboard in a hotel lobby, a man of Eastern European decent, either Hungarian or Czechoslovakian, approached and asked if Vernon wanted to play a game. As the two played, one word led to another, and Vernon confessed that he was interested in gambling and cards. The man responded that the interest was mutual. He himself gambled a great deal, and told Vernon that he knew a lot of people who could do good second and bottom deals. Cheats often share information with each other. They have few to confide in and constantly search for new techniques to augment their arsenal. Vernon would comment,

This is a strange thing but it's something the public doesn't really know. Only the ones that are inside, in the racket themselves, understand how this work is done. Now as a rule they don't confide in magicians at all. If they do they have a pseudo explanation of how the thing is done or they throw him off. But I've enjoyed the confidence of a lot of these fellows because I have had things that they want to learn themselves, that they think they can adapt to the card table, and as a consequence they're greedy for money, they will show something, in other words to get something from me.

Vernon discovered that his opponent could do some very fine things with a deck of cards. His was a level of expertise Vernon had not encountered in years, and then perhaps only once or twice before. The cheat had learned his technique in Europe, from his father, who was also a card player. The cheat was rather self-effacing: "If you want to see some great work," he said, "you ought to see 'Old Dad Stevens.'"

Dai Vernon: A Biography

"Who," Vernon asked, "is 'Old Dad Stevens'?"

The names of gamblers are bandied about the profession. Vernon was surprised he had never heard the name before. He pressed the man for more information. He learned Stevens was a regular at the Waiters' Club on State Street. Stevens played cards there most Saturday nights and he never lost.

Vernon asked, "Is he a waiter?"

The man replied, "Hell, no, why should he be a waiter? He's worth over a half a million dollars."

Vernon replied, "Then what's he doing at the Waiters' Club?"

"Oh," the cheat said, "he likes to play cards. He comes down there every Saturday night and trims all the waiters. He beats them all."

Vernon asked, "Well, how can they stand for this every Saturday night, being beaten?"

The man said, "They think they'll catch him sometime. They just say, 'Well, Stevens, I know you're doing something, but I can't see what you're dong.' That's how good he is; they can't catch him."

Vernon asked, "Is there any chance I'd be able to meet this fellow?"

Unfortunately the man was leaving town and unable to escort Vernon to the club. He told Vernon to just walk in. No one would bother him. He could just hang around. He then described Stevens, "He's an old guy; he's the oldest one in there—probably seventy-four or five years old—very quiet looking fellow. He is rather thin and wears a derby hat."

That Saturday, Vernon headed for Waiters' Club, spotted an old guy with a derby hat, and explained how he had met a gambler while playing checkers and how he had heard that a Mr. Stevens never lost playing cards. The man acknowledged that he was Mr. Stevens and that he knew the gambler Vernon spoke of, but had not seen him in a while.

Vernon said, "Well, I'm very interested in cards. In fact, it's almost a mania with me. I hear you do some things with cards that are quite unusual."

Stevens looked at Vernon, and he said, "Well, I'll show you something." He took out a bankbook and pointed to the balance. It listed over $250,000 on deposit.

"You don't generally see an account like this for people who play cards," he said. "I decided very young that I'd make money and save it. Most people who gamble win money at cards and lose it shooting dice. Or they may win money at cards and they go out to a racetrack, or they think they're smart and can beat the stock market. I didn't make that mistake. I won money at cards and I kept it. I put it in good securities and stock."

Stevens was correct. Most gamblers live a peripatetic life, frittering away their resources. Even S.W. Erdnase confessed that he wrote *The Expert At The Card Table* because he needed the money.

Vernon countered, "And you don't generally see people who have it, show things like that either."

Stevens replied, "I'm kind of proud of it. I beat the racket. I've got that money in the bank, and I've got a home in Evanston worth that much money too. I have quite a little nest egg for my old age."

Vernon said, "Well, I understand you play poker here and you always win."

"Well," he said, "That's my fun. I like to keep my hand in. I don't go around gambling any more. I used to. I was known as the Mysterious Kid when I was young, and the reason for it was that I'd always go in and I'd win money and nobody ever knew that I was in on a crooked card move. I was just termed the Mysterious Kid because for some reason, I always won. They couldn't figure it out."

"I'd love to see you do something," Vernon said.

Stevens took Vernon back to the table where he usually played cards. As soon as he touched the pack, Vernon noticed that Stevens was left-handed. And, when Stevens dealt the cards, Vernon knew he was in the presence of the master. Stevens removed three Jacks from the deck, placed them on top and then dealt the cards alternately to Vernon and himself. Stevens got the three Jacks. Vernon knew he was using only three Jacks and was dealing them to himself, so he asked if Stevens would repeat the trick. Stevens did it twice more. Vernon, in awe, exclaimed, "You must have to deal fourths to do that!" Stevens replied, "You're pretty smart; you're right."

Stevens was the most accomplished card cheat of the twentieth century. He demonstrated not only a perfect understanding of technique and spent the thousands of hours to master it, but he also developed extremely sophisticated concepts and new techniques that extended the range of both card cheating and, through Vernon, magic. Stevens extended the technique in *The Expert At The Card Table* in ways no one, particularly Vernon, had ever imagined.

"To become adept at second dealing," S.W. Erdnase wrote, "is as difficult a task as can be given in card handling." Stevens could deal *thirds*—dealing the third card down from the top of the deck as if it were the first—flawlessly.

Erdnase also wrote that, "The blind process of riffling the two packets truly together... leaving the order of the whole the same, is quite possible, but very difficult to perform perfectly."

Stevens had *multiple* ways of riffle shuffling the cards together on the table without altering the position of a single card. Stevens could also perform the shift, transposing the halves of the pack after the initial cut, imperceptibly. His greatest innovation, however, was the riffle cull.

Stevens had Vernon shuffle the deck so that the cards were thoroughly mixed. He took the cards back and asked Vernon to name the value of a card; the nines were chosen. Stevens gave the deck a series of tabled shuffles, separating the deck into two halves and shuffling them together. The four nines were now on top of the pack.

Vernon said, "You must have been pretty lucky that time."

Stevens said, "No luck about it. I'll do it again. What cards would you like this time?"

Vernon said, "The fours." Stevens gave the deck a series of shuffles and cuts and then dealt the four fours from the top of the deck. Vernon was nonplussed. It simply wasn't possible. Stevens then repeated the demonstration several times.

The cheat who can deal seconds and bottoms, even thirds, still has to track and obtain the cards he wants for the deal. He first has to find the cards for the hand *and then* control them or transfer them to the desired location for dealing. S.W. Erdnase's own system, one whereby the cheat notes the position of cards in previously dealt hands and then assembles or culls the cards during the course of a shuffle so that they fall to a particular player or to the dealer during the course of play, had to be performed with an overhand shuffle. Sophisticated players, however, customarily shuffled the cards on the table. Stevens had invented a method whereby he could secretly spot, mark and redistribute to the top of the deck cards that formed a winning hand, *all while performing a series of riffle shuffles*. Vernon imagined that the only way someone could be that accomplished was to be locked up in Alcatraz or sent to Siberia for twenty years with nothing more than a pack of cards and his wits.

"I never thought I'd see the day when I'd see a man do something like that," Vernon said.

"Well, you won't see anyone else in the world do it. Eighteen years when I was a young boy I practiced this. Eighteen years before I went into action," Stevens replied.

Armed with his impossible technique, Stevens then made his fortune. At seventy-four, he attended the Waiters' Club just to keep his hand in the game.

"Sometimes," he said, "I give them their money back, if they're married men and they need it. Now some of these fellows are so avaricious, I love to beat them. They're so smart, they'd steal your right eye; but they can't beat me, I beat them."

It was hard for Vernon to imagine anything more beautiful than the Stevens' riffle cull. And yet, while Stevens appreciated Vernon's enthusiasm for his work, he added that if Vernon wanted to see the most beautiful thing ever done with cards, he should seek out a player named Ping Pong.

Ping Pong, Stevens informed him, had mastered the shift. "The shift," wrote Erdnase, "has yet to be invented that can be executed by a movement appearing as coincident card table routine." If Stevens was awed by Ping Pong's shift, Vernon thought, it must be a sleight to behold. Unfortunately, Stevens could offer no other information about the mysterious gambler. The move, Stevens said, was impossible to describe. The two men parted ways, but not before Stevens invited Vernon to visit him at his home in Evanston.

Vernon's encounter with Dad Stevens was a pivotal moment in the evolution of magic. Stevens and Vernon connected, not because Vernon had anything to offer Stevens, but because Stevens recognized in Vernon a kindred spirit, someone who had a deep understanding of the intellectual underpinnings of the profession and the tenacity to reach for them. If Vernon offered Stevens anything, it was being the repository for his life's work. Stevens, age seventy-four, must have recognized that Vernon, age twenty-five, was a worthy recipient. It is likely that Stevens' name and innovations would have gone unrecorded without Vernon. Vernon was like Sir Richard Burton discovering the Kamasutra. Ultimately, he was rewarded for seeking out the uncharted vistas and cultural remnants of an exotic culture. Unlike Burton, however, Vernon only shared Stevens' riffle cull with a few close confidants. He guarded the secret closely for over sixty-five years. Today it remains the most difficult technique in the realm of card table artifice.

Several days after his session with Stevens, his head still in the clouds, Vernon visited Hunt's, a gambling supply house in Chicago that specialized in selling marked cards and loaded dice. First, he asked whether anyone had ever heard of a man named Stevens. An older gentlemen behind the counter said, "You don't mean Dad Stevens? The Mysterious Kid?" Vernon said, "Yeah," and the gentleman replied, "I've never met him, but he had a tremendous reputation here." Vernon then asked about Ping Pong. According to the staff at Hunt's, Ping Pong had last been seen around French Lick Springs, a health spa and gambling resort in Indiana. Immediately, Vernon set out to find him.

He arrived in the town and checked into the French Lick Springs Hotel, a grand building where industrialists and entrepreneurs could ride in their own railroad cars up to the door. The room cost Vernon the sizable sum of eighteen dollars per day. It was, however, on the European plan: three meals a day and all the mineral water, hot and cold, that one could stomach. Even better, the hotel had its own gambling den. There, Vernon made further inquires but learned very little. Although several gamblers there had met Ping Pong—a little red-nosed fellow who drank a great deal—they knew neither his real name nor his nationality. They did confirm, however, that he was perhaps the only man who ever lived who could perform the shift at the table. He had an unorthodox method but one that was highly effective. At the end of the week, Vernon heard that Ping Pong preferred to play in West Baden, another health retreat and center of gambling, named after Baden Baden in Germany and located just six miles from French Lick Springs. Vernon departed immediately, but he was too late. Ping Pong had come and gone. The trail was cold. It was time to return to Chicago, seek out more information, and perhaps meet with Dad Stevens again.

Once back in the Windy City, Vernon checked in at his regular haunts, the gambling supply houses, and asked if they had any further information of interest. Before he knew it, he had been arrested.

The day had started innocently enough. Vernon met two small-time gamblers in a store and joined them for lunch at a nearby diner. After a few moments, two plainclothes policemen interrupted the trio's conversation and invited the sharps to police headquarters. They were wanted for questioning.

Vernon was outraged by the demands, demeanor, and language of the police officers and protested vehemently in his best Canadian accent. They had no right, he told them, to force the gentlemen to the station. Then and there, the policemen decided that Vernon ought to come along too. They grabbed him and escorted him to the station with the others. After some routine questioning, the gamblers were turned loose. Vernon, however, was detained. He had no identification, and his only possessions were a dollar thirty-nine in change, several fresh decks of cards and a small sharp pair of scissors. The police decided that they had made an unexpected haul and that Vernon was, in fact, "The Black Prince," a notorious international pickpocket. The police howled when Vernon told them that he used the scissors to cut silhouettes.

Vernon was permitted to make one phone call. He phoned Harlan England, known to his friends as Bud. Vernon had only met England a couple of weeks earlier. Vernon had been practicing some tricky sleight with a deck of cards to pass the dull dinner hour in front of his hotel lobby silhouette stand when he became conscious of someone peering over his shoulder. Turning around, he looked up into a pair of smiling blue eyes and heard a drawling Texas voice say, "You're pretty good kid, what else do ya' do?" A long conversation ensued.

> *Bud was a wiry little ex-cow puncher from Texas and consumed large quantities of Old Overholt, which seemed to have no effect upon him whatever, except to loosen his tongue and unlock the storage of his strange adventures in far corners of the world. Bud had run away from home at an early age and joined the army. He rejoined during the First World War and after being discharged became a grifter. He had a disability allowance from the government and was thereby provided with shelter and food without having to resort to a nine to five existence to secure them. He managed to earn a good living by playing cards and selling or pitching novelties at fairs or on street corners.*

The two discussed the merits of false cuts, bottom and second deals, and other sleights with a deck of cards devised primarily for the use of cardsharping. Now, with his one phone call from the police station, Vernon implored England to bail him out. England raced to the station.

> He knew and hated every cop in Chicago because they treated the notorious gangsters with great deference and handled them with kid gloves, taking out on poor little fall guys, picked up for peddling without a license, or on a bawdy Saturday night reveler, all the sadistic and frustrated viciousness of their natures. Upon his arrival old Bud cursed them out in superlative style and demanded that one of them accompany him immediately to the hotel to check on [Vernon's] story that he was a magician and silhouette artist.

Vernon was released. England then asked how he was holding up. When he discovered that Vernon had only one dollar and thirty-nine cents in his pocket, he pulled out his wallet, crammed to capacity with one hundred and five hundred dollar bills, and counted out three thousand dollars. He insisted that Vernon take the money as a gift. When Vernon refused, he insisted. "Do me a favor and carry it around for a couple of days, it'll make you feel better. And in the meantime, if you change your mind and decide to spend part of it or all of it, it's okay by me." England had the improvident habit of giving away hundreds, and more often thousands, of dollars to some of his buddies who were in a continual state of insolvency. Vernon spent about twenty dollars for rent and laundry, and less than a week later returned the balance to his benefactor who, by that time, was flat broke.

Vernon had had enough of Chicago. It was time to return home to New York, but how? Another new acquaintance instructed him on the relatively new art of hitchhiking: Wait at a filling station where motorists stop for a cup of coffee or visit the washroom. Strike up a conversation, make sure the person understands that he is not speaking to a derelict or criminal, and then ask how far he is traveling. Vernon decided to give it a try, and it worked. He was on his way.

Back in New York, he headed straight for Coney Island, where he discovered that Sam Margules was managing a magic show. Whatever worries Vernon carried with him from Chicago melted away; Sam would help. When Vernon walked into the dressing room to see Margules, he asked a tall, nice-looking, fair-headed fellow named Eddy Ackerman whether Sam Margules was available.

"No," Ackerman responded and then added, "Who will I tell him called?"

Vernon replied, "Vernon, Dai Vernon."

Ackerman, as if defeated, sullenly said, "Oh," and then went on the stage where he began packing his props into a bag. Vernon realized that this was the magician who worked the show.

"I suppose you wonder why I'm getting ready to leave?" Ackerman continued. "Sam told me I could have this job as long as one fellow didn't come to town. 'If Vernon ever comes in, you're fired automatically, because he's going to work here.' Sam says what he means, so I'm through."

Vernon said, "Don't be silly, I wouldn't take a person's job."

Just then, Margules returned to the theatre. He greeted Vernon with open arms and suggested he get ready for the next show.

Vernon said, "Sam, I just came in from Chicago. I hitchhiked. I need a shower."

Vernon never told Sam that he would work for him; Sam took it for granted. Ackerman was not a professional magician. He was a haberdasher by trade and fond of magic. Sam had given him the opportunity to break in new material and to learn how to perform. In Sam's mind, that opportunity had now drawn to a close.

Sam told Vernon, "Get in there, do the Cards Up The Sleeve. Here Eddy, lend him that Die Box. You know how to work the Die Box."

Vernon protested, "They're liable to throw things."

Sam was persistent. "All right, you dodge them. What do you care; you flop, so what? What are they going to do, kill you?"

Vernon acquiesced to Sam's pressure. He walked out and performed the Cards Up The Sleeve, the Miser's Dream, and a few other tricks.

After the show, Sam said, "You are going to work here, and you're going to sell a package of magic. You know how much money you can make selling a package of magic?" Before he could respond, Sam told Vernon that Harry Usher and his wife, Frances, who performed a mind reading act at another location on the Island, banked $400-$600 per week. Vernon balked and reminded Sam that the Ushers sold "astrological charts," not magic.

Sam said, "Shut up. You're going to make a lot of money. I know a nice new apartment; I'll get you a nice, clean room. I'm going to introduce you to a fellow named Raoul. We are going to make up a package of magic to sell. Don't pick out good tricks. Give them the Chinese handcuff, a keyhole puzzle and tell the fellows 'what they see through the keyhole is nobody's business.' There will be nothing in there, just the card, but that makes people curious and they'll want to buy. Sell them the flip-flop card and the Diminishing Card that folds up. Make up a package that may cost you three cents, perhaps less, and sell it for a quarter. That's good profit."

Vernon bought several boxes of envelopes and packed them with the tricks that Raoul provided. After each performance, he would demonstrate a trick or two and say, "Now anybody who wants any of these tricks I performed, come up and help yourself."

Sales were disappointing. Then Harry Usher came in and introduced himself to Vernon.

"I watched your entertainment in here. My name's Harry Usher. You are going to make a lot of money if you stay in this field for the summer, more than you ever made in your life. You have sincerity. If you're a phony, even this Coney Island crowd will pick you out like that. But if you're sincere, people have faith in you, and you can tell them anything."

He then advised Vernon to discard the envelopes.

"You're not selling them, throw those envelopes away. People are suspicious; they don't think they are getting all the merchandise. Coney Island is the flimflam place, everything's fake. They probably figure they are only getting a sheet of instructions. If you want to use the envelope don't fold the card, leave it standing up. Put the Chinese handcuff in this way. When you hold it up it looks like a Christmas tree. Make up the package so you see every piece of merchandise, put a rubber band around it to hold it in place. Do each trick and put it in the envelope. 'Now, who wants the one I was I using?'

"Now," he said, "they know that they've seen you use this and they know it's authentic; that you are not demonstrating one thing and selling them another. This has a ring of truth. Your sales will jump up one hundred, two hundred, five hundred percent."

Vernon followed Usher's advice. It worked like magic. He couldn't make change fast enough. Sam would come as soon as the show was over and count the change. He would advance Vernon some money for daily expenses and then pocket the rest. He was doing this for Vernon's own good. Sam knew that if he handed Vernon all of the money, it would be gone as fast as it had appeared.

Vernon loved to gamble and socialize, and would eventually fritter the money away. Sam banked the money and handed it over to Vernon at the end of the season. The total was over $700.

Although Vernon had only been away from New York for a year, the city had experienced enormous growth and the pains that accompany it. In January 1919, Alfred E. Smith, a poor boy from the Lower East Side and a hero of the labor reform movement was sworn in as the first Irish American governor in America. The city was bursting with people as more than three million converged on Manhattan to take part in the delirious victory celebration as veterans returned to American soil and, in particular, to New York. On August 26, 1919, American women finally won the right to vote. Labor movements sprung up, and in early December 250 outspoken activists, including famed anarchist Emma Goldman, were transported to Ellis Island on grounds of treason and deported to Russia. Dr. James William Elliott, the Undisputed Challenge Card Champion of the World, was a sympathizer. New York displaced London as the investment capital of the world. With Vaudeville in full swing and its central booking office located in Manhattan, performers flocked to the city to impress the agents and operators. Some, like the Australian John Gerard Rodney Boyce, landed at Coney Island. Boyce changed his name to Jean Hugard and leased a small theatre in Luna Park to present his show "A Night in Pekin." Another change, one that would have a profound impact on the creation and performance of magic, was the continuing rise in power of the amateur magician. Amateur magicians had always aspired to duplicate the magic effects performed by their professional brethren. Now, however, the roles began to reverse.

At a meeting of the National Conjurors' Association held on November 6, 1918 at Martinka & Co., now under the management of Otto Waldmann, Jean Hugard was baffled by a series of extraordinary card tricks performed by a little-known amateur magician, Henry Gavin. Hugard was so dumbfounded that he took 1500 words to describe the experience in the January 1919 issue of *The Sphinx*. Hugard concluded his article by saying,

> *Mr. Gavin has since shown me many more of his card miracles, but the foregoing will justify me in saying that his work is the cleverest and most finished that has come under my observation. Mr. Gavin is at present interested in the art purely as an amateur. Should he decide*

to devote himself to it as a professional I have no doubt he will win his way to the topmost rungs of the ladder of conjuring fame.

Henry Gavin was born Arthur Gavin Finley in October 1887. His father, William, was a saloonkeeper and his mother, Margaret, ran a boarding house on East 34th street. The name Henry Gavin was an amalgamation of his mother's maiden name and his own middle name. In 1908 Finley started a mail order magic business, selling and advertising magic tricks under the name Henry Gavin in the pages of *The Sphinx*. He also joined the local magic clubs under this name. He was now, however, a commercial artist, having spent his early twenties in Paris, studying the latest trends. A student of Vernon's, an oil company executive named Peter Ten Eyck, suggested the two should meet. Vernon called on Finley at his Madison Avenue studio and, after much prodding, gained entry. Eventually Vernon's persistence paid off. Finley showed Vernon a "think-of-a-card" effect that baffled him completely. Vernon learned, however, that Finley had no aspirations to become a professional magician; he was a commercial artist. Vernon told Finley that he still wanted to become a professional portrait artist, but Finley did his best to discourage him. Finley's suggestion echoed the advice Vernon had received from Charles Gibson several years earlier.

In January 1920, Dr. Elliott died of pulmonary complications. The magic world needed to anoint a new "King of Cards." Houdini, as was always the case, claimed to be the king even while Elliott was alive, a boast not taken seriously by anyone other than the escape master himself, and his sycophants. Houdini even used his power and influence to commandeer the publication of *Elliott's Last Legacy* from Clinton Burgess, a society entertainer for the New York 400 and a prolific contributor and scribe for magic magazines who was given the task by Elliott's kin of translating the Doctor's personal notebooks (full of methods and ideas for tricks) into prose. Houdini was the last person Elliott would have wanted to be the editor of his life's work. In Vernon's opinion, published in the "Magic and Magicians" column in *The Billboard*, the new king of cards could only be one person—Arthur Finley.

It has been my good fortune to view at close range the work of all the leading professionals with a pack of cards, also many exceedingly clever gamblers who are extremely difficult to approach, as their knowledge is their livelihood, and they are very reticent about "tipping their mit" [sic], to use their own vernacular. Some of these fellows have certain sleights and moves entirely unknown to the magic fraternity, and they are among the cleverest and most subtle manipulations ever invented.

Only a few of the professional magicians have any knowledge whatsoever of these finer moves in card handling and that knowledge does not run beyond a few elementary "stocks," "dealing seconds" and some extremely apparent and little used "false shuffles"; if they had this knowledge they would not be willing to devote the hours and hours of incessant practice necessitated for their complete mastery — moves that must pass as natural under the closest scrutiny, and without the employment of misdirection.

The late Dr. Elliott was thoroly [sic] versed in the secrets of the professional gambler, and by their judicious use was able to nonplus and completely bewilder the even well-schooled magicians of his time. Furthermore, he realized the vital importance of making all sleights and move under cover of perfectly natural movements. He had absolutely no use for any fanciful or exaggerated gestures of any kind. "Be Natural," was his favorite slogan.

No one but Dr. Elliott's closest friends can conceive the years of practice he put in on single trifling little moves to bring them to perfection.

All the time he was practicing another was doing likewise. His name is Arthur Finley, and today I haven't a doubt but he is the rightful successor to Dr. Elliott.

He is a well-known New York artist and cards with him are merely a hobby yet he far excels all others in this most difficult branch of the art.

To see him make the "two-handed shift," execute the "side slip" or "false shuffle" would be a revelation to many. His work is as near perfection as anything I have ever seen, and this perfection was attained by persistent and painstaking practice — years of it.

Besides a complete mastery of all the standard sleights he has hundreds of entirely original problems of his own which rank with the best of them.

Magicians should by all means make his acquaintance.

(Signed) Dai W. Vernen [Vernon], "Sleightly Known."

Although Finley married Mary Carlile Lewis, a woman who would rise through the ranks of the New York fashion world to eventually become a role model for many American women, his real soul mate was, in many respects, Vernon. Finley was seven years older but just as committed to sleight-of-hand, particularly with cards. And his temperament was a perfect match for Vernon's. They met frequently and ventured forth to magic emporiums and societies of secrets, of which there were several in Manhattan. With his Coney Island funds rapidly depleting, however, Vernon had to find some new means to support his habits. Teaching the odd executive with an eccentric interest in card tricks was not enough.

Perhaps it was time for Vernon to also venture farther afield. He decided to visit other towns and cities. He would cut silhouettes at fairs and festivals and, where possible, convince department stores to engage his services as the resident silhouette artist. He would stay as long as the traffic was there.

A deck of cards was rarely out of his hand, and even while waiting for business at the silhouette-cutting stand, it was not uncommon for another amateur magician to discover his presence. Local chapters of the Society of American Magicians, known as Assemblies, had sprouted up across America. Assembly presidents would often invite Vernon to their meetings. They were interested in learning about the players and personalities in the New York magic scene, and Vernon was rarely at a loss for words.

In Cincinnati, for example, George W. Stock, the president of The Cincinnati Magician's Club, spied Vernon cutting silhouettes at Pogues Department store and invited him to attend the local club meeting. There Vernon met Stewart Judah and John Braun, two dedicated amateurs, and continued conversing with them well after the meeting had adjourned. Braun eventually had to depart, sensing that he owed some responsibility to his employer to arrive the next morning at work on time. Judah and Vernon, however, continued their conversation beneath a street lamp into the wee hours.

They stood on a downtown street corner, demonstrating card tricks for the police officer on the beat, the only audience available after midnight. The two eventually retired, but they vowed to continue their conversation over dinner before Vernon left Cincinnati. Braun attended the dinner.

> *I'll never forget the impression Dai made on me. I was seeing magic for the first time—it was a different kind of magic than I had seen in theatres, Chautauqua, or vaudeville, except Nate Leipzig's unfathomable magic, which looked different in his hands from the book descriptions.*

> *Both Stewart and I had a copy of Erdnase, and Vernon could say, "You name what you want to see and I'll do it for you," and as far as we could tell, he was doing it. I drank in everything that evening, and had to go home on a 'night owl' streetcar (after mid-night they ran 'night owls' every hour) and I was woozy next morning, but not so woozy that I couldn't recall and jot down a sizable pad of notes on what I had seen (the night) before.*

Judah and Braun were not the only magicians dumbfounded by Vernon's magic. Harry Houdini would soon be added to the list.

On February 6, 1922, Vernon and Sam Margules, who was also visiting Chicago, attended a banquet in honor of Harry Houdini. The two joined sixty other magicians, members of the Chicago Assembly of the Society of American Magicians, in dress suits and dinner jackets, in the Crystal Room, a mirrored ballroom in the Great Northern Hotel. They were all there to bask in the light generated by the self-proclaimed greatest entertainer in the world. Houdini was at the peak of his powers, having built an enviable career escaping from restraints of every shape and form. Although he was a vigorous forty-eight years old, the pace he set for himself had been exacting. Being tossed off of a bridge wrapped in a web of iron was difficult and dangerous. His bones ached. He had experienced so much success that the *need* to get out there and perform again and again had become diluted. The public was interested only in each subsequent stunt being more sensational than the last. Although he was performing at the Majestic Theatre, exposing Spirit Mediums—people who proclaimed to be able to contact the dead both verbally and physically, all of whom Houdini regarded as fraudulent—he was also in the midst of re-engineering his career.

Houdini recognized that the future of entertainment lay in another medium—cinema—and he had come to Chicago to promote "The Man from Beyond," a silent film produced by the Houdini Motion Picture Corporation in which he played the forerunner of the modern day action hero who, after having been frozen in a glacier for 100 years, emerged to rescue the beautiful heroine from the brink of Niagara Falls. The film would not be a success. Houdini was a sensation on the stage, not the screen. Audiences seemed to know intuitively—even then—that trick photography and cinematic hanky panky should receive credit along with the star on screen.

Houdini strode into the reception like a political figure on the campaign trail. Bess, his wife, followed in his wake. The sound of applause and flashbulbs popping ushered them into the room. Magic in the 1920s had its public and private stars. Houdini was the former, and the roomful of magicians, mostly well-heeled amateurs, profited from the association. Dr. A. M. Wilson, the editor and publisher of *The Sphinx*, greeted Houdini at the door.

Margules attended the dinner not only because it was *the* magical event in Chicago but also because he worshipped Houdini, having seen him in New York many times, both onstage and off. Houdini had even given Sam one of his tailcoats, the formal attire he wore on stage. Sam wore the coat in his own shows swelled with pride, despite the fact that the fabric was tattered and the garment was ridiculously ill-fitting. Houdini was short and Sam a bear of a man.

The celebration started at 11:00 pm, and the magicians took their places at the tables as soon as the honored guests arrived. Two long banquet tables bracketed the head table where Houdini sat with Dr. Wilson. Sam Margules and Vernon sat near one another, far from the focus of attention. After the perfunctory speeches and a grand dinner, various magic personalities performed for Houdini. At approximately 3:30 am, Houdini agreed to close the show by performing his stock display of flourishes with a pack of cards. The February 1922 issue of *The Sphinx* carried this testimonial:

> *And then, to fittingly close an event which we will ever treasure in our memories, Houdini displayed the impossible with a pack of cards; it was a revelation to many of us to think that this man, who has made his reputation in a distinct branch of our art, can emulate*

The Man Who Fooled Houdini

Houdini poses with his own likeness.

practically every sleight used by the greatest card specialists; passes (and) revolutions that you never thought of—ribbons—waterfalls, and many original effects which it would take years to duplicate.

After the performers retired from the stage, the formality dissipated. Those magicians that remained performed pocket tricks for each other and gossiped about the latest wonders and wizards.

Margules went straight for Houdini. He dragged Vernon along with unbridled enthusiasm. Margules, although not a sophisticated man, recognized talent when he saw it, and he saw in Vernon the most gifted card handler ever. Naively, Margules thought that Houdini would be interested in meeting him.

Houdini glanced at Vernon, sizing the newcomer up. Vernon was fit and agile. He had the body of an athlete and was dressed smartly in suit and tie. Without a word, Vernon knew what trick Sam wanted him to demonstrate. Vernon took out a pack of cards, Aristocrats, printed in a cool blue with white borders. He removed the cards from the case, placed the card case on the banquet table, and spread the pack between his hands. The cards seemed to dance in perfect alignment, moving gracefully from one palm to the other. Houdini glanced at Sam as if he were doing him a huge favor, then thumbed through a few cards and removed one from the spread. It was the ace of clubs.

Vernon removed a pen from his pocket and handed it to Houdini. "Please sign the card."

"Do what?" Houdini asked.

"Sign the card. Write your name on the face."

Houdini was perplexed. If required, the custom was to tear off the corner of the card and leave it with the participant as a testament of its singular nature. No one asked that a card be signed in ink. Vernon had experimented with inks, however, and had purchased a new pen, one with a chamber that contained indelible ink, ink that would not run or smear on the stiff paper of a playing card. Houdini, intrigued, scrawled "H.H." on the pasteboard. Vernon took back the pen, replaced its cap, and returned it to his pocket. He then motioned for Houdini to hand over the card.

Vernon placed it face up on the deck. He blew softly on the ink to ensure that it had dried and then, slowly and deliberately, turned the card face down. Without ceremony, Vernon lifted the signed card from the top of the deck, pushed the second card slightly over the right side of the pack and then inserted the signed card beneath it. He then squared up the cards so that the entire deck was in perfect alignment. Vernon gave the deck a purported magical squeeze and then turned over the top card. It was Houdini's signed ace of clubs. The trick was the tonic that aroused Houdini's attention. He asked Vernon to repeat it.

Vernon did the trick a second time. He held the card at his right fingertips and then, just as he was about to insert it below the top card, he paused and tilted the face of the card towards Houdini so that he could see that it was indeed his card. Vernon pushed it home beneath the top card and squared up the deck. Giving the deck a gentle squeeze, he created a soft sound effect by riffling his right thumb up along the end the deck. Vernon slowly turned the top card face up. Once again, H.H. had risen to the top.

Houdini interjected, "Oh, I've got it. You have two aces of clubs."

This was not the first time Sam had heard such a remark. He had seen Vernon perform this feat on other occasions. Sam reminded Harry that he had initialed the card. In addition to being the self-crowned *King of Cards*, Houdini often boasted that he could not be fooled if he had the opportunity to see a trick performed three times. Sam now understood the challenge.

There was a titter of excitement in the air as Vernon removed the H.H. card from the pack and inserted it beneath the top card once again. Sam knew that if Harry could not figure out how the trick was performed this time, Vernon would make his reputation as the man who fooled Houdini. This promotional tag would rapidly enhance Vernon's public profile in the way that Howard Thurston, the most famous illusionist in America, had kick-started his own career by fooling Herrmann.

Vernon, however, was not interested in the personal accolades or promotional possibilities. He had learned at an early age that there was no correlation between public profile and personal ability when, at age seven, he mystified Howard Thurston with a card trick drawn from Thurston's own book of magical secrets. Houdini, though, was far more aware of the stakes at hand. He came to Chicago to promote his career only to now find himself being fooled repeatedly and badly by an unknown magician with, as the press would likely describe it, a simple card trick. His mind raced, grasping at explanations. He had certainly seen and performed an astronomical number of card tricks, and while rank and file amateur magicians disdain card tricks, Houdini knew he was witnessing something much more sophisticated than it appeared. "Again," he said.

For the third time Vernon inserted Houdini's selection beneath the top card and made it reappear on top. "Well, Harry?" Sam asked. Houdini wasn't about to admit defeat. He called Bess to his side. "Bess, watch this. He has a clever card trick." Like the wives of most magicians, Bess had no great desire to see a card trick, but she knew her role and played it for Harry's benefit. That benefit, of course, was the opportunity for Houdini to see the trick a fourth time. Bess nodded to Sam and then turned towards Vernon.

Vernon showed Bess the card bearing her husband's initials, initials she knew very well. She watched politely as Vernon inserted the card beneath the top one, made a magical gesture and then turned over the top card. She gave an honest expression of surprise when the card appeared on top. She turned to Harry with a little grin, the grin a child makes when the magician pulls a coin out of her ear.

"Come on, Harry," said Sam. "Admit it. You are fooled."

Houdini stood silently—thinking. Bess asked Vernon whether he could do the trick again, but Vernon sensed that it was time to stop. The most powerful weapon in the magician's repertoire is surprise. "Never do the same trick twice," was the phrase coined specifically to prevent informed observers like Houdini from reconstructing secrets. Doing the same trick five times in a row was a challenge, plain and simple. Repeating the trick also went against a philosophy espoused by S.W. Erdnase in *The Expert At The Card Table*: "Excessive vanity proves the undoing of many experts. The temptation to show off is great. He has become a past master in his profession. One single display of dexterity and his usefulness is past in that particular company, and the reputation is liable to precede him in many another."

Vernon was not interested in showing off. He repeated the trick one last time—but for Bess only. Once again, the card appeared on top of the deck. The lines on her face, the result of the wear and tear of touring and watching her husband endure physical pain, vanished from her brow.

She turned to her husband, not understanding the significance of the challenge, and inadvertently added insult to injury. "Harry, can you do that one?" Houdini ignored the question.

"Again," Houdini commanded. Vernon's muttering that five times was probably sufficient was overruled by Sam. "Admit it, Harry, he's got you."

Suddenly, Bess and Vernon connected. Bess realized that her husband was in danger; not physical danger, but the danger of losing his pride. Bess knew that pride was the real secret to Houdini's success. When inscribing promotional photographs, Houdini often wrote that his brain was the key that set him free. Bess saw the same look of determination on his face that appeared every time he was challenged to escape from a new set of handcuffs. His determination, the unwillingness to admit defeat at any cost, was what motivated him.

Vernon was not interested in humiliating Houdini in front of his peers, the group of magicians that had gathered around to watch him perform. They couldn't comprehend the gravity of the situation, anyway. Vernon also realized that the constant repetition had raised his own stakes. What if Houdini figured out how the trick was performed? What then?

"This is it," said Vernon. "This is the last time." Vernon knew that the slightest tremor in his hands would betray his position. For the final time, Vernon inserted the card beneath the top one. He riffled the end of the deck with his right thumb as before. Slowly and deliberately he turned over the top card—his trump card. H.H. was back on top. Houdini looked at Sam, at Bess, and then at Vernon.

It was late and time to go. Houdini strode out of the banquet hall, Bess close behind him.

Margules and Vernon parted ways. Margules returned to New York and Vernon, with no ambition to jump to the professional ranks by marketing himself as "The Man Who Fooled Houdini," continued his peregrinations, searching for gamblers with arcane knowledge, sleights and subterfuges. As was becoming his custom, financial support came from cutting silhouettes. It was not long before chance again reared its head in a mysterious way. While walking around a fair in Palatine, Illinois, he spotted the man from Coney Island who had borrowed—stolen—his beautiful English raincoat. The man recognized Vernon immediately. Vernon was so annoyed—he had thought about the swindle time and time again—that he hit the man, throwing one solid punch, and immediately walked away.

Vernon met his next crew of hustlers en route from Louisville to Lexington, Kentucky.

> *I'm not a horseplayer. I may have a lot of vices, but playing the horses isn't one of them, although I love races and I enjoy going to the track occasionally to make a few bets. Well, one of the few times that I really bet a little money was at a track in Louisville, Kentucky. I played a parlay, and in those days I didn't know much about parlays except that you bet three horses, and if they all won, you came up with quite a bankroll. Well, luckily, two of the horses I bet on were long shots, and I collected about $1,700.00 for about a $30.00 bet. I was a pretty happy individual, and when I went up to cash my ticket, everybody was standing there applauding.*
>
> *Well, some guys there must have spotted what they thought was a young sucker. I had quite a bankroll, because they doled it out in tens and twenties and it looked like a cabbage. Anyway, I stayed around Louisville for a couple of days at the Tyler Hotel and from there I was going to Lexington where I was going to cut some silhouettes. When I got on the train, the train had no sooner pulled out when*

a rather nice looking young fellow came over to me and said, "Say, do you play bridge?" And I said, "Well, I play, but not well." So he asked, "Would you like to join us? We need a fourth for a game" I didn't suspect anything at the time, because he looked like a college kid or something. They had a parlor car, so I went back there and they had a little table set up there, and I noticed that the two guys sitting there weren't like this other kid at all. One of them looked like an old sharper, and the other was a real grifter-type.

Well, I smelled a rat right away. So I sat down and we played bridge for a little while, and then the older guy said, "Listen, I don't understand this game. You fellows are too good at bidding. Let's play poker. We don't have much time on this train anyway." I figured that this was it, but they had no way in the world of knowing that I even knew one card from the other, so I put on an act and shuffled with the old "haymow" shuffle and occasionally dropped a card. Now this other guy was doing a pretty bad milk from the bottom and running up the cards, and he'd put them down to have this partner of his cut, and he'd put them back and say, "Cut them clean. I don't like cards messed like that," because obviously the guy had missed the crimp. I even saw him check the bottom card a few times to make sure. Well, the funny part is, I'd get a Jack in the hole, and a Jack face up, and I'd say, "Gee, it's hot in here. I've got to get a drink of water," and I'd turn my hand down and walk away. Well, it was getting tougher and tougher all the time not to get hooked into one of these hands, because I knew darn well if I didn't bet one of these good hands, they'd suspect something. So I managed to stall along until finally I got a chance to do a few things, and I really won a couple of nice pots because I double-crossed them.

Finally, this old guy turned to his partner and said, "Listen, I'm an old timer in this racket and you fellows should be smarter. This fellow knows more than he's supposed to know." Well, by this time I had over $70 of their money, and he said, "Come on, we're on a short bankroll. We only have about $125 between us, and we've got to get to Lexington and make some money. Will you please give us back our money?" Well, I looked at him and said, "Listen, if you'd won and I told you I needed the money, would I get it back?" Anyway, I thought about it for a while, and then I said, "What's your best game?" And he said, "Six card knock rummy." So we played a few hands at $25 a *hand, and we seesawed back and forth, and I finally wound up with about $25 of their money.*

While Vernon was out-hustling hustlers, the world of magic was undergoing its own transformation. The public was no longer interested in performers who merely manipulated playing cards; they wanted to see women sawn in half. Indeed, despite Nevil Maskelyne's misgivings when the English magician and magical inventor P.T. Selbit performed the illusion at a special performance at St. George's Hall, London in December 1920, Sawing In Half developed a stranglehold on the public imagination. It was one of the few illusions that could physically attract an audience into a theatre independent of the personality of the performer. It was also an illusion that could be both pirated economically and promoted on a grand scale.

Horace Goldin, a Polish Jew raised in a farmhouse just outside Vilna, Poland, who would eventually stage command performances before the crowned heads of Europe, developed his own method for performing the effect. He then licensed his version of the illusion to other magicians for use in their own shows. Goldin, who charged fifty dollars per week plus a percentage of box office receipts vehemently attacked anyone else who performed the illusion, including the originator P.T. Selbit. Goldin obtained an injunction that prevented Selbit from performing his own trick on his 1921 American tour.

One license was sold to Sam Margules. Sam wanted to feature the illusion at a theatre he was setting up for Harry Schwartz, a friend with a few dollars to spare, on Coney Island. Sam knew how to sell blood and guts. The illusion drew capacity crowds, and when the rain came and business was slow, Margules made arrangements with the Coney Island Hospital to drive an ambulance back and forth from the theatre. The ambulance would rush down Surf Avenue, bell clanging, and stop in front of the theater. Attendants would rush in with a stretcher and come out with some dismembered form tucked beneath the sheets. It was a sensational stunt and crowds flocked in.

There were a couple of subtle differences between Selbit and Goldin's illusions. Whereas Selbit could perform his version with one woman, Goldin required two. Eugenia Hayes, the future Mrs. Dai Vernon, became one of them.

Dai Vernon: A Biography

Eugenia, known as Jeanne, was born in 1902. A pretty, petite blonde, she was traumatized at age twelve by her parents' divorce, which placed her in the middle of a vicious and vindictive custody battle. When her father and mother finally separated, she went to live with her mother in Sheepshead Bay, a community near Coney Island. Her mother died shortly thereafter, and, by the summer of 1922, Jeanne was living with her aunt at Brighton Beach. As she walked down Surf Avenue, a barker, seeing her pass, departed from his script and beckoned her over. She ignored the man, as she had been brought up to do, believing he was flirting with her. Thirty minutes later, on her walk home, the barker spotted her again. This time he insisted that he was not trying to be fresh. He told her that he was searching for someone her size to work in a magic show. The barker suggested that she go inside and speak with the company manager. Intrigued, Jeanne went inside and met the man in question, Sam Margules. As soon as Margules saw her, he knew that she was it. At 4' 9", she was small enough to be part of the team.

Jeanne went home to tell her aunt. Horrified, her aunt instructed Jeanne to return to the theatre and inform Mr. Margules that she would not be allowed to work at such an establishment. When the disappointing news was delivered, Margules was not prepared to take no for an answer. He returned with Jeanne to face her aunt and obtain her consent. Margules promised the aunt that he would look after Jeanne as if she were his own daughter. Jeanne joined the troupe. She was one of four girls expected to work from 1:00 p.m. until 1:00 a.m. for twenty-five dollars per week. She was scheduled to perform every two hours with her partner Kitty, a girl whose family owned some concessions at Coney Island. Kitty weighed eighty pounds; Jeanne weighed approximately ninety. As Kitty had a slightly longer neck—an attribute that helped with the illusion—Jeanne was assigned 'the lower half.' This more than suited Jeanne, as she did not have to appear on the stage nor on the bally platform outside the theatre.

Jeanne enjoyed being part of the troupe, although sometimes, to the complete bewilderment and utter consternation of Margules, the illusion didn't go off as well as it should have. Jeanne would sometimes fall asleep in the box and it would take more than a few loud thumps on the platform to wake her up. Unfortunately, these minor disasters occurred when Sam was most anxious to impress

Goldin's Sawing In Half Show at Coney Island. Sam Margules stands on the bally platform.

visiting magicians with the inimitable manner in which his little troupe performed under his able direction. Sam eventually discovered that Jeanne often crawled into the secret compartment with a box of popcorn or a hot dog and an ice cream cone. As the ventilation was poor and the performer often verbose, the close, dark quarters, in combination with the food, often made her drowsy. When Horace Goldin, the licensor, was visiting the show, Sam took extra precautions that caused Jeanne much discomfort. She wrote,

> *Once inside, an odor receded, then rolled in, in great waves that became progressively stronger. It finally became unbearable and in my frantic anxiety to get out of the (box), my knees were pushing against the trap in such a manner that poor little Kitty had to exert all her meager strength to hold it down until the time came for her to release it.*

Sam had plugged all but two of the air holes with Limburger cheese. Sam was, however, true to his word and looked after Jeanne as if she was family. Jeanne wrote,

> *Sam had the build of a young bull, a voice like thunder on a summer day, and a heart as tender as a dove's. His complex character was a striking example of the law of compensation. What he lacked in gentlemanly demeanor and sound judgment, he made up for in*

Dai Vernon: A Biography

kindheartedness, generosity and unfailing good humor.

Vernon eventually returned to New York and made a beeline for Coney Island. He heard about Sawing A Woman In Half and asked around for the name of the theatre where it was playing. Upon arriving, he was delighted to learn that Sam Margules was the manager. Jeanne was on hand to see him stroll in,

> *From the enthusiastic welcome that he received, you might have thought that he was a conquering hero home from the wars or a sailor home from the sea. After being obstreperously welcomed and rapturously embraced by various members of the cast of Horace Goldin's "Sawing a Woman in Half" company...he apologetically consented, after a great deal of coaxing, to do a few simple little tricks. All the girls gravitated to him like steel filings to a magnet and he was completely surrounded by a cackling fluttering group.*
>
> *This fabulous creature was Dai Vernon, a slim young man in his late twenties, with coal black hair that grew in an utterly devastating widow's peak and deep set sparkling grey eyes that gave the effect of being lighted from behind, by indirect lighting inside his skull.*

Jeanne, Vernon and Kitty.

Although impressed by his appearance, she was not impressed by the card tricks.

> *Each succeeding trick was greeted with sickening squeals of delight. "Chickens," I thought, as I stood by myself in a far corner, apart from the agitated mass of clucking females, completely disgusted and thoroughly bored.*

Suddenly, Margules pushed her into the melee. Sam insisted that Vernon perform a special trick just for Jeanne.

Vernon said, "The trick that I am about to do for your special benefit, young lady, is one absolutely guaranteed to fool even the most intelligent spectator and, since in all honesty, I cannot place you in this category, the trick will undoubtedly be doubly successful."

He then performed a 'sucker trick,' one in which, by design, the performer makes a miraculous recovery at the spectator's expense. Jeanne, however, refused to take the initial bait. The trick unraveled and Vernon was deflated. He said, "It's a well-known fact that the dumber you are, the harder it is to fool you." Even so, Jeanne was delighted.

Sam drafted Vernon into the troupe. He was required to perform fifteen to twenty minutes of general magic designed to hold the attention of the patrons inside the theatre while the talkers persuaded others on the outside to join them for the grand illusion. Vernon's renditions of classical effects, which he presented with a matter-of-fact but charming authenticity, incorporated new techniques and subtleties. Although Jeanne kept her distance, others, particularly magicians, came to visit.

> *Word got out that there was a young magician doing a trick they couldn't quite see through. Some of the Carnival workers would come through the back door, without paying; the great majority would stand, there were only seats in front. One day, who do you think were standing there against the wall? Thurston, Horace Goldin and Houdini.*

Vernon was thrilled that these three masters had come to see his show. By the end of the summer, Margules and company were invited to perform at the carnival in Havana Park, Cuba. Vernon and Sam set sail but Jeanne stayed home.

Shortly after they opened, Vernon decided once again to change his name. Cubans, like New Yorkers, had their own difficulties pronouncing Dai Vernon. Inspired by the globetrotting Davenport Brothers, Vernon became Dallas Davenport. Sam thought the name was ridiculous and simply called him "Dickie." As at Coney Island, Vernon performed his general magic act before the main attraction. Occasionally, Vernon relieved Sam and conducted the illusion himself. And, just as in New York, each performance brought its own challenges.

> *When we did sawing a woman in half, we had an American girl,*

who was the head whom we brought from New York, a very pretty girl. But the feet, we got a native girl. Now the first girl we got was the homeliest girl I have ever seen in my life, she was cross-eyed and had every blemish a girl could have, but her feet were all right. In spite of the fact she was in the box for only a few brief moments, her mother had to chaperone her, and the mother, whom she had probably inherited her looks from, was also cross-eyed. Her mother would sit on the stage and insisted on keeping her daughter in sight constantly to chaperone her, and even when she went in the box, for the brief moment when they switched the box around, spun it around, her feet disappeared for one second, her mother would even watch, but as soon as she saw her daughter's feet again she would sit and chaperone her. We never gave a performance but that this cross-eyed mother wasn't sitting on the stage watching her daughter. We finally got rid of her and got a prettier girl but...her mother came with her too, but it wasn't so bad because she was an attractive girl and her mother was fairly attractive...

When Havana Park fell under the control of gambling interests from Akron and Dayton, Ohio, and graft became a cost of doing business, Margules elected to return to New York. The troupe returned with him. Vernon, however, decided to stay in Cuba. He saw the possibility of cutting silhouettes.

It was like a gold mine. I made a fortune and got independent as the devil. I was making money hand over fist and the city offered me space in museums to work. "Ah, artista! Oh, magnifico! El rey del mundo." They knew I did tricks, too. I was quite a celebrity. I don't think they had ever seen anybody cut silhouettes; it was a novelty. The city gave me a place to work right in front of the American Club, even put in a special light, all for nothing. I used to leave money in piles and some bills and go and sit almost half a block away; natives would come and look at the picture nobody ever stole a penny.

Just as many modern artists have scrawled thumbnail sketches on napkins and exchanged them for goods and services, Vernon discovered he too could use his craft as currency. For example, he rarely paid for meals. He would do tricks for his waitress and the restaurant owners. After an impromptu show, they refused to accept his money. Many Cubans were superstitious about magic and as such, Vernon was regarded as a sort of medicine man while on the island. Although Vernon performed at many private parties, most of all he enjoyed the nightlife. He gambled in the casinos and attended shows. He saw his share of unusual novelty acts, including Superman, a variety performer who, while standing naked on stage, would maintain an erection through sheer concentration and then ejaculate on command. Superman performed three shows a night. Vernon confessed later, however, that he only stayed for two of them. It was certainly a different culture. When he started dating Cuban woman he also discovered that being considered "American" had its advantages.

> *In those days you could go and visit a Cuban girl and you could—I used to play the piano sometimes a little, in those days—you'd go in and the parents would leave you alone with their daughter and then when it got later, they say, "It's getting late now and they'd call their daughter to bed perhaps, but they'd leave you alone with their daughter, but the natives, they'd never walk out of the room, if the father left the mother would come in or the uncle. I always attributed it to the fact that perhaps they wanted their daughter to get into trouble perhaps with an American and have to marry him, because they wanted to marry their daughters off to Americans.*

If, however, the girl loved music and he took her to the opera, he was also expected to take the extended family, a parade of five or six people, and purchase the most expensive seats in the house. After eight months he had had enough and decided to return to New York. The trip home would not be easy.

When Margules purchased their tickets, he anticipated that the entire troupe would return within six months. Vernon discovered that he had overstayed his journey; the ticket had expired. He would have to find an alternative passage home. As a Canadian citizen, he solicited assistance from the British Consul in Cuba, a man named Brooks. The Consul suggested that if Vernon wanted to save money, he could become a member of the crew on a ship bound for New York and desert the ship once it reached port. Vernon did not care what the job was, as long as he got back to Manhattan.

The Consul arranged for Vernon to act as a steward on a ship. Once again, Vernon used the currency of magic to his advantage. He became quite popular on board and was treated like a passenger, given a more comfortable bunk, and wonderful food. He admitted to the crew that he was planning to desert the ship in New York. Although the crew enjoyed his company, they realized that he was no seaman. They said there was no need to desert ship; they would sign his release as 'incompetent.'

Back in New York he reconnected with Margules. The timing was perfect. It was the late summer of 1923. Margules had been asked by Horace Goldin to stage the Sawing In Half at a charity bazaar in Bayshore, Long Island. Vernon could join the troupe to cut silhouettes at the Bazaar. As it was a three-day event, he would be able to generate some quick cash.

Sam also telephoned Jeanne and asked her to rejoin the troupe. Her salary would be ten dollars per day, meals and daily transportation to and from New York City included, and the opportunity to reconnect with old friends, including Kitty. What Sam failed to mention was that he had invited Vernon to join them. She discovered this on her own.

> *One evening while strolling aimlessly about the grounds, I noticed a compact little group of people clustered together under a bright hanging light. Upon edging closer, I discovered that the center of attraction was my heartily disliked acquaintance of the past summer, Dai Vernon, the magician from "Sawing A Woman in Half" but he wasn't magishing, he was cutting silhouettes. I stayed to watch and after some time, when the crowd had begun to thin out, I heard a voice say, "Did you ever in your life see such eyelashes?" The voice came from a female and she was nudging her companion in an effort to direct her attention to me, at who she was brazenly staring. I suppose she had some reason for staring for at that time my eyelashes were so long that if I glanced up without raising my head, my eyelashes used to become entangled in my eyebrows.*

Jeanne was extremely proud of her eyelashes, believing that they made up, in a very small way, for her small stature. Vernon also heard the other woman's remark, for he turned with interest to see the exotic creature. His eyes met hers with a look of startled surprise. Vernon stopped cutting silhouettes to speak with Jeanne and then asked her to wait a few minutes more as he closed up for the night. Jeanne thought that he seemed genuinely pleased to see her. He was.

The Man Who Fooled Houdini

I made $109 and was just closing when I see this girl. I didn't recognize her—these l-o-n-g eyelashes, an inch and a half long, and I thought they were artificial, but they weren't. Her face looked familiar; I never saw her face, very seldom, because she was always hiding; she used to come in, do her job and then run back to her Aunt. I said, "I know you somewhere;" she said, "At Coney Island."

I said, "My goodness, I never noticed your eye lashes before." Of course on the silhouette I cut the eyelashes off. When she opened her eyes they'd get caught up there. I'd never got in conversation with her. She seemed to be intelligent. I made a comment and said, "People call these salutes at Coney Island but they are silhouettes."

She confessed that she had never seen Vernon cut silhouettes but had read the history of the craft. She was aware that they were named after Etienne de Silhouette, the finance minister in the court of Louis XIV. She added that she was interested in the arts and was contemplating going to art school herself. Vernon was amazed. It was, however, time for her to return to New York.

Vernon accompanied Jeanne back to the main stage, and later, after joining Sam Margules, Kitty, Horace Goldin and some others, asked her if the two could meet again in a few days back in Manhattan. She agreed.

On their first date, Vernon presented Jeanne with a pair of silhouette scissors, some black gummed paper, a supply of mounts, and her first lesson in cutting silhouettes. They met frequently in the fall

Jeanne Hayes arm in arm with Vernon.

of 1923. Despite their budding courtship, Jeanne stated that Vernon complained continuously about the way that she treated him.

> *He maintained that I was cold and cross and mean and that he had never, in his extensive experience with girls, been treated so shabbily. He told me that he had never before found it necessary to make the advances and that he usually had to fight them off.*

A letter dated Wednesday, 10:30 p.m., November 6, 1923, East Onondaga Hotel, Syracuse, New York, however, tells a different story.

> *My Very Own Darling Sweetheart,*
>
> *Both of your dear letters arrived safely, one at the Post Office, yesterday—the other here at the hotel to-day. Jeannie dearest you're wonderful—each and every letter that you have ever written to me has been one that even the most highly educated "lady of the land" could justly feel proud of if she had written it. Anyone who had never ever seen you, or heard of you, could see reflected, clearly, vividly and unmistakably, in your letters—your "finesse," your rapier-like keeness [sic] of mind, your alertness to every little thing that transpires and most of all that indescribable, irresistible "something," something magnetic that would captivate any poor mortal no matter how immune or how cold.*
>
> *Jeannie my virtues are few, probably negligible, however, I can be appreciative and I most certainly, thoroughly appreciate you—anyone of course would, but I notice things—minutest little details of excellence, that I feel positive others wouldn't. To me, Jeanne darling, you mean everything. My thoughts, my desires, my very being throbs and longs for you. I do so wish to make my little girl happy. Sometimes when I allow myself to think in a cold logical way of what a shadow of my former self I am it hurts. In the past I was never in any way conceited or imagined myself a 'Beau Brummel', but I did have a certain amount of pride in being from a good family and being always well groomed and apparently of a vivacious and pleasant disposition. It is not the change in me that hurts directly but the fact that you—my own sweet darling little girl, only know the "old shell"—the "silhouette." Jeanne darling I have been writing*

along putting my addled thoughts on paper and I'm going to "ring off" as it is utterly hopeless for me to convey to you the torrent of love and mingled remorse that I sometimes feel.

Vernon concluded,

Well my exquisite little loving lady, if I could write like you I'd send you—at least thirty pages, but letter writing is my weakness as you know, but I shall promise to think of you constantly incessantly and intensely until I see your sweetly pretty little countenance on Sunday. I pawn myself to you and burn the ticket so it's up to you.

More than all my love your "Dai"

Vernon was smitten. In a half-joking manner designed to conceal his insecurity, he asked, "How would you like to travel all around the country, get married and do this silhouette work?" Jeanne indicated that she would like that very much, and they became engaged. Unfortunately, Vernon had little money with which to provide for his future wife. His approach had always been to generate money with short-term solutions rather than steady and reliable employment. So, to earn some extra money, Vernon agreed to sell some of his secrets, for twenty-five dollars, to two New York magic personalities Robert Sherman and John Davis, who operated a magic shop dubbed Sherms, in the Hudson subway. The duo published *Secrets*, a small booklet that described twenty-five card tricks "that anyone can do." They sold the booklet over the counter to amateurs with an interest in card tricks. Although his friend Arthur Finley had published and sold various tricks privately, that is through the advertisements placed in magic industry journals, this was Vernon's first venture tipping his 'secrets' publicly.

In February 1924, Vernon returned to Ottawa to inform his mother and brothers of his pending marriage. On Monday evening, March 3, 1924, at St. George's Church Parrish Hall located at the corner of Metcalfe and Gloucester streets in Ottawa, Vernon presented "Sleight of Hand and Silhouettes." Admission cost a quarter, and although the tickets indicated that the sale of silhouettes would benefit the Red Shield Drive, past practice would indicate that fifty percent of all proceeds would go directly to Vernon.

He returned to New York by train the next day. On March 5, 1924,

Vernon escorted Jeanne to The Little Church Around the Corner. Before they were married, as they were alone, they had to pay the Church four dollars to provide two witnesses. Jeanne wrote,

> *The sum total of our assets after parting reluctantly with the witness fee plus a small monetary gift to the minister was two dollars and thirty-nine cents. Our worldly possessions consisted of the contents of several suitcases, several pairs of bright shiny silhouette scissors and several packets of black-gummed paper.*

Ever optimistic, Vernon considered the pieces of black paper worth their weight in gold.

Chapter Four
Inner Circles

"All you have to do to make money is to think 'dollars want me' and the dollars will find you." Vernon was talking to his new bride. Jeanne tried the magic formula but it didn't seem to work. Now that she had taken in the waistlines on all of her dresses and banished the thought of sirloin steaks from memory, it was time for her husband to earn some money. So, Vernon turned to his familiar bag of tricks; he sauntered down Broadway to rent a spot to cut silhouettes.

Fortunately, he discovered the Little Blue Bookshop, a store that specialized in selling "Little Blue Books," a series of pocket-sized publications advertised as a "University In Print." These books, which included condensed versions of such titles as *Dr. Jekyll and Mr. Hyde* and *Lady Windermere's Fan* and more practical, non-fiction titles like *Side-Show Tricks Explained,* were extremely popular. Little Blue Bookshops sprouted up in Washington, Philadelphia, Chicago, Cincinnati, and other major American cities. The store on Broadway had a large back room, perfect for cutting silhouettes.

Vernon offered the shopkeeper a percentage of his sales in exchange for use of the space. He then gave the manager a quick demonstration of his craft. Vernon had used this ruse many times before. This way, no cash deposit was required for the space. The demonstration worked. Once again, Vernon could exchange cut-out scraps of gummy black paper for the long green acceptable to the butcher, the baker, and Consolidated Edison (the candlestick maker), and he was free to come and go as he pleased. He kept very irregular hours.

Dai Vernon: A Biography

When we were first married—I used to leave her alone—course, all magicians leave their wives alone a great deal at night because these meetings always take place around midnight and go into the early dawn sometimes—when magicians congregate and anybody who's not a magician has no idea of how harmless they are, just a lot of fellows getting together, exchanging ideas—and this can go on for hours sometimes—and it's fascinating to those "in the know" in the business, exchanging ideas—concocting new tricks—but the wives of these fellows simply can't understand—they think they're out probably prowling around with girls—out on wild parties—but I assure you it's a very innocent form of amusement. But the wives don't see it that way.

Vernon also continued to gamble. He would troll Coney Island, Atlantic City, or poker tables in New York, optimistic that he would encounter a crooked gambler or a faro player who could enlighten him as to some new artifice or subterfuge that he could apply to magic. As for Jeanne, he suggested that she occupy her time by attending college or a finishing school. She was not interested in either. Jeanne preferred learning from books. When the manager of the bookstore was short-staffed and learned that Jeanne was an avid reader familiar with many of the titles he had in stock, she joined his staff as a saleslady. She welcomed the steady income, even if it was only eighteen dollars per week.

Vernon also developed another sideline to keep his wife busy; she would mark playing cards for card cheats. While magic dealers and the *National Police Gazette* advertised that the cards were "for the exclusive use of magicians and any gamblers found using them for the purpose of cheating at cards would be prosecuted to the full extent of the law," that was the exact market for which they were manufactured. Jeanne was quite skilled at marking cards. She had studied art briefly at Cooper Union and, as her husband learned when he taught her to cut silhouettes, she was an apt pupil.

Jeanne would lay the cards out, along with her special pens and inks, on a long table at the back of the book shop, visualize a pair of shoes or a dress that she had seen on display in a neighboring store window, and then set off on the painstakingly detailed work required to make the back design of each card appear both uniform but, to the trained eye, different from the others. If the business of books was particularly slow, she set up an assembly line. She would sort several decks into suits and value and mark each grouping. This way, she did not have to pause between each card in each grouping to revise the mark. She would, of course, have to reassemble the decks, place each back into its original case, and then reseal them. Although he had extraordinary penmanship, Vernon rarely assisted Jeanne in this endeavor. He was too busy entertaining a constant stream of visitors—magicians, gamblers, and cheats.

Once, one of the visitors knocked a pile of cards on the floor and then politely retrieved and replaced them on the table. Jeanne finished the day's work, and the evening messenger picked up the cards and paid her for the work. Two weeks later a gambler, Gooey Louie, entered the store with his nose out of joint—literally. Apparently two dozen decks of cards had been mismarked and misassembled. The dealer who commissioned the work quietly left town for a vacation in Atlantic City, but not before he pointed this irate customer in Vernon's direction. Vernon, ever gallant, directed the man to Jeanne; she was the one, he advised, who had physically marked the cards. Jeanne tendered the only explanation possible: the man who knocked the piles of cards off the table weeks earlier must have inadvertently placed them back on the table in a haphazard manner. Unfortunately, she marked the backs and reassembled the cards into packs without double-checking them. Gooey, whose name was derived from the softness of his heart, looked at the petite young girl and forgave her. Jeanne Verner described in her journal Louie's magnanimous reprieve:

It's okay kids, don't let it worry ya. We all make mistakes. Dats why dey put rubbers on pencils. I just wanted to check up on ya. No hard feelins. I'll be seein ya around and don't take no rubber nickels.

Gooey Louie was not the only odd character that Vernon ushered into their circle. Jeanne encountered a depth of eccentricity that far exceeded anything she encountered at Coney Island. Through her husband, these magicians, cheats, and hustlers became her extended family. There was, for example, "Slip the Jit Harry," a dapper little man with a moustache who always wore a derby hat. Harry was a short-change artist, a person who traveled the country miscounting or 'short changing' money. Garnet Lee was another. Vernon had once described her as the most beautiful woman he had ever met. Jeanne was taken aback when she first met her. Garnet

Lee was beautiful. At least, she sighed, her husband had good taste in women. Once, when Jeanne visited Lee at her apartment, Lee offered her some unsolicited advice: dump Vernon and find a well-endowed man, one with money. Jeanne discounted the idea after learning that the damp sheets hanging over the transom at Lee's place were erected to keep the odor of the opium from creeping into the hall of the dingy railroad apartment. Later, she asked her husband, "How do you know such people?" Vernon replied that it was all part of the game of searching for methods of doing magic. Jeanne asked if other magicians were just as dedicated. "No," he told her, "I just do a lot of research." Jeanne shook her head in disbelief. There had to be an easier way to become a magician. Jeanne eventually developed a mantra to calm her nerves. The mantra was inspired by yet another of her husband's acquaintances.

> *Well, I brought this fellow in—this character I'd been playing poker with—and introduced him to my wife—and he looked all around the store—and said, "What are all these?" I told him these were books—all the world's best literature—in condensed form—some of it—some in several volumes. He said, "Books, what are they for?" And my wife said, "Typical of your friends...books—what are they for?"*

So whenever Jeanne was faced with the odd, eccentric, or deranged and she wanted to signify her dismay, she would turn to her husband and say, "Books—what are they for?"

Books, however, were her refuge. Unfortunately, some titles proved detrimental to her mental health. She read Kraft-Ebbing's *Psychopathia Sexualis*, for example, and was convinced that she was surrounded on all sides by murderous maniacs bent on her destruction. This phobia lasted a week or two until she continued reading her way through the store's inventory and another publication rerouted her imagination.

Vernon's circle of friends was not restricted to those he met at the poker table or those who dropped in at the Little Blue Bookshop. It also included the proprietors and countermen of the many magic shops that dotted Manhattan. Vernon and his confreres, Arthur Finley and Sam Horowitz, haunted all of them. Magic emporiums still had back rooms, but the only secrets they stored were those stocked on the shelves out front. Vernon, Finley, and Horowitz formed their own back room, one that traveled from shop to shop.

Inner Circles

The trio would visit the various emporiums, perform their latest effects, and swap stories over the counter with each proprietor. The oligarchy of magicians, one that granted access based on professional standing, became a meritocracy, one where access to secrets was based purely on knowledge and skill. The trio was quick to recognize talent and invite it into the fold.

One Saturday afternoon, at Frank Ducrot's shop on Thirty-fourth Street, Horowitz told Vernon that he had recently met a young man, John Scarne, over in New Jersey. His nickname was "Flukey Johnny" because of his luck with cards. His favorite game was Banker and Broker, in which the deck was cut into several piles, bets were placed, and the player who picked up the heap with the highest bottom card won. Somehow, Scarne always managed to pick up a heap with either a king or an ace. "Next time," Vernon instructed Horowitz, "Bring him with you." Two weeks later, he did. Scarne played his game, and although Vernon recognized the scam, he admired Scarne's style and skill and suggested he join their circle, a tremendous compliment for a boy who had just turned twenty. Those, however, who were denied access could only catch a casual glimpse of the magic or hear snippets of dialogue, much like Vernon did when he first saw Max Malini at the Rideau Club in Ottawa. Imagination would have to fill in the gaps. Word quickly traveled from amateur to amateur and from shop to shop that Vernon, Finley, and Horowitz could perform miracles.

Max Holden, a magician and shadowist (someone who earns his livelihood from making hand shadows), was the first to publish a report of their work. Holden was a widely respected columnist for *The Sphinx*, and magicians, both amateur and professional, often turned first to his column, "Trouping Around In Magic," to read about the latest and greatest in magic. In his April 1924 column, Holden reported meeting Finley, Horowitz, and Vernon at Ducrot's magic shop and witnessing many new effects and sleights performed "by this clever trio." This was the first of many trade testimonials.

Many professional performers in New York were not surprised by the accolades. Some, those who had met Vernon when he was a boy in Ottawa, knew him from his days at Coney Island, or from meetings of the National Conjurors' Association, charted his progress and admired his deft touch. Others, particularly amateurs and professionals outside of his circle, found him brash, cocky, aloof, and pretentious.

The one circle that Vernon wanted to penetrate was that of Max Malini. For Vernon, Malini had become another obsession. And so he employed the same dogged enthusiasm hunting down stories, tips and tricks about Malini as he did doping out card table artifice from advantage players, but without as much success. Malini was elusive, not because he avoided socializing with fellow magicians, but because his travels took him around the globe and his performances were generally private affairs performed before wealthy industrialists, politicians, or potentates. Malini was also a wily character.

In November 1923, Vernon met Dr. Gordon Caldwell Peck of Grand Falls, New York at the Onondaga Hotel in Syracuse. Vernon was in town cutting silhouettes. Dr. Peck, a dentist, had earned, inherited, and married into a great deal of wealth. He was also an ardent amateur magician with a deep interest in sleight-of-hand, particularly the work of Malini. Vernon and Peck stayed in touch after parting ways. Less than a year later, Peck informed Vernon that he had made arrangements to meet Malini. The plan was to get together with Malini at the Waldorf Hotel, buy him a few drinks to loosen him up, and take him to the beautiful home of a wealthy business associate on Fifth Avenue. There, they hoped Malini would perform.

Peck and Vernon met Malini on the second floor of the Waldorf, and there they sat, drinking and discussing magic. Malini spoke of his travels to Europe, Africa, and Asia. Vernon and Dr. Peck waited patiently, praying that Malini would perform a miracle or two. As the conversation wore on, Dr. Peck removed a silver cigarette case from his jacket. Malini perked up and said, "I'll show you a little trick—do you have a cigarette there doctor?" Dr. Peck nodded in affirmation and opened the case. Peck smoked Bogusloskys, an unusual and expensive brand of cigarette imported from Russia; the tobacco was wrapped in tan paper emblazoned with the crest of Russian czars.

Malini took a cigarette out of the case, split it open lengthwise, and dumped the tobacco out onto the table. He laid the ragged piece of paper down on his hand and said, "Doctor, I want you to watch this, watch as closely as you can." He slapped his hand down on the table and continued, "There's nothing concealed between the fingers." Malini demonstrated that his hand was absolutely

Society entertainer Max Malini.

empty. He took the paper in the other hand and then showed the back and front of the other one. Malini tore the paper into pieces, rolled it up into his hand, blew on it, and then opened his hand. The tan paper with the crest of the czars was still there, but restored. Dr. Peck's jaw fell open. As he was familiar with the trick and, from his vantage point, he could see much of Malini's technique, Vernon wasn't exactly fooled.

Malini, however, scooped up the loose tobacco from the table and made a mound of it on the palm of his left hand. He crowned the mound with the restored paper. He then rolled his open palms together as if rolling a piece of clay. "Now Doctor, watch." Malini opened both hands. Both tobacco and paper had disappeared. Vernon was absolutely astounded. Malini reached across the table and lifted up an ashtray. There, to everyone's surprise, was the pile of tobacco.

Shortly afterwards, Sam Florsheim, the shoe magnate, entered the bar. Malini beckoned Florsheim to join their table. Florsheim was not particularly interested in magic but was a friend and admirer of Malini. Malini said, "Vernon, show them a little card trick."

As Florsheim had probably seen Malini perform some very good card tricks, Vernon knew that his would have to be special. Malini was a difficult, if not impossible, act to follow. Vernon asked Florsheim to select a card, and, although it appeared to be a free selection, Vernon used a subtle psychological gambit to force Florsheim to select the nine of hearts. Vernon was not about to take any chances in the present company.

"Now, Mr. Florsheim" Vernon said, "I want you to take the pack in your own hands, return the card to it and shuffle the cards to your heart's content."

Florsheim did as requested. Vernon then took the cards back into his own hands and secretly maneuvered the nine of hearts to the top of the deck.

Vernon continued, "Just by pressing the pack, I can make your card work its way right up to the top."

He asked for the name of the card. Florsheim said, "The three of clubs."

At first Vernon thought he had perhaps forced the wrong card. He then realized that he didn't make those sorts of mistakes. He said, "You're kidding me a little aren't you," and repeated the initial question, "What was that card you just drew?"

Florsheim said, quite emphatically, "The three of clubs."

Just then Malini intervened, "I bet you thought he took the nine of hearts." He then reached over and took the nine off of the top of the deck. Vernon was dumbfounded. It wasn't possible. Afterwards, when Vernon reconstructed the evening's events, he realized that Malini had orchestrated the mishap. He had instructed Florsheim, well before he joined the group, to name at the denouement a card different from the one he had actually selected. Malini would then intervene and produce the correct card. When it came time to perform, particularly in the presence of a potential client, Malini had to distinguish himself from his peers; even more so if the potential client was accompanied by an amateur. Malini was not alone in adopting such tactics. Houdini also did everything in his power to sabotage his competitors. Vernon was angry with himself for being so naïve and trustworthy. It was as if his lovely English raincoat had been taken from him a second time.

Few professional magicians associated with amateurs. Even though many belonged to the same fraternal organization, the Society of American Magicians, or the recently formed International

Inner Circles

Brotherhood of Magicians, professional magicians often held their amateur brethren in contempt. At a public reception at the Hotel McAlpin, organized by the Parent Assembly of the Society of American Magicians, Houdini had to be removed by force from the premises after striking another magician for suggesting that he take a lesson or two from an amateur.

Houdini had just performed a few card tricks. His technique, however, had not kept pace with the standards set by serious sleight-of-hand card aficionados in New York. When Houdini palmed a playing card from the pack, the card was visible to all but him. Margules suggested, in a kind-hearted manner, that Houdini take a lesson or two in palming from Vernon. Houdini snapped. How dare Margules suggest that Houdini take a lesson in magic, particularly card magic, from anybody? Houdini had just released *Elliott's Last Legacy* and, in his mind, was still the sole "Undisputed Card Champion of the World." Houdini then lost his composure, cursed Vernon, calling him an amateur, and punched Margules. Others, including Al Flosso, Vernon's friend from the Dreamland Circus Sideshow, intervened and escorted Houdini, wailing and flailing, from the building. Margules was devastated, not by the punch, as he was a large man, but because his idol, the magician he had worshipped since he first became interested in magic, was so irrational. Vernon wasn't devastated; he was disgusted. He lost what little respect he had for Houdini. Imagine, a grown man hitting another, without warning, over a card trick.

It was time to leave New York.

Vernon heard that the Little Blue Bookshop operated a store in Atlantic City. Having cut silhouettes on the boardwalk at Atlantic City many times, Vernon sensed an opportunity to return. He negotiated a rental arrangement similar to the one he had in New York and left with Jeanne for the sun and surf of the seaside resort. The couple enjoyed the beach and boardwalk, sailed on a boat owned by Bert Morey, a wealthy amateur magician and, when money was tight, returned to the Little Blue Bookshop to cut more silhouettes. While plying his trade one afternoon, Vernon heard the sound of a Canadian accent and introduced himself to the man, an engineer who was visiting Atlantic City with a group of other engineers from Canada. The man invited Vernon to join his group at their hotel later that evening, where Vernon recognized an old schoolmate. The mate asked whether Vernon still performed magic.

Jeanne and Vernon at the Little Blue Bookshop in Atlantic City.

As a deck of cards was rarely out of his reach, Vernon entertained the engineers with several tricks, including Cards Up The Sleeve, a routine he had learned from *The Expert At The Card Table* and had perfected at Coney Island. A crowd gathered in the lobby to witness the performance. He closed his impromptu set in a particularly spectacular manner. Two cards were selected and returned to the deck. Vernon tossed the deck into the air and, with rapier speed, plucked the two selections from the cloud of cards before it tumbled to earth. He received a huge ovation. After he finished, a woman asked to speak with him.

"My name is Frances Rockefeller King," she said.

Vernon recognized the name but, as he thought she sounded rather pretentious, he feigned unfamiliarity. Miss King mentioned that she was impressed by Vernon's impromptu performance and that she would like to speak with him at greater length. Vernon suggested she come by the shop where he cut silhouettes. She could speak to him there tomorrow.

In 1924, King was the preeminent talent agent in New York, perhaps the entire United States, when it came to private events. She had started her career as a chorus girl but became an administrative assistant to Vaudeville czar B.F. Keith after she was injured in an automobile accident. Keith admired her efficiency and assigned her the task of booking all talent employed on his circuit for both private parties and social events. She catered to the New York 400, and when they requested entertainers, she provided them with "name" entertainers such as W. C. Fields, Will Rogers, Billy Robinson, and Bing Crosby. Of course Vernon had heard of her. For years his friends had suggested that he contact Miss King at her office at the Palace Theatre. Now, she was knocking on his door.

The following day, Miss King visited Vernon. She waited patiently as Vernon finished cutting the silhouettes of other customers, then sat down and instructed Vernon to cut hers. Vernon said that he charged fifty cents a silhouette, two for seventy-five cents. She nodded for him to proceed. Vernon cut the silhouette. Miss King, admiring the craftsmanship, said, "That's very good. You have other talents besides the magic. The magic you did is phenomenal." Vernon replied, "I don't do magic professionally."

Miss King then asked Vernon whether he was interested in earning $5,000 for a couple of months' worth of work. Vernon was not quite sure what she meant or what might be involved. Miss King informed him that she would guarantee him at least that amount of income if he allowed her to book him for private parties in New York over the winter. He could perform magic and cut silhouettes. She told him to visit her when he returned to New York.

Miss King removed a silver dollar to pay for the silhouettes. Vernon refused the money. She insisted, however, on paying. He gave her a fifty-cent piece for change. Miss King noticed Jeanne Verner, who had been eavesdropping on the conversation. She asked Vernon to break the fifty-cent piece into two quarters and provide her with a strip of adhesive tape. She placed a piece of tape around each quarter and then initialed the tape. She handed one quarter to Jeanne and the other to Vernon.

"Keep this," she said, "it is going to bring you luck."

Weeks later, in September 1924, Vernon received a telephone call from Miss King. She asked that he return to New York immediately, as she had a very important engagement for him to perform that weekend. Vernon, frightened or foolish, advised her that he could not leave Atlantic City on such short notice. He was expecting a busy weekend at the shop. His only real ambition, much to the consternation of his wife and friends, was to enjoy the surf. Unfortunately, the engagement was very important. It was a private party in Long Island in honor of the Prince of Wales, the heir to the British throne. Miss King was quite annoyed, calling Vernon a "will of the wisp," and said that she would give the engagement to someone else. Joseph Dunninger, now a mindreader, got the call. Vernon had first met and admired Dunninger's work as a magician in 1915. Dunninger impressed the Prince by reading his mind and taught him a few magic tricks as well. The major New York papers covered the event and were euphoric. Dunninger was a hit. He presented "mindreading" in a thoroughly modern manner, and as his performance before the Prince captured the public's imagination, his fees jumped substantially, to $1,000 or more for a single engagement.

Vernon returned to New York in the fall but had exhausted his funds by December. Perhaps it was finally time to visit Miss King. She was surprised to see him but had an engagement for him Friday night if he was free. A millionaire had just purchased Aeolian Hall and was giving a dinner at the South Shore Country Club to celebrate the acquisition. Several other Keith acts were on the bill. Vernon would appear as a guest, circulate around the party and perform card tricks.

Although he had performed a stage act at Coney Island and often mingled his magic with silhouettes, this would be his first real professional engagement. He was aware of Miss King's reputation and the reputations of the other entertainers on the bill. His nervousness, something he claimed to have inherited from his mother, got the better of him, and he tried to wiggle out of the engagement. He informed Miss King that he did not have appropriate attire. She would not accept no for an answer, however, and provided Vernon with a letter of introduction to a prominent tailor. The tailor would insure that Vernon was dressed appropriately and Miss King would settle the account later.

Arthur Finley accompanied Vernon to the subway station on the day of the engagement to make sure that he boarded the train. Vernon offered Finley his fee of $100 if Finley performed in his stead. (Most magicians were lucky to receive a fee of fifteen or twenty dollars to perform at a private party.) Finley said he wouldn't do it for five times that amount. He reprimanded Vernon. "You are such a fool. You've got no competition in magic. Do you realize if you were a singer, a piano player, a violinist, or a photographer, you'd have competition? You can be great in your field, you can make a good living and enjoy the things you like." Suitably scolded, Vernon boarded the train.

He sought solitude as soon as he arrived at the club, and found it in a large rotunda. He took out a pack of cards and began to fan them. Frances White, a Broadway star famous for her rendition of "Mississippi" and one of the evening's feature performers, was pacing up and down, calming her nerves by humming a song to herself. She saw Vernon with his cards.

"I hate you magicians," she said. "There you are sitting there so cool and calculated, so relaxed, and here am I, a nervous wreck. I can perform on Broadway before a crowd and it doesn't faze me, but in front of all these millionaires in dinner jackets, all this wealth and pomp, I am just trembling."

Apparently Vernon wasn't the only one. Even the most celebrated stars battled nerves before each performance. It was a natural state. Vernon left the rotunda, entered the party, and circulated amongst the guests. Miss King was pleased by the reports she heard the following day. She sent Vernon out on other engagements, sometimes to perform magic and other times to cut silhouettes, sometimes both. Miss King was very clear about what she expected from both her performers and her clients. She said, "Mr. Vernon, if you ever go to a date and they ask you to wait in the kitchen or the hallway until you are called, you walk right out. Leave, Mr. Vernon, as you say that your performance is over. You'll get your check from me just the same. When you work out of this office I tell my clients that I don't book entertainers; I book artists, and I expect my artists to be treated the same as any of the guests."

As Miss King would not accept an engagement that paid her performers less than $100, Vernon worked for many interesting people. At one private party on Park Avenue, Vernon was relaxing in the library when a woman entered and asked if he was the man who was going to do the card tricks later that evening. Her husband was crazy about card tricks and was known to perform a few himself. Vernon asked for his name. The woman replied, "Oh, you wouldn't know him. He's a fiddler." Her husband, the fiddler and card trick enthusiast, was Fritz Kreisler. Entranced by the magic, he followed Vernon around the party, trying to absorb each and every trick.

Vernon also had the pleasure of entertaining Charles M. Schwab, first at the inaugural dinner of his presidency of the Carnegie Steel Veterans Association and later, and on several occasions, at his home. Vernon was impressed with his humility. Schwab was proud of his roots, a poor boy who started out by shoveling coal for Andrew Carnegie. Now he was the president of their association. Schwab offered Vernon $10,000 if he would teach him how to pull a card from the bottom of the deck without getting caught. Vernon asked Schwab why he would want to learn such a technique.

Schwab had a standing feud with another steel magnate, Judge Gary. He said, "We play poker, Judge Gary and all of us, and we have some pretty stiff games. We bet two or three thousand dollars on a card sometimes. It's good sport, you know; we have a lot of fun. But if I could just be in a pot with Judge Gary sometime—just sometime—and pull a card from the bottom of the deck and win the pot, perhaps with five thousand in it, and take the money, I'd say 'Judge, I cheated you—I pulled that card from the bottom, but you're not getting your money back!'" Now Vernon could understand why. He had also performed for Judge Gary, numerous times, and found him quite hypocritical.

Judge Gary had a syndicated column. Advice to young Americans: Get up early, rise at four in the morning, don't waste five minutes, have an early breakfast, exercise, never touch liquor, don't smoke young America, don't this and don't that. But old Judge Gary—every party I was ever at, his wife would say, "Now come on Albert, you've got to go home, you're getting too drunk."

The shows Vernon enjoyed most, however, were the difficult ones, the shows where he was forced to improvise to meet a challenging spectator or taxing conditions. One such audience was the Knights of St. Kelly, a group that met at the Union League Club, made up of bankers or businessmen who enjoyed playing poker. Miss King informed Vernon that they often booked a variety act or two through her and this time had decided on a magician. Miss King warned Vernon that they could be a difficult audience.

"Mr. Vernon, I want to warn you, they had Malini there one time, and Malini almost quit—they made it so hot for him—I don't think they are particularly interested in entertainment from a magician. They think they'll have a lot of fun; every trick he does, they'll make it tough for him. He won't be able to do the tricks. In other words, irritate him—catch his tricks."

Vernon said that he would be happy to take the engagement. He didn't mind that it could be potentially embarrassing. After all, Miss King said he would be paid no matter what the outcome. So Vernon made his way to the Union League Club on the appointed night and the chairman of the group introduced him by tapping the table with his knife and informing his brethren that that they were going to see some magical entertainment from one of the world's experts—particularly with cards. He added, "some of you fellows who think you're good poker players, he'll show you you're not so good." As soon as the chairman introduced Vernon by the name, however, somebody piped up and said, "What, vermin? We've got to put up with vermin?"

Vernon smiled, made some introductory remarks and opened his set with a rope trick. The group hollered, "We can't see!" There were about 150 men sitting at round tables. Vernon moved a little to one side. They yelled that they still couldn't see. "Higher," they said, "Get up higher!"

Vernon strode to a table in the center of the room, pushed the cutlery aside and stood on top. Even so, the audience continued to heckle. Eventually, though, they quieted down and enjoyed one of his best performances. Vernon improvised the set, performing standing on the top of one table before dismounting and continuing the performance from the top of another one. It was an unusual way to work the room. They group was impressed with his poise and magic. One said, "Mr. Vernon, I'd like to shake your hand. We had a little fellow here one time named Malini. We caught him with a card right in his hand. We were shuffling, and he had a selected card right in his hand. He had it palmed. We liked him. He was a lot of fun but we caught him that night." The man added, "We didn't catch you and you handled this crowd very nicely. They're a rowdy bunch, but somehow or other, you handled them and quieted them down."

Occasionally, Vernon was sent to engagements outside of the city and, whenever possible, would couple them with a silhouette cutting job. When engaged to perform for George Eastman (of Eastman-Kodak) in Rochester, Vernon also arranged to cut silhouettes at the Onondago Hotel in Syracuse. Jeanne accompanied him and they extended their stay at the hotel by several weeks. Jeanne soon discovered that not all eccentric magicians lived in New York.

The fire chief, who evidently had read some of the magic magazines and must have got hold of my name somewhere, came into the hotel and he asked, "Have you ever seen my illusion? I levitate a fire engine." In those days they had those great big nickel-plated things that weighed many tons. I really thought he was kidding. Anyway, we talked after that, and my wife said, "Boy, we certainly have some characters in magic."

So the next day, there was a big fire, and we were sitting in the lobby of the hotel. Well, after a few hours, we heard the engines coming back from the fire, and all of a sudden, in walks the chief. He had a black raincoat on, and a helmet, and his face was all dirty, and the tears were rolling down his cheeks, and he said, "Vernon, come on right now. I want to take you over there right now because I'm afraid I'm going to miss you. You're leaving town tomorrow." So here he is, fatigued and almost knocked out, and he takes my wife and me down in his chief's car with the siren roaring, and we go down to the fire station. It takes him about 20 minutes to set up, and he's giving orders to all the firemen, and then he says, "Now wait, you stay in this part of the building," and he takes me in and there's this great big fire engine standing there. Now he's giving guys private signals and everything, and all of a sudden, this fire engine creaks and creaks and goes up about two inches off the floor.

Then he had trouble getting this big hoop out of another room. It could hardly go through the door, and he had to bend it a little to get it through the door. Then he takes this thing, and it rattles, and he passes this god-darn hoop all over the thing, and when he takes it off he says, "What do you think of that?"

Vernon returned to New York and used the funds that he had received working for Miss King and from cutting silhouettes to sustain a rather bohemian lifestyle in the city. The money, however, always seemed to disappear faster than expected. He could have solicited more work if he wanted it. He had the perfect opportunity to promote himself as the premier sleight-of-hand performer in New York. As Arthur Finley said, he had no competition. He simply was not interested, however, in the business of show business. Vernon had heard enough horror stories. Other performers complained bitterly of agents who only looked after themselves. A performer's fee may only represent twenty or even as little as ten percent of the fee that the agent charged a client. Most performers with rent to pay or a family to feed would accept virtually any engagement, regardless of the fee, to make ends meet. And the agent always had an explanation: he had to split, for example, the fee with the hotel manager or caterer. Vernon would rather run out on the rent, a common practice, or cut silhouettes than have to deal with what he perceived was the indignity of the profession.

At a party, Vernon met George Otto, an "office act" billed as the Violinist From The Court of the King of Spain. An "office act" did not have to solicit work. It was a salaried position, like a nine to five job. The performer was sent out on the circuit by the head office. Vernon, he suggested, should develop an "office act." Otto offered to speak to Pat Casey, the manager of a theatre in Brooklyn where Vernon could break in the act.

When Vernon arrived at the theatre and looked at the call sheet, he did not see his name listed. He was watching the show from the wings when he heard the stage manager call forth, "Edward Brown? Edward Brown, where are you? Where is that damn magician?" Vernon recalled reading "Edward Brown, a novelty actor" on the call sheet and realized that it must have been referring to him. He hurried on stage.

The act featured a blend of tricks that relied on both apparatus and sleight-of-hand. Vernon opened with a cut and restored ribbon effect and then performed and 'explained' how to change the color of a handkerchief. He then performed a series of card tricks: the Diminishing Cards, the Cards Up The Sleeve, and the DeKolta Card Shower. He finished with the Clock Dial, an old chestnut in which hands on a clock were spun rapidly around the dial, and then stopped magically at a predetermined time. Vernon had a novel twist to the feat. The hands always stopped spinning at the exact time of day Vernon finished the act. He would say, "I'm glad that you appreciate my act, but my time is up" and then walk off stage.

In May 1925, while performing his "office act," Vernon had the opportunity to meet his boyhood idol, T. Nelson Downs. After he returned to America from his triumphant tour of Europe, Downs trod the boards of vaudeville, stopping in Ottawa, where Vernon saw him as a boy. Several years later, Downs retired to his hometown of Marshalltown, Iowa, where he invested in real estate and enjoyed a life of leisure, managing several rental properties in the quaint little town. His passion for magic, however, continued unabated. He took the occasional show, mostly for service clubs in and around Marshalltown and charged fifty to eight-five dollars per performance. He had also corresponded for many years, sometimes thrice weekly, with the late Dr. James William Elliott, each reminiscing about their glory years and carping about former competitors who were still active on stage. With Elliott's passing, Downs found himself out of the loop. Yes, he corresponded regularly with several young magic enthusiasts from the Midwest, answered the occasional fan letter, and gave magic lessons to those such as Eddie McGuire from Arctic, Rhode Island, who could muster the funds to travel to Marshalltown to spend a few days with the master. But Downs needed new tricks to keep his mental fire alight.

Downs knew from Max Holden's column, and from the reports of other performers who had seen them work, that Finley, Horowitz, and Vernon were worth meeting. A mutual friend, Bert Morey, arranged the get-together. Vernon was thrilled. He immediately noticed that, although Downs had retired from the stage, the personality that enabled him to hold the rapt attention of an audience of several thousand had not diminished. First, Vernon decided to perform a few of the tricks he had learned from *The Art of Magic*, the book that had been ghost-written for Downs and had inspired him as a boy. Downs was fooled. He asked, "What are you doing there?"

Vernon replied, "It's from your book."

Downs said, "What book?"

"*The Art of Magic*."

"Hell, some of that stuff doesn't work."

Vernon responded, "Sure it works. You read it, didn't you?"

Downs said, "Hell yes, but I didn't think some of it worked."

Vernon was tickled to death that he'd fooled Tommy Downs. For a follow-up, he performed the trick he had used to fool Houdini. Again Downs was staggered. Vernon repeated the trick several times. Downs was annoyed with himself. Although he was still regarded affectionately as the King of Koins, he always thought of himself as a "card man."

When Downs heard that Vernon was performing on stage, he asked Vernon to describe the act. Vernon said, "I'm finishing with a clock dial."

"Don't do anything like that," cautioned Downs, "You're an artist. I'll never forget when I played the Palace, some fellow said that

I could catch coins at the end of a wand. I loved the idea and was going to put it in the act but another said, 'Downs I'm surprised at you, an artist. You don't use those toys.'"

As soon as Downs saw Vernon's act, however, he changed his opinion. "Vernon, that's the greatest thing I ever saw in my life. There was dead silence, and the audience was looking at their watches. We could only hear the swish of the hand; it was beautiful, dramatic. Vernon, nothing can stop you, you're going right where I went."

Vernon asked, "Where is that, Tommy?"

Downs answered, "Right to the top."

Shortly after he returned to Marshalltown, Downs received a letter from Sam Horowitz. Horowitz explained the mechanics of "The Card That Always Returns To Top," the trick that fooled him—and Houdini—so badly. Downs cussed, writing back to Horowitz that he had performed the same feat as far back as 1917 or 1918. He added in a letter to his friend Eddie McLaughlin that he had even sent both the trick and the method to Eddie McGuire in 1923. He just didn't recognize the trick in Vernon's hands.

Despite Downs' prophecy, Vernon did not reach the top. Neither the name nor the act fit. After several performances he changed the name of the act to "Vernon—European Magic," and although his magic was very direct, Vernon wasn't a stage performer. He did not have the larger-than-life personality that could dominate a stage, and he wasn't particularly funny. It took years to develop a solid turn on vaudeville. And besides, vaudeville was in decline. At its peak, when Vernon first saw performances in Ottawa, vaudeville performers were treated like artists, with one show scheduled per day (except for Wednesdays and Saturdays, which included a matinee). Eventually, the theatres scheduled two performances per day, one in the afternoon and the other in the evening. By 1925 performers were required to do three or four, sometimes as many as five shows per day. Vernon hated hanging around the theatre all day long with no time to change his clothes or socialize with friends. Further, the money was not what it used to be. At one time performers would be booked in advance for up to forty-five weeks. Now, few acts—Houdini and Frank Van Hoven, the Man Who Made Ice Famous, being two of the exceptions—could command large fees on the variety stage. The market was flooded with entertainers aspiring to be the latest sensation. Most worked sporadically and acceded to a punishing schedule reminiscent more of dime museums than of the legitimate stage.

Fortunately for Vernon, Miss King continued to book him to perform close-up magic at parties and clubs around New York. And there were also the speakeasies. The Volstead Act may have barred the public sale and consumption of alcohol throughout the nation, but New Yorkers continued to drink. Over 32,000 clubs and watering holes sprung up to service this market, in flagrant violation of the law. It was a golden opportunity for someone like Vernon, a performer whose specialty was close-up sleight-of-hand. Although he was reported to be working these clubs, Miss King did not service this clientele, and Vernon loathed dealing with other agents.

Vernon found professional satisfaction in other ways, as well. He was content with the accolades he received from the magic community. Max Holden, in the March 1926 issue of *The Sphinx*, wrote:

> *Without a doubt the greatest card man of the age is Dave Vernon, you can never detect a false move or a pass whilst the cards are in Dave's hands. Some time I hope to be able to write up his act.*

If Holden had a difficult time describing Vernon's close-up act, it was because he did not have one. When it came to time to perform magic at close quarters, Vernon drew on his vast body of knowledge and technique to improvise. Knowing he could extricate himself from any challenging situation, he would mix and match techniques. This approach represented new ground, one that was difficult, if not impossible, for other magicians to follow. Those who could rarely attempted to duplicate the feats on a paid engagement. The techniques, they argued, were too risky. Inspired by the first English translation of the secrets of the great Austrian magician Hofzinser, for example, Vernon learned to control a spectator "by gaze." A person would select a card, return and shuffle it into the deck. The performer would start dealing cards to the table. Using his demeanor and expression, Vernon could unconsciously motivate the spectator to stop the dealing procedure at the exact moment the chosen card hit the tabletop. With considerable study and practice, Vernon became skilled at reading people and anticipating their every move or action. He had developed a deep understanding of the psychology of deception.

In May 1926, Larry Gray returned to New York after six years in

Inner Circles

California. Gray was one of the unsung stars of variety entertainment. A superb mimic, perhaps the greatest mimic that Vernon ever saw, he had developed a finely honed comedy act in which he impersonated famous celebrities such as W.C. Fields, Ed Wynn, and Will Rogers as they performed magic tricks. His impersonations were uncanny, and the tricks that each character performed were equally astounding. Although he played some big-time houses on the West Coast, he often supplemented his income by cutting silhouettes, having learned the trade from Vernon at Coney Island.

When Vernon and Gray reconnected, it was as though Gray had never left New York. They would stay out all hours of the night discussing magic and performing card tricks. Whatever Jeanne Verner thought of her husband's relationship with Larry Gray, she had other matters on her mind. On May 26, 1926, Vernon escorted Jeanne, in a cab, to Sloan-Kettering hospital and, on arrival, handed her over to the staff. She was about to deliver their first child. Vernon asked if he should wait, imagining a room full of fathers pacing back and forth, cigars at hand to celebrate. Unfortunately, an intern instructed Vernon to return home. He would not be needed until at least five o'clock, at the earliest, the next day. Once home, Vernon asked Larry Gray if he would spend the night with him at the apartment. Vernon was awakened by a phone call in the early morning and informed that Jeanne that had given birth to an eight-pound baby boy.

Vernon's mania for magic, his obsession for tricks, was well known in New York, and his friends wouldn't hesitate to ridicule him if given the opportunity. With the birth of the boy, Judson Cole, a prominent vaudeville magician and humorist, seized the opportunity to do just that. According to Cole, Vernon and Gray were exchanging card tricks all night, and the phone rang just as Vernon was saying, "Now Larry, you cut the cards in two piles, pick up one and count down the number you name." Vernon answered the phone, heard the news and then immediately returned to the trick at hand. Cole exclaimed that even the birth of his first child couldn't distract Vernon from completing a card trick. Jeanne heard the story when she returned home with the baby. Vernon denied the allegation. Jeanne surmised, however, that the story was probably not far from the truth.

Living with Vernon was extraordinarily difficult. He would stay up most of the night and sleep most of the day. Although his friends would marvel at his effortless skill, he displayed no ambition to make it his career or to use it as a means to provide for his family. His unconventional approach manifested itself in more ways that just his magic. When the nurses in the hospital asked the new parents to enter a name for their child on the official registry, they could not provide one. They couldn't agree on the name. Jeanne suggested two, and Vernon nixed both. He hated the name Robin: a cousin of his father's named Robin had caused the family great grief by extending a three-month family visit into a sojourn of six months, all at his father's expense. His mother, Vernon said, would never forgive him if they named the child Robin. Vernon was equally dismissive of Jeanne's second selection, Guy, a name that was always the focal point for schoolyard taunts. As they couldn't agree on a name, the nurses simply wrote "Male Verner" in the birth registry.

It is ironic that as it became harder and harder for most magicians to find venues in which to perform, the ranks of amateur magicians were growing by leaps and bounds. Their numbers were about to swell further with the introduction of a mail-order course of magic tricks. First developed by Walter Baker but then taken over by Harlan Tarbell, the 60-lesson course cost $79.95. After absorbing each week's set of instructions, it was claimed that you too could become a master magician. In June 1926 *The Sphinx* carried the following advertisement.

> *Attention—You who are deeply interested in the fascinating Art of Magic will be gratified to know that at last you can learn, not just tricks, but the very principles of Magic, Legerdemain, and Prestidigitation. In the Profession of Magic one man becomes a sleight of hand artist, another becomes a master illusionist, and still others specialize in different branches of the art. Each one has perfected for himself one or more principles. The Tarbell System, Inc, has perfected all the fundamentals of the Science of Magic and teaches these principles by means of carefully chosen tricks and illusions... Never before has Magic been taught from this scientific and professional standpoint with this remarkable completeness, thoroughness and clearness.*

As Finley, Horowitz, and Vernon continued to visit their regular haunts, more and more amateurs followed their every move.

Inner Circles

We used to stay together as a group in the magic shops. We discussed the latest innovations. We were always amused, too, because the fellows who were rather far behind in magic wanted to join us. These fellows were copycats, even the mannerism of turning a card, with prying eyes they would emulate everything we did, even the way we would sit on chairs. I said I would try an experiment with these copycats so I leaned over to Horowitz and Finley and put a card in this way: half-way into the pack, put the forefinger on the under and spun it around, made it rotate in its own plane and pushed it in. But we whispered as were doing this. The next week all the fellows were watching and said: "They pushed the card in this way now they turned it, I don't know what this does but it is very secret." We were so amused because it had no meaning whatsoever. Years later, now I see some fellow do this. They had no idea it originally started out as a gag to do some little peculiar movement which onlookers or eavesdroppers would look on and say, "This is something, but I wish I knew what went with it." This is how curious they were and how they copied everything.

Vernon knew, however, that his audience was composed primarily of magicians, and he took great pains to fool them. He even rekindled his schoolyard trick of setting the stage for an impromptu challenge. He would, for example, toss several cards down a street grating where a man was working, knowing that he would return by the grating in a short time with one of his friends. On the return trip, Vernon would stop to make a point in the conversation and hope that his friend would notice the cards scattered down the grating and issue the challenge to name a particular card. Vernon would, of course, comply. He'd name the card and then solicit the participation of the fellow cleaning the grate to turn it over. It was the sort of miracle people remembered. For Vernon, magic performed spontaneously on the street had much greater impact than the magic performed on the stage. It took time and trouble to orchestrate but was worth the effort, particularly for enhancing his reputation as a man who could perform impromptu miracles. Unfortunately, while such stunts create a reputation, and word of mouth travels quickly, impromptu performances did not generate income for Vernon, his wife, and their still unnamed first child.

In the summer of 1926, Vernon decided to forgo his annual pilgrimage to Atlantic City, stay in New York and open, with Larry Gray, a place on Broadway where they could cut silhouettes. Their store, located between 53rd and 54th Streets, became a Mecca for magicians. There they would entertain as many as sixty visitors in a day. Max Holden announced the operation in his July 1926 column:

> *Larry Grey [Gray] and Dave Vernon are playing on Broadway, or rather working on Broadway, where they have a store and are busy cutting silhouettes. Needless to say it is a hangout for magicians. Leipzig, Jud Cole, Sam Horwitz [Horowitz], Alan [Allan] Shaw and many others are to be found there.*

The silhouette store became the social club where magicians could swap stories and tricks. Vernon also learned a tremendous number of new tricks. He experimented with them, added his own improvements, most of which involved streamlining cumbersome techniques or eliminating discrepancies, and then performed them for others who dropped in to visit. Vernon was interested in improving these effects. Each trick was like a block of marble. He saw within the block a mystery, one that he could chisel out and bring to life. He was interested in chipping away the extraneous.

Suddenly, every new effect in the magic world was being attributed to Dai Vernon. Unfortunately, Vernon neither claimed nor disclaimed credit; he simply performed the tricks. Others just assumed that Vernon was the originator. This often created friction between friends. One trick, described by Max Holden in the July 1926 issue of *The Sphinx*, tested the relationship between Vernon and Arthur Finley.

> *Dave Vernon has a clever effect. He lays the three kings face down on table, then has one card selected and placed face down on table without looking at cards. He now explains that the card selected out to be of the same denomination as the other cards; the selected card is now turned over and found to be a ten. Then someone says, "you are wrong this time, Davie," but when the three cards which we saw laid down a minute before, and were then kings, he turns them over and there are three tens to correspond to the other ten.*

Although the public shows no interest in the authorship of magic,

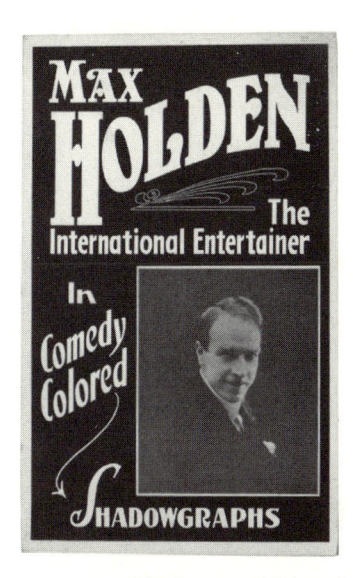

Shadowgraphist and columnist Max Holden.

magicians are territorial when it comes to claiming credit for the development of their tricks. For an audience, the effect itself is what matters, not who invented it. Further, many laymen have the false impression that magicians draw their material from the same bag of tricks. The public has not been taught how to critique or evaluate magic, nor has it been given the tools to do so. Magic tricks do not fall under the protection of either copyright, trademark, or patent protection, and there are no performance rights associations hovering around clubs and restaurants charging a royalty fee for the use of the choreography or technique employed by the working magician. In fact, most magicians are not interested in the origin or evolution of their own craft. The only remuneration magicians can receive for their inventions is proper credit. As such, magical inventors and historians take great pride in assigning credit where due. It was Arthur Finley, not Dai Vernon, who created the trick that Holden described in his July 1926 column.

Finley was annoyed that Vernon performed the trick for Holden. Holden's column was eagerly read by magicians around the world looking for the latest trends in magic. Magicians would read the description of the effect—his effect—and would try to reconstruct the trick. Finley was not against exposure of magic secrets. Years earlier he had sold the secrets to several of his own tricks, advertised in *The Sphinx* under a family name Henry Gavin, and had even promoted his own course in sleight-of-hand, teaching the fundamental techniques of card magic. What irked Finley more than anything was that his work, his creation, would be butchered in performance. Most magicians were lazy and would not spend the requisite time to learn the proper technique. The effect was so startling that it would forgive or conceal the absence of technique. Finley was distraught because he had worked so very hard to construct a sequence of events that were both magical and unexpected, and the power of the effect and its construction would be diluted by abominable performances, performances that would lower the bar of perception that a jaded public already had of magicians.

Houdini was again the touchstone. While preparing a new stage show for the road, Houdini asked for Stewart Judah, Vernon's acquaintance from Cincinnati, to teach him a beautiful effect in which a piece of tissue paper was torn, restored and then transformed into a snowstorm of paper that floated across the footlights. Vernon accompanied Judah to the theatre where Houdini was waiting. Houdini was quite dismissive; he thought he could learn the trick quickly and insert it into his show that evening. He had no understanding or appreciation of the finesse which the trick required in order to achieve the desired theatrical effect. Houdini, confident that he had mastered all that he needed to know, performed the piece that very evening. It was a disaster. He bungled every aspect of the trick and, perhaps wisely, dismissed any notion of permanently adding it to his repertoire.

Finley was also disappointed that Vernon taught the routine to other magicians after it had been given to him in confidence. Vernon was too cavalier and in Finley's mind, should have known better. The two still met, but less frequently, mostly in the company of mutual friends.

The silhouette shop continued to attract magicians. Nate Leipzig was a regular visitor and others, like Louis McCord, who toured as Silent Mora, would drop in whenever they were in town. The shop became dotted with promotional posters and photographs signed by each magician.

> *My walls were covered with pictures of magicians. I had a big picture of Dante, one of Kellar, one of Hermann, photographs of all the local*

magicians and in the corner I had a little visiting card with a picture of Houdini. Written below was the slogan "My brain is the key that sets me free." I always liked that slogan. I don't think Houdini came up with it—probably some newspaper person. Anyway, Harry Houdini came into the store and looked at all of the big pictures of Dante, Kellar, Hermann and so forth and he hollered, "Where's my picture, Vernon?" I took him to the corner, showed him the little card and told him how much I loved the slogan. "What, that small card?" he cried. "I'll send you a picture!" The next day a messenger brought in a great big crate and later Houdini came in asking if I had received his picture. I told him that I hadn't had a chance to unpack it yet. Well, he wanted to take all of the pictures down and rearrange them so that he was directly in the center. The nerve! Of course, I didn't do it. Larry Gray and I chose to hang it in a more appropriate place.

By this time in his career, Houdini had become the butt of many jokes and pranks within the community. Few took him seriously. Magicians took great delight in locking Houdini in a bathroom or cupboard and challenging him to escape. Houdini, of course, couldn't, and would kick and scream until someone opened the door. As the first modern media star, however, Houdini knew his priorities.

Vernon said, "Harry, no small child would be fooled by your vanishing elephant."

Houdini replied, "Vernon, very few see the actual performance. They only hear about it and marvel that such a thing is possible. Keep your name in the press, not every week, but every day if possible and be sure that they spell it correctly."

Vernon's name was well known, too. Unfortunately, magicians were the ones talking about him, not the public. Conjurers would enter the store and ask him for direction. Could he help them with their technique? Could he provide them with a new trick or two? None of the requests helped pay the rent. Larry Gray, although a superb performer, was satisfied with having mastered a handful of techniques rather than, as S. W Erdnase would say, every sleight in the calendar. Gray set up his own personal driving range in the back of the store and pounded golf balls into the curtain. He left most of the magicians to Vernon. Eventually Vernon and Gray realized that it was rather stupid to have a big store like that and do nothing but have a table back there and a place for magicians to congregate.

> People were always tramping in and out of this door on Broadway and bringing friends in and I thought we might as well make this place pay a little—we are paying rent here, $300 a month, and why not make a little money. So Jack Davis and Bob Sherman were selling magic in New York at that time—they had a place in the Hudson tubes and also in Grand Central Station, a magic store—so I said to Bob Sherman, if you like you can have a magic counter—it was screened off from where we cut the silhouettes, and you can have a magic counter in there. You don't have to pay any rent, but give us a percentage of what you sell.

So Davis moved in some stock and they set up a counter where they could sell magic. Once in a while a magician would visit the store, go to the magic counter and Vernon would walk over to talk to him. Other times, Davis would call Vernon over when a visitor would ask to see him. It became so bothersome, magicians calling to ask Vernon how to perform a trick or asking for further direction, that he said to Jack Davis, "Don't call me to the back unless it's somebody interesting that you think I'd like to meet, or some gambler or some person that has something interesting. I can't be quitting the silhouettes all the time and going back there because I get into these long drawn-out talks and I'm losing money."

One day in late July, Jack Davis came forward and said, "There's some Englishman back here—he doesn't know you, but he's just come from Vancouver or somewhere, and he's very good with cards. He does a few things very well."

Vernon came out to meet him. The man introduced himself as Richard Pitchford. His stage name was Cardini. Vernon thought "Card-ini" was the most ridiculous name that he had ever heard for a magician.

Cardini said, "This gentleman here tells me you're interested in cards."

Vernon responded, "Yes, I am, and I'm more interested in cards than I am in these silhouettes."

"Do you do anything with cards?"

Vernon said, "Well, I fool around with them."

"Would you let me see what you do?"

As there were cards on the counter in the magic shop, and he was

Inner Circles

the only one there, Vernon took the cards and made a fan.

Cardini asked, "Will you do that again?"

Vernon wondered why the man wanted him to make a fan again. Still, he complied with the request.

Cardini asked, "Would you do that again please?"

Vernon repeated the movement a third time.

Cardini said, "That's funny you make it in one movement."

Vernon replied, "I don't understand what you mean."

He answered, "You make the fan in one movement. When I make a fan I make it this way, then I bring it down this way with the other hand, like this. And I don't see how you can make a fan in one movement."

Vernon said, "Well, I don't know, I never thought about that."

And then Cardini asked, "Now can you make a blank fan?"

Vernon said yes, and made the blank fan.

Cardini responded, "Very good, very good. Can you do anything else with the cards?"

Vernon said, "Yes, I do a few things."

"Do you do any tricks?"

Vernon performed several for him. Cardini was baffled. He asked Vernon where he had learned them. Vernon informed him that he had experimented with cards his entire life.

Cardini asked, "You have? What's your name?"

Vernon told him his name, which drew a blank stare. Cardini said, "I don't read the periodicals, you know. Can you back palm cards?" and Vernon said, "Certainly."

He asked, "Can you do a split fan?"

Vernon said, "Yes," and he made a fan, asking, "Do you want to see some good fans?"

Larry Gray was practicing golf in the back, knocking the ball up against the curtain, when he heard Vernon call for him. "Larry," he said, "here's a fellow countryman of yours. He'd like to see some back-hand palming."

Now, in addition to being a first class mimic, Larry Gray had an extraordinary ability to back palm playing cards. Just weeks earlier, Clinton Burgess, the editor of *Elliott's Last Legacy*, and yet another self-described "Card Manipulation Champion of the World," entered the store to challenge Gray to a card duel. Gray dispatched Burgess with literally a wave of his hand—one that concealed a playing card. Vernon had seen Cardini manipulate the cards and

Swan Walker looks on as Richard Pitchford (Cardini) tips his hat to Dai Vernon.

he knew that he would be no match for Larry Gray.

Gray said, "Oh, I'll show you a few," and he proceeded to manipulate the cards, making them vanish and reappear at his fingertips. Cardini exclaimed, "My word, my word! Who is he?"

Vernon said, "He's my partner in cutting silhouettes."

He asked, "Where did he learn?"

The two thought they would have some fun with the Englishman with the funny stage name. "Everybody up and down Broadway," they said, "does this kind of thing."

Cardini was crestfallen. He had spent years perfecting the arduous technique of manipulating playing cards, first while recovering from shell shock in a World War One Veterans' Hospital, and then while on tour throughout Australia. He had just worked his way to New York from Spokane, Washington, at the suggestion of Harlan Tarbell, to break into first class theatres in New York. Here, unknowingly, he had run into two of the finest card manipulators in the world who were telling him that everyone in New York could do his type of work.

"My word," Cardini exclaimed. "Do you do other kinds of magic?"

Vernon said, "Yes, I fool around with all kinds of magic."

What hope of succeeding was there, Cardini asked, if everyone in America was as good as these two guys—who cut silhouettes?

Suddenly, out of the blue, Cardini exclaimed, "Well, I'm a betting man, and I'll bet you I've got a smaller, prettier wife than you have."

Vernon asked, "What has that got to do with it?"

Cardini said, "You're pretty good, you've got me beaten with the cards, and your partner too, but I've got a prettier wife—a smaller, prettier wife."

Vernon said, "Well, I don't know, you may have a prettier wife but I know you haven't got a smaller wife."

Cardini said, "My wife's only about that high."

Vernon said, "So is mine."

Cardini responded, "I'll be back here tomorrow with my wife. You bring your wife."

He walked out of the store. Vernon and Gray started laughing.

Cardini returned the following day and brought his wife, Swan, with him. Vernon brought Jeanne to the shop just in case. Jeanne was smaller than Swan and, in Vernon's opinion, much prettier. Fortunately for Jeanne, she and Swan struck up a friendship. In Swan, she met someone who had a sense of the trials and tribulations associated with being married to a magician.

When Vernon, Cardini, and their wives became fast friends, it was the dawn of a new era in magic. In October 1926 Max Holden wrote,

> *The Master card effect of the season is the Slow Motion Card Vanish invented and perfected by Dave Vernon. A freely selected card is taken and the right hand pushes the card down into the left hand, meanwhile backs of hands being towards audience; now the hands are slowly turned around and fingers apart and card is not there, fingers are snapped and hands turned around and lo and behold up jumps the card in the hand at command—where from? Yes! No. I want to say right here again that Dave Vernon is absolutely the greatest card man of this or any other age.*

On October 31st, Harry Houdini died in Detroit, Michigan after battling peritonitis, the result of a burst appendix. It could have been treated earlier, but Houdini stubbornly resisted until it was too late. Ironically, the onslaught of appendicitis was exacerbated by a punch to the stomach that Houdini received, rather than gave, during a backstage question-and-answer session with a student from McGill University, Montreal. The press reported that Houdini took his secrets with him to the grave. T. Nelson Downs begged to differ. Less than two weeks after Houdini passed away, he wrote to Eddie McLaughlin, "the truth is Houdini really believed himself a wonder with a pack of cards and as a matter of fact all the boys knew he was "rotten" of course all that newspaper stuff about Houdini carrying all his secrets to the grave is pure bunk—100% balahoo. There are No Secrets in mechanical magic. All the principles of all illusions are known to all magicians."

In November 1926, Holden nominated Vernon's Slow Motion Card Vanish as one of the "Five Super Magical Effects of 1926," and Nate Leipzig, Allan Shaw, Wallace Galvin, Judson Cole, Sam Horowitz, Arthur Finley, and Al Baker all assembled at the Vernon and Gray silhouette shop to demonstrate for each other their latest sleights and effects. The group became known as the Inner Circle. Holden coined the term in his December 1926 column.

> *When they [magicians] pay a visit to New York they expect to see wonders. I may be permitted to say that if they are acquainted with the right magicians they will be well received. We have a kind of an Inner Circle of Magic in N.Y.C. Al Baker, Sam Horowitz, Larry Gray, Arthur Finley, Jud Cole, Wallace Galvin, Cliff Green, Nate Leipzig, Allen [Allan] Shaw, and several others, all magicians and performers. Leslie Guest and his side partners, friend Judah, Dr. E. L. Bulson and many others make it a point to visit N.Y.C. just to keep in touch with some of the boys of our Inner Circle, and I am sure they see some real magic and are not disappointed.*

It was now official. New York had an Inner Circle, and although Holden omitted Vernon's name from the list, he would soon be crowned its King.

Chapter Five
Shadows With Shears

His friends were in agreement. "Listen, Vernon. Why don't you tell that Englishman to go back to England? He'll never make the grade."

The Englishman, Cardini, was actually Welsh, and, although Larry Gray and Vernon misled him as to the general level of expertise of their North American confreres, Cardini was highly skilled. It was sheer circumstance that the first two magicians he met in New York were his superiors. Although Vernon disliked the stage name "Cardini," he recognized talent when he saw it. Naysayer New York magicians, which included such seasoned professionals as Judson Cole and Nate Leipzig, were wrong. Vernon believed that Cardini could be a star if he developed the core of his act, the exquisite manipulation of billiard balls, playing cards, and cigarettes—in pantomime. The only thing holding Cardini back, thought Vernon, was his patter and the hackneyed shopworn tricks that filled out his program. Vernon offered his counsel.

> *Dick, you have a beautiful act. Only one thing mars your act, and that is the talk that you have with it. If you didn't talk, you would be one of the greatest stars on the stage I've ever seen. Don't feel hurt about this—I'm a Canadian and I'm a British subject and I can tell you without hurting your feelings. If an American told you you'd probably say well, "They're jealous of an Englishman," or something, but, I'm an English subject and I tell you, Dick, these puns and this type of humor is very corny around New York, and it's not funny, and when you come on and do this cigarette act it's beautiful. But as*

soon as you open your mouth and start to talk you might as well fall flat on your face because you create this beautiful illusion and then you talk and oh, it's sad.

Vernon relished the role of being a consultant—the man behind the curtain—rather than the performer. He had often shared his secrets and had, on occasion, accepted formal students. He enjoyed providing advice to other performers whose work and efforts he respected and who, in turn, respected his own expertise. He did not consider himself to be a very good performer. Unless it was an impromptu performance where he could improvise, entertaining in front of an audience made him nervous. He preferred to sit on the sidelines and let someone else get the applause. He liked to feel that he had helped his friends and that something he had told them had contributed to the audience's approval. Besides, accolades on stage were fleeting.

As a boy, very early in life, at a football game when I'd made the winning goal or a touchdown, boys would pick me up. I suppose I enjoyed it at the time, but felt it was an empty thing. I think other people feel it more than the person themselves—it isn't so great for the person. I appreciate a compliment from a person who's really clever or a true critic.

Vernon saw Cardini often. Jeanne and Swan became confidants, and their bond strengthened further when Swan gave birth to her first child, Richard. Jeanne's still unnamed child, "Male Verner," now had a playmate. Cardini was admitted to the so-called Inner Circle, the group of magicians identified by Holden, which included Arthur Finley, Sam Horowitz, Al Baker, Nate Leipzig and, of course, Vernon. Vernon kept hammering Cardini on the notion—reinforced with the not-so subtle recommendations of people like Miss King—that he should discard the commonplace and focus on his strengths. Cardini, given the opportunity to tour the hinterland with a variety review, set off to do just that.

Some old-timers, those who longed for real vaudeville or the grand shows of touring magicians such as Herrmann, Kellar, and Thurston, had no interest in the Inner Circle. They considered Holden's praise false and faint, and showed little interest in Vernon, his technical facility, or his performing skills. He had no act or ambition, and was essentially a magician's magician, not to be placed on a pedestal. Vernon was an amateur afraid to perform on the stage. These backward-looking performers, however, failed to grasp the transformation of the entertainment industry. The new magic was urban, performed in nightclubs, revue shows, and one-night engagements for local social or civic groups—"club dates"—by performers who could deliver short, snappy and engaging interludes or presentations with little or no apparatus. New York City was the epicenter, and Vernon was, when he wanted to be, one of its preeminent performers. His improvisational style, the ability that permitted his audience to just "think of a card," was fast paced, spontaneous, and ever-changing.

Vernon soon grew tired, however, of the improvisational format. He had abandoned the notion of pursuing a career on the stage and was content to keep second-class agents at bay by cutting silhouettes. He would wait for premium engagements offered to him by Miss King. Besides, he enjoyed contemplating card tricks, socializing with his clique of magicians, and hunting for obscure gambling artifices, which were becoming increasingly difficult to find. It was not that gamblers and cheats were in short supply, just that those he met offered him little that was new in the way of subtlety or technique. He had seen it all before, and by much better practitioners.

Max Holden continued to champion Vernon in his column, "Trouping Around In Magic," in *The Sphinx*, perhaps the most widely read column by a magician for magicians. Amateurs and professionals turned there first to discover who was working and where, and the type of magic that was being performed. Holden seemed to enjoy tantalizing his readers with descriptions of Vernon's latest miracles. In October 1927, for example, he described yet another.

> *A spectator shuffles a red deck, then a blue deck, selects a card from one and removes the mate from the other pack. For instance, if the five of diamonds was chosen from the blue pack, he would remove the five of diamonds from the red pack. Very fairly the red and blue cards are shown and placed face up on tables a few feet apart, yet at command the cards change places; the red one is now the blue and what was the blue is now red.*

Holden's thumbnail descriptions of Vernon's magic left much to the imagination. For some readers, interpretation was a good thing. Charles Earle Miller, a teenage magician in Indianapolis, was one such reader. Miller challenged himself to create methods that could duplicate Vernon's feats. Others discounted both the magic and the magicians Holden trumpeted. The effects as described were impossible. How could they not be? Many came to dislike Vernon, annoyed that they were not members of his circle and privy to his secrets. They believed, erroneously, that a magician's success was measured in secrets and that, as they themselves were members of the fraternity, they were entitled to know how Vernon did what he did.

T. Nelson Downs was an anomaly, a professional magician of great standing who shared the amateur magician's obsession for secrets. Although Marshalltown, Iowa was far removed from the theatres of his initial triumphs, Downs continued to perform both on stage and off. His obsessive nature, the fire required to excel in the craft, had not diminished even in retirement. He continued to perform "club dates" in and around Iowa and cajoled his sycophants, Eddie McGuire of Rhode Island, Faucett Ross of Missouri, and Eddie McLaughlin of Iowa, into feeding his addiction, demanding that they acquire, copy, and mail him any new tip, idea, or secret they discovered, even if the disclosure would breach a vow of confidence. Downs could not stand to be fooled. As the King of Koins and, in his opinion, most sleight-of-hand, being deceived was beneath him. He had to know it all, and there was a lot to know. It was the dawn of an incredibly prolific period, not just for Vernon, but also for the vanguard of new personalities, mostly amateurs, that flooded the market with their wares and secrets.

Although Vernon was reputed to be the best and most original purveyor of intimate magic, he rarely tipped his mitt, at least publicly. There were plenty of others willing to sell secrets, both their own and those belonging to others. Theodore Squires from Waverly, New York, who adopted the stage name of Ted Annemann, was one such merchant of mysteries. William Larsen and T. Page Wright from southern California, and seasoned veterans such as Al Baker, churned out tricks and ideas, first for magic magazines and then for their own group of devotees. Most of these secrets were advertised first in the pages of *The Sphinx,* and then sold, for astronomical prices, as carbon-copied typescripts. They proved popular because they centered on props that could be acquired with little financial investment—playing cards, coins and other small objects. The manuscripts, which were coveted and carefully guarded, were often used as illicit currency for trading with other devotees. Amateur magicians (whose ranks had swollen because of the popularity of the *Tarbell Course in Magic,* the rise of amateur magic societies, and the evolution of mail order magic as a business) had an insatiable desire for the newest, latest, and greatest. In the April 1927 pages of *The Sphinx,* Max Holden wrote a short piece entitled "The Right Side of Magic."

Magic is probably the greatest hobby of the present day. The love of magic will cause a person to spend hours on practice and study and money will be spent with no thought of expenses, just so a certain effect will be perfect. A simple little trick may have taken years to bring to perfection. A Magician may perform and do a remarkable trick which has everyone guessing, and the result is magicians are willing to pay for that trick and everybody is satisfied as the trick has been secured in a legitimate manner, but that trick is deliberately taken by unscrupulous people and they under sell, trade and swap, then that is not playing the game square.

When a Magician perfects an effect and offers it for sale and it sounds good to you, buy it and keep it to yourself, do not pass it on or swap it, as a secret is no longer a secret when it has been broadcast to everyone.

Holden's plea to play square, however, fell on deaf ears, and his friend Downs, totally preoccupied by secrets, was one of the biggest culprits. He kept McGuire, McLaughlin, and Ross busy sourcing, copying, and sending him the latest. Still, it was not enough. He was still smarting from his initial encounter with Vernon in New York in the spring of 1925. He made plans to return there almost as soon as he had arrived back in Marshalltown. In October 1926, he wrote to McLaughlin and stated that they had to plan a trip to New York, to see "the ones that are really worth meeting: Vernon-Horowitz." His desire to return to New York was reinforced by Holden, who repeatedly wrote to Downs that Vernon was the man to watch.

Downs orchestrated his return. W. W. Durbin, a political strongman for the Democratic Party from Ohio who maintained an obsessive interest in magic, or at least the power associated with organizing its brotherhood, had usurped control of the recently formed International Brotherhood of Magicians and organized a convention for magicians—predominantly amateurs—where they could gather and perform for each other. The first was held in June 1926 in Kenton, Ohio. The second was scheduled for June 1927 in Lima, Ohio. The plan would be for Downs to meet McLaughlin and Ross at the conclave; Downs would perform there and then the trio would work their way, passing through Cincinnati, Baltimore, Washington, and Philadelphia, to New York. They would spend time in New York with Vernon and Horowitz and then head to Providence, Rhode Island to debrief McGuire. The return trip home would take them through New Haven, Buffalo, Niagara Falls, Detroit, and then Chicago. Downs had it all mapped out. They would travel by car, stay at various Elks Clubs, and be back home by the thirtieth of that month. As Ross only had three weeks of leave from work, the trio agreed to cut Washington and Baltimore from their itinerary. On May 3, 1927, Downs wrote to McLaughlin, and explained his strategy for dealing with Vernon and Horowitz.

> *What they want is to cop any ideas I may have. Vernon & those Ginks will "Open up" besides they've got NIX that I can use of this I am positive—however should I possibly be mistaken we will get anything new they may have.*[1]

Despite Downs' protestations to the contrary, Vernon continued to produce new and unusual effects. In his May 1927 column, for example, Max Holden described Vernon's latest:

> *A pack of cards is shuffled, and cards spread face up and one card mentally chosen. The cards are again shuffled and cut. Now the pack is again cut and on the card being named the top card of the bottom cut is turned over and there is the card.*

The trick that Holden described became known in later years as Out of Sight, Out of Mind, and represents, in many ways, the high

---

[1] Grammatical and spelling corrections in excerpts from private correspondence have been limited in the interest of maintaining the original flow and character of the language.

Shadows With Shears

*Faucett Ross (left) and T. Nelson Downs,
vaudeville's King of Koins.*

water mark of Vernon's exploration of improvised card conjuring. Holden described just one possible variant. The real secret was the way Vernon was able to limit the range of choice a spectator had in thinking of a card without the spectator suspecting that his or her decision was not entirely free. This made it easier for Vernon to divine the information secretly, penetrating a person's innermost thoughts, and then use his deft sleight-of-hand to produce or reveal the card in a startling manner. The effect was truly miraculous.

While Downs was making his final preparations for the excursion East, McGuire, sensing perhaps that Downs, McLaughlin, and Ross might cut out the leg to Providence, wrote to Ross and dangled an extra incentive for them to make the trip. Ross passed the information on to Downs by letter, dated June 2, 1927.

Received a letter yesterday from Edw. McGuire and he urges us to be sure to visit him. Says he has most of the dope on the new effects of Horowitz, Baker and Vernon and will slip them to us when we get there.

McGuire had attempted to develop a friendship with Horowitz

independent of Vernon on previous occasions, to no avail. Now he adopted another tactic. He would approach Horowitz as an equal, someone to whom he could offer up his own secrets or, in this instance, the secrets of Max Malini in exchange for what Horowitz could share with him. Although McGuire had only a cursory knowledge of Malini's actual methods—he had foisted himself on Malini during the great magician's performances in Rhode Island—Horowitz would know none of that. McGuire wrote Horowitz on stationery that audaciously described himself as Malini's manager. The gambit worked, and Horowitz's response was quick. He invited McGuire to his home in New Jersey and dazzled him with a barrage of card tricks. But when McGuire was not forthcoming with the secrets he'd promised to divulge, Horowitz offered none of his own. McGuire then attempted to pay for the secrets to the tricks he had just witnessed. Horowitz declined. "Good effects," he said, "are scarce and if a clever magician was to see or witness them worked, he would devise his own method of producing a desired result." McGuire left undeterred. He wrote Downs and said "I think I can get his stuff, if I go about it right."

Downs, McLaughlin, and Ross made the trip to Kenton, Ohio in Ross's Chrysler Roadster. Downs performed as planned and basked in the adoration of the throng of amateurs. In their world, he was still a bona fide star. After the convention, the trio continued their journey East; Downs in the passenger seat, smoking LaPalina cigars and sipping whiskey from his flask; McLaughlin in the rumble seat, draping a raincoat over his head to protect himself from the elements. They arrived in New York on schedule and checked into the Elks Club near Times Square. After they had settled into their hotel, Downs spoke with his friend, Bert Morey, and confirmed that their meeting with Horowitz and Vernon had been arranged.

Vernon and Horowitz dazzled them with unexplainable mysteries. Ross and McLaughlin, like most magicians before them, were floored. Downs, on the other hand, was not yet ready to abdicate his crown, particularly in front of his acolytes. He nodded after each trick, all-knowingly, as if he were on the right wavelength. Afterwards, when the trio was back in the car and Downs was asked for his opinion of the work, he said "Well, he does all that [Charles] Jordan stuff. He gives it a twist of some kind." He then assured his companions that he had all of the secrets on file back home in Marshalltown. Downs, however, had no more clues to the methods than his confreres. Charles Jordan was an extremely clever man, a pioneer of magic based on subtle mathematical principles, not sleight-of-hand. Vernon and Horowitz had carved their own paths independent and distinct from Jordan.

Even though McLaughlin and Ross witnessed some astounding magic, their initial encounter with Horowitz and Vernon could not be described as a success. The duo was hoping that they would learn some secrets. After all, Downs had boasted that Horowitz and Vernon would open up in his presence. It hadn't happened. Vernon had recognized their ploy, and whatever information he was prepared to share with Downs had evaporated in the presence of McLaughlin and Ross. Vernon recognized that Ross, in particular, was well educated and interested in the arts. Still, he did not part with secrets so easily—particularly to strangers.

The trio left New York and headed for Providence, hoping that perhaps McGuire could enlighten them. Unfortunately, McGuire was no further ahead than they were. Still, they spent an enjoyable week with him in Arctic, just outside of Providence. Through him they also met Walter Scott, a professional musician, a Hawaiian steel guitarist, who also had a long-standing interest in magic. McGuire had met Scott years earlier through the Rhode Island Chapter of the National Conjurors' Association. Scott was also interested in gambling techniques and had perfected quite a few, some of which he had learned from hustlers and others that he had developed on his own. Although he had retired from advantage play in 1924, Scott continued to practice his technique and gave Downs a private demonstration. When it came time to disclose his technique, however, Scott was just as cagey as Vernon and did not tip the work. Downs informed McGuire, McLaughlin, and Ross that, next to his own second deal, Scott's was the finest that he had ever seen. For Ross and McLaughlin, however, Scott's best trick was the production of several bottles of whiskey from his overcoat. Soon enough, it was time to head home. They jumped back in the Roadster and headed for Buffalo, entered Canada at Niagara Falls in order to circumnavigate both Lake Erie and, like Scott, the Volstead Act. The trio reentered the United States at Detroit with liquor in hand. Downs may have learned very little on the journey, but like a seasoned baseball player, spoke of next year and started making plans to return to New York.

Vernon decided to spend the summer in Atlantic City and finally christen his son. The boy, approaching his first birthday, still had not been named. His parents could not agree on one they both liked. Finally, they settled on Ted, a compromise. Jeanne hated the name "Theodore" and Vernon liked the name "Edward." Both liked short names. The boy was christened Edward Wingfield Verner, or Ted for short.

Just before the christening, Vernon met Bess Houdini on the boardwalk. He told her that he and his wife were about to have their son christened. When Bess asked whether they had a godmother for the boy, Vernon admitted that they didn't.

Bess said, "Well, please let me be the godmother. I've done everything but I've never been a godmother."

At the christening, the minister was entering information into the ledger and asked for the name of the father, the mother, and the godmother.

Bess said, "Bessie Houdini."

The minister looked up and repeated the question. "What was that last name?"

Bess replied, "Houdini, H-O-U-D-I-N-I."

The Episcopal minister asked whether she was related to the Houdini.

She said, "I was his wife."

The minister was star struck.

After the christening, Bess accompanied the young couple and her new godson for lunch at the Traymore Hotel. When the waiter removed the plate of gruel placed before Ted on the highchair, he discovered a $100 bill and mistakenly thought the banknote was his gratuity. Bess reprimanded the waiter and said that the money was for the little boy, who had just been christened. Jeanne and Dai were as surprised as the waiter at the sight of the bill and thanked Bess for her kindness and generosity. After lunch, they parted ways, Bess returning to New York, and Dai and Jeanne spending the summer in Atlantic City, cutting silhouettes and enjoying the sun and surf. That fall, they would return to New York to fill more engagements for Miss King.

In May 1927, Miss King had booked Vernon to perform at a house party in Norfolk, Virginia. It was for a venerable, well-respected judge and his prominent Virginian family. After Vernon's performance, he was invited to spend the weekend on the estate. While there, he noticed a series of silhouettes of family members and their

Shadows With Shears

A comic representation of Vernon at work, cut by Vernon himself.

ancestors on display. Many had fallen into disrepair. Vernon intimated that he could do work of that nature, and eventually cut silhouettes of the family and replicated many of the old and tattered profiles. The family was thrilled and invited him to return later in the year to perform both his magic and cut more silhouettes, this time for family and their guests. That fall, the judge kept his word. Vernon returned to their abode for another lucrative engagement; Jeanne stayed in New York with Ted.

The family introduced Vernon to many prominent people connected to various Church movements and charitable organizations. Remembering the success he had cutting silhouettes during the war, Vernon offered to cut silhouettes and donate fifty percent of his proceeds to the charitable cause or organization that sponsored him. It worked. Organizers recognized his talent and, more importantly, his ability to raise funds. The first stop on his tour was Asheville, North Carolina, under the auspices of the St. Agnes Guild of the Trinity Episcopal Church. Vernon was a huge hit. The *Asheville Times* carried a glowing account of his work in their November 6,

Dai Vernon: A Biography

1927 Sunday edition.

For the past several weeks passerbys [sic] on Haywood street have gathered in large numbers to watch a young man at work in front of a window cutting silhouettes of Asheville persons under the auspices of the St. Agnes guild of Trinity Eposcopel [sic] church. E.W. Vernor [sic], the silhouette maker, has done a big business here. He had expected to stay for only a week, but his unique work created such a demand here that his visit has been extended week after week. He expects to leave Asheville Wednesday.

The art of cutting silhouettes, which appears so remarkable, is one of the lesser of Mr. Vernon's sidelines... Where Mr. Vernon really creates a sensation is in his sleight-of-hand. He is recognized as one of the finest magicians in the country and he has performed before the most critical magicians in the world... . One of his favorite pastimes is the performance of mental tricks, and one of his most interesting subjects, he says, is mental telepathy.

Vernon has given several exhibitions in Asheville. He has performed at parties, and he gave a brief demonstration of his work before the Civilian Club. He will entertain next Wednesday at the Junior League dinner.

But all these arts, developed to an unusual state of perfection, are only sidelines. Vernon says he hopes to be a painter of portraits.

And then, in an interesting twist that one would think would rile most magicians, Vernon, the hoarder of secrets, performed and then taught the reporter a trick, the same trick that J. Warren Keane had once performed for him in Ottawa. Perhaps, as he indicated in the body of the article, he could reveal the real secret because nobody would believe the explanation to be true. The newspaper detailed the exchange.

"I'll tell you a trick, and then expose it to you," Vernon told the Times reporter.

"This trick, I've been working on since I was ten years old. It took me years to learn it. Now I can make it work eight times out of ten. I've

showed it to the best magicians of the world and they have turned pale in astonishment, and I showed it to the ordinary audiences and they've dismissed it as, "oh, you read my mind."

This is the trick: Mr. Vernon takes a deck of fifty-two cards, pulls one out and lays it beside the others. Then he requests someone to think of the card. The person responds and the single card proves to be the one named.

"Presumably," he said, "that trick is impossible. It couldn't be mind reading because the other person doesn't know what the card is I laid out of the deck. The other alternative would seem to be the projection of thought.

"Here's how it is done. Sometime during the evening I pick out someone in the crowd and engage him in conversation. I get on a subject that is intensely interesting to him and while he is concentrating on our conversation, I give him a slight glimpse, just a flash at a card. He mustn't really see the card. He must see it only subconsciously. Eight times out of ten he will name that same card when I ask him to name one."

Mental telepathy is one of his favorite subjects. He is inclined to believe that such a thing is possible and that the science will some day be developed. He has an open mind on the subject. But as for all the tricks, purported to be performed by it, he declares there is just a trick in all of them.

Seasoned show business performers were puzzled by his success. How could he attract such crowds and generate such publicity? Perhaps it was because Vernon was the antithesis of the show business persona. He was well spoken and well educated, not bold, audacious, or presumptuous. He performed exquisite magic and cut fine silhouettes. He also made his patrons a great deal of money, not personally, but for the charities that they supported. Vernon continued the practice of contributing fifty-percent of all proceeds made cutting silhouettes to the cause or organization that employed him. The committee members of most of the organizations that retained Vernon's services were usually women who were married to business leaders of the community. It was not uncommon for Vernon to be profiled in Sunday morning papers, for example, because the Chair of the Auxiliary Committee that employed him also happened to be married to the publisher of the paper. Vernon was also invited to set up shop in prestigious locations, rent free, because of the social network that engaged him. In short, he worked for people who had power.

Near the end of his sojourn in Asheville, when Vernon was just about to close up shop, a man and his wife entered with their five children. Vernon started to tell them it was too late for silhouettes when one of the boys spotted a pack of cards laying on his stand and asked what they were for. Vernon gave in and cut portraits of them, and then performed a few tricks for the children. Their father was quite impressed and asked Vernon if he could perform the following day at his luncheon club. Vernon informed him that, as a professional, he was required to charge a fee. The gentleman agreed but warned him that one of the club members was well versed in magic and would probably tell everyone exactly how everything was accomplished, a challenge Vernon welcomed. He attended the function the next day and prefaced his performance with some introductory remarks.

> *I understand you have a member who knows all these tricks and that he is conversant with all the methods used by magicians. I hope he'll refrain from telling you how they are done until the performance is over.*

Vernon then performed a thirty-minute program without interruption or incident. At the conclusion of the performance, a tall aristocratic gentleman stepped forward and remarked, "I want to congratulate you for a remarkable performance; not so much for the tricks you did, but for the way you handled the committee. You had two well-known men in town and you treated them like gentlemen. This is my main complaint with a lot of magicians. They often make spectators the butt of jokes, but you made them enjoy it just as much as the audience."

This man, Ellsworth Lyman, was the amateur magician that Vernon had been warned about. Lyman was not only a keen student of magic, having created and sold secrets to the fraternity much in the manner of Henry Hardin, Charles Jordan, and Arthur Finley — but he was also a most gracious and wealthy man whose family could

Shadows With Shears

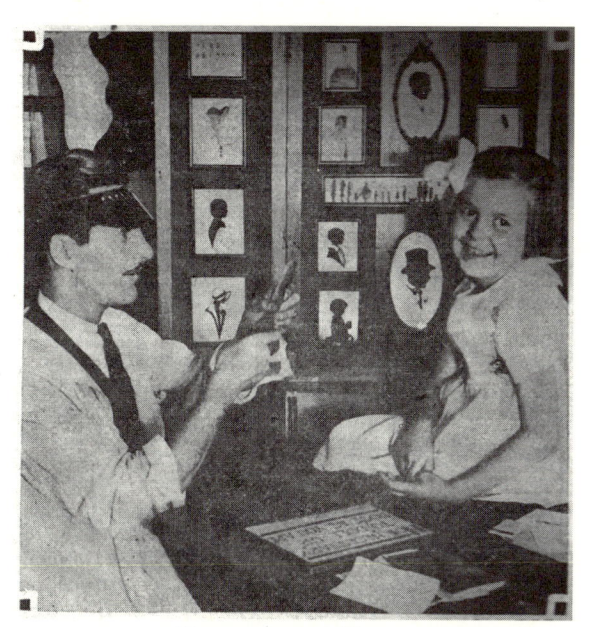

Vernon cuts a silhouette in an Atlanta department store.

trace its roots back to the Mayflower. Lyman invited Vernon back to his handsome estate in Biltmore Forest, and, although Vernon had to return shortly to New York for the December season, the foundation was laid for a great friendship.

Once Vernon was back in Manhattan, it didn't take Max Holden very long to put pen to paper. In his February 1928 column, Holden described Vernon's latest miracles for his avid readers and added, "no use in talking, those cards will do anything for Dave."

And again, in his April 1928 column:

Dave has a new changing card—a card is shown and by simply turning the card around it changes to an entirely different card. As I said before, Dave's cards are trained.

Holden wrote in his May 1928 column:

The magicians of New York City seem to have the edge on other centers for original card problems. Dave Vernon of N.Y.C. and formerly of Ottawa, Canada, to my mind is the cleverest man with cards in this or any other country. Being familiar with the work of Leipzig, Merlin, O'Connor, Milton, Sheldon of Germany, Horowitz, Braden, Jack Miller, Wicks of Australia and my friend T. Nelson Downs, I must hand the crown to Dave Vernon when it comes to skill with the pasteboards.

Here, however, Holden unknowingly threw down the gauntlet to Downs. When it came to skill with playing cards, Holden had crowned Vernon "king." It was time for Downs to return to New York and attempt to reclaim the crown.

He would travel once again with Ross and McLaughlin, first to the magic convention hosted by Durbin, to be staged this year in Lima, Ohio, and then East. Despite his obsession with secrets, Downs had an extreme dislike for magic conventions, magic societies, and magic dealers. In his candid correspondence with McLaughlin, Downs stated, "none of these magical societies are worth a damn for the best interests of magicians and magic as a business or profession. On the contrary they are in a way detrimental as magi's get together and expose each other's tricks. They become common property and lose their commercial value because they all – do – the –same –tricks." The convention would, however, help defray some of the travel expenses. They would also save some more money by restricting their post-convention travel plans to just New York and Providence.

McGuire indicated to Downs that he might drive to Lima from Rhode Island to meet them. Downs recognized that the trip would be therapeutic in some ways for McGuire. He had lost both his brother and his mother in recent months. He was left now only with his sister, Marion, having lost his other brother in the Great War and his father in 1925. Downs also learned that Holden might join them on the trip. Ross informed Downs on May 23, however, that his employer would not give him the requisite time off. One week was all he could muster, and that was only because his name had already been printed in the convention program. He wrote to Downs,

One thing that I regret particularly is not being able to go to N.Y. and make an attempt to get some of Horowitz's and Vernon's card stuff. I was figuring on getting Horowitz to one side and offering him fifty bucks for a few choice effects then letting you kid Dave

Shadows With Shears

Vernon out of the rest.

Downs forwarded Ross' letter to McLaughlin and added a postscript:

Tough luck for Ross—well we will go alone—the two of us! ...In a way it will be better for us visiting McGuire & etc.

Unfortunately for Downs and McLaughlin, Vernon was not in New York when they arrived. As Holden would later report in *The Sphinx*, Vernon was in Atlantic City cutting silhouettes. He only returned to New York to play the occasional date for Miss King. Holden pointed out that Vernon was part of a select group of performers—Dunninger, Leipzig, and Baker among them—who were paid big money, that is $500 for two hours of up-close magic. With Vernon out of town, Downs took the opportunity to introduce Holden to McGuire. Holden gave McGuire's work a glowing account in the pages of *The Sphinx*.

Ed McGuire of Rhode Island, and a former manager for Max Malini, showed some wonderful skill with cards—triple, quadruple and quintuple passes, and next a real one-hand shuffle where you see each card falling separate. Second dealing and bottom dealing, also shown. When it comes to manipulative skill at cards Eddie is at the top. Malini and T. Nelson Downs have seen to it that he has had the proper training.

Downs and McLaughlin returned to the Midwest. Downs, the grand old man of magic, continued to trade his name for wares, offering signed promotional photographs in exchange for secrets. Many enthusiasts gave Downs their items out of respect for his contributions to the craft. His book *The Art of Magic* had lured more than its share of amateurs to the fold. These were not, however, the secrets that he really coveted. More than anything, he wanted the secrets of Vernon and Horowitz. Reports of Vernon's latest miracles continued to trickle in from friends and emissaries like Ted Arnold and Ellsworth Lyman. Vernon was content, however, to stay away from New York. He enjoyed the lifestyle of Atlantic City, and cutting silhouettes on the boardwalk proved to be quite lucrative. The transactions were short, generated significant cash, and gave him control over where and when he worked. The throng of magicians in New York could have the club dates.

Now, more than ever, New York was the center of magic. Many amateur magicians, buoyed by the knowledge and repertoire of their more learned colleagues, became semi-professionals, accepting paid engagements while maintaining their regular employment, in direct competition with (and much to the ire of) those professionals who called the city home. Some, like Ted Annemann, moved to New York to make their mark and started playing dates around the city. Annemann's specialty was mind reading, and the "think of a card" tricks inspired by Vernon soon became part of his own repertoire. Al Baker became, after a rocky start in which he accused Annemann of pirating one of his creations, Annemann's mentor. Annemann abandoned the character dress of the Hindu mystic and made great strides as a performer in more traditional haberdashery. Leslie P. Guest certainly noticed. He wrote in "Magic Here and There," *The Sphinx*, April 1928:

> *Drifting into Duke's (Frank Ducrot's) shop in New York I met Annemann of Waverly, N.Y. I have always considered him a first class pirate, ready to peddle any idea he got hold of regardless of primary ownership. While I still reserve some opinions on that subject, I will admit my impression of Annemann has materially changed. The boy is darned clever, and very few could follow his card mental work. He does some of those "Think of a Card" effects which leave no clue as to the method of operation.*

Another new face on the magic scene was Paul Rosini. Born Paul Vucic, Rosini had immigrated to Chicago with his family from Trieste. As a young man, Rosini had assisted several magicians, including Carl Rosini (from whom he stole his stage name) and Julius Zancig, the preeminent practitioner of second-sight or two-person mindreading, who by the late 20's was in the twilight of his career. Vucic was a dashing figure and a quick study. Although Philadelphia became the base of his operations, he made frequent sojourns to New York City. "Think-A-Card" material was also a major component of his repertoire.

The magician who garnished the most notices, however, was Cardini. Cardini had returned to New York, having replaced, as Vernon had suggested, patter with pantomime. His act had been honed to perfection, a jewel polished by the grind of repetition. With Vernon back in town, Holden accompanied him to Newark, New Jersey to see Cardini perform. He wrote,

> *It was my great pleasure to journey across to Newark and see Cardini and in company with Dave Vernon I enjoyed a wonderful show of real sleight of hand. I had looked forward for a long time to seeing Cardini and I certainly was more than satisfied. The production of fans of cards one after another in succession was a masterpiece, especially when it is noted that Cardini wears gloves...*

In March 1929, Cardini signed on with the Pantages circuit, adding a new feature to his act—the manipulation of lit cigarettes. Holden described it as the greatest cigarette routine in the business, and far ahead of the other self-proclaimed Kings of Cigarettes. Cardini had become, as Vernon predicted, a star. His act also became the most copied in the history of the profession. Now billed as Cardini—The Suave Deceiver, Cardini spawned generation after generation of manipulating mannequins who possessed neither his technical ability nor, more importantly, his powers of pantomime.

Now that Vernon was back in town, it appeared as though he was ready to establish some roots. He renewed his membership in a magic society, this time the Parent Assembly of the Society of American Magicians, attended meetings and even served on its social committee. He also continued to experiment and develop a host of new miracles. The 1920s were a period of intense creativity for Vernon as he minted his own magic. Gamblers used sleight-of-hand and various sub-rosa gimmicks to deceive their prey. Magicians also used sleight-of-hand and a different style of gimmick to deceive their audiences. Unbeknownst to his audiences and the magic community, Vernon was able to marry both the method and, more importantly, the gimmicks used by magicians and card cheats in subtle ways to create modern miracles. Others kept their eyes on Vernon, but Vernon also kept his eyes on them. He kept current with the latest magical inventions and then experimented with ways to elevate the work, applying techniques from other fields (like gambling) to improve the effects and make them his own.

The starting point for the next wave of effects was *Original Card Mysteries*, a small manuscript printed and published by Eric F. Impey in 1928. Impey boldly claimed many of the ideas in his manuscript as new effects that incorporated original principles. Max Holden begged to differ and accused Impey of pirating and publishing one of Al Baker's pet secrets. Holden later retracted the allegation and admitted that it was perhaps the case of two minds coming up with the same idea independently. Vernon recognized the value of Impey's ideas, regardless of their paternity. He also knew how to refine them, and this ability to refine the work of others became yet another hallmark of the Vernon touch.

It was time for a change. Vernon's interest and approach to magic had evolved. Initially, he had focused on extemporization, building up an astounding arsenal of sleights, many culled from the repertoires of professional gamblers, and then improvising. Cards were selected and discovered in ways that came to him on the fly. Once Vernon was confident that he could extricate himself from any scenario, at least when the scenario pertained to playing cards, he progressed to having spectators just "think of a card." He then relied on his agile mind to hone in on the spectator's mental selection and track it in the pack so that he could produce it in an unexpected manner. It would appear face up in the pack, at a particular number suggested by the participant, or at any position named out loud. For many, both magicians and spectators, this was the *ne plus ultra* of card and mental magic. For Vernon, the fun was in the chase. Once he had this skill at his fingertips, it was time to explore other avenues. The Impey manuscript provided the avenue. On page two, the author described a feat called "Mysto," and added the subtitle—"The Masterpiece." Vernon added it to his repertoire, but with his own technical and presentational refinements. Holden described the effect in *The Sphinx*.

> Mr. Dave Vernon of New York City has a clever little card effect. Fanning a pack, you are requested to mentally select a card. Pack is now squared up and cards dropped on table one at a time and your card has vanished. Of course, we all know what has happened, but we can't explain how a card mentally chosen should vanish, as it might have been the other card.

Unbeknownst to his confreres, Vernon had taken a trick that employed a mechanical pack, one doctored by the originator in such a manner as to enable him to produce the desired result—in this case, the vanish of a mentally selected card—but had improved it

Shadows With Shears

by altering the process used to manufacture the deck. He applied a substance used by card cheats—faro dealers in particular—and manufactured a trick deck. Vernon, the master of sleight-of-hand, was fooling well-posted magicians and laymen with a trick that was virtually self-working, provided you knew how to both treat and handle the cards, a prime example of subtlety over sleight-of-hand.

In his January 1929 column in *The Sphinx*, Holden wrote:

As I have remarked before Dave Vernon is the cleverest man with cards in this or any other magic sphere. Never a false move, pass or slip, but only a regular shuffle or cut and there you have the kind of work Dave Vernon performs miracles with...

Dave Vernon had three cards selected and the pack was handed out for the return of the cards and a shuffle by each member. Now, taking another pack, Dave asked the first member to think intently of his card, meanwhile Dave removes a card from the center of his pack and, asking the first member to name his card, and on turning the card in hand around, there was the same card, and so on with the remaining cards. This is one of the cleverest effects in cards I have seen for some time.

He then added in March 1929:

Dave Vernon gave an hour and a half show the other night at a home on Park Avenue and his show, you might say, was in his vest pocket. Two packs of cards, three silks, a few coins, four small rubber balls and a small pad of paper.

Sixteen people comprised the audience and Dave had to work right among them with the audience all around and there is no chance of forcing a card here, as among the "Upper Ten." It is strange how much they know about magic, and they do not want the ordinary magician, but the very best in the business, and they are willing to pay.

When Vernon read Holden's laudatory column in that March 1929 issue of *The Sphinx*, he noticed, by sheer coincidence, a contribution by Judson Brown that followed it. Brown, a Californian, was a contemporary and correspondent of Charles Earle Miller, the teenage magician in Indianapolis enamored of Vernon. Brown's contribution, a trick called "A Super-Reverse Problem," had also been inspired by Impey's manuscript. Here, the performer spread a deck of cards between his hands, each card lying face down. The spread was closed and the spectator asked to name any card. The performer then fanned the cards between hands, revealing that the card named by the spectator was now magically upside down, that is reversed, in the pack. After careful consideration, it dawned on Vernon how to alter both the presentation and the method of Brown's trick and turn it into a miracle.

Ever since J. Warren Keane had first fooled Vernon by tabling a card that Vernon had conjured in his imagination, he had explored ways of recreating the effect. As he confided in the interview with the reporter of the *Asheville Times*, he had only an eighty percent rate of success. Now, however, he had a surefire way, one that would guarantee success each and every time. He could now inform the spectator that he had reversed a card in the pack prior to the performance, then ask the spectator to name any card, and spread the pack to confirm that he had, in fact, done what he had said. Best of all, by applying a special chemical treatment to the cards, the same one employed by crooked faro dealers, in the same manner as he had with Impey's "Mysto" card trick, the effect was virtually self-working. It represented a major breakthrough in both technique and effect.

In April 1929, Vernon embarked on another tour of the South, this one much more extensive than his last. On April 7, he was in Richmond at 410 West Grace Street under the auspices of the Women's Circle of Centenary Methodist Church. He stayed there for close to a month, advertised as both a silhouette artist and the "New York Magician & Sleight-of-Hand Performer." He then headed to Chattanooga, Tennessee. The female leaders of St. Paul's Episcopal Church provided him with a studio at 632 Market Street to ply his trade. Money was coming in fast and loose. The May 9, 1929 edition of the *Chattanooga News* provided a glowing account of his work:

> ...this D.W. Vernon is truly an artist. There is much of the genius in the deft way he has of getting the personality of an individual into a bit of cut-out paper. It was a bright idea of Mrs. Sam Connelly and the members of her chapter to bring Mr. Vernon here from Richmond,

Shadows With Shears

because it seems it would be perfectly safe to say that he is, if not the best, certainly one of the very few best living silhouette artists in the world.

Some of the Vernon treatments of groups in silhouette will be found especially interesting, in that they involve an artful finesse of design and balance, something which is lacking from many such groups done by artists of less genius. His silhouettes of children have a very true sort of softness conveyed through the use of the severe black and white medium.

Mr. Vernon himself is a charming sort of a chap; tall, rather slender, he has deep-set gray eyes with rather dark lashes, if one remembers correctly, and a lackadaisical sort of a mouth that knows how to laugh. Altogether a pleasing, casual, nonchalant sort of a person who very obviously has seen many corners of the world and has managed to find something interesting everywhere.

This Vernon has so much individuality about him that he has made himself quite at home in this improvised studio. And he has the happy faculty of radiation of that spirit so that his clients who come in party clothes and with plastered hair shining, to have their shadows expertly concentrated by this wizard who conjurers neat miracles in portraiture with a teensy pair of scissors.

Really, no joking, this man has an individualized perfection of style in handling silhouettes. There will come a time, one will venture to say without contradiction, when a Vernon silhouette will be a treasure.

Vernon was held over three weeks and then moved onto Norfolk, Virginia to cut silhouettes at 341 Granby Street, next to the Southland Hotel. He was advertised as working every day between the hours of nine to five, except for Wednesdays, Fridays, and Saturdays. On those days, he set up shop, so to speak, at private homes in neighboring communities.

By July 18th, he was back in Asheville under the auspices of the Ladies of St. Agnes Auxiliary of Trinity Episcopal Church. He had a shop on Haywood Street, near Scrugg's drugstore. The shop was in the back of the Haywood branch of the Central Bank and Trust company. The local papers advertised that Vernon was in town to raise money for 'benevolent' purposes and that "in addition to his silhouette work, Mr. Vernon is a recognized magician and sleight of hand performer." Vernon informed the papers that his visit would be brief, as he planned to return to his studio on West 56th Street in New York later in the week. While in Asheville, Vernon was able to spend considerable time with Ellsworth Lyman. Lyman was a prominent member of the community whose interest in magic and magicians was well known. When interviewed by the local paper — the headline stating "Asheville Boasts Able Magician" — Lyman was quick to praise Vernon:

> *Vernon, who recently was in Asheville engaged in cutting silhouettes for a church benefit, Mr. Lyman described as the best magician on earth. He named a half dozen of the foremost. "They are all marvelous, but Vernon is the best," he said.*

The *Savannah Press* reported on Wednesday, December 4, 1929 that Vernon was an English artist, who works with a church in each city where he plies his trade. They also added, "Vernon had pledged himself to give fifty percent of his earnings to pay off some of the obligations the Christ Church School had incurred during 1929" and "He has recently spent some time in Washington, where he was doing work at the White House, and for that reason has been late in filling his appointment here." Vernon was a smash success in Savannah and was held over for a second week. He set up shop on Broughton Street, in an empty storefront no doubt vacated due to the effects of the Great Depression. Vernon used a variety of marketing strategies to keep business flowing. One scheme involved running a "Who Is This?" contest in which the local newspaper reproduced a Vernon-cut silhouette of a prominent community member. Vernon offered to cut the silhouette, for free, of the first person to correctly identify the subject.

He left Savannah for Jacksonville, Florida under the auspices of the Woman's Guild of the Church of the Good Shepherd and there set up another improvised studio at 32 West Forsyth Street. He had met great success there the year before for the same organization. The January 12, 1930 edition of the *Jacksonville Journal* reported:

> *Mr. Vernon is truly an artist. There is much of the genius in the deft way he has of getting the personality of an individual into a bit of cut-*

Shadows With Shears

out paper. The cost of a silhouette is such a nominal matter, and they can become such treasure, and have such an artistic value of their own, that people generally are rather pleased at a chance to get hold of some silhouette done by a man of Mr. Vernon's standing.

Vernon left Jacksonville for Tampa, sponsored by the service league of St. Andrew's Episcopal church before heading to Miami. By the end of March, Vernon had started his route home, stopping off in New Orleans where, according to the *New Orleans Standard* for Sunday, March 30th, Vernon made his headquarters at Seebold's on Carondelet Street. From New Orleans, his route took him to Arkansas. Although Vernon had been away from New York for several months, he had not been forgotten. Max Holden, writing in his column in *The Sphinx* for May 1930, under the new heading "New York News," still considered Vernon the king.

Nate Leipzig is around here and playing the better private engagements. Nate is probably the father of the modern school of card magicians, as every card man of today all give credit to Nate as being the perfect man with cards.

(Louis) Zingone is playing clubs around and also giving lessons in advanced card magic. Sam Horowitz is another card man of note, as also Johnny Scarna [Scarne], the last named probably the cleverest card man of all, but the crown goes to Dave Vernon, who is now in Arkansas.

Vernon next headed to Chapel Hill where, once again, his "Shadows with Shears" generated excellent publicity. The paper also commented, "Mr. Verner is also a sleight-of-hand man, and will arrange to give a performance the latter part of the week. If he can draw as big a crowd to this as he does with his silhouettes, he will make the affair a success."

And then it was on to Raleigh, sponsored by the Woman's Auxiliary and St. Mary's Guild of the Church of the Good Shepherd, where he was invited to set up his shop in the lobby of the Grand Theatre. Here Vernon donated a percentage of all proceeds towards the Parish House fund of the Church of the Good Shepherd. Again, he received excellent notices.

The silhouette man did a rushing business in Ivey's last week, and by the way, he is staying over two more days.

Hundreds of people sat down and had him cut their faces out of black paper.

We had ours made – Don't know when we have felt so foolish, sitting on a chair, with a crowd looking on, trying to appear composed, nonchalant and don't-care-ish, when we were as embarrassed as could be.

All the men who sat to be silhouetted explained in a sheepish way, that their wives sent them in to have it done, or else that they were doing it to help the church.

Another local paper added:

Mr. Vernon is a fast worker. With a tiny pair of scissors he cuts your likeness out of black paper while you sit in a comfortable chair and converse with him. But the conversation is not obligatory; he does the job just as willingly for a silent sitter. When the cutting is done he mounts the silhouette on cardboard like that which is used for photographic mountings.

With Vernon still on the road, cutting silhouettes back in Asheville and socializing with Ellsworth Lyman, McGuire and Downs could wait no longer. It was time to up the ante and obtain the additional leverage required to pry the secrets they so strongly coveted. McGuire and Downs had a plan, a conspiracy to both steal the crown from Vernon and persuade Sam Horowitz—and perhaps Vernon, as well—to open up. They arranged a special session in New York, one where their "discovery" could dazzle the Inner Circle with his prowess at the card table. If all went according to plan, word that there was a new player at the table, one worthy of being crowned King, would travel through the Inner Circle and then percolate through the pages of *The Sphinx*, particularly in Max Holden's column.

Their ace in the hole was Walter Scott, the amateur magician and retired advantage player whom McGuire had befriended and introduced to Downs, McLaughlin, and Ross several years earlier.

Shadows With Shears

McGuire had already tested the waters by parading Scott in private sessions with both Horowitz and Cardini. Both were impressed by Scott's ability. Neither, however, was particularly well versed in the higher orders of card table artifice, their knowledge limited to the tidbits of information and technique, rather than the "real work" that Vernon had studied. They were only interested in techniques of advantage players because they were an obsession of Vernon's. They did not seek out such information on their own or master every technique that Vernon catalogued. And they had certainly never spent time in the company of a gifted card cheat, one of the standing or skill of Dad Stevens, the way that Vernon had in Chicago in 1919 at the Waiters' Club. Scott would be the first "real" gambler that they would meet. McGuire knew that they would be impressed and that, given their standing within the magic community, the opinions of Horowitz and Cardini would carry great weight. Still, in order to carry off the scam, they required the participation of two others. The first was Max Holden. Holden would have to witness the demonstration and the reaction of Horowitz and Cardini. Holden could not, however, be privy to the scam. Only if he could genuinely believe in Scott's skill could he proclaim in his column that Vernon had lost his crown.

The other participant was Al Baker.

Twenty years Vernon's senior, Baker never rose through the ranks he thought were commensurate with his talents. Although uneducated and unsophisticated, he had a tremendous wit and could produce tricks that were exceedingly clever, particularly in the eyes of amateur magicians. Arthur Finley and Vernon used to joke that Baker created the perfect tricks for amateurs, tricks that required extensive preparation and incorporated methods at which amateurs could marvel. Baker struggled to make ends meet and dedicated a great deal of his time to creating magic that he could market to amateurs. Perhaps tired of the endless accolades bestowed upon Vernon, Baker acquiesced to Downs' request and agreed to participate in the scam.

Baker's task was simple. When called upon to provide the decks of cards for the demonstration, Baker was to supply packs doctored in advance by Scott. If the decks were unsuspected, Scott's work would appear to be in the miracle class. Also, to ensure absolute success, Downs and McGuire controlled who would or, more importantly, who would not, be invited to witness the demonstration.

At the session in Brooklyn. Seated, from left: Downs, Holden, Walter Scott (blindfolded), Horowitz and Eddie McLaughlin. Standing, from left: Baker, McGuire and Cardini

Two members of the Inner Circle, Arthur Finley and John Scarne, who, given their keen understanding of card table artifice, would have recognized the ruse for what it was, were not invited. On June 14, 1930, the session took place. Holden took the bait. He wrote,

> *Eddie McGuire of Providence accompanied by Walter Scott also came to N.Y. to meet Tommy Downs, and what a feast of magic we had. A special session at Al Baker's home with Cardini, Sam Horowitz, Downs, McLaughlin, McGuire, Scott and the writer. This is one event which was worth a lot as here we saw Walter Scott from Providence perform miracles with cards, and I pass the crown to Walter Scott. Without a doubt Walter Scott is the cleverest man with a pack of cards in the world, and I am backed up by Nelson Downs, Leipzig, Cardini, McGuire, Sam Horowitz, and all others who have witnessed his skill...*

Holden described why he passed the crown to Walter Scott:

> *Anyway, here is a description of a few miracles of Scott: A pack of cards borrowed and shuffled by Al Baker. Scott seated at the end*

Shadows With Shears

table take the cards in hand and deals out hands. I suggested 6 hands and 6 hands were dealt out. Now again the cards were handed to Al Baker to shuffle and again placed into Scott's hand and there was no chance to make a pass or do anything unfair with the pack. Again six hands were dealt out on a table. Again a shuffle by Baker and again six hands dealt out until there was a full poker hand or deal. On turning over the hand of Scott there were four aces and a king. We were all watching close and none of us could detect any false moves or anything unfair. Again the cards were thoroughly shuffled and again Scott held a royal high flush against the other hands which were all seemingly good hands. Now another pack of Al Baker's cards were borrowed and Al asked to shuffle and place in Scott's hand (one hand only). Now Scott says, "It is easy to tell the top card to me, but if I can look down and tell you that the fourth card down is an Ace what would you say?" and on Al looking at the fourth card it was an Ace. Again the fourth card from the bottom was also an Ace, and also cutting the pack into two heaps Scott handed me one heap and says, "You have one King and three Aces," and sure enough I had.

And to add insult to injury, Holden reiterated his stance:

I cannot begin to tell you of the miracles of Scott but he is really uncanny and I think that I have seen the greatest card magicians all over the world: Dr. Elliott, Baker, Leipzig, Hunter, O'Connor, Milton, Zingone, Dexter, Cardini, Jimmy Thompson, Noffke, Scareny [Scarne], Erens, Nelson Downs, and last of all Dave Vernon whom I have always admired and Dave to me is the greatest in cards but I now have to pass the crown to Scott and the others all agree with me.

Holden, who had passed the crown from Downs to Vernon, now stripped the crown from Vernon in absentia.

Vernon heard the news first through a letter sent to him by Sam Horowitz. He then read about the session in the pages of *The Sphinx*. He wrote Horowitz:

Rec. your most interesting letter—it was very nice of you to let me here [sic] from you. The boy must be good if you say so. If he has met you and Al Baker why should he care to meet me. I'm among the "has beens" now I'm afraid.

Vernon was no longer the prince of the pasteboards. The king was dead; long live the king.

Chapter Six

Phantoms Of The Card Table

Vernon finished his missive to Horowitz with a question about Walter Scott: "What class of work does he do and did he fool you with anything? Let me hear from you. Shall be here a couple of months at least." If Vernon had any notion of being past his prime, it certainly didn't last very long. He was simply not a demonstratively competitive person. Vernon competed with himself alone. Could he do things better—more efficiently? Could he eliminate the extraneous? He was interested in the work, not perfunctory titles. For his part, Horowitz was enamored with Scott and tried to broker a meeting between McGuire, Scott, and Vernon.

Vernon wrote again to Horowitz on July 14, 1930 from Asheville. He was there cutting silhouettes for a third season, under the auspices of the Woman's Auxiliary of Trinity Episcopal Church.

I wish to thank you ever so much for your efforts to enable me to see Walter Scott work.

I would gladly go to New York but just at present I am tied up in such a way that it is entirely out of the question. If there is any chance of Eddie McGuire and his friend coming out this way I shall of course be "tickled to death." I had often wanted to meet the former as I new [sic] he was very closely associated with Malini at one time.

Sam after seeing Walter Scott you must have felt very much the same as I did when I saw that old Mississippi gambler in Chicago. I am certainly glad that you have seen some of the work done. Annemann can't sell it. Thank goodness.

What second does he employ? Does he pull card from end, corner or side? Does he ever use Erdnase style pushing two over? What is his blind shuffle specialty and how does he "cover up?"

Please excuse all the questions Sam old boy, but I am hungry for a little incentive to do some work myself.

The old Mississippi Gambler mentioned by Vernon was, of course, Dad Stevens. Finally, his friend Sam Horowitz would experience the same rush that comes from being on intimate terms with someone whose work and talent is head and shoulders above all others. Vernon's reference to Annemann is equally telling.

As young wonderworkers who had developed profiles within the magic community peddled their wares, the sale of individual secrets, ones that depended on sleight-of-hand, subtlety, or both, as compared to mechanical marvels, had reached new heights. Vernon encouraged Horowitz to consider releasing his own manuscript.

Noticed what you said about Annemann and think it would be a great idea to put out something first and beat him to it.

Go right ahead Sam sell anything and use both our names on it. If you need any help financially or otherwise I'll do my best to help you.

The next time I go out to Biltmore Forest to see Lyman I'll see what he has of [Henry] Hardin's. The first thing he showed me last time I went out was a padlocked book put out by Annemann, also the trick from Lane's "Moe's Look at a card." If he can get three dollars for a trick like that you should be able to get a hundred. Go to it Sam and we'll advertise and sell for about five bucks or two-fifty perhaps would be a better price.

Vernon's main interest, however, was the second deal. In a series of rapid-fire letters, Vernon probed Horowitz for every technical nuance, not out of envy, but out of serious intellectual interest, the desire to add even more information to his arcane collection.

I've got the fever again pretty badly since you have told me of Walter

Phantoms Of The Card Table

Scott so I may have an idea or two.

Does W.S. deal as effectively with a margined card as with the all over back? How is he on shifts?

I judge from what you tell me in your letter that Walter Scott deals his seconds with very little perceptible movement of the top card — in other words a very "fine" second. In this form the thumb "hitting" out the card is not new to me, but if he deals anything like "Old Dad Stevens" did from the side and slowly, I know nothing about it.

Answer me this question Sam — If you saw Walter Scott deal a few seconds and you were not aware of what he was doing would you suspect the deal? If he does this I would rather see it than anything else in the world.

And in another letter, from July 30, 1930,

Sam I wish you'd tell me if he [Walter] deals a "fine" second or a "push over."

Does he ever use one where the left hand does nearly all the "work"? I have often used the index finger of right hand to "propel" card for a stud deal this brings card between first and second finger then thumb "levers" card face up, is this any thing like you meant Walter does when he deals with first and second finger only. This can be used on a very fine margin same as ordinary second. This method with natural hold (first finger at end of deck) I can deal invisible second but the "propel" of card must be rapid or the illusion is lost. This is the point I want to get at, does W.S. get the exact illusion of the top card coming off and can he use it, for instance, to bring a card at a selected number with no suspicion? If can do this I'd rather see it than anything else I know of? Can he deal the cards one on top of other as in a trick and use the second illusively?

Please excuse the "third degree" Sam but I've spent years of thought and study and some practice on the subject of this second card and I'm truly worried. When you mention the triple quadruple etc do you mean thirds fourths etc? This must be for the deal of a single card, (not continuous).

Horowitz was out of his league. Vernon had spent more time thinking about the second deal and could articulate its nuances like no other. Vernon had seen Stevens deal thirds and fourths, but not continuously, that is, without breaking the rhythm of the round.

Ultimately, that was the test. Could Walter Scott deal the second card in such a way that, as Erdnase would say, "there is not even a hint of suspicion"? This was the test that Vernon applied to every sleight in the calendar.

Vernon's correspondence with Horowitz was filled with joy, the joy of discovery displayed by a specialist who, until then, thought he had seen everything. He was excited by the technical minutiae of gambling moves. He was also interested in hearing more about McGuire and, in particular, his exploits with Malini. His letter to Horowitz on July 25, 1930 described some of his latest pet secrets.

> *Well Sam old boy I am going to explain a couple of little things that I would like you to try out, for yourself. I often intended to show you the palm while in New York but swore to myself to keep it absolutely for my own use, after seeing the way they "murdered" the two card turn-over. However you have been so decent about everything and I feel a sort of guilty feeling in not letting you in on something that to me is extremely useful and has enabled me to fool many a wise observer.*
>
> *It gave me a great kick to use it often, with Louis [Zingone], Al [Baker] and yourself a couple of times. It is absolutely unsuspected or I never could have got away with it. I do not mean that I fooled you with a trick but that I used the palm on a location where the pack is shuffled and I hold out the card.*
>
> *I do not believe I ever worked a date where I have not used the palm numerous times and never even been suspected...I have fooled Finley several times with it and have never told him. He'd have a fit if he thought I'd ever "palmed out a card on him."*

Vernon described a rear palm technique, one that would be appropriated and popularized decades later by other magicians. Horowitz was ecstatic over the technique and suggested that Vernon's name should be associated with the maneuver. Vernon disagreed.

Phantoms Of The Card Table

You mention the palm I sent you as the "Vernon palm." I should like another palm I use continually to be associated with my name rather than the former. It is one of the few moves that I have worked out that I'm really proud of—it approaches perfection as nearly as any move I know.

By August, McGuire had written a manuscript, *The Phantom of the Card Table*, extolling Scott and his second deal. McGuire forwarded a copy of the manuscript to Vernon. Vernon praised the manuscript in a letter to Horowitz dated August 30, 1930.

The Phantom of the Card Table is admirably written and exceedingly intriguing to anyone interested in cards. If Eddie wrote it he's very clever and if he intends selling secrets this method of exciting curiosity is the last word and far better than the most usual method of describing a lot of impossible effects.

Still, Vernon had some lingering doubts. Because Scott's approach to the second deal was not entirely unfamiliar, Vernon asked Horowitz again whether Scott really fooled him with any manipulation. A similar technique had made the rounds years earlier and, in fact, was described in 1914 by Theo Hardison in *Poker*. This book was possibly the source that had inspired the cheat who had taught the sleight to Scott. The manuscript also detailed Scott's method for manufacturing the 'punch,' a gambling device that placed Braille-like markings in the cards. While punch work had been well documented in gambling treatises, including 19th century works by Robert-Houdin and J.N. Maskelyne, Scott had refined the gimmick and its use in play. Vernon wondered why, if Scott was so fantastic, Scarne or Finley were not invited to the original super session. Both had been in town at the time and were members of the so-called Inner Circle. Although Horowitz was a friend and confidant, and Cardini was a superb manipulator, neither could be considered experts when it came to gambling artifice. No, the two authorities in New York, at least the two people whose opinions on such moves Vernon would trust were Arthur Finley and John Scarne.

Vernon's instinct proved correct. It wasn't so much that Scott was a fraud, but that his credentials had been presented, unknowingly at least to him, in a fraudulent manner. McGuire, Horowitz, and Baker manipulated the super session, each with his own agenda.

Scott was a musician; his instrument was the Hawaiian guitar. He had, many years earlier, been associated with advantage players and could deal, as Vernon would say, a "fine" second. He did so often, not to cheat *in* games but *before* games, to defraud others into bankrolling his team in play by using the second deal to display his skill. The suckers provided the working capital to Scott and his confreres. They expected Scott, based on his skillful pre-game display, to deal nothing but winning hands. How could he lose? Scott would then double-cross his backers. During the game, it would appear that wires became crossed and the financiers would lose their stake to other undisclosed members of the team.

In New York, Scott became a pawn, paraded by McGuire and Downs in the hopes that he would be the key that unlocked the door of the Inner Circle. In order to implement the deception, however, they had needed to control two factors. First, they had to ensure that Scott used his own cards, cards he had marked and punched according to his personal system. McGuire and Downs assigned that task to Al Baker. When the crew asked for borrowed cards, Baker kindly supplied decks that he had been given in advance by McGuire and Downs. Baker was not interested in penetrating the Inner Circle. He was already part of it. Perhaps Baker was more interested in seeing Vernon and his reputation being taken down a notch or two. Baker was a seasoned professional, one perhaps a little tired of seeing Vernon's name featured in Holden's columns. Besides, it would be fun to fool the others. McGuire and Downs also had to control the invitation list. Both knew that Finley and Scarne were extremely well versed in card table artifice. As members of the Inner Circle, both men would have most likely seen through the charade.

Vernon was not the only one expressing his doubts about the set-up. Faucett Ross, left behind in St. Joseph, Missouri, also had concerns. He had met Scott several years earlier and was trying to reconcile the man he had met then with the one that Holden now championed in his columns as the new King of Cards. He asked Downs outright. Downs wrote Eddie McLaughlin, another co-conspirator at the table, in a letter dated July 3, 1930, to inform him of Ross' suspicions.

> *Ross wants to know all about it. I told him to write to you that I didn't pay much attention told him that you & I & Eddie McG helped*

put Scotty over but he guessed it rite — that he had Max, Horowitz & most of 'em completely fooled but I didn't think he fooled Al Baker much.

Still, Max Holden continued to champion Scott. In his September 1930 column "Around New York with Max Holden," he wrote,

Louis Zingone, Al Altman and the writer drove up to Providence to spend a few hours with Walter Scott and Eddie Maguire [sic], and no need for me to introduce two of the finest and cleverest men in magic. Walter Scott is absolutely the greatest of all card workers, and Eddie Maguire his pupil and pal. Well, our visit of a few hours was to see some more of the wonders of Walter Scott and we also got a few pointers on the presentation of real magic. A drive of 400 miles to be in the company of Scott and Maguire was well worth the trip, and at this time I want to introduce Louis Zingone as another of our cleverest card men. Louis is much in demand in New York and is now at the Central Park Casino entertaining.

For all their efforts in promoting Walter Scott, Downs and McGuire still could not penetrate the veil of secrecy that surrounded Horowitz, and, more importantly, Vernon. This was particularly hard on Downs; he thrived on secrets. When Ross and his friend, Charles Maly of Indianapolis, pooled their capital to acquire a manuscript from Jean Hugard of New York, and had the designated purchaser sign a covenant not to disclose, share, or trade the secret contained therein, Downs wrote Eddie McLaughlin and insisted that he procure a copy of the manuscript from them.

I'd sure like to write Ross & get a copy of that 4 ace trick he & Maly paid Hugard $10.00 for & any others slip me copies. Yes drop in on your way to Creston & get these secrets from Ross. Do it now.

The proliferation of private manuscripts continued unabated. Some of the special manuscripts included feats associated with or pioneered by Vernon. More often than not, the original source of inspiration was not credited. In January 1930, Jean Hugard released one such manuscript entitled, "All Backs." He advertised it in the January 1930 issue of *The Sphinx*.

With any pack of cards you show that the faces have vanished, the

whole pack or any card apparently having backs only. No prepared cards and just enough skill to appeal to the artist. The best possible introduction to a series of card tricks for parlor, club or theater.

Vernon had performed the trick a decade earlier, and, in fact, had shown it to Hugard backstage at a theatre Hugard had established at Coney Island. Hugard asked Vernon at that time if he could write up the effect and sell it as a private manuscript. Vernon declined, believing that magicians should not inadvertently advertise the fact that double-backed cards exist, even if they were not utilized in the trick at hand. With Vernon out of town for an extended period, Hugard decided to breach the confidence and release the effect as his own creation. Hugard was not the only one to profit from Vernon's work.

Also in 1930, Nelson Hahne, a twenty-two year old magic enthusiast, wrote, illustrated, and compiled a booklet, *Here's Magic*. The booklet was published by Joe Berg, a spirited twenty-seven year old magician who had served an apprenticeship with, among others, the Chicago gambling supply firm of H.C. Evans and opened his own magic shop in the Windy City in 1925. At least two of the tricks described within its paper wrappers should have been attributed to Vernon. Holden described Vernon performing one of the effects, a trick Hahne called "The Cards With The Color-Changing Back," years earlier in his October 1927 column in *The Sphinx*. A second effect, one offered by Berg, was called "A Routine With A Double-Back Card" and was, in essence, the first published explanation of the trick that Vernon had used to fool both Houdini and Downs. Berg, most likely, was inspired to reconstruct the trick after seeing Vernon perform it for his colleagues at H.C. Evans during one of Vernon's many trips to Chicago.

Magicians, particularly those wishing to make a mark in the magic community, often embraced the notion, like a ship that flies a flag of convenience, that whoever first *publishes* the modus operandi behind an effect, earns the right to be called the *originator* of that trick. There is no evidence that Vernon took umbrage to this publication, however. First, he had been traveling quite extensively through the southern states and may not have seen the booklet. (The frontispiece indicated that *Here's Magic* was limited to three hundred autographed copies.) Second, Vernon had explored these tricks years earlier—fifteen years earlier when it came to "A Routine

Phantoms Of The Card Table

With A Double-Back Card"—and he was now exploring new terrain.

Vernon was annoyed, however, with another publication. This one, *Hull's Mental Discernment*, was advertised in the August 1930 issue of *The Sphinx*. Unfortunately, the advertiser, Ralph Hull of Crooksville, Ohio, was not the originator of either the effect or the method for sale. Vernon had originated it years earlier and Holden had even described a performance of it in his May 1927 *Sphinx* column. Hull had been intrigued by the description and pressed his friends, Stewart Judah and Ted Annemann, for more information about the routine. Judah was conversant with the secret and broke his confidence with Vernon.

The opening paragraph from Hull's instruction sheet stated,

This is not a trick in the real sense of the word. Rather it consists of an ingenious method of learning the name of a card mentally selected by any member of your audience, without any knowledge on the part of this person, or any one else, that this information has been imparted to you. You obtain this information without even asking a single question.

Hull's manuscript outlined—in extraordinary detail—the modus operandi behind not only one of Vernon's signature routines but also illustrated, through many examples, Vernon's improvisational mode of performing. Hull added,

The originator of the experiment invariably gains the information, as many will testify who have seen him perform it. Each elimination is performed in a different manner, and this will keep the audience from getting any clue.

Vernon was annoyed that he did not receive any credit by name. He was simply the "originator" and Hull was the "writer." To help him cope, Vernon developed a self-defense mechanism. He distinguished those who profited from a breach of confidence from those who reconstructed the tricks on their own. Vernon wrote Horowitz,

Was a little peeved to see Hull's mss. some time ago—He thanks Judah and Annemann for help. I get no mention whatever. I do not

mind but I'm disappointed in Judah. Annemann is O.K. Any thing he uses of mine I did not give him and he has a perfect right. His book is very good. Congratulate him for me.

Vernon was referring to Annemann's recently released *Exclusive Secrets of Annemann's Conception*, a small manuscript that explained fourteen items and sold for the astounding sum of fifty-two dollars. Given that very few of the items in the manuscript were of Annemann's conception, the title was an ironic one. They belonged to members of the Inner Circle such as Sam Horowitz, Henry Christ, Nate Leipzig and, of course, Vernon. Still, as Vernon pointed out to Horowitz, Annemann at least had the ability to dope out the routines on his own. He added,

I have long since ceased to worry about such things as—after all it's a complement when people copy a trick move for move—the only solution is to always keep a few jumps ahead. Professional pianists have the same trouble, as soon as they originate some "tricky breaks" or add rhythm it is copied on a wholesale scale.

Vernon was correct; magicians were more than willing to copy on a wholesale scale. Ross wrote McLaughlin,

I just got a special delivery letter from Maly and he wants me to spend a day in Indianapolis with him alone. He will then turn over his complete collection of secrets to me and let me go through it and take what I want. No fooling. Maly has the largest collection of real stuff in the world today so I figure this is the chance of a lifetime. And, brother, don't think I won't take plenty.

But unless I'm alone I would get practically nothing. Now get this. Everything I get from Maly I'll see that you also get. That's a promise. All I want is a day alone and I'll get everything. I spent three weeks of hard work getting up patter and presentations for a full evening show for Maly & that's the reason he made me this offer.

I'm telling you this confidentially and please don't tell anyone. This is strictly between ourselves. Maly says he'd prefer to have the session before the convention as he may be out of town afterwards and I don't want to take any chances. I can get more of the real stuff from him in

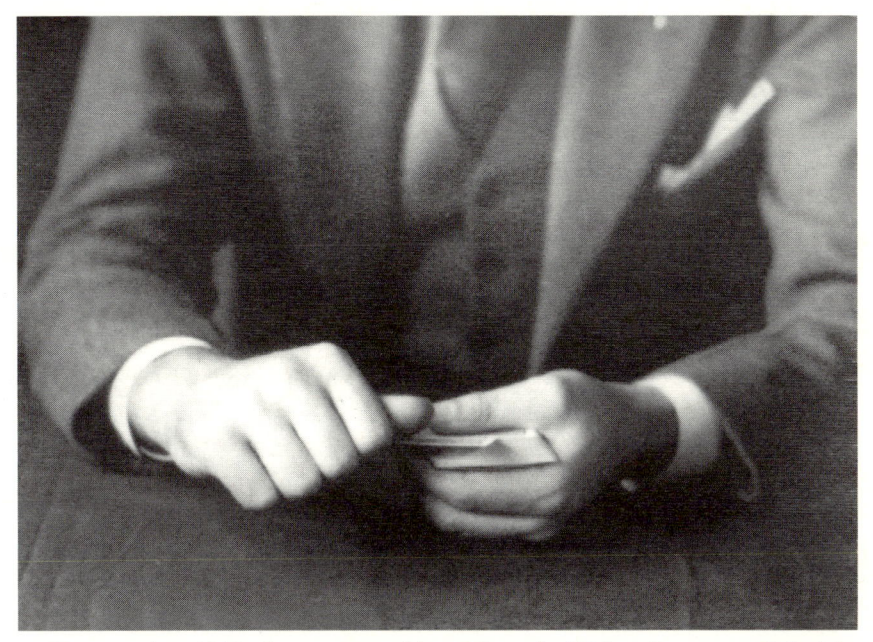

Vernon, circa 1930, demonstrates his work on the Walter Scott second deal for the camera.

a day then I could at a dozen damn conventions.

I figure my session with Maly will pay me for the whole trip. Once more, keep this strictly in your thumb tip. Maly is very peculiar in many respects and you have to handle him just right to get what you want. He's got everything and I don't mean maybe.

If amateur magicians craved for every little secret, perhaps it was time for Vernon and Horowitz to satisfy the need. Besides, as far as Vernon was concerned, the only magic worth performing was magic based on skill. Vernon was not opposed to releasing secrets that required minimal skill. He had released many in the booklet *Secrets* years before. He reassured Horowitz once more that, if he wanted to release a book, he could use any of his (Vernon's) material he wanted. Few would perform the material because few ever really mastered even the simplest of sleights.

Cardini, meanwhile, was back on the road with the Crazy Quilt Review, opening up for picture shows in grand theatres across America. When he performed in Cedar Rapids, Des Moines and

Sioux City, Iowa, Downs caught his act. Downs wrote to McLaughlin and encouraged him to see Cardini's act.

> *I went over on train & saw his 3 shows. Just exactly as I had him pictured in my mind. He's an artist. Capital A-R-T-I-S-T—Not A New Trick—In Fact—No tricks so-to-speak—just manipulations with small objects—Par Excellance—You know I've always contended—Trix – are incidental—any D--- Fool can do tricks. But How?*

Still, Downs' ego was in fine form, and he intimated that Cardini probably excluded coins from his act because he was aware that Downs was in the house. Downs took the time, however, to write up Cardini's act in great detail and forward it to his de facto personal secretary, Eddie McLaughlin, with instructions to make multiple copies. Downs wanted to forward a copy to McGuire, knowing that he would like to appropriate some of Cardini's cigarette manipulations for his own act. For Downs, secrets still represented hard currency. He wrote McLaughlin,

> *O.K. I told you to send those two poker trix direct back to Ross & tell him to write up Al's Self Cutting Deck—NOW DO IT. I'll send these two bum poker trix to him & you get the Baker dope and make a copy for me—McGuire keeps promising but don't come In With it.*

Vernon's focus was much more narrow. He was still interested primarily in card table artifice and, while in Asheville, he had had the good fortune to meet another professional advantage player (retired) who was a cut above the herd. His name was Shock, and he made enough from plying his trade for forty-five years to open a coin and stamp shop in Asheville. Shock was a fountain of arcane information.

Although Shock confessed that he once had the reputation of being the best second dealer in the South, he maintained that that title really belonged to Eddie Fish, a Dutchman in Chicago. "Machine gun precision, with the left hand absolutely still," is how Shock described Fish's work. Vernon performed a few moves for Shock, including the Scott second deal. The two were in agreement: the left hand absolutely must not twist or move up and down during the deal. It was a deficiency. Shock regaled Vernon with stories and

Phantoms Of The Card Table

information and showed Vernon the best "paper," that is marked cards, that he had ever seen. His specialty, however, was punch work. Vernon asked him how he got to be so good with "the peg."

Shock said that he used to travel with a mob that included an expert locksmith. They would travel from town to town, breaking into gambling establishments. The locksmith would open up the trunk where the establishment kept the chips and cards. They would remove the decks, spend the rest of the evening putting in the punch work and then return them to the trunk. For the ruse to succeed, however, the mob had to make sure that there was no sign of forced entry to either the building or to the trunk. The following day, the gang would walk in and go to work, using the doctored cards to great advantage. The gang preferred punch work because games were often held in basements with little lighting, just one or two flickering gas jets illuminating the table. Such conditions made it difficult to read markings. Punched cards, on the other hand, could even be read in the dark. A player could *feel* their identities and control their placement as they passed beneath his thumb.

Vernon met with Shock on several occasions, every time asking him the same question. "Shock, you used to gamble all the time. Did you ever see anything traveling around that's unique? Something, some dodge of some kind, something different?" Eventually, Shock came through.

"I'll tell you something that's very, very good," he said. "There's a fellow, I've forgotten his name, a character of some kind, he used to take a rubber band and a sharp pair of scissors and he'd cut it up into a thousand little pieces, just like little grains of pepper, and he'd work at this for four or five hours cutting up elastic bands, until his pocket—it was literally like a pocket full of tobacco. He'd have these and he'd put them in every suit—he'd have in his jacket pocket these little pieces of rubber band."

"Now," he said, "he'd put his fingers in his pocket to get his pipe or get a cigar and he'd dig his nail into this little pile and one or two of these little pieces of rubber would stick there, and after he'd finished shuffling, he'd ask the man to cut. You can't fail to cut every time at that little speck there. The pack will break there." Vernon tried the ruse for himself. It worked perfectly.

Vernon also asked Shock about the gambler named Ping Pong, the one he'd tried to locate in French Lick Springs a decade earlier. Much to his surprise, Shock knew Ping Pong and taught Vernon what Stevens had described as the most "beautiful thing ever done with a deck of cards."

Vernon wrote to Horowitz,

> *I have at last discovered what the "one thing" the late "Ping Pong" had that no one could ever copy. He could shift the cut with a most natural move. He used it in the "fastest company" and was never detected. Its simplicity is a thing of beauty, but to get or acquire the requisite speed would seem impossible. Shock (the gambler) said no one was ever able to do it but "Ping Pong"—he used to play with him twenty years ago and swears he could not detect the move.*

Finally, in September, the time came to leave Asheville. First he headed to Waynesville for a week and then Chattanooga. In Chattanooga, Circle No. 10 of the Woman's Auxiliary of St. Paul's Church sponsored his appearance. The *Chattanooga News* for Saturday, October 18th reported that Mrs. E.D. Walter, chairman of the Circle, had discovered Mr. Vernon several years earlier. The paper printed many examples of his work, particularly his silhouettes of children. Vernon included a silhouette of his own son, Ted, in the group. The following week, a rival paper, the *Chattanooga Times*, ran images of "Debutantes of Chattanooga's Social Season 1930-31" as cut by Vernon. It certainly wasn't difficult for Vernon to acquire prime storefront property from which to conduct business. The Great Depression had taken its toll and untold numbers of businesses folded their tents. Vernon managed to turn a good trade, pocketing enough money to allow him to buy a new car and wire Jeanne that she and Ted should join him in Savannah.

> *For a time I was going like a house on fire. Jeanne was in New York all this time. Finally one day in Chattanooga, Tennessee—I began to get so much money in my pocket—I was putting some in the bank occasionally, I bought a car, paid cash for it. Then I wired Jeanne, "Meet me in Savannah, Ga." I drove over and she came down on the boat with Teddy.*

As Vernon described it, Jeanne found life on the road to be full of inconsistencies and frustrating incidents.

> *Well, for instance—I used to like to go to art stores, and buy water*

Phantoms Of The Card Table

The Vernon family: Jeanne, Dai and Ted, photographed in 1931.

colors—and Jeanne would go along, and she would browse around in the stores—(she was an artist too, in many ways, she was a better artist than I was she was very talented) And Jeanne would say ... I'd like to have so and so—and the proprietor would say, "Oh, does your little girl paint too?"

Course I always thought that was funny—and remember I was ten years older than she—anyway, I remember, Jeanne used to get very indignant—as is the way with all small people—when someone crowds in front of them—my wife used to get very indignant—for instance, sometimes we'd go to the movies (we went to the movies quite a bit) and if we went to a movie for adults only, I'd go up and buy two tickets, and then they'd say, "I'm sorry, you can't bring the little girl in."

She used to say, "I'm a married woman."

We got in without any trouble.

Dai Vernon: A Biography

At least, however, her husband was making money. For others, as Downs would report in a letter to McLaughlin on October 28, 1930, business was down. Jobs, he said, were like hen's teeth: scarce.

Had letter from McGuire couple days ago (mislaid it) said he had couple letters to Ross returned to him—also said things in General Biz Bad but magic dead as a business and in his opinion the Tarbell System and Magic Societies especially (the) IBM killed it.

Despite his protestations about amateurs, Downs was still on the beat for magic tricks, most of which were produced by part-time professionals or hobbyists. Faucett Ross was still his main source of information, buying or acquiring in trade virtually every major release. McLaughlin remained Downs' ever-faithful scribe, typing out multiple carbon copies of each manuscript or instruction sheet, so that Downs could circulate the work in trade with others. Vernon, on the other hand, was content to try to perfect what had just been placed before him. He wrote Horowitz from the Park Hotel in Chattanooga.

Hello Sam—Have had to do a little work as I've been neglecting everything to practice piano and cards. I have worked out the Ping Pong shift to perfection. It's marvelous, shall send you photos and description when I hear from you. I want you Cardini and myself to be the sole possessor of it. Cardini has photos now but not correct move to go with them. My seconds are 98% and bottoms 50% perfect. Drop a line I'll write when I hear from you. Had wire from Miss King to play date in N.Y. but too big a jump. I shall get the photos of the Ping Pong shift from the car next time I go over to the garage. Want you to master this move as it's unknown as far as I can find out.

With the family reunited, Vernon moved on to Jacksonville, Florida, checked into the Mayflower Hotel and set up a studio to cut silhouettes. There he learned that Clyde Powers, the magic dealer who gave him carte blanche to the backroom, had died. He also learned that Max Holden had begun championing yet another newcomer, although the newcomer was not so new to Vernon:

Johnny Scarna [Scarne] of New Jersey is another clever worker with cards. Johnny is without a doubt one of the cleverest card men there

Phantoms Of The Card Table

is. One of his effects is a card selected and placed face down on the table. Now Johnny takes a Queen from the pack and places it over on the opposite side of the table and the two cards are caused to change places. One of the neatest bits of sleight of hand I have ever seen. Ellsworth Lyman a visitor from Ashville, N.C. and he reports the wonders of Dave Vernon who just left there.

From Jacksonville, Vernon headed for Miami. Performing in the hotels that dotted South Beach was the famous Max Malini. Vernon and Malini met on several occasions. Malini performed his act nightly, and Vernon sat in on the show at every opportunity. Malini even generously invited him onto the stage to assist with various tricks in order for Vernon to have a better understanding of the work involved in creating the illusions. Vernon also learned that Eddie McGuire, the man who billed himself as manager of Max Malini, was nothing more than a glorified ticket taker at a Malini performance in Rhode Island. McGuire had pestered Malini so much that Malini gave him a job to keep him out of the way. Malini did not have, nor require, a "manager." Whatever newfound cordiality that had developed between Vernon and Malini, however, soon vanished.

Miami Beach was chock full of nightclubs, and Vernon was asked to entertain at the opening of a nightclub at the Hollywood Hotel.

> ... I went over there, and I was nervous because I had to do a show for a lot of people and they wanted me to do cards, and I know that they couldn't see cards the way the room was situated, and they wouldn't be able to see the ordinary card trick. So I did the cards up the sleeve, which has good visibility, and I did stabbing the card—you know, blindfolded, and mixing them all over the table and stabbing them.

Vernon stabbed three selected cards on the point of a knife. When Malini caught wind of the performance, he reprimanded Vernon. They met the next day after the show at the Floridian Hotel, where Malini was staying, and Malini said, "Vernon, I don't want you to do my tricks."

Vernon was confused. He asked, "What do you mean, Max? I don't do your tricks."

But Malini was persistent. "You were out there last night at the Hollywood Club and you did my trick."

Vernon reiterated, "Max, I didn't do any of your tricks."
Malini disagreed, "You did the stabbing trick."
Vernon argued, "Yes, Max, but that's not your trick. For goodness sake, that trick is explained in books before you were born."
"One card!"
"Yes," Vernon said, "one card."
"Not ten!"
Vernon said, "I didn't do it with ten."
"But you did it with more than one card!"
Vernon agreed, "Yes."
"That's my trick."

Vernon finally conceded the point. After searching his inventory of tricks, he could not recall any other performer stabbing multiple cards. Malini was appalled by the fact that he had tipped Vernon on the work of some of his repertoire and that Vernon had had the audacity to immediately perform it. The protocol amongst professional entertainers was to avoid performing any trick that was associated with another individual, a signature piece, particularly in the same market. What Malini failed to recognize was that Vernon was not a professional in the traditional sense of the word. Despite his professed admiration for Malini, his showmanship, and his magic, culturally, he was a world away. Malini was a seasoned, Lower East Side Jewish entertainer. Vernon was an Anglo explorer searching for arcane information. Performances were secondary to Vernon.

There may have also been another reason for the falling out. Malini often augmented his income by selling secrets to simple mechanical tricks for inflated prices. He sold, for example, a mechanical coin trick—the Dime and Penny, a trick that Downs claimed to have invented—for $100 to businessmen who wandered into his lair. The trick normally sold in magic shops for a dollar or less. Vernon, it appears, had been cutting into his domain.

In a letter to Horowitz from the Hotel Pancoast, Miami Beach, Florida, Vernon wrote,

> One of the most important events is that Max Malini has come and gone. I caught his show at the Floridian—wonderful in every way except his Fish Bowl Production.
>
> His performance was divided into three parts with intermissions of thirty minutes. His handling of the egg bag is perfection to my mind

and he can manipulate the genuine egg better than most who use a shell.

There was an attorney staying at Malini's Hotel who Max was trying to line up for a few lessons but had previously made arrangements with me for a few lessons and I had plenty of fun trying to keep one jump ahead and not let Malini steal my pupil. I only showed him simple stuff—mostly—back palm with variations.

Although Vernon was in Miami to cut silhouettes, the field was not as fruitful as he had hoped. Taking on private students, even if it was for just a session or so, helped pay the bills. Still, Vernon would have perhaps made more money if he weren't so obsessed with the second deal. Another letter to Horowitz revealed his state of mind.

Suppose that you have dealt millions of seconds and bottoms since I last saw you.

I would love to see you "rip a few" as Johnny says. I can image how perfectly you operate because I know you will not rest until you have mastered every detail. The great thing in both second and bottom work is to deal with utmost ease. It is this ease of execution which when seen demonstrated by Scott—I feel sure that makes his work "stand out." This absolute naturalness is extremely difficult when carrying out or combining so very many little details. To really deal approaching perfection the second and top or bottom and top must be alternated almost unconsciously.

Vernon informed Horowitz that he would be leaving Miami in about a week.

Expect if all goes well to be leaving here end of next week. Will probably stop a week in Atlanta. Haven't made a single dime all winter but have had plenty of sunshine and Jeanne and Teddy look like a million so that's worth something.

Hope that you are able to make ends meet these hard times and that all your family are in best of health.

Give my kindest regards to Sam Margules, Al Baker, Max Holden and any of the 'boys' you may run into.

Miami this year has been "teeming" with would be "card sharps." However I met two—both Greeks who were very clever. One fellow—(do not know his name) tells me he is always around 42nd and Broadway when in N.Y. He could run up two sets of threes for anything up to nine handed best I ever saw. He was absolutely sure on the "comit."

Vernon was still pursuing advantage players, ready to add to his store of knowledge. No sooner had he spent time with one, absorbing whatever information he may have had to offer, then he was on the prowl for the next. Soon enough, Jim Whitley's name came to Vernon's attention.

Vernon learned of Whitley from a blackjack dealer at a Palm Beach casino. Whitley was an old-time faro dealer down on his luck. Once he had dealt the bank, the pinnacle of the profession until rampant cheating had led to the virtual exctinction of the game. Now, near the end of his life, Whitley was cooped up in a Miami hospital, trying to make ends meet. Because Vernon knew that faro dealers were the most skilled at card table artifice, he tracked the invalid down and learned that the old man had little life left. Whitley had even hocked his prized possession, a faro box, to a pawnshop for twenty-five dollars to help pay for his care. Vernon speculated that the gambler must have tipped to the proprietor of the shop the secret mechanics of the box, that is, how a faro dealer could allow anyone to shuffle the cards and still know in advance whether each card drawn was a winner or loser. Twenty-five dollars was a lot of money for a silver box used to hold playing cards. This was, after all, the Depression.

To finance the acquisition of the faro box, Vernon called on an old acquaintance from New York, Frank Pickard, now living in Miami. Pickard was the proprietor of Frank's Magic Shop. Vernon sold him the right to reprint *Secrets*, the same small booklet of secrets that he had compiled and sold in 1924 to another magic dealer to raise money to marry Jeanne. Pickard changed the name of the publication to *28 Card Secrets*, "the latest and revised edition exposing and expounding twenty-eight mystifying tricks that can anyone could perform with any deck of playing cards."

Phantoms Of The Card Table

In the introduction, Pickard wrote,

In this message to you I most sincerely thank my good friend, Dave Vernon, the well-known card wizard, who gave me the right to expose his "Secrets" in this book.

Should you become interested and use any of the effects described herein, I think you, too, owe thanks to Mr. Vernon. But for him "Secrets" would be still unborn.

If you should desire to further develop your knowledge of card tricks, I would like to recommend what is, in Mr. Vernon's and my own estimation, one of the best books on the market today, known as "The Expert on [sic] the Card Table," containing 100 drawings illustrating the proper way to manipulate a pack of cards. This book can be bought at any store selling "Secrets," or direct from Frank's Magic Shop, Miami, Florida.

Vernon acquired the pawn ticket from Whitley and went to the shop to repay the advance and reclaim the item. When he arrived, the proprietor informed him that the period for reclaiming the article had expired. The ticket was past due. Vernon offered the man the face value of the ticket, but the offer was declined. "That," said the man, "was what I lent on the box. I've had the box here for a long time and wouldn't dream of letting it go for that amount."

Vernon tried to negotiate. "What," he asked, "was he going to do with it?" He upped the ante but still struck out. Vernon left the store discouraged, but returned two or three times, each time increasing his offer. The pawnbroker, however, wouldn't sell, so Vernon planned one final assault. He packed his car with boxes, drove up to the establishment and, with Jeanne and Ted stationed on the sidewalk in front of the shop, told the man that he was leaving Miami, heading back for New York. He then took five perfectly new, crisp five-dollar banknotes and thumbed them out onto the counter. "This is your last chance. If you want, I'll buy that box." The man looked at the card box in its leather case, the family on the street, and the money. Finally, he acquiesced.

As soon as the man removed the box from its case, Vernon knew that the grandstand was worth the effort. He was ecstatic. The box was the most beautiful he had ever encountered. Still, he had to learn how to use it. There was no guarantee that Whitley would reveal the secret of its construction and use to him.

> *Faro dealers, they don't talk. This thing is handed almost from father to son. You've got to belong to the Guild. They don't hobnob with other card players. They're aloof. They consider themselves the intelligentsia or the royalty of the card world. And they are. They're always dignified old fellows, very beautiful card handlers.*
>
> *So this old fellow—this is a picaresque thing, not one out of twenty thousand, probably twenty million people knows—when I asked him to show me some of the work, he said, "Have you got old thing?"*
>
> *And I knew right away this was something—He said, "Have you got the old thing?"*
>
> *And I said, "No."*
>
> *He said, "Well, how can I show you? I can't show you; get old thing and I'll show you."*

Vernon knew that, without a full appreciation for the slang or argot of the vice, the old man would recognize him for what he was, a dilettante, not a worker.

> *Now, the old thing, this is not known even to the gamblers. Only faro dealers know this. I, by subterfuge, I discerned what old thing was and found out all about it by not pleading ignorance. I didn't say I didn't know what 'old thing' was. I didn't want to be that ignorant. He wouldn't have shown me anything, see, because I wasn't entitled to know, but by hook and by crook, by making him think I knew other faro dealers, he went into it.*

Surreptitiously, Vernon learned the meaning of the "old thing" and was initiated into the inner workings of the mechanical marvel placed before him. The box was a combination box, that is, a double-dealing box with both a needle and sand tell and a secret locking mechanism that would withstand the closest scrutiny. Originally, Whitley had paid $100 for the box, and that had been twenty years earlier, before the game of faro had fallen out of fashion.

Phantoms Of The Card Table

Although Miami may not have been an economic success, Vernon's sojourn into the southern states was, by and large—certainly artistically—rewarding. He had learned much from Shock in Asheville, including the mechanics of the Ping Pong shift, studied Malini at close quarters in his natural commercial environment, acquired the most beautiful gambling device he had ever encountered, and cultivated much inside information about faro from a seasoned practitioner. A missive to Horowitz contained his glad tidings.

Vernon set out in his Buick, weaving his way back towards Manhattan, setting up shop at various ports of call to finance the expedition. In January 1931, while Vernon was on Canal Street in New Orleans, encouraging patrons to "preserve your profile for your descendants" and offering to sell "inexpensive frames" along with the silhouettes he would cut—two for one dollar—Cardini returned to New York a sophisticated and seasoned performer. Max Holden heralded his triumphant return in his February 1931 *Sphinx* column,

> *Cardini the Peer of all Sleight of Hand Artists played a return date at the Palace and at No. 3 on the programme, stopped the show at every performance. (Stopping the show is a theatrical expression used where the artiste at the finish of his act receives so much applause that the next act is unable to go on until the artiste comes back and acknowledges the applause.)...The greatest act ever and a magician that we are all proud of. Cardini is booked for England, Scotland and the Continent November next.*

Vernon continued to hover in the southern states, having worked his way back to Atlanta, once again under the auspices of St. Mary Guild of St. Philip's Cathedral. This time he set up shop in the Thomas Florist Shop, 1934 Peachtree Street. The *Atlanta Constitution* for May 28th introduced him to their readers.

> *There are only ten first class silhouette artists in the country who can make your portrait from life, it is said, and Mr. Vernon is one of them. He works exclusively for the Episcopal church now, and already has brought in thousands of dollars with his scissors. In the past he has worked for other religious and charitable organizations, enriching them considerably.*

Dai Vernon: A Biography

While staying at the Cox-Carlton Hotel, 683 Peachtree Street N.E., he sent Horowitz an update of his itinerary.

> *Just a line to let you know that I'll be in Richmond Va. next week if all goes well. We are leaving in a few minutes. We shall stop off a day and night to visit Lyman in Asheville en route. Write to me in Richmond Gen. Del.*
>
> *I shall drop a line from there. Was too busy this week to write. Car was broken into and gabs stolen and plenty of other things to think about so please make allowances.*

By June 9th, he had arrived in Richmond and started cutting silhouettes at 412 East Grace Street for Circle 3 of the Centenary Methodist Church. There, he noticed a great deal of publicity being given to Reno, Nevada. Vernon and Jeanne decided, having no particular place to go, to head west to see what the action was like. It was a long drive through Kansas and Oklahoma. Vernon sent Horowitz a postcard of the oil fields from Tonkawa, Oklahoma, and informed him that he might stop off in Colorado Springs, Colorado for a couple of weeks. Horowitz could write to him there courtesy of General Delivery. He added that the three of them—Ted, Jeanne and himself—were having a wonderful time.

Colorado Springs was a welcome relief from the dry, hot weather of the plains. The weather, even though it was in the middle of July, was cool. The Vernons decided to stay a few days and enjoy their surroundings and the climate. No sooner had they arrived than Vernon heard of a carnival on the outside of town, a carnival that featured a magician—a very clever one, according to most reports—by the name of Paul Fox. Vernon pricked up his ears at the name. It rang a bell immediately. Paul Fox was the stage name of Paul Fuchs, a good friend of Al Baker.

> *Many years ago, at Bayridge, Al Baker told me he had a dear friend, Paul Fox in Colorado who was dying of consumption. I had heard his name mentioned often among magicians—he originally had a school of engraving in Chicago; he was very successful doing magic, got suddenly sick, stricken with T.B., was in the Glockner Sanitarium and had been given only six months to live.*

Phantoms Of The Card Table

Al Baker asked me for instructions on cutting silhouettes, intending to send them to Paul Fox to while away his time. So, for one of the few times in my life I did go to a lot of pains to put together some notes, sent some black paper, a pair of scissors.

Apparently, the climate and conditions of Colorado Springs had helped bring Fox back to good health. When Vernon first made inquiries he was informed that Fox did not give out his address and that he had no desire to meet amateur magicians. Vernon replied confidently, "I think he'll meet me," found his name and address in the phone book and placed the call. Vernon, ever coy, baited Fox.

"Hello, Mr. Fox. I'm from the East and very interested in magic."

Fox replied, "I'm sorry, I don't discuss magic with people very much. There are only two people that I'd be interested in meeting. One is Al Baker and the other is Dai Vernon."

"Well," Vernon said, "You happen to be talking to Dai Vernon."

Immediately, Fox, who was living in Colorado Springs with his wife Henrietta, became quite excited. He learned where Vernon was staying and rushed out to pick him up.

Fox was a kindred spirit, perhaps even more so than the close coterie of friends—Horowitz, Cardini, and Finley—that Vernon had in New York. Whereas Vernon was an artist with the shears and displayed superb penmanship, Fox was a master engraver, often commissioned by fine jewelers like Tiffany to ply his trade on their wares. Vernon played piano, more for his own recreation and amusement than professionally; Fox was a gifted banjo player, having studied with Eddie Peabody, another renowned player. Both men were also obsessed with detail and its place on the path to perfection.

Paul was an absolute perfectionist. One year Mahan's Jewelry Stores had made the largest sale of silver plate ever sold in this country. The dozens and dozens of platters, bowls, silverware sets, etc., were brought to Paul for the engraving of a monogram. I was visiting him one day and we were talking as he was doing the engraving. He was on the last spoon when he suddenly jumped up and I thought he was going into a fit. "My goodness, what have I done, what have I done?" he exclaimed. When I asked him what had happened he showed me the spoon and said, "Look at that!" I looked but could see nothing wrong with it. I had pretty good eyes and tended to be a bit of a perfectionist in the cutting of silhouettes. I looked carefully at the monogram and couldn't see a thing wrong with it. Paul said, "Put the loupe in your eye and look at it!" So I did, and I still couldn't see what he meant. "Look at the serif on the letter, don't you see it has a little burr on it?" Well, it was so minute that I don't think one person in a million would have noticed it, not even another engraver. However, to Paul, it was a catastrophe, the fact that one letter was a little less than perfection.

Fox persuaded Vernon to set up shop, a silhouette stall in Manitou, at the foot of Pike's Peak, Colorado's premier tourist attraction. Manitou, Vernon learned, was a Native American word for heaven, and heaven it was. Business boomed. Vernon had crowds all the time, and, even though it was the midst of the Depression, he hung a sign over his easel saying, "No Depression here." Reno could wait.

He sent Horowitz a postcard, "Above the clouds on Pikes Peak Cog Road," on July 22, 1931.

Certainly wish I could see you again. Paul Fuchs [Fox] and I see each other here nearly every day. He's sure one of the inner circle. Paul Fuchs is exceedingly clever and ranks with the best of them. Have many new ideas to discuss with you. Shall write soon. Business is great here and we can hardly sleep at night on account of the cold.

The work suited Vernon just fine. He would stay up most of the night discussing magic. The cool Colorado air, he said, made it difficult to go to sleep. He would sleep most of the day and then stroll in to work at his silhouette shop in the early evening to address the needs of the long line of customers, by and large women with children, waiting to have their profiles cut. More often than not, Fox would sit with Vernon, and the two would discuss magic while Vernon plied his trade. Although Vernon often wondered what his customers thought of their exchange, he knew none would be wiser from eavesdropping in on the conversation.

The two exchanged many ideas. For Fox, perfection was no detail and this fact suited Vernon just fine. Fox, for example, offered Vernon a suggestion for one of his most recent creations. The trick was the one in which Vernon would state that he had reversed a card in the deck prior to the performance and then ask the spectator to name that card. Inspired by the Impey manuscript and Brown's Super Reverse, Vernon's version was a surefire hit. Fox suggested, however, that Vernon could enhance the effect if he informed the spectator that the card he had inserted upside down into the pack prior to the performance was drawn from a deck with a different colored back. Vernon agreed, and this touch, the named card having a back that was a different color from the rest, transformed the trick into a genuine miracle.

Vernon learned many other things from Fox. Although he had spent years tracking down information about gamblers, extrapolating principles from their work, and applying them to magic, he had never really turned his attention to magic with apparatus. Fox provided him with a post-graduate education on the finer elements of this branch of conjuring. He learned, for example, that Fox was one of the first to manipulate cigarettes on stage—using an ingenious combination of sleight-of-hand and faux cigarettes. Fox presented Vernon with a set of the requisite props. Vernon elected not to perform the feat publicly, however, out of respect for his friend Cardini, now making a reputation with his own manipulative ability with tobacco. Vernon also learned that many items in the *Tarbell Course* had come from Fox's fertile mind. When Harlan Tarbell usurped control of the course from Walter Baker, he called on Fox for technical assistance. Fox was also the mysterious manipulator that Harry Kellar had once spoken of years ago, the only one who performed the production and vanish of playing cards in such a manner that it really looked as though he was catching cards out of the air.

Despite his great affinity for performing, Fox was an artist, not a showman. Ever since Vernon fell under the spell of *The Expert At The Card Table*, a tome that spoke of sleights in terms of elegance and artistry, Vernon drew distinctions between the two. He enjoyed watching great showmen; he admired great artists more.

> *There's a difference between just a performer, a showman, and an artist in my opinion. A showman can be flamboyant, loud, and in some way or other intoxicate the people or make them think he's great, but an artist is a different thing altogether. You take Rubinoff playing the violin, and he gets down on one knee and he jumps around and he does all kind of calisthenics, and some people say, "Isn't he great!" But Spaulding or Heifitz or Kreisler can stand perfectly still and just*

Paul Fox: perfectionist and prestidigitator.

bow that violin and create a lot more feeling than he can with all his gymnastics. It's the same way with magic, I think, as in any art. You don't have to do gymnastics to impress people.

Fox was someone who had the ability to do more but the will to refrain. The historical magicians that Vernon most admired were of the same school. Vernon also recognized that great artists suffer for their art, not just economically, but emotionally. Artists, like Robert-Houdin and Hofzinser, had to deal with showmen who would take credit for things to which they were not entitled and, even worse, butcher the material because of little understanding of the theory, structure, and technique behind the trick. It was easy to see how one could become bitter and disillusioned. Vernon vowed not to suffer the same fate.

Although Vernon wrote to Horowitz at the end of July to say that he expected to leave Manitou shortly and stop off in Denver or Salt Lake City en route to Reno, he spent the remainder of the summer and fall in Colorado Springs. Business was simply too good. He finally set out for Denver in December. The Denver Dry Goods Co. advertised his services in the local paper: "Have your silhouette made by the man with the magic scissors." The advertisement assured readers that, with the revival of the romantic period in women's clothing, so too had come the revival of silhouettes. Silhouette portraits, they advertised, were in vogue. And while Vernon may have been cutting hundreds of silhouettes, it was still magic that was on his mind.

Magic was also continuously on the minds of Ross, McLaughlin, and Downs. Ross wrote McLaughlin on November 4th,

Glad you got to see Cardini again & will also have opportunity of seeing him again. Received a letter from him Monday with the interesting statement that Dai Vernon is in Denver Colo at present. This interests me very much. Within the next month I had planned a business trip to Denver and of course I'd certainly like to look up Vernon. In fact I'd be willing to go most anytime between now & Dec if I thought I'd have a chance to see Vernon.

Listen when you see Cardini again ask him where Vernon is located in Denver and how long he expects to be there. I'm really anxious to know. Also try to find out what kind of a racket Vernon is working out there. Previous to Denver, he was in Colo Springs & Reno.

Enclosed is a write up of Cardini's present routine. It is fairly complete but there are several things in the cigarette routine that are missing. Now you'll see his act a half dozen times probably and with this outline as your guide please try to fill in what's missing. I would really like to have complete routine of his cig. work—move for move. I recall what a great job you did on Keating. Don't worry about his card and b. ball moves—it's just the cig. routine I'm anxious to get—move for move. This is the only copy I have so please return it.

Also please don't forget to ask him about Vernon, address, how long he expects to be in Denver, etc.

Evidently, Vernon must have heard from Cardini that Ross was interested in visiting him in Denver. Ross wrote Eddie McLaughlin,

Dai Vernon: A Biography

Yesterday I received a nice note from Dai Vernon saying the quicker I came out to Denver the better etc. So I guess I'm all lined up and I expect to run out on the bus (pass) within the next two weeks. I guess he's been rather "thick" with Paul Fuchs [Fox] who is now in Colorado Springs.

I don't expect to get much from Vernon. All these boys are a big disappointment to me in so far as the super-subtle stuff is concerned. Most of their stuff is simply stolen from ancient sources & polished up a bit.

Ross made the trek to Denver over the Christmas holidays. Downs wrote McLaughlin on December 22, stating, "No news from Ross for some time. He must [have] gone on to Colorado to see Vernon." Downs wrote McLaughlin again on December 29th.

Had a letter from Ross in Denver in which he said he had had a session with Vernon & seemed all 'het up' about it & was going have another meeting at Vernon's apartment & stay all nite that nite.

Said he was making notes of everything said Vernon still claims Malini is "The King Em All" Now I know Vernon is overrated. Fact is I've known since 1925 when I saw him do a trial show at Victoria, L.I. (A flop). He just cannot put a show over the footlights. Prof. Hocus with his bum funnel fire cracker—pop corn in hat and monkey which makes the kids scream when he peaks out thru curtains makes a living in magic such as it is while Vernon can't. Viola!

Magic is sure in a bad way when Blackstone Cardini Gwynne have to play most tank towns & split weeks it proves VOD-VIL is over—Thru—real show biz is a thing of the past.

Ross persuaded Vernon to return with him to Wichita rather than Reno. There, Vernon, Jeanne, and Ted acquired digs at the Harrison Apartments, a building owned by another budding magician, on Seneca Street. Vernon's unit, number 302, was adjacent to Ross's. For Ross, it was a dream that came true. He wrote McLaughlin,

He [Vernon] blew in Wichita January 15th and for three weeks, day and night, we did nothing but talk magic. One session lasted from

Phantoms Of The Card Table

three o'clock one afternoon until eleven the next morning.

At the end of three weeks he got located in the Innes Dept Store cutting silhouettes and his stuff is great although he cares nothing about it—just a means to making a living. He soon became very popular especially amusing the "elite" and after a couple of weeks he was successful—they waited for him in droves. He works very fast—never takes over two minutes. He never showed up at the store until eleven and worked until five thirty. He's very independent about the silhouettes. If he didn't like the looks of a person he'd refuse to cut them.

For Vernon, Wichita was full of surprises. First, he discovered that Ross, although not a technician, was a very good journeyman performer and, more importantly, had one of the most impressive collections of magic books and manuscripts Vernon had ever seen. Ross informed him that his principle sources of information were Charles Maly, Tom Bowyer, Sid Lorraine, Earl Violet, Doctor E.G Ervin, Tommy Downs, and Eddie McGuire.

Second, Vernon had his suspicions about Walter Scott confirmed: the entire New York session had been a set-up. In a letter to Horowitz, Vernon gently reprimanded him for falling for the ruse and tipping work. At least, Vernon said, McGuire did not share secrets readily.

Sam I'm very glad that Eddie is close with what he knows because I feel sure in your enthusiasm you "tipped" everything you could think of at the time. It is very evident that Eddie just used Walter as an "open sesame" to the doors of guarded secrets. He met with great success in most cases and I give him credit. I was sorry to learn that he thinks I would never have had anything to do with him if it hadn't been for Walter. If I was a good correspondent I would have written him years ago before Walter appeared on the horizon. He has been more than nice about writing me and I hope I can in the near future repay him with some information. But although I have dozens of new angles and ideas writing them is another story.

The third surprise in Wichita was the appearance of Charles Earle Miller. Miller became interested in magic in 1916 when, at age seven, he witnessed his brother perform a simple trick. It was the same year that Vernon first made a name for himself in New York. Magic became Miller's all-consuming interest at age fourteen, about the same time that Holden first started alluding to Vernon's magic in his columns in *The Sphinx*. Miller subscribed to *The Sphinx*, discovered the Welworth Magic Co. in his hometown and, more importantly, met Charles Maly. Maly was a close confidant of Ross and, so it seemed, had access to the latest secrets from New York well before others. Ross confessed that he had befriended Maly primarily to have access to the secrets in his library and share them with Downs.

Although Miller was fifteen years Vernon's junior, the two men were very much alike. Miller was a gifted student of magic. A prodigy by his late teens, he read the primary texts, displayed a natural ability for learning sleight-of-hand, and had the persistence to perfect it. For Miller, Vernon and the magic he performed as described by Max Holden represented the pinnacle of magical achievement. Miller was confident that he could reconstruct the routines. In 1931, Maly suggested that Miller, then twenty-one, should contact Ross. Miller, residing in El Paso, Texas, wrote to Ross,

> Mr. Maly has spoken of you several times and I was told to look you up if we came through Wichita on the way home. I promised Charles Maly of [sic] couple of tricks that were performed by Dave Vernon. Of course I only read the effects as described by Max Holden but I think that I have them right. Anyway, they work, and the effect is the same so there can't be much difference. It would be interesting to know just whether Mr. Vernon and Mr. Horowitz can do all of these wonders with borrowed cards. I know of methods for doing similar tricks with borrowed cards but there is usually a weak spot somewhere. Most of the things I have read about Dave Vernon give me the impression that he uses his own cards.

When they finally met in Wichita, Vernon was totally taken aback by Miller and his magic. Not only had he reconstructed the effects as described in the Holden columns, more importantly, he was right. As his letter to Horowitz years earlier intimated, Vernon had a grudging respect for magicians who, like Annemann, were able to dope out material on their own. Miller's capacity for reconstruction was beyond compare. Many magicians had speculated, for example, on how Vernon accomplished his storied effects. Miller

*The dapper Charles Earle Miller
of El Paso, Texas.*

was the first, however, to nail the correct methods. Vernon wrote Horowitz,

> ...the boy who has the "real dope" is young Charles Miller of El Paso Texas. Ross has hundreds of letters from him and he is a genius considering the fact that he has been shut off by himself most of the time. A few weeks ago he came all the way up here to see Ross and myself. He stayed for three or four days which were continual sessions. He claims the "crowd" at the coast—Judson Brown, MacMillan etc refer to the "mythical effects of the New York Card Men" and do not put any faith in reports so Miller decided to come up here and investigate by asking me all about it. He has real ideas. Manipulates coins and cards beautifully and although he suspected I had some information from Scott he was very nice about not being curious or interrogating me in reference to it. I would like to nominate him for the "Mythical Inner Circle" as he is really a No. 1.

Vernon was so enthusiastic about Miller and his work that he dashed off a second missive to Horowitz only a few days after the first, remarkable considering by his own admission that he was such a lax correspondent. Vernon instructed Horowitz to alert John Mulholland, the current editor of *The Sphinx*, that when Miller "visits New York he's going to have them all talking." Vernon added, "Say that I think he's the best I've met in years."

While the new guard beat a path to Vernon's door, the old guard, as represented by Downs, feigned disinterest. Downs wrote McLaughlin on January 21, 1932.

> *Just got a letter from Ross asking me to come down to Wichita—I'd never think of it even if I was feelin' ok. Just between you & I Vernon has got no gambling stuff or anything else of any practical value in magic—I'll just enclose Rosses letter & you can return it & I'll send it on to McGuire.*

The fourth and biggest surprise in Wichita was still in store. Unbeknownst to all, Vernon was about to stumble on the best-kept secret of all. Faucett Ross had received a tip about a gambler, held on murder charges in the Sedgwick County Jail, who was spending his time performing card tricks for his captive audience: the other detainees and the staff that manned the facility. Vernon's enthusiasm for hunting advantage players for arcane information was contagious. As soon as he heard the news, Ross rushed over to the Innes Department store to inform Vernon.

The gambler, Amador Villasenor, a Mexican advantage player and thief, had been incarcerated for a month, on charges of slaying one Benito Leija some eighteen months earlier. Villasenor had confessed to the killing but maintained that he had acted in self-defense. The authorities at the jailhouse bought his story but still had to hold him until due process had taken its course. They did not regard him as a threat.

Vernon got excited and headed immediately to the jailhouse with Ross. Ross knew the sheriff and, after performing a few tricks for the staff, persuaded the authorities to allow them an audience with the hustler. The authorities pulled Villasenor from his cellblock—the jailhouse housed eight hundred prisoners—and instructed him to run through his repertoire of tricks for the two magicians.

Vernon required little time to assess the man's skill. Years of hunting gamblers and persuading them to part with their wares had provided Vernon with a critical eye. Although Villasenor was a professional, he was no Dad Stevens. After the prisoner had exhausted his repertoire, Vernon asked him one question, the same question that he posed to Shock in Asheville and to every other advantage player or hustler, regardless of standing or expertise, that he came across.

"You've played cards all your life," Vernon asked, "Have you ever seen anything you don't understand? Have you ever witnessed anything unusual?"

Without any hesitation, in broken English, Villasenor replied, "In Kansas City, I see a fella. He deals cards from the center of the pack." The man said it with such conviction that Vernon knew that he was serious.

Vernon had heard of the notion of dealing from the center of the deck before. John Sprong had written him years earlier of the rumor of some Midwestern hustler who had the ability to negate the cut by dealing cards from the center of the deck. Sprong had even offered Vernon $100 for any information he could uncover about the technique. Until now, Vernon had dismissed the entire notion as poppycock. It surely must have been an urban myth, much like the often-old tale of a man who had cut off a portion of his finger in order to reduce the flash of his bottom deal. Vernon peppered Villasenor with questions, the most important one being, "How did the deal look?" Villasenor's response never varied. The deal looked, he said, "Perfect."

Vernon had chased perfection his entire life, and it had always eluded his grasp. Perhaps, he thought, there was someone else out there who had achieved it. He vowed to find him.

Chapter Seven
Centers And Secrets

"You must be crazy," the wily old sharp exclaimed. "It's hard enough to take the second card from the deck let alone one from the center. What mail order catalogue have you been reading?"

Vernon was making inquires in every backroom gambling den he could find in Kansas City, Missouri, on the hunt for information that could lead him to the man who had achieved perfection, the man who could deal from the center of the deck. Charlie Miller, the twenty-one year old, baby-faced, pudgy prodigy that Vernon had nominated for the mythical Inner Circle, accompanied him. Vernon had written his newfound friend, who had just returned to El Paso, about his meeting with the Mexican gambler in the Sedgwick County Jail, briefed him on the notion of the center deal, and outlined his plans to head for Kansas City to find the man.

Miller had been one of the few parties interested in joining the posse. Faucett Ross, whose exchanges with Downs had curtailed substantially since Vernon arrived in town, tried to persuade Downs to join them. Downs was ensconced in his own world, believing that the Jordan material in his possession remained the high water mark of inner secrets. He wrote McLaughlin:

> Ross hasn't sent me a thing of Vernon's. Just goes on raving & romancing about Vernon inventing 8 or 10 new ones every nite mostly poker stuff. Ross writes one he & Vernon was gonna make a trek to K.C. to see a fellow who deals from center of deck & also has a new machine for holding out cards for poker! (A lot of hooey in my opinion) & want me to make trip to K.C. & meet 'em says Dai talks

about me continuously & wants to see me. So I'm writing 'em both —very pressing invitation to drive on thru K.C. when thru with their K.C. Kard men & spend a coupla days here & they can look over my scrap books & get a line on Jordan's stuff etc—Told 'em I was not feeling well 'nuff to make the trip besides another trip to K.C. would crab the act as the Drs & everyone would want to "cut in" see?

Miller joined the hunt, however, because he recognized that Vernon's genius was rooted in his applications of card table artifice. Miller's knowledge of gambling technique was restricted to information, most of it hackneyed, promulgated by specialty publications housed in Charles Maly's library in Indianapolis. Miller had neither the inclination, the disposition, nor the opportunity to make sojourns into the gambling world. It was obvious, after meeting Vernon and hearing him deflect praise, admitting that most of his ideas had come from or been inspired by gamblers, that if Miller wanted to progress as a card handler, he would have to meet them as well. Here was his opportunity, a chance to learn from and with the master. Miller responded immediately to Vernon's missive. He would join the expedition.

Vernon, experienced in the hunt, prepared Miller as best he could. He laid down the ground rules. First, as their quarry was no Park Avenue sophisticate—he had, after all, been playing in a backroom poker game with someone who purported to be an itinerant Mexican laborer—Vernon suggested a tactic tailored specifically to their target. They would pretend to be big city advantage players who plied their trade on transatlantic crossings who had come to Kansas City to learn from the man that they had heard so much about on the ships. Second, although Vernon welcomed Miller's company, he realized that Miller didn't look or sound the part of a seasoned player. Miller's naiveté, both in looks and knowledge of card table artifice, could prove a serious liability.

Miller was a kind of mother's boy. He wouldn't curse or swear and if someone told a risqué story or showed a pornographic picture, Miller would become highly indignant and say, "I don't like to lose respect for you, please desist from this type of conversation." It was just the way he had been brought up.

Knowing the importance of argot and that the misuse of a term or phrase would torpedo any attempt to pry prized information from shadowed sources, Vernon instructed Miller that, if asked to flag his particular specialty, he was to reply in one of two ways. To a card mechanic, he was a dice worker; to a dice worker, he was a card mechanic. He was to keep it short and simple; say as little as possible and let Vernon do the talking. Unfortunately, despite the briefing, Vernon didn't fare much better on his own account. More often than not, he was subjected to ridicule. Part of the problem stemmed from the fact that there was no argot to describe the technique that Vernon wanted to learn. Every time he was describing the action to anyone who would actually listen, he was forced to describe the feat in the most unsophisticated language. He was looking for a man who could deal a card from the center of the deck. Talk like that made Vernon sound like a "square." While Miller was disheartened by the consistency and tone of each rejection, Vernon was a seasoned card detective and knew that enduring rejection was part of the process.

Kansas City was no French Lick Springs, a resort that housed a small community of hustlers who preyed upon itinerant marks. A hotbed of corruption and illicit activity, Kansas City was much more difficult to penetrate. It was almost as if the corn crops and stockyards planted by rugged agricultural entrepreneurs were designed to conceal an underbelly of gambling, drugs, prostitution, and jazz. The city was a feudal state controlled by an underworld kingpin, Tom Pendergast, his mob, and the serfs who inhabited this oasis of iniquity. Even traditional sources of information, the proprietors of gaming supply houses like the Kansas City Card Company at Twelfth and McGee, offered little assistance. All they could provide, other than traditional wares of milled and weighted dice, machines for holding out cards, and famous 'readers'—decks secretly marked by a group of Asian women skilled in fine penmanship—was a warm fireplace and a collegial atmosphere where those interested in advantage play could talk shop.

Vernon eventually learned that if anyone in Kansas City knew the information he sought, it would be John Lazia, the mobster assigned by Tom Pendergast to manage his illicit gambling operations. It would not be easy, however, to obtain an audience with Lazia. So Vernon headed back to the K.C. Card Company for a letter of introduction. Although the firm's General Manager, "Red" Langworthy, had professed no knowledge of either the artifice or man who could deal from the center of the deck, he did have a contact who might be able to arrange an audience with Lazia. Langworthy disclosed the location of a backroom card game where they could meet a man who had access to the potentate. Vernon and Miller followed Langworthy's directions, drove to the location, and knocked on the door.

A man growled from behind a panel, "Who sent ya?"

"Red Langworthy," Vernon responded.

"Who?"

"Red Langworthy at the K.C. Card Company!"

The door opened and Vernon and Miller were ushered down a long, dark corridor into a dingy back room where a couple of men sat off in a corner playing cards under a dim light, the type of light that would force a gambler like Old Shock in Asheville to embrace a punch deck rather than traditional readers. Then, like a spider summoned from its lair, a double amputee with a menacing glare coasted out of the shadows. His last name was Minshall; his friends called him Peg, an apropos moniker considering he was missing both of his legs. He was, despite his physical disability, an enforcer assigned to Lazia's operations. His talent was clear: he showcased a large .45 caliber revolver on the tray of his wheelchair and the toughest, meanest exterior Vernon had ever encountered. Miller had no trouble playing the silent type; he was terrified.

Vernon was quick to the point. He followed his script, informing Peg and his associates that he was a card mechanic that played the ships who was anxious to learn if Mr. Lazia knew of a man, a man from Kansas City, who could deal cards from the center of the deck.

As if on cue, the assemblage unknowingly followed the script that had been work-shopped at every other port of call in town. They laughed heartily, almost in unison, and reiterated the standard retort, "What mail-order catalogue have you been reading?"

Vernon's skills of improvisation immediately took hold. Now, instead of finding a thought-of-card, he was searching for a gracious way out of a more difficult situation. Vernon joined in their laughter and indicated that he, too, thought it was a crazy notion but one that he had to at least check out. He quickly steered the conversation to more familiar ground, stories of cardsharps and techniques that he had actually witnessed. His tap dance slowly gained an audience—the mobsters were interested in what he had

A covert Kansas City card game.

to say—and then the bubble burst. Turning his gaze towards Miller, but directing his question towards Vernon, one asked, "What's the fat boy do?"

Vernon looked at Miller, and Miller responded.

"I'm a dice man!"

The words were right, but, whether it was his age, inexperience, or fear of imminent danger, the timber of his voice pierced the air. He delivered each syllable like he had just sucked the gas out of a helium balloon.

All eyes darted back to Vernon. The improvisation continued.

Vernon gave a private glance back to the mob, raised his right hand towards his head, and made a series of short circular gestures with his index finger, gestures that informed the group that Miller was slightly crazed. Even this hardened group recognized from the nod that punctuated Vernon's visual sentence that some questions were better left unanswered. Vernon, however, thanked them for their time. He and Miller made a hasty retreat.

Miller was despondent. He had failed the test. He felt unfit to continue the quest, and decided to return to El Paso. Vernon did not dissuade him. Besides, it was also time for Vernon to return home.

Centers and Secrets

He had made little headway, was low on funds, and had a wife and child to see, if not support, in Wichita.

To raise money he turned his favorite trick, using his shears to transform pieces of black paper into perfect silhouettes, and resumed operations at the Innes Department Store, cutting silhouettes of the citizens of Wichita. It was three weeks before his wealth and the weather would permit him to return to Kansas City. This time, however, he would make the two hundred mile trek in style. He rented an expensive automobile—a Buick—one befitting a high-seas high roller on an inland excursion, and headed back to the K.C. Card Company to speak with Red Langworthy once more. As Langworthy was unavailable, Vernon turned to his associates.

Vernon was as proficient and as knowledgeable as anyone they had ever met, and when he pulled out his prized possession, the sterling silver faro box he had acquired from Jim Whitley in Miami Beach the previous year, even the most seasoned salesmen took notice. Vernon struck up a more intimate conversation with one counterman, H. B. Lee, known affectionately as Old Man Lee. Although Lee was in charge of dice, he had been around long enough to know about the game of faro and the place its eminent practitioners held in the hierarchy of cheats. Sensing that he had struck an empathetic chord, Vernon probed him for information—any information—he might have about a man who could deal from the center of the deck.

Lee said, "Think I know the only man in the world who can do this. He'll let you cut and replace, or even triple cut 'em, yet any time he wants, out they come."

Vernon kept a poker face. It was his first major break, and he needed to raise the stakes slowly to keep Lee in the game. Lee chipped in with some additional information: the man did not live in Kansas City. He lived some distance out of town. "Perhaps," Lee suggested, "you could phone him, long distance, or send him a wire."

Vernon laid his cards on the table. He needed more information. What was the man's name? Where did he live?

Lee reluctantly acquiesced. He wrote down the name, Allen Kennedy, and the town, Pleasant Hill. He had, however, no idea of the address. Vernon stayed the night in Kansas City and headed for Pleasant Hill the next morning.

Pleasant Hill was a small farming community located twenty-five miles southeast of Kansas City. Known for the endless fields of corn that seemed to stretch from horizon to horizon, the farmers of Pleasant Hill also raised cattle, hens, and hogs for the slaughterhouses in Kansas City. And, like the mirage that was middle-American values, Pleasant Hill had its own underbelly of corruption and vice. It was, in many ways, a farm system for advantage players hoping to jump to the big leagues, larger fields of green baize, in the big city to the north. Again, like Kansas City, its citizens were accustomed to running a tight ship. They kept their business—however unsavory—to themselves. The populace was highly suspicious of outsiders, particularly those who drove expensive cars. Their skittishness was accentuated by a current crisis, one that gripped the nation, and one to which Vernon, his head in the clouds, obsessed with finding a man who could deal to perfection, seemed completely unaware.

The infant son of Charles Lindbergh had been kidnapped on March 1, 1932, from his upstairs bedroom in the family's estate. Although the kidnapping took place in New Jersey, the nation was convulsed with the news, and newspapers across the country alerted their readership to be on the lookout for suspicious cars and people. When Vernon arrived in an expensive car and started to ask questions of its citizenry, town folk weren't sure whether he was a gangster or a member of the F.B.I.

> *When I arrived in this little town, my troubles had only started. Everyone told me something different, [I] met several who knew him as "Bill," but no one seemed to know where he lived. My first ray of hope was when someone told me he lived above a certain grocery store. The place was deserted and unoccupied. Next, I heard he lived behind a print shop. Again a false lead. Then I stopped a wise looking fellow on the street, and asked him if he knew anything. He replied, "If you did find him it wouldn't do you any good as he never talks to anyone." Then, "I'm curious to know what you want him for, what does that guy do anyway, some times you see him driving a taxi, and the next day he's a printer or an automobile mechanic?" So then I went to work on the garages where many knew him, but—where did he live?"*

Possibilities nearly exhausted, Vernon was on the verge of abandoning the hunt. He remembered, however, how difficult the chase

Centers and Secrets

had been on other occasions. He remembered being on the trail of Ping Pong in French Lick Springs, only to miss him by a week. And although he eventually learned Ping Pong's signature sleight, it wasn't the same as actually spending personal time with the master mechanic. Besides, there was no guarantee he would ever discover the secret of the center deal.

While he pondered his fate, sitting in his car parked across the street from a convenience store, Vernon noticed several small children, aged six to seven, emerging with ice cream cones in hand. One little girl, however, was quite distressed. Her ice cream had toppled from its perch. Vernon motioned for the girl to come and see him. He was prepared to buy her another cone. The girl, warned to shy away from strangers, shunned his invitation. Vernon, sensing her unease, withdrew a quarter from his pocket and tossed it towards the urchin. He motioned for her to pick up the coin and buy another cone. The girl emerged from the store moments later, with cone in hand and a smile drawn on her face. She walked within earshot of Vernon and thanked him for the cone. Vernon nodded and then, by rote, asked her, "You don't happen to know where a Mr. Kennedy lives, do you?"

"Mr. Kennedy lives," she said, extending her finger upward, "in that white house at the top of the hill."

Weeks later, when Vernon relayed this information to Charlie Miller, he wrote, "They say in the Scriptures 'and little child shall lead them,' so it came to pass."

Vernon drove up to the simple frame house, and knocked on the door. A somewhat rustic, rugged looking man wearing a pair of overalls opened the door. Vernon asked him whether his name was Allen Kennedy.

"Yes, I'm Allen Kennedy, what can I do for you?

Vernon recognized from the tone of Kennedy's voice that he was not a welcomed visitor. Kennedy then asked Vernon who had sent him. Vernon concocted a little story to stroke Kennedy's ego and gain admission, a story that he had practiced for the past several weeks. He related the tall tale of being a professional mechanic on the ships, one who had heard Kennedy's name spoken of in reverent tones. He informed Kennedy that he had heard Kennedy was the one man in the world who could deal from the center of the deck. Kennedy took the bait, excited that his reputation had extended East, and invited Vernon into his home. Kennedy turned to

The farm town card artist Allen Kennedy contemplates his next move in this rare photograph, Christmas, 1954.

his wife and said, "Put a deck of cards out on the table and see that everything is cleared away."

Vernon accompanied Kennedy into the dining room. Kennedy pulled up a chair for Vernon at one side of the table and seated himself at the other.

> *The first thing he did was just riffle the cards. He had the "touch," —most good card players seem to have this. He then showed me the three bottom cards of the deck, then asked me to cut. I cut near center, but did not carry the cut. He put the two halves together, and picked up perfectly naturally and dealt out four hands of stud. Before he commenced to deal the "turn" he stopped and remarked, "Did you see anything?" (You doubtless know that the "turn" is the term used to refer to the first round after the first two have been dealt each player. In other words each player has his hole card and one face up, then the dealer makes the turn.)*
>
> *I give you my word that everything looked absolutely natural, and the deal was careless and innocent in appearance. I told him all was O.K. so far. He then said, "Watch, now and tell me if you see anything,"*

Centers and Secrets

dealing the turn and two more rounds. Hard to believe, but the first card that "hit" me was one of the former bottom ones, then on the last round I saw another fall in front of me, and upon turning up my hole card there was the third one. This last was a real thrill as I realized that this was the first one from the center, and I had not even suspected it was there.

Not even suspected it was there!

So it was true. It was possible to achieve perfection. Kennedy was the man who had done it. Kennedy informed Vernon that it had taken him five years to learn the deal, and, to his knowledge, only one other man had ever accomplished the feat, a gambler from Joplin, Missouri, fifty years earlier.

But now Vernon embarked on an even more difficult task; he had to acquire the secret for himself. Unlike many gamblers who have perfected a move and are pleased to show their brethren the inner work simply because there are few who they can confide in and even fewer who appreciate the work involved in mastering something that appears effortless, there was no indication that Kennedy was about to reveal his secret.

Vernon's first inclination was simply to offer up a sum of money. He had sixty dollars with him and was prepared to give all of it to Kennedy. Then, just as he was about to reach for his wallet, he reconsidered. Perhaps there was another way. Kennedy was a full-time advantage player. Perhaps Vernon could show him a move or two from the inventory of sleights, subtleties, and ruses he had collected crisscrossing the country. Surely there must be something Kennedy would like to learn that he could offer him in exchange. Vernon picked up the pack of cards and started running through his own repertoire, tabling moves that he knew Kennedy was unlikely to have seen, but could profit by.

One sleight was the method of dealing seconds that Vernon had learned through correspondence from McGuire and Horowitz. Kennedy did say it was one of the best second deals he had ever seen but only if it could be done without the "see saw," the subtle rocking of the left wrist. Kennedy was right. Vernon agreed the left had must remain perfectly still for the deal to be truly deceptive. Fortunately, Kennedy was interested in another sleight, one of Vernon's own creation, a sleight in which Vernon could deal seconds but with a stud-style take, that is, retaining the top card secretly face down on top of the deck while dealing (turning) the card beneath it face up. Kennedy recognized intuitively there had been nothing in the literature to that effect. The move struck a chord because he was able to achieve a similar effect, but with much greater difficulty, as he dealt cards from the center of the deck. The two men passed the deck back and forth, trading sleights and subtleties like two jazz virtuosos trading riffs in their own private session. Kennedy tipped some of his pet secrets, including how he obtained secret glimpses of key cards before the deal. The secret Vernon wanted, however, still eluded him. Finally, Kennedy opened up. He taught Vernon the secret to the deal. It was a marvel of engineering, one that combined brute strength with the grace and poise of ballet. Vernon would never have believed it was possible unless he had seen it with his own eyes. He also knew that it would take him many months to perfect it. As they parted ways, Vernon showed Kennedy the sterling silver faro box in his car, and Kennedy handed Vernon a scrap of paper that set out his postal address and extended an offer to stay in touch.

As soon as he left the property, Vernon scurried to a post office and sent Miller a postcard that stated simply,

Have just spent the entire afternoon with Allen Kennedy. Kennedy is a man of mystery. HE REALLY DOES IT PERFECTLY. More later. It's a long story.

When Vernon arrived back in Wichita, he immediately set to work, not cutting silhouettes at the Innes Department Store, but on mastering the intricacies of the center deal. His behavior was erratic at the best of times, and now it was positively manic. He would sit and deal cards for hours on end. Jeanne felt abandoned. Even though she had lived and traveled with her husband for years, his weekend excursions had become more frequent and more prolonged. She knew that Vernon always had an eye for the ladies, yet when confronted, Vernon insisted that he did as he said. He had sought out a man who had a sleight that rivaled Dad Stevens' riffle cull as the most difficult sleight in the lexicon. What's more, he did it perfectly. Jeanne thought the story a dubious one at best, so Vernon vowed to introduce her to Kennedy. That way, she could see the wonder with her own eyes. Besides, Vernon thought, it would be a good opportunity for him to ask Kennedy a technical question

Centers and Secrets

that was plaguing his own progress in mastering the deal. Arrangements were made and the family set out for Pleasant Hill. Vernon cautioned both Jeanne and his young son Ted, aged six, that they were not to mention that he was a magician.

Kennedy ushered Vernon and his family into the dining room. Vernon introduced his wife and son to Kennedy and added that both had very sharp eyes. Would Kennedy be kind enough to deal a few centers for their benefit? Kennedy obliged and demonstrated the deal in the manner that had first fooled Vernon, leaving Jeanne as startled as her husband had been on his initial viewing. Kennedy turned to Ted and said, "Son, did you see anything?" Ted said, "I didn't see anything, Mister." Jeanne could not argue with her husband on this issue; Kennedy was extraordinarily gifted at dealing cards, particularly cards from the center of the deck.

Before the family and Kennedy parted ways, Vernon mentioned that his son could handle a deck of cards pretty well for a child of his age. Recognizing his cue, Ted took the deck of cards and performed a simple shuffle sequence that had been taught to him by his father, stacking the deck for a winning hand. Kennedy turned to Vernon and said, "Vernon, I want to congratulate you. You're really bringing that boy up right!"

Jeanne, Ted, and Vernon returned to Wichita.

Back home, Vernon focused all attention on his other family, the kings and queens that resided in his ever-present pack of cards. It was as though Jeanne, having seen the level of perfection possessed by Kennedy, gave her tacit consent to her husband's professed mania. Vernon estimated that it would take him eighteen months of incessant practice to master the deal. Everything—and everyone else—could wait. Downs, who firmly believed that Ross had become his mole in the Inner Circle, was frustrated by the lack of news. He wrote McLaughlin:

> May be Ross is waiting until Vernon goes & will then attempt to write up some of Dais card moves which I think have been over-estimated so far as being of any real value in magic. I told Ross to give me the low-down on Vernon's card stuff. (Never mind coins as I'm not interested in coins.) They were going to K.C. + I have a hunch they were in K.C. about Fri. Sat + Sunday last. I'm writing Violet now to find out + told him to give me details of anything he saw Vernon do. Eddie McGuire is nuts to hear of what Vernon has got new but as I

say Ross closed up like a clam all of a sudden. I told Ross to just give me the dry bones on Vernons gags if he had anything really new + no romancing + not a d--- word since in over 2 wks.

Ross did write McLaughlin, however, to bring him up to speed on Vernon's latest exploits: the Mexican gambler in the county jail, the revelation that someone could deal from the center of the deck, Vernon's wild enthusiasm and dogged determination, and his ultimate discovery of the man and the work.

Dai said that he had to show him almost everything he knew before the fellow would talk. Finally he did and Dai got the lowdown. That was nearly four months ago and since then he's been practicing on it constantly but thinks it will take until next fall to perfect it. He's nuts, like Tommy, on the gambling stuff and you'd be amazed how much he knows & can do in this line.

Downs wanted to see Vernon. The International Magic Circle, a newly formed magic society, spearheaded by the young, brash, barnstorming illusionist Harry Blackstone, was holding its annual conclave at the end of May in Kalamazoo, Michigan and had asked Downs to appear on the program. Downs had also been invited to perform at Durbin's International Brotherhood of Magicians annual convention to be held the following weekend in Kenton, Ohio. Although he hated the schedule of performances, confiding to friends that once he was considered "an artist" but now he was a mere laborer, Downs agreed to perform at the conventions—it would give Vernon and Ross an opportunity to join him both prior to and during the conferences. Downs made room reservations, one for himself and McLaughlin, the other for Ross and Vernon, so that they would not have to sleep in a car. Ross responded to the invitation positively, even though his enthusiasm for magic had waned slightly, a casualty from Vernon's constant barrage of card tricks. Ross also reassured McLaughlin,

Yep, I'm sure that Dai and I will be on hand as per schedule. Dai is all enthusiastic about the proposed trip and talks regarding it constantly. He's never been to one of these things and thinks he'll have a great time. He drove over to Kansas City yesterday to line up a new spot for the silhouettes. He wants to work for a couple of months to make

Centers and Secrets

enough to defray his expenses to the convention. As it is, he's been loafing except practicing with the pack.

I rather think Dai will show the boys a few things. In particular he has several items that will fool the wisest. I'm still worrying about his "spread" which is something like Merlin's but far superior. It's the nearest approach to real magic with cards that I've ever seen. I told him that I didn't want him ever to explain it as I preferred to worry about it. Dai has shown me a lot of stuff not only with cards but with many other things—more than I ever dreamed existed. You may be sure he will be glad to show you many items of interest.

By mid-May, however, Downs was starting to doubt whether or not he would have the opportunity to see Vernon and learn his secrets. Ross informed Downs that Vernon's new silhouette shop wasn't as profitable as anticipated, and that, with his wife expecting a new addition to the family in August, Vernon had to take things a little slower. Downs wrote McLaughlin.

Ross talks like Vernon may "Flop" on us! There you are! As a whole the magicians are positively the most irresponsible bunch on earth...If Ross & Vernon both "Flop" on us we will make the trip regardless—wont we & we wont be over-crowded.

On May 21st, one week prior to the convention, Ross sent Downs a Western Union Telegram.

Regret greatly we cannot make trip as Mrs. Vernon is ill and Dai is afraid to leave stop cannot come alone as my car is in bad shape stop Dai greatly disappointed and so am I but circumstances make it impossible stop good luck and let us hear. F.W. Ross

Ross sent McLaughlin a more telling portrait.

Guess you've heard news now that we won't be able to join you. Believe me that we wanted to go and we've discussed the thing from all angles. Here's the low down. Dai's wife Jeanne is not feeling well as she is to have a baby in a couple of months. She's all nervous and raises the divine when Dai leaves her for over a few hours. Her hospital expenses will cost several hundred dollars and confidentially

209

Dai hasn't that much at present. You know how he is—lives one day at a time & never looks ahead. However his wife did say if he would open a store here and raise a hundred dollars he could go. He opened but biz has been terrible despite the fact that we both worked to put it over. Jeanne simply refused to let him touch their savings and you can't blame her. Dai might raise some money working at the conventions but he wouldn't do it. He simply won't work when magicians are around. I secretly wired Tommy to send him a note suggesting this but it did no good. Did all I could to change his wife's mind but no luck. Believe me when I say that I've pulled every possible string. It's a damned shame but it can't be helped. There's no one to blame just circumstances.

Jeanne had every justification for trying to curtail her husband's excursions. Not only was she completing the second trimester of a difficult pregnancy, but she also feared that her husband would abandon her, leaving her stranded in the Midwest with a young child, a baby on the way, and no means of support. Vernon could be very stubborn and insensitive to the needs of others, two hallmarks, unfortunately, of many great artists. Vernon's insensitivity to Jeanne reached a new low when she vetoed another side trip, one that Vernon wanted to take with Ross.

Ross had recently obtained employment in the promotions department of an interstate bus company. His job was to perform magic in the bus terminals of neighboring communities, using the goodwill created by his show—and the magic tricks that he exposed and distributed to children—as a means to build brand loyalty for his employer.

Vernon thought it would be fun to tag along for a three-day excursion. Vernon and Jeanne had a heated argument with Ross present. Although Jeanne emerged victorious and Vernon agreed to stay, he decided to torment her.

"Look at me," Vernon said to Ross. "You notice I'm wearing pajamas. Well, the minute you walk through that door I'm going to bed and I'm going to stay in bed twenty-four hours a day until you return."

Ross said, "You mean you're going to sleep?"

Vernon replied, "Whether you know it or not, I can go to sleep for any length of time I decide."

Jeanne seconded his remarks. "Yes, he does have a remarkable faculty for sleeping for long stretches."

It sounded just too crazy to be true, but when Ross returned in the evening three days later, he made a beeline for the Vernon apartment. Jeanne greeted him with a puzzled look on her face and said, "He's asleep in bed. I've watched him very carefully, but I honestly believe that he's been asleep day and night for the past three days."

Ross asked, "You mean he hasn't been up at all—hasn't eaten or drunk anything?"

Jeanne said, "I've watched the supply of groceries very carefully and I know he hasn't touched them. I haven't seen him even so much as go to the bathroom."

"Well, maybe," Ross suggested, "he slipped out of the apartment while you were asleep."

"He couldn't possibly do it," she replied. "I've kept the front and back doors locked and hidden the keys."

Ross entered the bedroom, spied Vernon snoring away peacefully, and then shook him with considerable force. Vernon opened his eyes, somewhat startled, and gazed at Ross.

"Haven't you started yet?" he asked

Ross replied, "Yes, I've been gone three days and just returned."

"Well," Vernon said, "Maybe it's time for me to get up."

Dumfounded, Ross stood there while Vernon rose from the bed, dressed, and then immediately launched into series of card tricks. Jeanne was equally perplexed. Surely it was not possible for someone to sleep at will for three consecutive days. Like a "locked-room" mystery, there had to a reasonable explanation. Vernon said nothing, however, to betray the illusion.

Vernon still wanted to meet Downs and McLaughlin. Ross suggested that the two magicians shorten their own trip to the conventions in order to spend time with Vernon in Wichita. He advised McLaughlin,

> *I hardly need tell you Dai has everything. All the exclusive stuff of Finley, Leipzig, Dr. Kaldah, etc., etc. If you make it, I'll promise that you'll get it all. We'll have all night sessions and a real exclusive convention of our own with no punks around to bother us. You'll learn more of the "inside" stuff than you would at a thousand conventions. We'll have plenty of liquor and can raise all the hell we want without being bothered.*

> *At present Dai is in close touch with Finley & Horowitz and is getting all their latest stuff by letter. He has some close up stuff with silver & copper coins that would be worth the trip alone. Also the lowdown on the mental tests of Dr. Kaldah that is absolutely unknown & something you could stun the boys with. All of Leipzig's close up stuff that he used in the night clubs. Gee, there's no limit it. There are hundreds of things that will be new to you and Dai will break his neck to slip it to you fellows. I'm not exaggerating he really has it.*
>
> *Now let me know what you think of this and if you can do it will get busy getting all the dope together. Just cut the convention short and dash down.*

Vernon wanted to show Downs the center deal. Although he wanted to keep the information within a very tight circle, Downs was one of the few people who could appreciate the utility and beauty of the sleight. One of the others was Sam Horowitz. Vernon wrote Horowitz on June 1, 1932.

> *As soon as Jeanne has her Kodak fixed I'll have her take some pictures of the Centre Deal. The Finest Thing I Know. It would be utterly impossible to describe, without some photographs of the two essential positions and especially the "key" as Walter would say. If a sharper were to master this deal he'd never need anything else, to always get the money, of course provided that he played where the deck went around. This thing is far far too good to let out to any magis—even if they knew all the details I doubt if any of them would ever give it the practice required. Miller just about has the "dope" on everything and what is most remarkable he works out nearly everything himself. However I have sent him no information on the centre deal and he is "killing himself" I feel sure trying to fathom it. I'm going to put him to a few tests before I show him certain things. I've been foolish before on occasions so this time I'll be overly "cagey." However Sam do not misunderstand me. Miller is a friend of mine now and I like him very much and admire his ability. I have shown Ross a great many things but although I see him every day and night or nearly so, I have never once let him catch me practicing the center deal.*

Downs had no intention, however, of making the trip to see Ross and Vernon. No, Vernon would have to come to visit him. Despite

Centers and Secrets

their difference in age and education, they shared certain traits. Both were extremely confident in their own abilities. Although he was obsessed with obtaining Vernon's secrets, Downs still regarded Vernon as the student and himself as the master.

By June, with the silhouette shop barely holding its own, and no other economic opportunity on the horizon, Vernon decided to return to Colorado Springs, where he had enjoyed some measure of prosperity the year before. It would also give him the opportunity to spend time with Paul Fox. Ross, sensing that Vernon could quite likely be gone for several years, implored McLaughlin once again to make the trip to Wichita.

If you are interested in the linking rings, Dai has some wonderful things with them...In two weeks Dai leaves for Colorado and next spring goes to California. So you probably won't get the chance to see him again for several years. Therefore don't fail to make the trip.

P.S. If possible try to get here by a week from tomorrow (Sunday) Dai won't be working and he'll spend all his time with you & Tommy. Everything is all set for the big session and be prepared to learn a lot. You can make the whole trip in 4 or 5 days.

McLaughlin and Downs failed to appear. By mid June, with Jeanne seven months pregnant, Vernon headed with his family for Colorado Springs. Although Downs feigned disinterest, he pressed Ross for a portrait of Vernon. Ross described Vernon and his peripatetic interests in a letter.

Dai worked about two months at the store then loafed for over a month and finally the last month he opened up a shop of his own but didn't do so well although he made a living out of it. Confidentially, the trouble was that he met the checker champion of Kansas and spent most of his time during business hours playing checkers or else playing pool with me. He's a funny guy. For example, he'd spend a lot of time in the rear part of the store practicing walking on his hands or balancing himself on a chair.

Also if he likes you there's nothing he won't do for you. He was always wanting to buy me something or lend me money. On the other hand if he doesn't like you it's too bad. I think he disliked Carter

Harrison more than I did and consequently he refused to do a single trick for him while he was there. He wouldn't even go to the door when Harrison knocked. So far I don't think he saw Harrison over eight times altogether in five months and then it was only to say hello. He'd been living in Harrison's place nearly six weeks before Harrison even knew he was there.

On the other hand he liked Loring Campbell very much and for weeks we were together almost every night. However he never showed Campbell anything as Campbell knows nothing & apparently cares nothing about the subtle stuff.

Dai thinks Malini is the greatest of them all and says if he could do what Malini does he'd forget all he ever knew. Hence he refers to Malini's close-up stuff and not his regular show. Says he's dogged Malini's footsteps for years but that he could never get Malini to open up. He thinks that Larry Gray is the greatest entertainer with a deck of cards although he isn't so skillful but is a real showman.

Damned shame you missed Vernon. You'd been crazy about the gambling stuff he does—a lot of new ideas—and he would have been glad to have shown you the works. He lives with a pack in his hand and does nothing but practice & experiment. Besides that he's a real guy.

If Ross had any notion that Vernon was out of his life, he was mistaken. Vernon enjoyed Ross's company and he encouraged Ross to join him in Colorado Springs. He sent Ross several postcards, each one enticing him with more riches. Paul Fox, Vernon informed him, had several new ideas that he would be willing to share. Vernon also promised to puzzle him with a few new moves, exclusive material that he failed to tip to him in Wichita. As the man in the middle, Ross was also invited by Downs to visit Marshalltown. Ross postponed that trip, informing Downs that he first must visit Vernon in

In Colorado Springs, Vernon holds his newborn son Derek.

Centers and Secrets

Colorado Springs. He promised, however, "to get Dai's permission to show you [Downs] some things that, at present, I'm not a liberty to divulge." Ross gave a report on his return.

> *Just got back last night from a two-week sojourn in Colorado. Spent ten days in Colorado Springs with Dai Vernon. He turned over a bed to me and I had a great time. Dai's wife, Jeanne, gave birth to a seven-pound boy last Monday night at nine o'clock. Both okay. We took her over to the hospital about seven thirty that night. She had the baby without anesthetics and an hour afterwards she was talking a blue streak and smoking a cigarette. The kid has very long fingers and Dai thinks he'll be a great magician.*

The boy was born August 14, the day after Jeanne celebrated her own thirtieth birthday. Both Jeanne and Vernon, given their nomadic lifestyle, were thankful it was a boy. Although the labor was taxing, the selection of his name was not nearly as traumatic as it had been with Ted. Ross suggested that the boy be named after the great Austrian magician Johann Nepomuk Hofzinser. Vernon said that he did not want to saddle the boy with a name like Johann. The parents quickly agreed on another name: David Derek Wingfield Verner. Vernon and Ross, however, soon took to calling the boy "Neepie"—short for Nepomuk. The new arrival did little, however, to disturb Vernon's pattern of behavior. Ross reported to Downs that Vernon still wanted to arrange a meeting and give him the low down on the center deal. Also, Vernon was still obsessed with checkers and harbored the ambition of becoming a great player. Vernon paid little attention to his family, and only then when it was connected to his magic. Vernon was appalled, for example, when Jeanne sewed two of his egg bags, bright red little cloth bags used to make eggs appear and disappear, to a belt as part of a native American costume for Ted, who wanted to play the Indian in a game of Cowboys and Indians with the other children.

While Paul Fox enjoyed a certain prosperity performing in Colorado Springs, charging twenty-five to thirty-five dollars per engagement, Vernon was content to practice two things: his technique and checkers. The few shows that he did undertake were given without financial consideration. When Franklin Roosevelt, for example, was touring Colorado, Vernon had the opportunity to perform for the presidential candidate first hand.

Roosevelt's silhouette cut by Vernon in Colorado Springs in 1932.

Just before Roosevelt was elected, he appeared on crutches and a cane at the Broadmoor hotel to make a speech in Colorado Springs. Paul Fox and I had the pleasure of entertaining him. He was under the weather from speech making and did not stay long, but we did tricks for Eleanor and Elliott. A few days later, a local lawyer, [Chet Horn] asked me if I would make a silhouette of the President. I went over to the hotel, the President posed, I cut two, he was still posing and I decided to make more—and have him autograph them. Somebody behind me was saying, "Be careful, he has a beautiful aquiline nose." I was getting annoyed and was just about to turn around to say, "Madam, you make the nose I'll make the rest of him." I felt a kick on the side of my leg and a fellow whispered in my ear; I glanced around and there was Eleanor behind me.

Vernon gave two to Roosevelt, one to Fox, one to Horn, and kept several himself, one of which was autographed.

Always an apologetic correspondent, Vernon used his time in Colorado to catch up on his letter writing and broker the exchange

Centers and Secrets

of words and ideas between members of the Inner Circle, a group that now included Charles Miller. Vernon received several letters from Cardini, Horowitz, Baker, and Miller. He introduced Miller to Horowitz, Baker, Finley, and Sprong. He also took time to write up the details of the center deal and forward the information to both Downs and Miller. Both men, no strangers to the rigors of practice, became obsessed with mastering the intricacies of the sleight.

In October, with his friend Cardini setting sail for a four-week engagement in England and a tour of France, Vernon left Colorado Springs to cut silhouettes at the Denver Dry Goods Store. He had planned to stay there until Christmas and then head for Miami and, possibly, Cuba. While in Denver, Vernon received several tricks from Horowitz, including "Duo Flight." Vernon indicated in a postcard to Horowitz that he was contemplating releasing some of his own pet secrets. It was the only way, he wrote, to stay a few jumps ahead of "the 'boys' who try to make a few pennies or win a little credit with the ideas of others."

This willingness to release more detailed secrets of his craft to the magic fraternity represented a major shift in his thinking. Vernon had always been reluctant to part with his secrets. He had never written or sold anything in the way of magic. Even the booklet *Secrets* was written and sold by others. Vernon respected the power of the imagination. He remembered how disappointed he had been as a boy when the illustrators of children's books failed to render the story in the vivid manner he had painted in his own mind. That acute sense of disappointment was rekindled when he heard Charlie Chaplin, the silent screen movie star, speak for the first time. Vernon was not alone. Many were surprised that Chaplin talked like a great many other people—not particularly well. He was an ordinary person. Vernon was afraid that he would suffer the same fate. The publication of his secrets would puncture the mystique. But, with the economy in a funk, two children to support, and magic dealers like Frank Lane selling secrets attributed to Annemann for fifty dollars, perhaps it was time to cash in. Besides, he thought, many of his sleights, dodges, and routines were already percolating through the magic community without credit. Vernon decided that he would approach Frank Pickard in Miami, the man to whom he sold the right to reprint *Secrets*, with the idea of releasing a manuscript of new material.

Vernon set off for Miami earlier than expected, as business

was dry in the Denver Dry Goods Store. Ross, when informed of Vernon's plans, suggested that he stop in Kansas City en route. Ross wanted to throw a party on his behalf. Vernon accepted the invitation and, while visiting Ross, confided that he was thinking of releasing some of his secrets in manuscript form. Ross suggested Vernon not wait until he reached Miami; Ross could help him write, print, and distribute the manuscript then and there.

By early November, Ross and Vernon had culled ten items from Vernon's oeuvre, all involving cards. They included, among other things, a blindfold poker deal, a psychological gambit that appeared to be direct mind reading, the vanish and recovery of a playing card (which Max Holden had nominated as the best trick of 1926), and a miracle card location in which the performer handed the chosen card to the spectator after the spectator, while out of the room, selected it and shuffled it back into his own deck. They had planned on selling twelve copies, with each illustration drawn and hand colored by Vernon, to a discrete and wealthy clientele. They also proposed selling each copy for twenty dollars. Downs thought they were crazy. "Fellows, do you realize there is a Depression? You couldn't sell a manuscript for twenty dollars. Millionaires are selling apples on Wall Street."

Instead of advertising the manuscript in the trade journals, Ross and Vernon planned to capitalize on the established trade route for private manuscripts. They obtained a list of potential purchasers from Eddie McLaughlin and circulated to each name on the list a four-page document that described each effect—"A Prospectus of the Dai W. Vernon Super Card Subtleties"—and was written, as was the manuscript itself, by Ross. Ross set out the terms and conditions for the sale of the manuscript in the document's "Foreword."

> *If the ten most competent magic critics in America were asked to name the greatest living card expert their choice would undoubtedly be that of Dai W. Vernon of New York City.*
>
> *It is a positive fact that Mr. Vernon's work has completely dumfounded all the best informed card men of both America and Europe that have been privileged to witness it. The reason is simply that Mr. Vernon's finest conceptions are based on essentially new and revolutionary principles of his own originations and have been guarded by him with religious secrecy.*

Centers and Secrets

Two pages from Vernon's Ten Card Problems, *which came to be known as the "Twenty Dollar Manuscript."*

Therefore, the announcement that Mr. Vernon has at last consented to release his ten best card problems for a nominal sum should come as something of a genuine sensation to lovers of super magic.

A few things to remember:

1. These ten effects are the ones that Mr. Vernon sincerely considers to be his best and will prove a genuine revelation regardless of how much you may know about card magic.
2. They are dependent on sheer subtlety rather than skill and there is nothing included that does not come within the scope of your own ability.
3. This offer is being made known to less than fifty reputable men in magic and consequently will not be advertised in magazines etc. The sale will positively be restricted to twelve buyers and these in as widely distributed portions of the country as possible. This to eliminate "swapping" and to prevent them from becoming commonplace.

4. Every effect is fully described with drawings and many suggestions and additional ideas are included.

5. The price of the entire collection is twenty dollars in the form of certified check or money order and none of the items will be sold separately.

6. Orders may be sent directly to Dai W. Vernon, 1115 Munnell St., Wichita, Ks.

On November 21st, the duo sent the prospectus, along with a cover letter signed personally by Vernon, to fifty potential purchasers. Vernon's cover letter read,

> Dear Sir:
>
> Knowing that you are interested in subtle and exclusive card problems I feel certain that the following will be of genuine interest to you.
>
> Countless times in the past I have been offered various inducements to part with some of my original card effects. These offers I have always steadfastly refused.
>
> However, now for certain reasons, I have at last decided to release my ten favorite and most closely guarded effects.
>
> These have been carefully incorporated into attractive manuscript form by my good friend Mr. F.W. Ross, a highly competent writer of wide experience.
>
> Mr. Ross has spent many months preparing this material under my personal supervision and I must say it has been admirably done.
>
> Enclosed is a carefully written prospectus of the ten effects that I offer you. In this every effort has been made to eliminate exaggeration and misrepresentation.
>
> The price of the collection complete is twenty dollars.
>
> You undoubtedly know the intrinsic worth of exclusive material sufficiently to realize that this constitutes a genuine value.

Centers and Secrets

Very truly yours,

Dai W. Vernon

The response was terrific; Vernon received $400 in the first week. Forty percent of their list—twenty people—responded to the initial offer. How, however, could he satisfy demand when the prospectus stated that the sale would be restricted to twelve buyers? The solution, Vernon and Ross decided, was to only number and autograph the first twelve. Ross' girlfriend, Marjorie Shockley, worked off-hours to type up the manuscript, cut the stencils, and mimeograph copies at her place of employment, the Brown Crummer Investment Company. She ran off twenty copies. Vernon then numbered, autographed, and hand-colored the illustrations in the first twelve. The remaining copies were sent to subscribers as is. Although they may have fudged the numbering, they did keep one promise. They did not advertise the existence of this manuscript, now called *Ten Card Problems*, to the general magic community.

R.W. Hull, the amateur magician from Crooksville, Ohio who had profited by selling Vernon's approach to magic in *Hull's Mental Discernment* two years earlier, was, not surprisingly, the first person to send in his money order. Downs and McLaughlin, who expected complimentary copies from their friend Ross, were surprised to learn that Ross, the writer, did not even own a copy. As he explained to Downs in a letter dated January 8, 1933,

> *Dai and family is still here but silhouette biz practically nil. Confidentially the only thing that saved his life was the sale of the manuscript which amounted to over $400.00 and a few orders still drifting in.*

> *Now T. Nelson, here's the truth. I don't have a copy of that manuscript. Dai has acted peculiar as hell about the whole thing. He's made up his mind not to pass out any complimentary copies to anyone. I know for a fact that he hasn't done so. His best friends such as Horowitz, [Finley] etc. did not receive a copy although they asked for one. My girl ran off twenty of them and Dai took immediate possession of original copy, stencil and the mimeographed copies. He said weeks ago that he was going to give me an autographed copy but*

> to date he hasn't done so. Of course I know what's in it – I wrote the thing and to ease your mind let me say that there are only two real items—the poker trick and the card location using the old deck and getting a natural break by pressure. I slipped you both of these while in Marshalltown. Four other items are old stuff and these others use prearranged setups and are all served gas. However, when I feel half way decent I'll write up these three things but will bet you won't even read 'em. Dai's best stuff is the gambling sleights and gags & the best of this is the center deal. None of this material was explained in the mss.

Vernon did give away two copies, but not for free. He traded one copy for twenty dollars worth of merchandise to Floyd Thayer, the West Coast craftsman who specialized in manufacturing props, particularly those turned out of wood, for discerning magicians. Vernon acquired a set of wooden billiard balls and some silk handkerchiefs. He was contemplating developing a stage act. A second copy was given to Julian Proskauer, a prominent amateur magician but printer by trade who had a business relationship with Royal Heath, the business manager for *The Sphinx*. In return, Proskauer arranged a full page of free advertising in the magazine. The advertisement that appeared in the December 1932 issue made no mention of *Ten Card Problems*. It announced instead the immediate release of "five choice and original impromptu problems that had hitherto been reserved for Vernon's own personal use." There was no mention or description, however, of what those choice and impromptu problems might be. Vernon and Ross had no idea themselves. They just recognized that the opportunity for a free full-page ad in *The Sphinx* was too good to pass up. So Ross used the tools he had acquired from the advertising trade and drafted copy that capitalized on Vernon's mystique.

> *Contrary to usual advertising practice a specific description of this offering will not be made. However, it is felt that Mr. Vernon's reputation as an originator of subtle and exclusive magic is sufficient guarantee that prospective purchasers will receive full value and satisfaction.*

The ad also stated that the collection was offered in the form of a carefully written and illustrated manuscript, and included "those little details so essential to flawless execution." The cost was three dollars, "a mere fraction of their real worth to the individual seeking magic of quality and distinction." For all of Vernon's concerns about losing the mystique associated with his name, few orders trickled in, surprising given the success of their previous effort. Perhaps they had alienated some of their clientele by advertising a second manuscript so soon after releasing the first. Although demand was negligible, Vernon and Ross still had to write, illustrate, mimeograph, and distribute the manuscript as advertised.

Five Close-Up Problems described several novel tricks and techniques including "Follow The Leader," a feat inspired by a trick of Hofzinser's described in a letter by Ottokar Fischer of Vienna to Downs; "Short Change With Long Green," a routine inspired by the short-change artist Slip The Jit Harry and his ilk; and "A Perfect Coin Vanish," a reengineering of a sleight by T. J. Crawford, one that enabled the performer to vanish a coin in a perfectly "natural" manner. Once again, Marjorie Shockley was pressed into service. Vernon kept a tight reign on distribution; those expecting a complimentary copy, including Ross, were again disappointed. Although advertised to the magic community, *Five Close-Up Problems* was not reviewed in *The Sphinx*, most likely because Vernon did not send a complimentary copy to the staff reviewer, Milton Bridges.

Vernon tried to placate Horowitz.

> *Before long I hope to send you a copy of the twenty-dollar manuscript also the "Five Problems" as advertised in the December Sphinx. Only had fifteen of the first mimeographed and sold all so shall have to have one or two more made up, as I promised Doc Peck one. He sent his check for twenty but I of course mailed it back to him.*

> *Perhaps you will be surprised to learn that I have received many very long letters from Warren J. Keene [Keane]. Let the "boys" forget about him—keep him under cover as it were—because he has some of the prettiest things I've ever heard of in magic. This boy is in much deeper than I ever dreamed but he absolutely refuses to hob nob with the magical fraternity. Please don't tell any of the fellows that I correspond with him. You may see him in Vaudeville again shortly.*

> *I am very anxious to hear from you after you have attempted the center deal. Letter from Tommy Downs saying he is sending it to you.*

> *Had wanted you to keep the letters but he seems very anxious to hang onto them. He has apparently no conception whatsoever of the true method although he attempts to do it after his own ideas. I'll tell you some funny things about his when I see you. I would give anything if you could only see Kennedy the user of this deal "in action." Perfect. Jeanne could not detect it either—also his peek was perfectly covered from all angles.*

> *Sam please do not get the idea I am going to part with any good stuff. My reason was that some of these things were already being told on the Q.T. and others about to be. I have things now that money could not buy. I have an original color change I would sell for $100.00. It is perfect as far as natural goes.*

On February 13, Vernon finally forwarded copies of both manuscripts—in duplicate—to Horowitz. He instructed Horowitz to pass on one set of each manuscript to McGuire, to whom he was still grateful for sharing the *Phantom of the Card Table*, even though Downs had confirmed his suspicions that the session that introduced the work of Walter Scott to the New York Inner Circle was a sham.

> *Downs claims that the whole thing was his idea to fool the "New York crowd"—he met Scott the year before, Ross also, and told him to mark up some cards, also "punch" a few and then go with Eddie to N.Y. and fool the boys. Downs then told him that all the inner circle would tip off all the good stuff to Eddie. In turn he was to pass it on to Tommy.*

Vernon's newfound success certainly did not change his routine. Ross wrote McLaughlin,

> *Recently read a letter that Dai's wife wrote Marjorie. From it I gather that she and Dai have been scrapping constantly—don't think he's been getting in before five or six in the morning and has been gambling. He just can't seem to stand a little prosperity.*

Even Ross was beginning to tire of the routine. He wrote Downs,

> *Dai still here but hasn't tried to do a lick of work for three months—*

Centers and Secrets

still living off receipts of the mss. However he's down to his last fifty so he's going to have to do something soon.

Wish you were down here at that as you'd have a good time. This guy Dai stays up all night doping out new trix and sleeps all day. He shows me all kinds of stuff but, honest to goodness, I pay no attention to it. No kidding, I'm completely fed up on magic. The mention of it sickens me. I just get up & do a few bum tricks, give the railroads hell and draw my paycheck—sometimes! Ultimately I hope to become the publicity director of the company and chances look rosy—if the concern doesn't go broke like everything else. After that, the magic can go to h-ll. Of course I can never hope to rid myself completely of the curse—but wish I could.

Ross wasn't the only magician with more pressing concerns. Rank and file magicians everywhere were up in arms. The R.J. Reynolds Tobacco Company had just initiated a national advertising campaign that placed beautifully illustrated magic tricks and their secrets, drawn by Paul Carlton, former magic shop demonstrator and now graphic artist, in over 1,200 newspapers across America. The tricks also appeared in leading national magazines, including *The Saturday Evening Post, Literary Digest, Fortune, Colliers, Liberty, Billboard, American Magazine,* and *The New Yorker*—all to promote Camel Cigarettes. The campaign, "It's Fun To Be Fooled... But It's More Fun To Know," created by William Esty & Company of New York, incensed magicians, and led prominent members of the magical community such as John Mulholland (publisher of *The Sphinx*) and Julian Proskauer to lobby state assemblies to table bills to curtail the gratuitous exposure. W.W. Durbin, President of the International Brotherhood of Magicians tried to mobilize the magic community to strike back. He wrote Downs to enlist his support.

Dear Mr. Downs,

The R. J. Reynolds Tobacco Company of Winston-Salem, N.C. have started a campaign of advertising in which they are exposing magic. We have noticed three of these that have come out lately and there is much dissatisfaction among magicians and followers of magic and the wonder is that the R. J. Reynolds Tobacco Company would pick on magic and magicians to boost their Camel Cigarettes instead of using a more legitimate way.

We feel that all of our members and friends ought to get busy and write to them, setting forth their point of view and show to them that this is unfair to expose the ancient art of magic and that they gain nothing by it. Write a nice gentlemanly letter and complain about this and tell them that you believe they have made a mistake and that they ought not to do it. I feel if we get many protests in to them that they will see that the magic art has many followers and if anything can stop them, this will.

Shall be pleased to hear from you.

Fraternally, W.W. Durbin

Although Downs was obsessed with secrets, at least collecting them, he reprimanded Durbin, and intimated that magicians had only themselves to blame.

I told Durbin in as much as we magicians are ourselves the worst offenders in exposing our trix of trade putting up booths + stores on the streets at our conventions, selling trix promiscuously to the public I would consider it very presumptious on my part to make any suggestions to the Reynold Tob. Co. as to how to run their business.

Downs recognized that the value of secrets fluctuated with the market. The ones that magicians, particularly amateur magicians, cherished were of little value because of their commonality. Magicians were quick to copy any performer, act, or effect under the false notion that success was transferable. Real secrets, ones that were dependent on either the skill or personality of the operator, would continue to remain unavailable or concealed from those who could do the most damage—not the laity who scanned an advertisement that revealed some minor miracle. But amateurs failed to understand the significance, nuance, and power of subtle secrets. That is why, although Vernon joked that "Tommy never gives the boys a chance to forget him," the two titans of sleight-of-hand, Downs past his prime and Vernon entering his, needed to meet. Although they both loved and respected the same craft, only one could truly be king. That meeting of minds and skills finally arrived in April 1933 when Vernon and Ross made the pilgrimage to Marshalltown.

Ross and Vernon checked into the Stoddard Hotel. They then met up with McLaughlin and Downs at Downs' home. As Vernon made the perfunctory tour of Downs' personal scrapbooks, he reiterated his love for Downs' *The Art of Magic*, one of the magic books that had ignited his imagination as a youth. Ross chipped in the news that John Northern Hilliard, Downs' ghostwriter on that tome, was fast at work on another project, a larger book, one that would contain the pet secrets of Leipzig, Horowitz, and others. Hilliard had an "angel" in Minneapolis who was willing to publish it, even if it meant doing so at a loss.

Vernon then performed some of his latest miracles. It was evident to both McLaughlin and Downs, who had last met Vernon in New York six years earlier, that Vernon's work had evolved. Vernon's interests, always esoteric—improvisation, arcane card table artifice, doctored decks and, of course, the center deal—kept his audience off-balance. McLaughlin was completely bamboozled. If Downs, however, was impressed, he didn't let on. As before, Downs nodded all-knowingly and muttered that much of the work was housed in his collection of Jordan material. Vernon did not take the bait. As in his two previous encounters with Downs, he did not offer to explain the modus operandi behind his miracles. The two maintained the tacit game of one-upmanship. Vernon may have had him beat at cards, but when it came to coins, Downs believed he was still the undisputed King. Downs performed his signature piece—the vanishing and recovery of eight large silver coins from his bare hand.

Vernon had seen Downs perform the piece before. It was a masterpiece. Downs displayed a coin at his left fingertips, closed his right fingers into a loosely clenched fist, and then inserted the coin into the opening between his thumb and index finger. He rubbed his fingers slowly against his palm, as if dissolving the coin like a clump of sand in the wind. He then opened his hand and gracefully showed, rotating his hand back and forth, with his sleeves rolled back and his fingers extended perfectly straight after each turn, that the coin had disappeared completely. He repeated this feat with each coin, dissolving each one into the ether in the same mystifying manner. He then reproduced each coin, slowly and mysteriously, taking time between each reproduction to show that his hand was completely empty. McLaughlin, Ross, and Vernon applauded the performance. It was eloquent and haunting. Vernon did not ask that it be explained, and Downs did not offer

It was getting late and Vernon and Ross were preparing to return to the Stoddard Hotel. Downs turned to Vernon and said, "Vernon, are you going to tip some of that card work to me before you leave?"

Vernon replied, "Tommy, I'll make you a trade—you show me the lowdown on the coins on the back of the hand—the gimmick—and I'll show you the card tricks you want to know."

Silence engulfed the room. Downs had built his reputation on being a master of pure sleight–of–hand; the piece that he had just performed was a signature effect. Vernon knew, however, that no one alive could have performed such a dexterous feat without the assistance of some mechanical aid.

Vernon pressed. "Tommy, you must use some kind of gimmick—a horse hair or a clip or something—you can't backpalm as many coins as that so beautifully."

Downs response was unequivocal. "I do this by dexterity—the fingertips. Watch. I'll do it again."

Downs removed the stack of silver coins from his vest pocket and challenged Vernon. "Look," he demanded, "Are those legitimate coins?"

Vernon was silent. McLaughlin and Ross were not sure how to react. Downs had never confided to them that he employed a mechanical aid in the routine.

Downs started to scurry through it once more. It was evident to all, however, that this encore performance lacked the brilliance of the original presentation.

"There you are, do you see a gimmick?"

Vernon piped up, "Well, Tommy, you did that very well, but it wasn't the same effect without the gimmick. There's no use trying to fool me that way. I know you use some kind of gimmick—there's something."

"Damn it, Vernon," Downs exclaimed, "I don't use a gimmick. I'm a sleight-of-hand man."

Vernon stood his ground.

"We're among friends," he said. "I know you use a gimmick, and I merely want to see it."

Downs teetered—his hand moved ever so slightly towards his vest pocket—and then toppled. He had never shown anyone his

Centers and Secrets

little "assistant." His greatest feat was convincing all others that his reputation was based on pure skill. Heartbroken, Downs removed the gimmick from its hiding place and tossed it on the divan. McLaughlin and Ross were in shock. Downs had been deposed.

"Damn it, Vernon," Downs muttered, "I told you I can do it without this."

No one, however, was listening.

Chapter Eight
Midway To Manhattan

"When I play stud poker at the Stoddard Hotel," Downs declared, "I give the sucker a couple of jazzboes back to back and take a pair of cowboys for myself. This deal is the greatest."

As Vernon had predicted, Downs was nutty about the center deal. It was an elixir of youth, a reminder of the type of arduous sleight-of-hand that he once practiced to while away the hours as a railroad telegraph operator in small-town Iowa. Like a budding guitarist who boasts of the calluses that form on the fingers of the fret hand, Downs was ecstatic that he too developed a blister on his second finger—as Vernon had—when he practiced the deal. It was a sure sign that he was on the path toward perfection. Despite his efforts, Downs never grasped the finer points—the subtle stuff—that made the deal work. Vernon did not want to curtail Downs' enjoyment of the process by correcting him. Downs, pleased he was a card man, also discounted the previous session. He wrote McLaughlin the next day.

> I don't think Dai had a thing new to show after you left most of the time was spent looking over my scrap books & library after you left. Aside one or two things I can't remember what Dai really did of practical value in magic in giving a show.

Downs' notion of what constituted "giving a show" was rather antiquated. Traditional vaudeville had crashed along with the market years earlier, and the grand touring shows of yesteryear were finding it increasingly difficult to make ends meet. Howard Thurston had announced his "retirement" from the stage, stating that he was going to concentrate his energies on producing the radio dramatizations of his escapades and pursue the film business with his daughter, Jane. This shift reflected the current state of the market. Few performers could sustain a career with "a turn," a short variety act of eight or ten minutes. Most were forced to hip-hop the country as opening acts for feature films. Amateur magicians, with stars in their eyes, had little idea of how unsatisfying the work could be. Performers traveled great distances and performed numerous shows before unappreciative audiences, which included latecomers who purchased concession items and had trouble finding their seats before the big picture show. As Downs had often moaned, performers were now laborers, not "artists." Those who presented large-scale illusions, "Tall Grass Showmen," were shunted to the hinterlands and focused their efforts on the cities, towns and villages that received little entertainment—of any sort. Still, despite Downs' professed disinterest in Vernon's technique, he could not get enough information about Vernon and his whereabouts. Ross gave him an update.

Yep, Dai still here. All he does nowadays is to practice and invent new things in magic. Think he'll stay here as long as the dough holds out. Ultimately, he hopes to cut silhouettes at the World's Fair in Chicago. Have sort of lost my interest in the subtle stuff although I certainly see & hear about plenty of it. Dai is now framing a new club card act and also a manipulative act with balls, lighted cigarettes, etc. He has stuff with lighted cigs that Cardini would break his neck to get—a fact—but it's all Paul Fuchs [Fox] ideas.

Vernon and Ross also caught up with Cardini on tour. They were scoping out the Century of Progress Exposition, also known as the Chicago World's Fair, as another field that Vernon could hopefully harvest by transforming little black pieces of paper into gold. Cardini had his own woes to report. Ross relayed the information to Downs.

Arrived in Chicago & got in touch with Cardini pronto. He's still doing the old line but has cut down on the cards & balls & works the cigarettes more strongly. Also act looks much smarter & sophisticated. Said he jumped from London to N.Y., played a week

> at Buffalo & then into Chicago. Has a whole scrapbook of European newspaper clippings & I guess he slicked over there. However, he told us confidentially that he did not make any big money. Also said he was all burnt up and the N.Y. home and would like to peddle it. Also says he wants to quit his present act. Sez he has a new one that he's been working on for past three years. I told him point blank that if he cut out the cigarettes he'd never get another week's steady work. To my mind he'd better stick to the old act. Told us that his new act was a talking one and we all know Cardini can't talk. Says he has a chance to go back to Europe in the fall & probably will do so. He's getting very bitter against magical societies & organizations and particularly against his imitators such as LePaul, Pablo, Keith Clark, etc., etc. Admitted, however, that LePaul was a better card manipulator than himself.

Vernon and Ross's reconnaissance mission to the Fair yielded little. They searched for a booth or shop located in a high traffic zone where Vernon could follow past practice, demonstrate his skills for the proprietor, and suggest a split of the proceeds generated by the sale of silhouettes in exchange for unfettered access to the store. The task was more difficult than they had imagined. The Fair was spread out over 427 acres, featured over fifty large-scale buildings, fifty sideshows, as well as theatre performances, movies, sightseeing trips around Chicago, and the opportunity to see professional baseball. There was too much ground to cover, and simply not enough time to pinpoint a suitable location. On the trip back to Wichita, Vernon arranged to cut silhouettes in Burlington, Iowa, the home of Eddie McLaughlin, which gave him time to decide whether to take his chances on the Fair or to head back to Colorado Springs and Paul Fox. Vernon left Wichita at an opportune time. Ross had just been diagnosed as impotent and entered a deep funk. Ross wrote Downs on July 21, 1933.

> Dai & family left here nearly a month ago and as yet I haven't written them a single line although I've heard from them three times. I can't quite figure it out because as you know I used to write a lot of letters and got a real kick out of it. One reason I suppose is that I've almost completely lost interest in the magic art. The more I see of it the more disgusted I get. Also the more magicians I meet the more disgusted I get. I honestly don't believe I'd cross the street to see a magic act.

Midway to Manhattan

Although Vernon arrived in Burlington to cut silhouettes, he spent most of his time discussing magic with McLaughlin, leaving Jeanne and the children to socialize with Martha McLaughlin and the McLaughlin's son, Timmy. Vernon gave McLaughlin copies of both *Ten Card Problems*—an overrun—and *Five Close Up Problems*. He asked McLaughlin to forward both to Downs for his perusal. When Downs finally had the chance to see what all the fuss had been about, he wasn't impressed.

> ...looks like Rosses foreword & description of Vernon's miracles is the best part of Vernon's $20 list. Dai has some very ingenious ideas—but I don't think most of them are of practical use in magic. I mean in giving a magic show—you must have 100% sure fire trix that can't go wrong? Take the first trick his 5 card mental force it's not sure fire and no 2 with the daub? How do we assume the customer has "his own deck of cards"? I noticed Dai had a lot-o-ideas that did not work when he tried em on me—but he said they always worked on the other fellow? Yes—Dai has some very subtle ideas and does some very clever stuff for us magicians but strange to say he could not put over a show on the stage.

That was the crux of the problem. Whereas Vernon was content to take risks and improvise, Downs needed "surefire" material, making Vernon an easy target. The material was high risk; the execution required what Erdnase would describe as "unflinching audacity," a quick wit, and the capacity for management. Downs' milieu had always been the stage; Vernon's was the card table. The stage performer builds an act that runs with precision—like a watch. The performer of intimate magic—subtle stuff, as Ross described it—could be more flexible with both time and material. Unaware that, despite his own misgivings, Downs had added Vernon's blindfold poker deal described in *Ten Card Problems* to his repertoire, Ross tried to bridge the gap. He wrote Downs on July 31, 1933.

> Re: The Vernon Mss. Of course this wasn't worth twenty dollars but you couldn't blame us for selling it for that if we could find enough suckers to pay it. At that there were four good things explained—the rest was mostly filler. The Poker Demonstration and Slow Motion Card Vanish would be worth $20.00 to a real card nut that liked this sort of thing. Yep, Dai Vernon is a good guy—none better—also a real

233

genius in certain respects but he's certainly not a practical performer and don't believe he could ever get up before a thousand people and really entertain them if his life depended on it. Well, magic is just a hobby with him. He enjoys tinkering with little ideas and doesn't profess to be a second Houdini etc so I don't think he should be criticized. At that, he's his own worst enemy. His one great mistake was ever to get married. It's not fair to his family for him to live the way he does. He should be single and have an income like your friend Bert Morey. Then he could spend all his time with a pack of cards and no one would be any the worse off except maybe himself.

At Burlington, Vernon weighed his options and decided to head for the Fair. Although it opened on May 27, there was still plenty of time to establish a silhouette business, as the Fair was scheduled to stay open until November 12. Also, with its dual theme—the celebration of the birth and growth of Chicago and "Science Finds, Industry Applies, Man Conforms," which focused on "the unprecedented discovery, invention and development of things to effect the comfort, convenience, and welfare of mankind"—organizers had sold over two million admission tickets in advance. Expectations were high. The city of Chicago had also booked over 300 conventions during the course of the Fair.

Vernon's journey got off to a rocky start when the car he was driving was rear-ended by a truck. Fortunately, no one was seriously injured, and the trucker admitted liability and paid for the repairs. When Vernon and family eventually arrived in Chicago, Vernon had trouble connecting with a booth. The Fair was too large—eventually attracting over four million visitors—spread out over too much terrain, and there was too much competition. Business was bad wherever he set up. Perhaps it was also because silhouettes were both old-fashioned and expensive—fifty cents for one, two for seventy-five cents and four for a dollar—when compared to other attractions. One fifty-cent general admission ticket, for example, gave the patron access to thousands of exhibitions and displays, many of which showcased the latest developments in science and technology. Fair-goers who could afford to pay for extras seemed to prefer to pay for more sensational attractions such as the provocative dancer Sally Rand and her famous fans. Even the illusionist Charles Carter, who sank thousands of dollars into building a "Temple of Mystery," closed shop early, his magic a pale comparison to the latest scientific wonders like a pioneer demonstration of the principle of television. Max Holden, who proclaimed once again that Vernon was the crowned king of cards—perhaps because he had been informed that Walter Scott had obtained the crown under false pretenses—wrote in *The Linking Ring*, the journal of the International Brotherhood of Magicians, "it seems that the visitors were able to see so much magic of a scientific nature that just plain magic lost its appeal."

Although the Fair was no economic bonanza for Vernon, it did give him the opportunity to meet Frank Toby. Toby, once the sheriff of Dodge City, had a stellar reputation within the gaming world as a manufacturer of "furniture," or gaffed gaming equipment. Vernon was more interested, however, in asking Toby about the game of faro, having heard that Toby was running a bank—a faro operation—in conjunction with an off-track betting establishment at the Fair. How, Vernon wondered, could he contact Toby? Through sheer happenstance, Jeanne provided the answer. She recognized the name.

> *When my wife was a little girl in Sheephead's Bay, Coney Island, it happened that this Frank Toby had his workshop next to where my wife lived with her aunt. This little girl would wander away from her home and, she didn't know it, it was some kind of a shop. She liked the man very much, of course he was an elderly man, his name was Frank Toby. He was over six feet tall and he had a tremendous diamond ring he used to wear. My wife, this little girl, was fascinated with this ring, and he used to tell her stories about the West, you know, and he was always talking about coppers. My wife said she always thought he was talking about pennies. He was talking about police—coppers. He said, "Well, we'll close the shades because the coppers have a way of...you know." He was making gambling furniture for Cannes and Monte Carlo, and in those days (Kid) Canfield's gambling places in New York and Palm Beach. He made the finest furniture that was ever made in this country, I mean as far as gambling. And he also was the only man that ever lived they say that could load a solid ivory ball with a steel center. Solid ivory. They don't know to this day how he did it.*

Jeanne was sure that Toby would make a beeline for her once he heard the news that the little girl from Coney Island was all grown up and at the Fair. She was right. Toby came to call, just as Jeanne had predicted, and the two had a grand time catching up on the past. Toby had been forced to shut down his furniture business in New York after a disgruntled competitor, Arthur Popper, complained to the authorities. Toby was now in Chicago, as Vernon had heard, running a faro game. Vernon had a particular question he wanted to ask Toby. He was interested in how faro dealers could, each and every time, shuffle the cards perfectly, that is alternating the weave one by one so effortlessly to displace any natural splits—pairs of cards—that appeared in a previous round. Toby took Vernon's cards and demonstrated the shuffle. He grasped the deck from above, divided it neatly into two perfect halves, butted the ends together, and then, with a slight flexing of his fingertips on the ends of the deck, caused the cards to bow and then weave perfectly one after the other. He could control the speed of the mesh, fast or slow, the latter being the norm so that each player could satisfy himself with his own eyes that the cards had been shuffled fairly. Toby then taught the technique to Vernon. Vernon's education in the game of faro was now complete.

The Fair was also a source of inspiration for Jeanne. After seeing a display of masks in an exhibition hall, she wondered how they were fabricated and painted. The masks appealed to her artistic sensibilities. Although her days studying art at Cooper Union were long past, she still had the desire to express herself artistically. Mask making seemed an answer. She vowed then and there to learn as much as possible about how to create them. It would be a way of exercising her imagination, a release.

When the Fair ended, Vernon was unsure of his next move. He had received a note from Al Baker, along with a copy of Baker's recently published manuscript *Al Baker's First Book*, and thought that perhaps he and Baker should travel to England. Vernon had longed to meet English magicians. Not surprisingly, Jeanne did not endorse the idea. She wrote Ross's girlfriend Marjorie Shockley, and declared that she would leave her husband for good if he traveled to Europe with Baker. Cooler heads prevailed, however, when she realized that her husband couldn't possibly obtain a passport. Vernon was an illegal alien in the United States and, as he had no formal documentation that declared whether he was an American, Canadian, or British subject, he could not risk leaving the country. So Vernon stayed in Chicago, visited with local magicians, and

Midway to Manhattan

frequented its magic shops—sometimes with humorous results. One afternoon, in one such emporium, a new employee started to demonstrate a trick from *Ten Card Problems*, completely unaware that his target was the original creator. Vernon played along until Joe Berg entered the store and greeted Vernon with open arms. The young clerk, realizing his mistake, slithered away silently from the scene. In mid-December Vernon made arrangements to cut silhouettes over the Christmas season at a major department store in Evanston, Illinois. He promised Jeanne that, after Christmas, the family would return to New York. His timing was perfect.

While the Fair may have advertised itself as the showcase for science, technology, and design, the place to see substantive change and progress was Manhattan. During Vernon's five-year hiatus, William Van Alen completed the Chrysler Building and H. Craig Severance built the new corporate headquarters for the Bank of Manhattan Company. Both were daredevil feats of engineering and jostled for the title of tallest structure on earth. The Empire State Building replaced the Waldorf-Astoria, the hotel where Vernon believed that Malini had betrayed him. Rockefeller Center, a galaxy of buildings, theatres, and public spaces, became the hallmark of elegance, self-assurance, and sophistication that was Manhattan.

The political landscape had also changed. The Jimmy Walker era of corruption and patronage at City Hall ended with the election of Fiorello La Guardia in 1933. La Guardia brought a manic energy to the concept of urban renewal, setting a benchmark for others across America. January 1934 also ushered in the repeal of the Volstead Act. Although New Yorkers had coped with Prohibition through a network of underground clubs and speakeasies, vice was once again allowed in the open. New legal clubs and facilities opened quickly. One of the first impresarios on the scene was Billy Rose.

Rose, a Depression-era P.T. Barnum, planted his big tent firmly on Broadway. In the fall of 1933, with the repeal of Prohibition imminent, Rose leased a theatre on 54th Street, just west of Broadway, ripped it apart, and converted it into the Casino de Paree. The club opened in mid-December to glowing reviews, *Variety* labeling it "the most unusual café in the world." Rose had always loved variety artists and had much success staging shows both on Broadway and, most recently, on tour. The Casino was no exception. His December 29, 1933 advertisement in the *New York Times* stated, "Friday Night, we present a Full Length Musical Extravaganza in Two

Acts, with a New cast of principals, including Bill Robinson, Smith and Dale, George Givot, Al Siegel's Saxon Sisters, Cardini, Hinda Wassau, Holland and June and two magnificent orchestras with Ben Pollack and Don Redman." Everything—show, dinner, and dancing—was included for one price: two dollars. There was no cover charge. Other entrepreneurs opened swanky nightclubs, not just in New York, but across America. Variety entertainers now had a new home. The premier club, however, was Rose's Casino de Paree. Magicians auditioned to perform there and, as Vernon detailed in a letter to Faucett Ross, Rose could be a tough taskmaster.

After the Fair closed I hung around Chi (seeing the magicians and so forth) until Christmas when I went into Lord's Dept Store in Evanston, Ill and cut silhouettes for a couple of weeks after which we pulled out for here—The Big Town.

The second day after we arrived I was strolling on Broadway and I bumped into Cardini and were we surprised? He insisted that I go with him to the Casino de Paree to see Louis Zingone have an audition. (The time was the afternoon and I happened to be up.) Well to make a long story brief, Billy Rose told Louis who had both his agent and manager with him, that he would never never never do. I'll try and tell you how it came about.

Cardini, Billy Rose and myself were sitting together and there were about a hundred waiters and the rest of the regular acts in the audience. Louis after various instructions to the orchestra and so forth started his routine. Forgot to say that I had shaken hands with him and he told me he had practically given up magic as he was now a real showman—knew how to deliver gags—get belly laughs—wow them—lay them in the aisles—and—and—and.

Well he went through his offering without anything going wrong and even out did his usual performance according to an aside by his agent—hub.

Billy called him down to his seat and over he came flanked by his two 'yes' men. Cardini and I stepped back slightly to give them a little privacy...

Midway to Manhattan

Rose speaking—"In the first place you do not know how to handle talk and your material is very weak. Of course in my opinion there are not more than a half dozen men in the show business that can talk. Furthermore if you did work here, which of course is out of the question, the spectators seated at the tables would make more funny remarks than you could possibly concoct for your act. You know we get the cream of the New York crowd here and they know what's what and would never go for that stuff of yours. Now as for the tricks you do—I may be mistaken but I think I can step around the corner on Broadway and buy that rope trick for a dollar and you can't even do it well. The egg trick you do I have seen for years on the Big Time by a fellow who could really sell it and your other stuff is very mediocre. However you seem to handle cards as if you knew something about them but you have no act." Poor Louis—after telling me he had improved so and that I would never believe it was the same Louis when I saw his act.

Vernon and Cardini watched several other acts audition and then Cardini introduced Vernon to Rose as the foremost practitioner of close-up entertainment. Rose was quite cagey. He said, "Well, if Cardini says so you must be pretty good. I think Cardini's got one of the finest acts I've ever seen in this line." He then looked at Vernon kind of quizzically and asked, "What can you do for this club?"

Vernon said, "I might be able to do some intimate magic. Perhaps if I had a table in the corner where people could walk up and sit down I could show them some intimate tricks. Or, I might be able to go to a table with some of these people who are dining and do some tricks. I've never had any of this kind of experience, but I've played a lot of engagements for Miss King."

Rose asked, "You worked for Miss King?"

"Yes."

Rose said, "Well, you must be pretty good."

Rose had already hired fortunetellers, handwriting analysts, and quick-sketch artists to circulate throughout the club. Magic performed table-to-table might not be a bad idea.

Rose took Vernon, along with Cardini, up to his office. Rose opened the drawer of his desk, removed a brand new deck of Bee cards still in the cellophane, and handed them to Vernon. He said, "If you can do something with these cards, you must be all right."

Dai Vernon: A Biography

There is no record of what tricks Vernon performed for Rose, most likely because the set was improvised. Rose, however, was completely bewildered by Vernon's magic, and instructed him to report for work the next evening—in tails. Vernon confessed that he could not start so soon, as he had just arrived in town, hadn't even found a place to live, had a car full of baggage to unpack and did not own a set of tails. Rose, however, would not take no for an answer. His mind was racing. He said, "Rent a suit. I want you to wear tails. Wait a minute; I've got an idea. I want something different. How about a little mask to distinguish yourself from the guests? It will give you an air of mystery."

Vernon, who as a boy had admired the virtuoso sleight-of-hand magician l'Homme Masqué, liked the idea.

"All right," he said, "but I can't possibly come in tomorrow."

Rose gave Vernon a day's grace and added that he was the luckiest man in the world to have both Cardini—on stage—and Vernon—going table to table—in his club. For club work, Rose was right: Cardini and Vernon were the best. There were other performers, like Joseph Dunninger and Fred Keating, who had greater professional standing, but none were as suitable or as gifted for the Casino De Paree. Dunninger, who had been booked by Miss King in Vernon's stead for the performance before the Prince of Wales, parlayed one success into another, first for Miss King and then other agents, as he transformed himself from practitioner of all magic trades into a master of mentalism. His quick mind—something Vernon recognized from their first encounter in 1915—natural talent, and ability to market himself as a successor to Houdini, particularly where the supernatural was concerned, provided him with steady media coverage and the high society private engagements that flowed from it.

Keating, a dashing figure, was inspired by the craft when in 1908, aged eight, he witnessed a performance at the Eden Musée. Keating ran away from home at fourteen to travel with Howard Thurston, made his professional debut as a solo performer at age fifteen, and by 1929 had obtained extremely favorable notices performing in variety shows around New York. His tricks were traditional—the East Indian Needle Trick associated with Houdini and the Vanishing Birdcage of Bautier de Kolta—but his presentations were not. Billed "The Aristocrat of Magic," Keating presented magic with wit and panache. By 1934 he had forged a career as a mainstream actor

Midway to Manhattan

Vernon cut a dashing profile while working table-to-table in nightclubs.

both on Broadway and in Hollywood.

As instructed, Vernon showed up for work on Friday night and performed his magic table-to-table. He soon abandoned the mask, however, as women kept trying to snatch it from him. Evidently, the mask did not add the air of mystery Rose and Vernon had hoped it would. To compensate, Vernon experimented with his wardrobe, switching to a French Foreign Legion outfit, complete with all the trimmings, pockets, and profondes. He soon reverted back to more formal attire.

During his first week at the Casino, Vernon also cut silhouettes, particularly for celebrity patrons. He certainly met his share, including Jimmy Durante, Ed Sullivan, D.W. Griffith, Gene Tunney, Clark Gable, and Cary Grant, to name but a few. After that, except for the week when the Egyptian wonder-worker Gali-Gali was featured, Vernon performed magic exclusively, his focus being on performing feats with everyday objects. Effects included passing coins through the table, the vanish and recovery of a salt shaker, the passing of a ring on and off a wand, the discovery of copious amounts of coinage beneath articles on the table and, in a rare de-

Cardini poses for a studio portrait ca. 1930.

parture that utilized a prop, The Cups and Balls. Vernon edited the content and structure of this parlor trick, one that had fallen from favor, appropriating sleights from classical sources and from master practitioners such as Louis "Pop" Krieger and Malini, and made it suitable for performing at close range. Soon, other magicians followed suit.

> So I started to do regular cups and balls, and then every other magician in New York started to do them. Nobody was doing the cups and balls at that time, except Pop Krieger, and he was dead. And I was the only one doing cups and balls, and then it got to be kind of a vogue—everyone and his brother tried to learn it, and the dealers put in cups. Before that you couldn't even buy cups in dealing shops except old fashioned ones that were from years ago, and they'd have them as a museum piece in the case, but nobody sold it. Then it became quite popular around New York.

Midway to Manhattan

Vernon also performed a slew of his favorite card tricks. He caused four signed cards to jump from the pack to four different pockets of his suit, performed Arthur Finley's Matching The Cards, and tabled a prediction of a card that would always match the name of one nominated freely by a member of the audience—the trick that incorporated a special deck and a presentation that he had refined over the years with Paul Fox.

Although his repertoire was vast and often improvised, the stories that Vernon wove in with the magic, the stories of gamblers and con artists he had met in his travels, made the material come alive. The stories had the ring of authenticity, because they were, by and large, true. He did, however, when occasion warranted it, embellish stories for greater impact. He regaled his audiences, for example, with the tale of meeting a one-armed gambler and how he learned—almost to his regret—how the gambler lost his limb while trying to cheat another player. The story with the biggest impact, however, was the tale of the trick that had fooled Houdini. Vernon would recount the story of his encounter with Houdini and recreate the effect, causing the signed card to jump repeatedly back to the top of the pack. Audiences loved it. Vernon then started to experiment; he performed other tricks and claimed that they were the ones that fooled Houdini. Much to his surprise, the reaction was always the same. No matter what trick he performed, if he called it the "Trick that fooled Houdini," the audience would exclaim that it was the greatest trick that they had ever seen. When it came to magic, the public could not discern good from bad or difficult from easy. The most difficult sleight-of-hand would always be overshadowed by a simple effect if it was "the one that had fooled Houdini." The story made it so. Vernon's passion was not the same as that of the public. As Ross had indicated to Downs, Vernon had no interest in being the next Houdini; he preferred being a student of the art.

As a student, Vernon loved, as much as anything, having the opportunity to watch and learn from other performers. When it came to manipulation and, in particular, the synthesis of magic and pantomime, Cardini was perfection. Vernon saw Cardini's act at the Casino hundreds of times. Cardini would be booked for several weeks, leave to perform in another Broadway review, and then return. According to Vernon, Cardini was at his best at the Casino, as everything there was built to order: the atmosphere, the spot, the trimmings, and the music. Everything was harmonized.

The Casino offered other advantages, too. First, there were plenty of places to hide. When tired of toiling in the trenches, Vernon found he could avoid work by ducking downstairs to The Nudist Bar or upstairs to the main room. Second, the Casino gave him the opportunity to meet a wealthy and cultured clientele. One, Garrick Spencer, became both his student and friend. Vernon described Spencer in a letter to Ross:

> *My best friend here is Garrick Spencer attorney for the Brooklyn Times, also for the Woolworth interests. I hang out in his apartment at 70 Park a great deal. He's particularly good at the art and practices all the time. I met him while at the Casino. He never touched a card before that and now deals a perfect second and does nearly all the tough moves and puts over his tricks a la Malini. I gave him lessons after first sending him to Al for instruction.*

Vernon's passion, particularly for the pasteboards, was contagious. Whereas Fred Keating exclaimed in the January 1934 issue of *The Sphinx*, "Magic today is an art gone Rotarian" and laid the bulk of the blame on amateur magicians and magic societies, Vernon cultivated a coterie of amateurs who, like him, studied the craft for the shear love of it. Most professionals, once they develop their repertoire, stick with it. Vernon demonstrated that there was art in variation, particularly with cards, and he continued to explore these variations just as a composer like Bach would explore the art of counterpoint. Variations on themes, sleights, and subtle gambits inspired him, and he, in turn, inspired others. The Inner Circle embraced hobbyists who absorbed and mimicked Vernon's obsession.

> *As far as I know, I don't say it in any egotistical way, but I kind of changed the thinking. I made it more of a hobby for people because there's so much more to it. People were more intrigued with cards and they spent more time with them; there were so many different dodges that could be used. If you just had five things and you learned to do them very well, it was kind of empty. You were tired of doing the same thing over and over again for your own personal satisfaction. So as I say, for personal satisfaction or enjoyment, of enjoying a hobby, although perhaps you might not be able to use it to a great extent entertaining others, it gave a lot of personal enjoyment to people*

trying to play with cards as a hobby.

Now back in Manhattan semi-permanently, Vernon rekindled his friendship with Sam Margules. He had considered Margules part of his extended family ever since their days together on Coney Island. An enthusiast more than an amateur, Margules had carved a niche for himself organizing gala performances and benefit shows for New York area magicians. Margules, however, was also part of Dunninger's extended family, having befriended and assisted him at the Eden Musée when both men were in their teens. Margules often had supper with Dunninger and his mother at their home on Sunday evenings. It was there that Dunninger scooped one of Vernon's treasured secrets, a secret that would help him cement his reputation as the premier mentalist in America. The secret involved that special deck of cards, the presentation created by Vernon and honed by Fox, in which the performer, in this case Margules, made a bold prediction of a future event, the name of the card that Mrs. Dunninger would freely suggest. When Margules spread the deck of cards face down on the floor and revealed not only that his prediction was correct but also that the prediction had been drawn from a deck of a different color, Dunninger stepped on the cards to prevent Margules from picking them up. Dunninger scooped them up, examined them, and deciphered the secret. He then immediately set off to tweak the presentation to suit his performing style, creating the impression that he could hypnotize a subject into naming a card that he had taken from a different pack and inserted upside down in the deck. The trick became, in Dunninger's hands, a masterpiece. Vernon harbored little ill will. He was extremely fond of Margules and knew that Sam was no match for Dunninger or his ambition.

Although vaudeville had disappeared and large-scale touring magic shows were in retreat, amateur magicians could not satiate their thirst for secrets. Magic clubs that gave local practitioners the opportunity to perform like amateur thespians in local theatrical societies flourished. Second-tier performers and amateurs with means produced countless magazines and newsletters to cater to this ever-growing contingent. Ted Annemann, for example, always in the shadow of the enigmatic and dynamic Dunninger, began publishing *The Jinx*, a four-page mimeographed newsletter that provided the community with clever tricks, mostly of a pseudo-psychic variety.

Prominent professionals, however, were still reluctant to part with their secrets. As Ross had mentioned earlier, John Northern Hilliard, the ghostwriter of the seminal *Art of Magic* was compiling material for an even larger opus, one to be published by Carl Jones, a scion of a newspaper publishing in Minnesota. While many magicians—mostly amateurs—were more than happy to contribute their pet secrets to Hilliard's proposed publication, professionals like Nate Leipzig were still smarting twenty years after the fact that their repertoire had been pilfered and put in print. Now, Max Holden—the performer, writer, and magic dealer who had once admonished the magic community to play fair when it came to disclosing and performing the secrets of others—quietly became a culprit, first as the man behind the Camel Cigarette campaign, secretly feeding the advertising agency with the methods behind select secrets, and second as the driving force behind the publication of compilations of tricks and techniques targeted for amateurs of more advanced standing.

Holden realized that there was a ready market for books in certain areas of magic and commissioned Jean Hugard to write them. The pairing was a perfect fit. Hugard was extremely knowledgeable and literate, and what's more, was in need of a new source of income. His last attempt at a full evening show at Luna Park in 1929 had been an economic disaster, and now his eyesight was beginning to falter. It was also evident from his previous commercial exploits that Hugard would have no qualms about exposing the secrets of others.

Holden suggested that Hugard write a compendium of great magic sleights and routines for the trade, which Holden would publish. The first, a mimeographed manuscript called *Card Manipulations* appeared in 1933 to great acclaim. The second, *Card Manipulations No. 2*, was released in 1934 and contained a more than passing reference to Vernon and his technique. In describing the double lift, the first major technical description of this closely guarded sleight, Hugard wrote,

> The perfect way to do this sleight is to push off two cards as one without first separating them from the other cards with the thumb. This is very difficult, but Mr. Dai Vernon, the famous card expert, not only does it, but is able to push off two, three or four cards, as one, at will. By this means he apparently places the top card in the middle

of the deck three times in quick succession, each time showing it has returned to the top. In his hands this is one of the most amazing feats possible with cards.

After eight months and a change in management, Billy Rose having been squeezed out of his operation by some of his financiers, Vernon left the Casino De Paree. He treated himself to a small upright piano and divided his time between practicing magic and the keyboard. He also accepted the occasional engagement through Miss King. King, the agent who had persuaded Vernon to join her stable of artists a decade earlier, had shifted the bulk of her business away from live theatricals and more towards coordinating the participation of artists on radio broadcasts. Still, her office with her young apprentice, Mark Leddy, was considered the premier booking agency for private entertainers in New York. In December 1934 Vernon received an offer from Bertram Weal of the Madison Hotel, a renowned hotel, apartment complex, and nightclub, located at 15 East 58th Street and home to such New York stalwarts as Lucius Bebee, Robert Benchley, Peggy Joyce, and the Gimble family, to present his sleight-of-hand as part of the hotel's New Year's Eve entertainment. His performance that evening was so well received that the management extended his engagement. Vernon became the opening act, performing his intimate magic table-to-table, before the appearance of the feature attraction. Most nights, the feature attraction was Kate Smith. One critic, "Zit," proclaimed,

[Bertram Weal] personally picks the talent which entertains his society patrons. He picked a boy by the name of Dai Vernon, who, to my way of thinking, is one of the greatest table entertainers of magic that one would want to see. A fine looking boy, pleasing personality, with wonderful gift of speech and above all entertaining with no presumption other than to mystify you and show within a space of a foot from your eye how quickly the hand moves.

At the Madison, Vernon performed the repertoire he had honed at the Casino De Paree, the Cups and Balls and his extensive repertoire with cards—the Rising Cards, the color changing pack, the vanish and recovery of cards from unexpected places, "stop tricks" in which the spectator would instruct Vernon to stop dealing cards only to discover that Vernon stopped on his or her very selection–as well as a variety of puzzles, stunts, and stories with everyday objects. One trick that caused both bewilderment and consternation was built around a simple toy, a small round red box with a pull cord, manufactured by the S.S. Adams Company. Whenever someone pulled on the cord, a voice would say, "You picked the ace of diamonds."

Once, one of the wealthy female patrons asked, "Mr. Vernon, do you ever sell any of your tricks?"

"No," he said, "I don't think I do."

The woman was more direct, "Would you sell any of your tricks?"

Vernon thought perhaps the woman had a little boy who did magic. Still, his answer was "No."

She said, "I want a trick to do at the card parties, bridge parties. I'd love to do one trick."

Vernon said, "You don't have to buy it, I'll show you," and he started to show her a simple card trick when she interrupted him.

"No, no, I want a special trick that you do in here occasionally."

Vernon replied, "Well, I don't know—the tricks I do aren't too easy."

She said, "Oh, no, I mean the little box you have that reads the mind."

Vernon said, "Oh, well, I could teach you to do that trick, but I'm sorry, I can't part with the box." Vernon didn't want to part with the box because they were quite rare. The toy had to be modified by hand to deliver the appropriate phrase and Vernon was having a difficult time replacing the well-worn one he had at hand.

The woman was persistent. "Well, if I gave you enough money for it, you'd sell it."

"No," Vernon said, "I wouldn't sell it for one hundred dollars."

The woman upped the ante and offered Vernon $150. Vernon, scanning the woman's wardrobe, assumed she could afford it. It was an offer he could not refuse. Now, however, he had to figure out a way to show the woman how to perform the trick. Vernon informed the woman that he could meet her after he had finished performing for the evening. He would be out of the club by 8:00 pm. The woman gave Vernon the number of her room, informed him that she was having a few friends up for cocktails, and that he could join them, teach her how to do the trick, and pick up his check. Vernon called at the appointed time, met some of the guests, enjoyed a cocktail, and then went to a corner of the room to show the woman the trick. The first thing he had to teach her was how to force a card: how to make a spectator pick the one card that matched the voice recording produced by the little round box. The woman was confused.

"Now why do you do all that?" she asked.

Vernon tried to explain. "Well, the person's got to get the ace of diamonds."

"I don't understand what you mean," she said. "You just had me take a card."

"Yes, I know," he tried to explain, "but I couldn't teach you how I did it because it is too technical."

"But," she said, "I want to do it the way you did."

She took the cards into her own hands and had Vernon select one. She then pulled the string on the box. The voice said, as it always did: "You took the ace of diamonds." Unfortunately it was not the name of the card Vernon had selected. Vernon tried to explain once more. "You've got to make them take the ace of diamonds."

"Why," the woman exclaimed, "I thought it read your mind."

Vernon, his frustration growing, said, "No, it doesn't read your mind. It's a trick. All these things I do are tricks."

"Do you mean to tell me it always says 'You took the ace of diamonds'?"

"Yes."

"Oh," she said, "it's not worth anything."

Vernon reminded her that she seemed to have liked it enough to offer him $150.

"Well," she said, "I thought it read your mind. I thought how wonderful it would be at the bridge table to let a woman take a card and have the box tell me the name of it."

The woman was quite apologetic and offered to pay Vernon for his time, but he would hear nothing of it. On the ride home, thinking over the incident reminded Vernon of how often the simple effects are the most mysterious, particularly when performed for people with imagination.

Vernon performed nightly at the Madison Hotel for six months, circulating from table to table during the cocktail hour, finishing each night around 10:00 pm, early enough in the evening to still socialize with his magical confreres into the wee hours of the morning. One new confrere was Dr. Jacob Daley, an ear, nose and throat specialist who was inspired by a colleague to embrace magic as a hobby in 1934 to relieve the stress associated with his medical practice. Daley had taken lessons from both Baker and Horowitz, and had become a frequent patron of the Madison Hotel. Vernon recognized that Daley was a dedicated student of magic, pursuing difficult sleights with dogged enthusiasm. Vernon also socialized with other professionals, visiting performers at the clubs where they were performing. This time, however, if recognized by the patrons of these other establishments, unlike the episode with Max Malini in Miami Beach, Vernon did not encroach on the territory of the resident performer. At Texas Guinan, for example, a nightclub owned by an impresario of the same name who was famous in the 1920s for greeting each patron with the salutation, "Hello sucker," Vernon had the opportunity to watch Leipzig perform. Afterwards, when Vernon was recognized by another patron and asked to perform, Vernon declined graciously and reiterated that Leipzig was the house performer. Perhaps now that Vernon was more firmly ensconced in nightclub work and aware of the constant and inopportune enthusiasm displayed by other magicians, he understood the common courtesy that performers exhibit towards one another, avoiding both each other's material and domain. Leipzig thanked Vernon afterwards.

While Vernon was performing nightly at the Madison Hotel, Jeanne was rearing the two children—Ted and Derek—and in the late evenings developing her own expertise. Since returning to New York from Chicago, she spent time visiting libraries and had studied the rudiments of mask making. She soon started to experiment and develop her own body of techniques at home. Her first masks were made out of papier-mâché, but they were too heavy to be worn comfortably. Jeanne then tried to mold the masks from large sheets of paper. These masks, conversely, were too brittle. Finally, she developed a process where she would first model a face in clay and then cover it with a layer of special Japanese paper torn into three or four-inch squares bound with an adhesive. She then applied a paste, her own concoction, which would not make the mask too brittle or leave an unpleasant odor. She would apply three or four layers of paper squares, shellac the mask when it was dry, and then paint it. She even developed her own way of mixing the paint that gave the mask a soft finish, one that resembled the texture of human skin.

Midway to Manhattan

Initially, she created masks for friends like Cardini. She then expanded the range to include famous figures like Marie Dressler, Enrico Caruso, and Florenz Ziegfeld. She completed over fifty masks during the time that her husband was performing at the Casino De Paree and the Madison Hotel. A number of the masks were commissioned by a Broadway producer for a musical number, "There's A Broadway In Heaven." Unfortunately, the musical was a flop.

When Vernon left the Madison Hotel in June 1935, he had performed consistently for close to eighteen months—his longest streak performing magic for the public—but he had little money to show for it. A letter to Ross was telling.

> *Since then I have done nothing by private engagements for Miss King and direct booking. Have not cut a silhouette since I was first in Casino. I have been getting some nice work recently. A short time ago I worked for Wm. English president of the Sugar Exchange (booked direct for 'C') also played the Princeton Club, Yale Club, Union Club, also Union League. Worked twice for the Morgans also several insurance companies and several of the Park Ave. crowd. However*

This finely crafted mask, hand-made by Jeanne, was a near-perfect replica of Cardini's famous face.

I never seem to amass any fortune and I always seem to be in debt. Tomorrow I collect for two dates and already Jeanne has told me where most of it is to go. But think of the fun we have.

Vernon was not the only one having difficulty making ends meet. His young apprentice, the prodigious Charles Miller, was also finding it a challenge. Miller, who had moved to Los Angeles with his mother only to return to El Paso to embark on a career as a professional magician, found little success. He wrote Ross about the possibility of teaming up with him in Wichita.

Yes, Ross, I really am in the profession, but I am not making any money. I came to El Paso to team up with a friend of mine. The only trouble is that he is married and that means that he has to get out and make some money and cannot take a chance on making anything with magic. His wife doesn't seem to like it, anyway, except on the side. If it were not for the fact that I have a bed here in our office, it would be very hard for me. As it is I can live very cheaply and still have time to practice. I am handicapped by the fact that I do no large effects and my friend is also handicapped by having played most of the schools here two or three times with the same show. He is [sic] just about worn it out and cannot buy any new effects. I really am anxious to team up with you for a short while.

As you know, I have never gone in for anything other than pure sleight of hand and small effects, and this makes it very hard for me. Another thing is that I have no clothes. By this I mean that I haven't even a tuxedo and right at present do not see how I can get one. I probably could borrow enough to get one if it were absolutely necessary, but naturally, I don't want to borrow unless absolutely necessary. Let me know at once about this. If I ever make enough, I shall have plenty of nice clothes.

I have found out many things about presenting sleight of hand. One thing is that they don't seem to care how poor an effect is as long as it is entertaining and they haven't seen it before.

Do you live in an apartment, Ross? Could I sleep on the floor for a few days? I have a friend hear [sic] who told me the other day that he would get a railroad ticket for me if I would let him know a couple of days in advance.

Please let me hear from you just as soon as possible. I am anxious to make good and my mother is very anxious to have me be a successful performer, also.

Ross could offer Miller little, and, dejected, returned home to his mother in Los Angeles. It was a fortunate turn of events, for there Miller soon tumbled on to a new mentor—Max Malini.

Malini was performing in Los Angeles when Miller, with his friend Judson Brown by his side, made an unscheduled appearance at Malini's hotel room door. Malini was impressed by Miller's devotion to magic, his obvious technical skill and, just as importantly, the close relationship Miller had with his mother. For Miller, Malini represented a father figure, both in and out of magic, and one who offered a whole new approach to performing magic. Unlike Vernon, who jumped from trick to trick and from technique to technique, Malini focused on performing a core repertoire to perfection. Malini allowed Miller to accompany him for eight months, day in and day out, as Malini attended to his business. He also taught Miller to perform his [Malini's] repertoire and, more importantly, permitted him to perform it publicly. Miller wrote Ross,

Don't you know, Faucett, that it is the man—not his methods—that makes him famous. He is really in a class by himself when it comes to this. Really Faucett, I have come to the conclusion that Max is absolutely right when he says to work any effect in the simplest cleanest manner possible. He can make the most barefaced trick seem like a dream in his hands. I wish that I could have a personal talk with you. I could tell you some of the things that he has taught me that would seem so natural that one wonders why they can't do them. Max is one of the dandiest fellows I have ever met in my life and I owe him a lot. I owe him a lot for he has really taught me how to make a small effect seem like a masterpiece to the spectators. For nearly eight months I saw him nearly every day. We took several trips to different places together. He certainly is a wonderful fellow, and I wish that he were here now. Malini gave me a marvelous introduction the other night at a party given him by Frank Fewins. And what is more he made a beautiful speech about Mother, and believe me, it certainly made me happy. I have come to the conclusion that it is better to do just six effects perfectly than to do several more. Malini says that he can do but six tricks. He says the other things are just fooling the people. I am lining up some real nice dates now, although there isn't much money in them. Keep this strictly to yourself, as I don't want anyone to hear it. I am indebted to Malini for "breaking me in." He got me a cheap date in a cocktail bar where I worked one evening doing just close-up stuff.

The show I do now is almost the same as that given by Malini, with the exception that I have added several effects. Once, I had to give the same program that Max worked. I ran out of material. He says it's all right, so I don't feel bad about it, and I give him credit in several of his tricks. As I stated before: I gave a program similar to Malini's and you would be surprised at the impression it makes. I have been trying to locate a good agent but it is about like trying to invent an invisible shift. Yes, Dai wanted all the data on Max. Now tell that guy not to eat Jewish food just so he can do his tricks.

If Vernon was envious of Miller's newfound access to Malini, he did not show it. In a letter to Ross, Vernon wrote,

Malini—ah. There's a magician. I still consider him the master. No one creates the effect that he does. I've met people from all over who talk of the wonders he has performed for them—not his show however. Real magic cannot be done at a distance—it cannot possibly impress people the same way.

Malini performed magic that Vernon loved, magic that had to be seen up close to be appreciated. While Malini may have performed this magic purely to drive ticket sales to his public performances and enhance his reputation, Vernon admired Malini's impromptu magic, as it represented the high water mark of the art, not commerce.

Miller was not the only sleight-of-hand performer whose career was now on the upswing. Paul Rosini, the dashing and charismatic mind reader from Philadelphia, was now generating favorable notices for his magic and mind-reading in both Philadelphia and Manhattan. With nightclubs sprouting up across the country, particularly in hotels as the proprietors expanded the services and amenities that could be extended to their guests, Rosini found more and more venues amenable to his style of performing. Hotels such as the Adelphia in Philadelphia, the Park Plaza in St. Louis, and the Palmer House in Chicago featured variety acts as integral parts of their floor shows. Vernon, however, had little interest in working these venues, particularly as they required the performer to appear before hundreds of people rather than in the intimate setting of a single table. Vernon was content to leave the broader field to other performers and those with a more public or dramatic persona, including Rosini, who performed the material of Malini, Leipzig, and Vernon.

Vernon's eighteen months of relative prosperity only reinforced the notion that he did not enjoy performing the same effects, day in and day out, as did most performers. Vernon's passion was studying the art of magic: collecting arcane bits of information as well as streamlining classic effects and the techniques and presentations of others. Even the media picked up on his reclusive nature. George Ross, in his column "Trails on Broadway" in the *Charleston Daily Mail* for January 18, 1936, wrote,

> *Among the master magicians of today, there are, of course, Cardini, John Mulholland and in his own field of abracadabra, Thurston. But although he is little known to the layman, a conjuror named Dai Vernon is the magician's tutor in hocus-pocus. Vernon is credited with having invented and created more ingenious card tricks than any other living sleight-of-hand artist; he introduced the stunt whereby a blue deck of cards is changed to red without any substitution.*
>
> *The bible of card manipulators is a book published at the beginning of the century called The Expert at the Card Table, by S.W. Erdnase. Vernon mastered every sleight in this difficult text when he was 12 years old. And yet he will not appear anywhere professionally and no amount of coaxing will prevail upon him to do so.*

In another profile, "To Hold the Mirror up to Nature," the author described Vernon:

> *He could make millions as a gambler—but Dai Vernon decided to be a magician, specializing in cards. He fooled Houdini; today, magicians admit that no man equals him with cards. Today, he seldom gives public performances—he appears only at small private parties to*

> *practice the most difficult "over the table work," where his audience can get as close to him as they like. That work is the cream of the business; only the best get it. Unlike most magicians, he doesn't want publicity, because he doesn't need it.*
>
> *He is one of the few honest living men who can "center deal" successfully—that means, dealing from the center of the pack while apparently dealing from the top. That comes in very handy in crooked poker. Vernon could use the trick to make a crooked fortune. But he doesn't gamble—doesn't even play bridge.*

With more time on his hands, Vernon decided to release another one of his pet secrets to the magic community, this time in the pages of *The Sphinx*. The trick, An Ace Trick for the Expert, appeared in the August 1935 issue, along with a pen and ink portrait of Vernon, trademark cigarette dangling from his lips. In it, he disclosed a new technique—a new style of palming—to the magic fraternity, a technique that had its roots in the gambling world. Vernon also stressed that it required practice to achieve naturalness, echoing the mantra he had learned from Dr. Elliott in 1915.

On April 13, 1936, the era of the grand stage magic spectacle, which had been on life support for years, and more recently had been reduced to being the opening offering in movie palaces, came to an end. Howard Thurston, the man who had once fooled Herrmann and who, in turn, had been fooled by Vernon (when Vernon was a boy in Ottawa), died. Thurston's passing gave the media the opportunity to reflect on this age-old profession's state of affairs and its future. The Corning (N.Y.) *Leader* for April 25, 1936 declared, "Magic Moves To The Night Clubs As Illusionists Desert Old 'Props'"

> *Outstripped by science at wonder working on a grand scale, magic is shelving elaborate apparatus and turning back the clock to sleight-of-hand. In night clubs, hotels and grills, before intimate groups at private parties, there is scant room for diving tanks and bisectable girls in boxes. Modern sorcerers must work in the open as their predecessors in black art practiced where they could gather a street corner crowd. The trade sees Thurston's death as closing the era of great "illusionists." The line ran from Herrmann the Great, through Harry Kellar to Houdini and Thurston.*

Midway to Manhattan

Vernon performs for "patrons" at the Kit Kat Club, including his wife, Jeanne (at his immediate right).

Blackstone's is called the last big-time, full-length magic show traveling the road. In contrast the new school of wizards are suave parlor tricksters who purposely reduce the size of the illusion and minimize dependence on "gimmicks" or props. Tops include Ade Duval and Cardini, a Welshman.

Fred Keating, of Hollywood, employs tricks merely to keep his hands occupied while he titillates the customers with adult patter—as Will Rogers punctuated his wisecracks with a rope. Dai Vernon and Nate Leipzig make most of their appearances before night club crowds.

A photograph of Dai Vernon performing at the Kit Kat Club, a fashionable New York nightspot, shot by Associated Press photographer and amateur magician Irving Desfor, accompanied the article. Although the photograph was a staged promotional shot—Jeanne Verner sitting at the table pretending to be an astonished participant—the image captured the transition magic was making from stage to nightclub. Other writers, with perhaps more of an insider's understanding of the world of wonder, laid the cards more openly on the table. Magic was at a crossroads. Robert Reinhart, a respected actor and sometime magician, wrote an extensive piece in the New York *Herald-Tribune* for April 26, 1936, one that illustrated all the foibles and frustrations of the fraternity.

> *The recent death of Howard Thurston raises the obvious question — who, if any one, will be the next world-famous magician? On whose shoulders will the distinguished robes of Alexander Herrmann, Harry Houdini and Harry Kellar fall? One may reach the easy conclusion that the modern miracles of invention have made the minor miracles of the stage magician seem trivial. Such reasoning suggests that magic is a declining or even a dying art. Is this actually the case?*
>
> *Unhappily it must be admitted that magic, as a form of theatrical entertainment, is a declining art, but this is not because of the present public, either children or adults, has had its fill of it. The fault lies with the exponents of magic, who have not brought its presentation up to date. It is obvious enough that the theater has made great strides in the present century. It is equally obvious that the art of presenting magic has not.*
>
> *Until some visionary producer or manager comes along who has sufficient imagination to see the entertainment possibilities in a modern production based on magical effects, presented in twentieth century theatrical style, there will probably be no successor to Thurston. Some individuals may continue in his tradition but the successor to Thurston must begin where the latter left off.*
>
> *For those so afflicted, the urge to "do magic" is strong. There is no likelihood of this art disappearing, even though it be a precarious profession. Throughout the country there are several hundred men who earn their living, usually not too prosperous, by conjuring, or playing the part of a magician. Some even find a way to combine it with other kinds of work. The "magic bug" is at least as tenacious as a similar bacillus which produces the phenomenon we call "stage struck," from either of which the victim seldom recovers.*
>
> *A few of these performers of magic appear in theaters, some in cabarets or night clubs, and a number entertain at clubs, lodges, private dinners and at children's parties. It may be stated with reasonable assurance*

that there will continue to be these club or drawing room magicians, at least enough to satisfy the demand for children's entertainments and for small occasions of an intimate nature. There is no denying the technical skill and abilities of many of these performers, but their presentation for the most part leaves worlds to be desired. This applies also in almost every case to those who appear in theaters, for here, too, the lack of the modern approach is evident.

To this general statement there is one exception, and here we must pause to praise Richard Cardini, whose flawless presentation, stage deportment, mystery and pantomime have been so widely admired. Yet Cardini is after all but a specialty artist, whose fifteen or twenty minute performance is a far cry from a full evening's magic show.

Years ago Robert-Houdin defined a conjurer as an actor who played the role of a magician. After having been associated for nearly twenty years with magic and magicians, I find it difficult to think of any modern conjurer who fits this definition. Fred Keating perhaps, for he came nearest to it, but he was always the suave, charming young man who appeared as much surprised at his effects as were his audiences. The decline of the opportunities for vaudeville artists and a wide number of imitators forced Keating to desert the "black art" for the legitimate stage, and subsequently for the more lucrative cinema.

There are perhaps fifty organizations in the country the memberships of which are composed largely of magicians, some professional and some amateur. They combine the social aspects of a lodge with the aims of a little theater group. These societies hold regular meetings and often stage performances, but even the best of them are not of a high quality, judged by any standard. In these organizations are also such closely related miracles mongers as side-show artists, fire-eaters, ventriloquists, jugglers and Punch and Judy performers, and those generally associated with the "outdoor show business," the carnivals and amusement parks.

Many great performers have started in the circus or side-show tradition. Houdini and Thurston were both at one time side-show performers. Keating once traveled with a circus as a magician. The magician of today, however, while he must know the technical aspects of this field, preferably should have a theatrical background.

> *It has been my privilege to know many of these artists well, performers who are direct descendants in heritage of the first traveling showmen. Out of their related arts and out of puppetry grew much of the theater, which is really the greatest and highest achievement of magic. For here is real illusion concerned with living people.*
>
> *The arts of the theatre are the highest development of magic. For magic itself again to become popular, it must draw closer to its blood relation, the theater, with which it shares a common origin—the inherent desire of mankind for illusion. In so doing it may still produce one of the greatest forms of entertainment, illusion within illusion.*
>
> *It therefore will be necessary for some theatrical producer with wide knowledge of theater to avail himself of all this technical knowledge, and to combine forces with those who have the technical knowledge of legerdemain, and then to find a man who can act and carry out the part of a magician. This will be the man about whom to create the character of "magician," and the man who logically should be Thurston's successor.*

Reinhart went on to explain the difficulty faced by those who dare produce magic:

> *In the past magic shows have grown gradually, the performer developing as an institution and his program growing with him as he developed or was successful. No one, to my knowledge, has successfully staged a magic show in the way that a legitimate play is produced, by knowing from the start what was going to be produced and having the capital to finance this end. To produce such a magic show would cost at least as much as an ordinary play, and the possibilities of making a financial killing are much less, as the scale of prices is considerably lower.*
>
> *There is, however, another angle to a magic show. It is like the circus in that once the original investment has been made, it lays the foundation for shows in future years which will not change much from the original, and such a production can go on the road for years.*

Midway to Manhattan

Thurston, after reaching the top in his field, lived to see a serious decline in the popularity of his art as he knew it. This does not mean that magic is dead. The multitude of people who support even the mediocre programs of the magical societies and hundreds who practice magic as a hobby testify to the contrary.

Reinhart was right. Magic societies were living in a dreamland, guilty of the same willful blindness that many magicians experience, believing that their secret machinations were invisible to all but themselves. Several performers were doing superb work, but their chosen arenas were invisible to the public. Most members of the Inner Circle had achieved a level of grace, deception, beauty, wit, and humor in their intimate work that surpassed much of the magic staged in other epochs. Their performances, however, were fleeting, existing in the moment. Such intimate performances were designed to be experienced, like the best of Max Malini's repertoire, up close. With no means of recording their splendor, they could not be seen by or broadcast to large audiences.

Still, Vernon had to earn some living. Garrick Spencer made two suggestions. First, he suggested that Vernon create an act and he offered to finance its development. Vernon recognized that developing a professional act was a tremendous challenge. He had created one a decade earlier and had shopped it around but with little success. Although the act had individual touches, the material was conventional, and the forum—the vaudeville stage—was not to his liking. A new act had to meet different criteria.

First, it must have universal appeal so that it could play not only in nightclubs but also, if possible on stages in the United States and abroad. Second, it had to feature magic with objects small enough to transport yet large enough to have a presence in grander venues. Third, its narrative arc had to be communicated through magic, costume and music rather than dialogue. Fourth, it had to be different from that of his friend, Cardini, quite a challenge as the manipulation of cards and, to a certain degree cigarettes, was Vernon's forte. Finally, as legerdemain, Vernon recalled, was essentially a psychological process intended to appear mysterious and to evoke wonderment, the new act had to transport his audience and rekindle their sense of wonder, the same sense of wonder he had experienced as a child witnessing Harry Kellar at the Russell Theatre in Ottawa. Vernon accepted Spencer's offer and vowed to develop an act of great artistry and commercial viability for the stage.

Second, Spencer suggested that both the magic fraternity and the public needed a means of distinguishing good magic from bad and a way of safeguarding the dissemination of secrets. He suggested the creation of a professional guild—a self-regulating body—one that could monitor and recognize the level of expertise and control the flow of secrets. Vernon embraced the second suggestion and in May 1936 mustered the members of the Inner Circle into a more formal society.

George Ross announced the formation of this new society in his column, "In New York," in *The Frederick Post*.

> *So last week, a small clique of magic men split the ranks and formed their own fraternity. Cardini, Nate Leipzig and Dai Vernon are some of the members in the new secret order called the Academy of the Art of Magic. They are pledged to keep their gali-gali to themselves.*

Membership, the group decided, was accorded to those who, by character and ability, had added outstanding distinction to the art. Initial members were Al Baker, Richard Cardini, Arthur Finley, Paul Fox, S. Leo Horowitz, G. W. Hunter, J. Warren Keane, Nate Leipzig, Max Malini, Charles E. Miller, Garrick Spencer and, of course, Vernon. This group was a curious mixture of young and old, amateur and professional, wealthy and impoverished. All, with the possible exception of Spencer, were artists.

The question remained, however, whether they or their organization would have any impact on the art it hoped to advance.

Chapter Nine
Over The Rainbow

"So, I produce this ball from a cone, and then another, and then a ball so big that the cone can't cover it, so I take off my hat, cover the ball and change it into a coconut. I throw the coconut into the air, and it changes into a monkey."

Jeanne looked at her husband in disbelief. "A monkey?"

"Yes," Vernon replied, "a monkey, and I would teach the monkey to bow. I would walk off, lead the monkey off stage and go out and bow. Then, the monkey would walk out and he'd bow. Then, I'd pull him off. This would go on, the monkey trying to take the credit, and then you would go to pull him off and give him a little spank. This would be sensational."

The concept, if nothing else, was original and, as John Booth, a young magician residing in Hamilton, Ontario indicated in his "Magic of the Moment" column in the November 1936 issue of *The Linking Ring,* originality was in short supply. Although a tsunami of secrets rose unabated within the magic community as magic societies flourished, magic depots churned out tricks with an emphasis on ease in performing rather than on digital dexterity. In addition, a host of new publications provided fodder for the masses, most of the material derivative. Nightclubs sprang up across America, employing scores of magicians who each needed fresh material for their own market. Magicians became masters of sampling, borrowing themes and motifs from others, sometimes as a homage, other times for more mercantile reasons, often re-orchestrating them as one's own. Although it would be decades before copyright legislation regarded the product of sampling as a form worthy of protection, most magicians adopted this approach to creating tricks and routines. Booth wrote,

> The "urge to live" makes us all imitators with the gift of originality. To make a living most of us magicians, dealers and writers must live off the inspiration and perspiration of others. As much as we recognize the ethical wrongs of our actions toward the more original of our brethren, still this necessity to make a living forces the hand that might otherwise not prostitute the magic that we are pleased to call "art."

And then there was the issue of exposure.

Horace Goldin was no stranger to the courtroom, often suing his brethren magicians for "stealing" his signature tricks. This time, however, his sights were set on a more prominent defendant: the R.J. Reynolds Tobacco Company. A national campaign advertising Camel cigarettes, tagged "It's Fun To Be Fooled... But It's More Fun To Know," had made it clear that most magic secrets were readily available. In this case, the secret in question was Goldin's prized "Sawing a Woman in Two," exactly as it had been used by Sam Margules on Coney Island. Margules, called as a witness for the plaintiff, was forced to admit under cross-examination that magicians often published their secrets in books, books that were available in libraries to anyone expressing a passing interest in reading them.

Even if magicians could place their work within the domain of copyright protection, they had no organization to represent their interests, no entity that could police the use of material and levy charges for its improper use. Magic clubs offered little assistance; members were enthusiasts, amateurs keen to use the very secrets that most professionals wanted to keep hidden. Of course, what most professionals neglected to remember in this new age, the age of the nightclub, was that amateurs had developed many of the tricks used by professionals. Whereas most professionals detested amateurs, Vernon acknowledged that, in this new era, magic's most prominent practitioners (those who moved the art forward) often came from this class.

> In my opinion, all through the ages, the amateurs made the contributions to method and technique; the professional found the

commercial or amusing or entertaining way to present the tricks. But many of these effects, ideas, I'd say ninety per cent, came from amateurs. They have the enthusiasm, the interest in creating new effects then the professional takes them and sells [performs] them. Amateurs burn the midnight oil working. A professional just wants to know how he can commercialize and get a good effect; he is not as particular about his method. As long as it's good enough to get the money or to register with the audience, he is not particular about the artistry.

As for the Camel Cigarette campaign, Vernon noted that magic was more sophisticated than a mere collection of secrets. "Skill," he said, "cannot be exposed." What really bothered Vernon were inept performers and unscrupulous dealers, not because they exposed or sold a mechanical contrivance or sleight, but because they retarded the progress of the art and marred the public's perception of magic's most accomplished practitioners, not as magicians, but as artists. Vernon disliked anything that made magic seem trite.

Robert Reinhart had a different take. In his March 24, 1937 *Variety* column he wrote,

Magicians are a peculiar species. As a group they are highly clannish. Usually practicing of effects results in their becoming enraptured with their own proficiency and they drift off into a dream world in which 'the trick's the thing' rather than the cash audience. Many of them spend their time creating effects which will fool the other magis and which is known as magician's magic. From a show business point of view this is a sheer waste of time. Like the proverbial absent-minded professor they are lost to the world in the depths of their own researches. Chief research man in the business is probably Dai Vernon, who practically refuses any work but private engagements as it might interfere with his practice. His wife even calls him the 'professor.'

Reinhart added,

It is generally conceded however by those in the know that Vernon's technique, useless as much of it may be commercially, is tops in the field. Presently Vernon is working on an act which has been booked unseen on his reputation, and while there is no use predicting

whether it will be good or bad, it may be confidently stated that if he ever produces it it will be the best magic around and entirely original in its presentation.

Reinhart was correct: Jeanne did sometimes address her husband as "The Professor," a sobriquet bestowed on him initially by Garrick Spencer as a playful way of chastising him for his role as oracle to the many acolytes that beseeched him for information. Vernon recognized, however, that while tricks may have been plentiful, wonder was in short supply. The question of how one captures and communicates wonder was difficult to answer. Fortunately, David Bamberg's appearance at the Cervantes Theatre in Spanish Harlem gave Vernon a clue.

Bamberg was part of a long line—seven generations—of Dutch magicians. He had had unfettered access to the great magicians of the age, both in America and in Europe, and displayed the talent to fill the void left by the passing of Howard Thurston. Bamberg made his first stage appearance at the age of eight when Thurston, with whom his father, Theodore Bamberg, was touring, requested that the boy perform a card trick from the stage. Thurston predicted then and there that the youth would become a great conjuror. Bamberg then served an apprenticeship under Julius Zanzig, acting as assistant to the world-renowned mind reader, a role that would later be played by Paul Rosini. Now, aged thirty-two, Bamberg was invited by an American promoter to return to America with his full evening show.

Magicians were captivated by Bamberg's artistry, returning again and again to see the show. Ted Annemann wrote in the pages of the *Jinx*, "Those who have seen it opine that it is the most beautifully dressed show to hit these shores. The opening ran almost three hours and the illusions, for the most part worked into sketches, are of a type, and carry an atmosphere totally different from what American audiences have seen." Max Holden, in a breathless description of the show in *The Linking Ring*, described it as "the greatest magic act that ever hit N.Y.C. with showmanship, personality, costumes, scenery and all apparatus beautiful." John Mulholland, editor of *The Sphinx*, agreed: "To me, the whole show was the realization of the dream of what a magic show should be...a liberal education in magic." He added, "For the first time in my life, I have seen magicians so impressed that they talk only about the beauty

David Bamberg, at center, performs the Floating Ball.

and skill of the presentation, instead of the mechanics of the tricks. In case you ever hear of anyone who doubts that magic is an art, send him to see David Bamberg."

Vernon regarded the show as the most beautiful he had ever seen and attempted to describe both Bamberg and his production:

> *He was a young man, a very nice looking man, and he was like a fairy prince, like perhaps the Prince of Wales [Edward VIII] was when he was a young man. He had the whole world at his feet. And he changed into these beautiful costumes; he must have made thirty-five changes during the show. He had these costumes, these museum pieces, and every time he'd step off the stage he'd come back in a different, gorgeous Chinese costume. He not only had fantasy, whimsy, mystery, he had comedy in his act. He had very funny bits where he'd shoot a bear and the bear would fall down dead. He'd shoot it and the music would change and be sad, and everybody would feel sad that he'd killed this bear. Now he'd reach down and cut the bear open and reach in and take out a heart — I mean a real looking heart — and massage it and look at it and pet it, and put it back in the bear, and pat the bear, and the bear would jump up and walk off the stage.*

Well, this intrigued people, because they were all sorry for the bear, and a moment later with his magic power he'd take its heart out and massage it and put it back in place and the bear would run off. But the illusion was good—the feeling was good—the plot was good; he had lots of amusing things that other magicians didn't have. Everything he did was well done.

Vernon immediately proposed Bamberg for membership in the Academy of the Art of Magic; Bamberg was pleased to accept. In his memoir, *Illusion Show,* Bamberg wrote,

I attended some memorable sessions and was privileged to see high quality manipulative magic far superior to anything I had seen before. I hadn't been around for years and most of it was new for me and they took a keen delight in driving me crazy. Dai Vernon made me suffer for a time with the new "Do As I Do" card trick which had me baffled because of the many variations they used; but finally Dai took pity on me and explained it. Sam Horowitz had developed a new style over the years, entirely different from Vernon's but just as effective, and he gave me many a sleepless hour, and any evening with Al Baker and Nate Leipzig was something never to be forgotten. It was the beginning of the modern school of manipulation, in which apparently no moves are made and things seem to happen of their own accord. There was no doubt the American school of card manipulation was the finest in the world.

"Bamberg had what all great artists have," added a friend of Garrick Spencer, "the ability to make people believe that they love to be out there entertaining the audience. Everybody in that audience feels that he's working directly to them. Very few people can create this feeling in a big theatre. He knows the true secret. He diffuses love for the audience."

If only Vernon could import Bamberg's sense of wonder and his love for the audience into his own work. It was a tall task. When he did perform at private functions around New York, Vernon performed in the same manner as others, that is one trick after another, altering repertoire based on the mood of his audience and his own temperament, with little regard for the overall theatrical effect of performance. He performed much of the material he had honed at the Casino De Paree and the Madison Hotel—the Cups and Balls,

Over The Rainbow

a trick with small sponges, a torn and restored cigarette paper, the Ring on Stick, and dozens of card tricks. As an encore he did occasionally venture into more theatrical terrain, leaving the room momentarily to return as a Chinese magician, wearing one of Jeanne's fine masks and a Chinese robe, and performed the Chinese Linking Rings, a trick that he had experimented with since he was a child. The mask and gown provided the trick with a fresh look, a theatricality that enhanced the wonder inherent in the feat.

Magicians continued to speculate about Vernon's new act and a thumbnail description soon leaked out through the pipeline that ran between Paul Fox and Faucett Ross and, as a result, the broader magic community. Ross described the new act in a letter to Eddie McLaughlin.

He'd [Fox] had several letters from Dai who outlined pretty thoroughly his routine for the night club and that's arousing so much speculation around N.Y. Haven't gotten quite the straight of it but will feature the linking rings. Will also do the sponge ball routine with two spectators holding netting a la Mora. The routine will be similar to one with small rubber balls but, of course, much more visible. Another item will be some manipulations with a solid two inch billiard ball and climaxed with the visible transposition of ball and handkerchief from hand to hand a la J. Warren Keane. Will not do Cups & Balls as he says Galli-Galli [sic] killed the trick around N.Y. His finish is original and really wonderful. No one else could duplicate it please don't mention it to any one. He comes back for a bow and suddenly appears to grow—he visibly grows to a height of about eight feet! The secret is that Jeanne has made a perfect mask of Dai's face. After bowing off (wearing cape) he returns. In meanwhile has put on the mask with lazy tongs gimmick which is concealed in cape. Walks out again for bow, stands very still, music plays, and by some manipulation, the false face is elevated and a perfect illusion results. Can you beat it? I promised Paul not to tip this to anyone so please don't mention it to anyone although, as you are, me or anyone else couldn't possibly utilize it. Oh yes, Dai will also do the coin pail using one of Paul's pails. The music helps to put it over.

As Ross's description illustrates, the act was not settled and it lacked a unifying theme, a theme that could capture the imagination of his audience.

In May 1937, Sam Margules provided Vernon with an opportunity to make a little money. Margules sold the Seagram-Distillers Corp. a promotional giveaway that involved a magic trick, one created by Vernon. Margules charged $250 and split the fee with Vernon.

On June 11, 1937, Vernon celebrated his birthday in the company of Sam Horowitz, John Mulholland, David Bamberg, Chang (a friendly competitor of Bamberg's from South America), and their wives. Bamberg was leaving the next morning for South America. He was frustrated by the financial and artistic demands placed on his show in America by the William Morris Agency and decided to break his management contract with the agency. It was Chang, however, who persuaded him to return to South America rather than venture to Australia. Chang said that the world was ripe for war and that South America would be a far safer haven. Vernon, comfortable in America, decided to spend the remainder of the summer in Colorado, banking on sales of his silhouettes. Paul Fox would also be pleased to see him and hear a first-hand account of his recent exploits in New York.

Vernon set up shop once again at the foot of Pike's Peak in Manitou, cut silhouettes and had numerous sessions with Fox. Fox was thrilled as Vernon had much new material to show him, and he became particularly enamored with Vernon's routine for the Cups and Balls. The only flaw, he surmised, were the cups. They were made of tin that had been folded around a form and soldered up the side. Fox had an idea for improving their design and, by the end of the summer, presented Vernon with a set, spun in brass by the Marshall Manufacturing Company in Denver, that was more elegant and ergonomic that any of its predecessors. Their time together, however, was not all fun and games. Fox was frustrated by Vernon's cavalier approach to life, career, and family and told him so. After the confrontation, Fox injured himself, cutting his fingers on a pair of Vernon's shears. Vernon left Colorado Springs for St. Joseph, Missouri, expressing little remorse for what had transpired. Fox confided his dismay in a letter to Ross,

> Note what you had to say regarding Dai and am forced to agree with you although I have wanted to think other wise, and feel that he was on the road to big things for I shall always regard him as the outstanding magical genius of the age: but never the less and not

Over The Rainbow

withstanding he is a darned fool without any sense of proportions whatsoever.

I don't feel that I am very qualified to make an unbiased comment, however for I feel that I have been an arch victim of his darn foolishness—and if all indications and prognostications hold out I'll probably suffer the rest of my life for it.

If this had been an "honest" accident—I could charge it off but it was the result of one of Dai's "build ups."

The night before Dai had been bragging about squandering five or six dollars on the hangers on and bums around Manitou—and that afternoon I had taken him a letter from Jeanne—saying the lights had been turned off and that she had fallen over a chair in the dark and injured her leg—and that she only had $2 to her name and that they had to eat.

Like a chump I tried to tell Dai that he should have more of a sense of financial responsibility toward his family and cut out the gambling and feeding and buying drinks for all the bums. So when he saw that I was properly wrought up—he pulled the gag of asking me if I had a half dollar for change—I gave him the half and he gave me six dimes—I called his attention that he had given me six he said he knew it—and tried to give one back to him. When he refused to take it I got sore and tried to force him to take it back—by stabbing at his pocket and running the scissors through the fingers.

I guess you are tired of hearing all this over again in detail but it has almost gotten to the point of being an obsession with me, after the suffering it has caused me—and no relief in sight.

Dai's attitude, of course was that it was my fault and, that he had nothing to do with it, as I should have kept the dime.

These things make me wonder if Dai's apparent big heartedness and generosity is what it seems on the surface—in view of the way he has neglected to utilize his unusual talents to really provide for his family—because, after all, there is a real responsibility there—the old story—(and so tragically true) may apply—of the "big hearted" guys who in the past used to stop at the corner saloon on the way home on Saturday night and squander their pay check on drinks for the house—while the wife and children went without food and the decencies of life.

You know I have always tried to honestly boast [sic] Dai—but my enthusiasm hasn't always been shared by others. Am mindful of the attitude of those more practical minded whose attitude has been "what of it!" One individual through here in the last two years, when I tried to prophesize that Dai would eventually do a great act—and soar to great heights—said it wasn't in him to exert himself to that extent, and that he would end up by just playing around and not attending to business.

I hope you won't hold it "agin" me for writing as I have Ross. You are becoming more and more my "safety valve"—and I don't believe you will abuse my confidence. However, I haven't said anything to you I wouldn't tell Dai to his face. But I don't want it twisted around by any outsiders.

I feel you know my sincere regard for Dai, and I have really worried about his letting others get ahead of him even though he has been so wonderfully endowed by nature. I feel that Dai should have been sufficiently thankful for his inborn and inherited abilities to really use them—instead of preferring to follow the lines of least resistance by practically refusing opportunities that were almost thrust upon him.

Vernon ventured to St. Joseph primarily to visit Faucett Ross and cut silhouettes. There, as Arthur C. Spratt would apprise the readers of his "Amateur Department" column in *Genii* magazine, Vernon dazzled the local magicians with his craft and generosity.

About the only news of importance is that the great Dai Vernon has been residing in St. Joseph for the past six weeks to fill an engagement at the American Royal Show, in Kansas City, and will possibly remain in Kansas City for a while.

Dai was a guest at the last meeting of our local club, and boy did we see Magic or did we see Miracles? The latter word would best describe the effects he performed. His ten cards up the sleeve is a masterpiece,

Over The Rainbow

as his Cup and Ball routine. He performed with coins, balls and what have you.

You should see him deal "Seconds" (several methods).

You should see him deal "bottoms" (or "Rip a base" as Charlie Miller used to say.)

You should see him deal "From the center of the pack."

Perhaps you think I am 'Nuts,' but after his exhibition at our club meeting, I immediately dumped my magic in the river, and will soon retire to the farm.

All joking aside, he is one grand fellow. In the last month it has been my pleasure to spend several hours with him, talking magic, etc. I shall always cherish the memory of those hours spent with Dai Vernon. He is a scholar and above all, a gentleman.

Vernon also promised Spratt "not a trick, but a new principle in Magic, not to be found in *any* textbook on Magic, and never before used" that he could publish in his column. Eventually Vernon left St. Joseph, Missouri for Peoria, Illinois, where he was engaged for a couple of weeks to cut silhouettes. He then returned to New York, flush with cash. Home, Vernon continued to putter, handing Annemann a trick, "Up and Down," for the pages of the *Jinx* (likely the trick he had promised to give to Spratt), content to sit idly by as others like Jean Hugard continued to profit from his work. Hugard had compiled and edited a book, *The Encyclopedia of Card Tricks*, which included, among other pieces, rewrites of the secrets Vernon divulged in *Ten Card Problems*. Industry practice was such that "contributors" were meant to be content with accreditation. Fortunately for Hugard, Vernon had little interest in being paid for his ideas. Sadly, he had little concern for the economic or emotional plight of his family.

Though Vernon accepted few engagements, Miss King continued to call. When he did accept, his absentmindedness sometimes tempered the success of his performance. Miss King engaged his services, for example, to demonstrate gambling techniques for an intimate group of businessmen. Vernon showed up at the hotel ninety minutes beforehand and decided to pass the time in a restaurant across the street. While enjoying a coffee and a sandwich, he thought it would be a good idea to practice the routines on a group prior to the professional engagement. In short order, he gathered a crowd in the restaurant with his pasteboard prestidigitation. He discovered, unfortunately, that this focus group was also the audience he was expected to entertain at the hotel. His only remedy was to phone Al Baker and implore him to perform the paid engagement as if he were "Dai Vernon." Baker did as requested. Miss King was not pleased with the unannounced substitution but, as her client was satisfied with Baker's performance, she handed the check to Vernon so that he could endorse it over to Baker.

Eccentric people continued to parade through the Vernon apartment like it was the Little Blue Bookshop on Broadway a decade earlier. Now, however, instead of Gooey Louie, Jeanne had to contend with Count Orloff. The Count, who maintained the fiction that he was the direct descendant of Russian nobility, challenged Jeanne's notion of child rearing. He suggested that she keep, like he did, an Egyptian sarcophagus, complete with mummy, beneath her children's bed so that her boys could absorb the wisdom of the ages by osmosis.

And then there were the card tricks. Jeanne wrote,

> As an audience I have been called forth wet and dripping from a shower, to witness and enthuse over the way Mr. M [Vernon] has so brilliantly concealed a card in the seat of his trousers, and which he so cleverly regains possession of, at the psychological moment, by sitting on his hand, inadvertently. If he can fool me, a bored and rebellious audience at best, one who knows his every change of facial expression, every snort, blink, and grunt, then he is assured of success in fooling a lay audience to whom his strange mannerisms and unnatural contortions are without any particular significance. If, by any false move or fleeting shade of expression on my face, I am so unfortunate enough to betray the fact that the gathering pool of water at my feet is distracting my attention from the joyous contemplation of the little miracle he is performing for my special benefit, he flies into a rage, retires from the world and quietly contemplates the advantages of spending his remaining days in seclusion of a monastery.

Vernon pestered his wife and children with enough card tricks that his family soon regarded them as a form of punishment. Even if Vernon was trying to soothe his children by performing a minor miracle, Jeanne would reprimand her husband, "How dare you torture that child! Remember, he's mine too." Jeanne herself was not above using the threat of a card trick to her advantage. One evening, well after midnight, while Vernon was having a session with an enthusiast, Jeanne noticed Derek had risen from his bed and peeked into the living room. Derek had heard the racket of dice being picked up, whipped back and forth in a dice cup, and then deposited, stacked neatly one on top of the other, on the tabletop. Jeanne, who was reading in a nearby chair, instructed her son to return to sleep. Derek finally took heed when his mother threatened him, "Derek if you don't go to bed I'll have your father show you a card trick." The boy let out a scream and ran back to bed, never to return.

Vernon could be cruel both by accident and by design. Once, when Ted Verner placed second in a city-wide swim meet, his father reprimanded him for wasting his time. Vernon said that the boy should not have called him to come and see the race unless he could finish first. Vernon also seemed to enjoy toying with emotions. At Christmas, for example, Ted dreamt of receiving a giant Erector set. The box he spied under the tree on Christmas morning, however, was a tiny one and, as it turned out, was merely a starter kit. Only after Ted had unwrapped the present and registered his disappointment did his father pull the larger set from beneath the couch and present it to the boy.

The dysfunctional nature of the Vernon household reached a high point with the appearance of Compeer. Remembering an organ grinder with a little monkey that passed a hat for money, Vernon thought he could teach a monkey to perform tricks, both close up and on stage. He went to a pet store, observed two monkeys interact with their mother, and tried to fathom which of the two was more intelligent. Eventually, he made a decision and purchased the animal. The proprietor reached into the cage with gloves, the mother wailing all the while, and pried the chosen one from her care. The monkey was placed in a parrot cage wrapped in heavy brown paper and then into a sack. Vernon gave the parcel to Jeanne and asked her to take the monkey home to Brooklyn. As soon as Jeanne entered the subway carriage, the monkey started to yell and scream. The conductor asked Jeanne to leave at the next station. Once Jeanne was on the platform, the monkey would stop screaming, only to start again as soon as she boarded the next train. Each conductor in turn asked her to leave his train. Eventually, after getting off and on at every station en route to Brooklyn, she made it home. Despite the traumatic trip, the monkey soon regarded Jeanne as its surrogate mother. Jeanne wrote,

> *The baby monkey was named Compeer in honor of the brothers of the fraternal order of The Society of American Magicians, who use this endearing form of address. Little Compeer had been snatched from the protective arms of his mother at the tender age of eight weeks and in his infantile endeavor to find a substitute, promptly switched his demands for love and attention to me. He insisted on being carried about in my arms all day and on sleeping with me at night. As Mr. Magic and I shared a double bed, through lack of floor space and not old-fashioned sentimentality, this led to serious domestic complications and a threatened trip to Reno.*
>
> *Having two hellion sons and, out of desperate necessity, numerous books on child psychology, I tried to adapt some of the suggested training methods to a working plan for sidetracking Compeer's nocturnal demands. Either my adaptation was faulty or Compeer's atavistic instincts were superior to modern child psychology. They certainly proved less complicated and more to the point. In fact they were completely successful. He simply let loose with a series of blood curdling yells which continued unabated until he was taken into bed. He then quieted down and snuggled himself into a smelly little ball of brown fur and slept peacefully through the night.*
>
> *I discovered quite by accident some time later that Compeer wasn't particularly selective about his bedfellows, he just objected to sleeping alone. A Maltese kitten was the solution to this problem. The domestic crisis passed and Mr. Magic's threatened trip to Reno never materialized.*

Eventually, Vernon's mother, with whom he maintained a checkered correspondence, became involved in his day-to-day affairs. She couldn't conceive of how anyone could exist without regular employment and the structure of going off to work everyday just as her late husband had done in the Copyright Branch of the Department of Agriculture. What did her son do with his time? How did he earn a living and support his family? She had to come to New York, along with her middle son, Napier, to see for herself. Napier was looking forward to the trip. He had started a new position as a commission-based stockbroker after losing his position as a sales manager with the *Ottawa Evening Journal* (during the difficult economic times, the newspaper was releasing those who did not have families to support), and he had not seen his brother in years. Napier hoped the trip would be therapeutic for both him and his brother. Upon his family's arrival, Vernon took them on a tour of New York. At Jones Beach, Napier proved he was just as agile and acrobatic as his older brother when it came to walking on his hands along the shore. The trip turned tragic, however. Napier contracted pneumonia, dying only days later. Mrs. Verner returned home to Toronto (where she had been living with her youngest son, Arthur) to mourn the loss of Napier. The loss of her eldest and favorite child to the world of show business suddenly paled in comparison.

As Vernon continued to waffle and drift, some of his staunchest allies started to waiver.

Paul Fox, whose personal life had taken its own turn for the worse with the onslaught of arthritis in the hand that guided much of his engraving work, wrote Ross, "I think it smells to high heaven the way Dai has been about the 'act' with all the splendid backing from (Garrick) Spencer." Fox suggested in his missives to Ross that history indicated that it is not what you do, but how you do it. The most successful performers, such as Malini and Rosini, performed standard effects but mesmerized their audiences with personality. Fox's pessimism may have been rooted in his own lack of confidence, the notion that he and Vernon were, in many respects, two of a kind: magicians who believed that the magic should be just as mesmerizing as the personality of the performer. Spencer did not waiver, however. He believed in Vernon and continued to offer his support.

And then came an epiphany.

One evening, Spencer and Vernon found themselves discussing the merits of the Cups and Balls. Both men loved the effect but agreed that it was not a suitable trick for a nightclub floorshow. First, it was now over-exposed; many contemporary performers featured the trick. Second, the trick, according to Spencer, was simply too confusing for a nightclub audience, a crowd that would often talk and drink throughout a performance, to follow. It would be much more effective, he suggested, if it could be performed with just one cup and one ball. The audience could then follow the sequence of effects with ease.

Spencer's comment prompted Vernon to canvas his encyclopedic knowledge of magic for a routine that could be performed with just one cup and one ball. Tom Osborne had just sketched out such a routine in his recent book, *Cups and Balls Magic*, published by Kanter's Magic Shop of Philadelphia. Vernon recalled reading its predecessor—an effect published in 1909 by another New York area performer, Burling Hull—in a booklet titled *Deviltry*. Hull's notion was quite simple: the performer would vanish a billiard ball and then make it reappear beneath a paper cone that had been shown empty moments before it had been placed on a table. Hull reprinted this sequence the following year in a more elaborate work, *Expert Billiard Ball Manipulation*. Two variations on this theme appeared in *The Sphinx* shortly afterwards. Vernon remembered that one of the variations, a contribution by Scottish magician De Vega in the January 1911 issue, was particularly interesting. De Vega offered a novel way of making the ball vanish. He would place the ball on the back of his right hand and then, in the act of covering the ball with the cone, secretly remove the ball without any false moves or difficult sleights.

Vernon forged a cone from paper and, with one of the billiard balls he had acquired from Floyd Thayer years earlier at hand, experimented with the technique. The magic flowed from his fingertips like a jazz musician extemporizing on a standard. In this case, however, the piece could hardly be called a standard. The melody had been abandoned for over twenty-five years. It was a theme buried in the recess of his mind. Vernon discovered that he could not only make the ball vanish and reappear but also, magically, penetrate the crown of the cone. He could even make the ball change color and, if need be, shape. Enthused, Spencer suggested that the cone become a motif for the act. What costume or character they asked, did a cone conjure up?

The answer: A Harlequin.

Harlequin or *Arlequin,* a character whose *Comedia Dell'Arte* dramatic roots are often connected to the comic representation of a medieval demon, had become, by the early part of the twentieth century, a visual icon for playfulness, mischievousness, and devilry; in short, it was the perfect character for performing magic. Vernon now had his theme, a thread from which he could weave a tapestry of magic.

Performing as Harlequin had other advantages. First, the character and the type of magic he would perform were far removed from the manner and magic performed by Cardini and his imitators. Harlequin was also a universal icon, one that transcended many cultural boundaries and one that, when combined with music, Vernon was confident could usher his audience into that world of wonder. Best of all, from Vernon's perspective, the Harlequin created an alter ego; Vernon was not required to be the Harlequin off-stage.

Separating an off-stage character from an on-stage persona, particularly in the variety arts, was difficult. Most were expected to be "on" at all times. Often the performer himself promoted this. Alexander Herrmann and Max Malini were rarely off-stage, electing to perform magic on the street and in restaurants in order to draw attention to their work. Although Houdini did not perform escapes at the drop of hat, made sure that those around him were aware that they were in the presence of *the man*. William Robinson, who had achieved fame as Chung Ling Soo, a Chinese conjuror, maintained the fiction off-stage, speaking to the press through an faux interpreter in order not to risk alienating the affections of his audience by disclosing that he was an American playing the part of a Chinese magician. Vernon could remain a nondescript New Yorker by day and transform himself into a Harlequin at night. He enlisted Jeanne to design the costume. It had been years since she had been inspired to attack a project with such relish. She welcomed the opportunity to conduct research into *Commedia Dell'Arte* and tap her talent as a visual artist.

Jeanne set off to design the costume, while Vernon and Spencer continued to muse about the structure and content of the act. The Chinese Linking Rings had always fascinated Vernon. As a boy, he had seen William Hilliar, the founder of *The Sphinx*, perform the trick on the grounds of the Canadian National Exhibition. Vernon had even fabricated his own rings out of iron before acquiring a set from a magic supply depot. His interest in the trick had never wavered, and he continued to develop original twists and turns with the trick, prompting Faucett Ross to write about them in 1932 to friends within his circle. Although the Harlequin character precluded him from performing his most recent routine, one performed in Chinese robe and mask, Vernon was confident that he could choreograph elements of it into a new sequence, one suitable for the new character and costume. Much would depend on the music. It had to be perfect.

Vernon and Spencer considered music an integral element of the act, one just as important as the magic or the personality of the performer. Few magicians worked entirely to music, and most of those who did performed their magic to snippets of popular songs or original music written for their turn. Spencer suggested that Vernon choreograph magic to classical music, and Vernon embraced the idea. He remembered the thrill he experienced as a child at concerts he attended in Ottawa, and imagined that people would be just as intrigued by a Harlequin who performed magic to great music as he was as a boy by the man who waved the baton in front of the orchestra.

It helped that both men were interested in music, Vernon primarily in ragtime and jazz and Spencer in the classical repertoire. For the rings, Spencer suggested Vernon compose a routine to the "Carillon de Westminster," the closing movement of the Third Suite of Louis Vierne's *Pieces de Fantaisie*. Vierne was, for much of his career, the resident organist of Notre Dame Cathedral in Paris, and was known for his virtuoso skill and ability to compose ethereal, impressionistic symphonic works for the organ. "Carillon de Westminster," inspired by the chimes of Westminster Cathedral in London, was his most popular composition. Vierne wrote the piece in 1926 for his inaugural tour of the United States. Spencer provided Vernon with a 78 rpm recording of the work, and Vernon set off to develop a routine, the linking and unlinking of solid bands of steel, to the recording.

Vernon's approach to the trick was fresh. Just as the Cups and Balls begat the cone and ball, Vernon distilled the Chinese Linking Rings down to its essence, reducing the number of rings—first to five, and ultimately to four—in the routine from the eight, ten or even twelve rings manipulated by most magicians. It was a minimalist approach, one that emphasized grace, elegance, and beauty rather than the brute force most exhibited by clanging one ring against another.

Second, as the routine was choreographed to a specific score, one that required Vernon to weave the tonality of the rings with the chimes in the original score, Vernon was forced to redesign the ap-

Over The Rainbow

paratus used for the trick. Traditional rings had a tinny sound, not at all in character with the chimes of Westminster. Fortunately, Paul Fox had a solution: hollow rings—tubular bells. Vernon used ¾ inch Shelby tubing, a pure steel tube with very thin walls, and found a firm that was used to handling Shelby tubing in the manufacture of dirigibles and could weld two hollow tubes together without plugging the ends. (Plugs would dampen the tone.) The firm made Vernon a set of five rings, each one twelve inches in diameter.

With the ring routine in progress, Vernon focused on the act's opening sequence, the one with the cone and ball. Advantage players had always stressed the importance of transitions—how they get "into the move" and "out of the move." The same issue applied to magic; how could Vernon make the transition into and out of the trick with the ball and cone? Fortunately, another Tom Osborne manuscript, the *3-1 Rope Trick*, caught his attention. (Kanter's Magic Shop would publish an expanded edition of the Osborne manuscript in December 1937.) The trick, the magical transformation of three cords into one, was simple and direct. Vernon would display three sash cords, sometimes red and other times green, of equal length and then gather them together in his left hand. After a suitable magical gesture, he would take hold of two ends, separate his arms, and display that he had fused the cords together into one long piece. It was, he thought, a terrific opening number, and it created an opportunity to move into the routine with the ball and cone by gathering up the cord in his left hand, stroking the bundle with his right, and producing a billiard ball at his fingertips.

Vernon then placed the cord aside, removed a handkerchief from a pocket, and performed a series of feats (inspired by J. Warren Keane) with the billiard ball and handkerchief. He eventually produced a leather cone, six inches in height, from beneath the handkerchief and embarked on his minimalist version of the cups and balls, a bewildering series of manipulations with the ball, cone, and handkerchief. He concluded the sequence by producing a saltshaker from beneath the cone.

Once the cone had been handed off to Jeanne, Vernon poured a large quantity of salt from the shaker into his clenched left fist. He then magically made the salt disappear as he threw it into the air. Moments later, it rematerialized, Vernon snatching it out of thin air with his right hand. He removed a small decorative tray from his pocket, held it in his left hand, and allowed the salt to stream forth from his right hand on to the tray.

The Salt Pour was an unusual effect. It exemplified how old chestnuts are altered over time as many minds attempt to simplify technique and clarify effect. Vernon had first read about the trick in 1909 in Downs' *The Art of Magic*. The trick was performed close up rather than on a stage and relied on pure sleight-of-hand and unflinching audacity. Emil Jarrow, a vaudeville performer and sleight-of-hand expert, adapted the trick for the stage in the 1920s, substituting tobacco for salt. In 1931, at the annual conclave of the International Brotherhood of Magicians held that year in Columbus, Ohio, a magician from Minneapolis named Henry Gordien performed the trick, again with salt and close-up, but with a new method. Faucett Ross approached Gordien for the secret; Gordien readily acquiesced and showed Ross the appliance he used to perform the trick, giving him permission to perform the routine. Ross wasted little time in relaying the information to Paul Fox and was surprised to learn that Fox had already turned his inventive mind towards improving the trick years earlier. Ross also communicated his findings to Vernon. Now, years later, Vernon put it all together, choreographing a sequence with salt that was suitable for the stage. It became the final segment of his opening mélange of magic for the Harlequin Act, a sequence he performed to, at Garrick Spencer's suggestion, the "Overture" to Tchaikovsky's *Sleeping Beauty*.

Vernon now had his opening segment (sash cord, cone and ball, and salt) and the middle segment (the Chinese Linking Rings). He needed a grand finish, something unusual, graceful, and spectacular.

The character and costume of the Harlequin did not permit him to elongate his body pursuant to his original intention. Vernon then became intrigued with the idea of scaling playing cards that would explode, unfurling a snowstorm of flowers and confetti, over the heads of his audience. The cards, loaded with confetti and paper flowers that would spring to life, proved difficult to construct and had an unreliable release mechanism. He knew, however, that he was on the right track. Fortunately, Vernon was a student of magic, all magic, and had witnessed great performers from a variety of cultures as they toured North America. He recalled a Japanese magician, possibly the great Ten-Ichi, stage in Montreal a beautiful piece with a butterfly and a fan.

The performer created a butterfly out of paper, and then appeared to bring it to life through the skillful flicks, twists, and turns of a fan. Traditionally, in the hands of a master Japanese magician, the butterfly would then settle on a potted plant and discover a mate. The two butterflies would then dance in the air and come to rest near water, where one accidentally drowned. The other, a mate for life, next took its own life. The performer then transformed the butterflies into a torrential snowstorm of paper that cascaded over the heads of the audience. The Butterfly and Fan was, and remains, a poetic and visual high watermark for the art. Vernon thought he could distill the trick down to its essence and eliminate the love story while still retaining its visual strength, one with the same emotional arc that David Bamberg employed in his routine with the bear: gaiety followed by sadness followed by surprise and wonder.

Vernon researched the flight of butterflies. Charles Miller sent him two beautiful fans, one red, the other blue, both trimmed with gold, which he had purchased in San Francisco's Chinatown and a metal form, designed by Paul Fox, that would punch out scores of butterflies from rice paper so Vernon could create the trick's finish. Vernon discovered, unfortunately, that draughts and air currents made it difficult to perform the routine as envisioned. Not wishing to discard the concept entirely, he visited the Bronx Zoo and explored the possibility of producing live moths, letting them loose for the finale, when they would fly to the lights. He eventually discarded the notion of using butterflies altogether and turned to an even more simple narrative line, one described superficially by Hatton and Plate in their seminal 1910 work, *Magicians' Tricks How They Are Done* and, more recently, by Harlan Tarbell in 1926 as the Chinese Paper Mystery and Wintertime In China as part of Lesson Four of the *Tarbell Course of Magic*. It was the same routine that Vernon's friend, Stewart Judah, had tried to teach Houdini to use for what turned out to be Houdini's final tour.

The performer displayed a twenty-four inch by six-inch strip of white tissue paper and slowly tore it into several pieces that were then folded into a small package. The performer made a magical gesture and then opened the package. The strip was now restored to its original condition. He then repeated the sequence of tearing the strip of paper into small pieces and folding them together. Instead of opening the package, however, he dunked the paper into a glass of water, scooped out the saturated ball with a small stick, and wrung the water out of the bundle. He then picked up a fan and transformed the bundle into the snowstorm of paper, the motion of the fan rocketing confetti-like tissue over the heads of the audience. Vernon choreographed the entire sequence to music suggested by Garrick Spencer: a segment of the acclaimed violin virtuoso Jascha Heifetz's 78 rpm recording of Camille Saint-Saens' *Rondo Capriccioso in A minor, Opus 28*.

The Harlequin Act now had a beginning, a middle, and an end. Spencer commissioned Felix Meyer, a friend and acclaimed musical arranger, to orchestrate *Sleeping Beauty, Carillon De Westminster* and *Rondo Capriccioso in A minor, Opus 28* into a single arrangement with enough charts to outfit a nightclub ensemble. Jeanne Verner, by this time, had also completed the rendering for the costume. She tabled two designs: one of Harlequin performing a trick with a handkerchief and a second one of Pierrot performing a trick with a billiard ball. Vernon would be the Harlequin and Jeanne would be Pierrot, his assistant. Spencer handed the renderings over to another acquaintance, a costume designer and theatrical tailor, for execution. The designer said, "I understand exactly: you have to wear a large cape, you throw it open and they see a beautiful emerald green silk lining, you swish the other side and it's bright red. This startles people, they sit up, they scream."

Initially, Spencer wanted the color scheme to be restricted to black, white, and gray. Vernon and Spencer, however, were soon swept away by the designer's enthusiasm and authorized him to construct a white satin costume with splashes of color and ribbons, and a cape that was fourteen feet in length. The costume required Vernon to wear hosiery, one red stocking and the other green, green eye shadow, and a skullcap. Jeanne's costume, Pierrot, was understated but elegant, completely appropriate for her role as assistant. It was now time to workshop the act in front of an audience.

Ross wrote McLaughlin on May 6, 1938.

> *I had a long letter from Dai last week in Philadelphia. He played two weeks in Harrisburg Pa; being held over the second week and says the engagement was a real success. Then he jumped to Philly for a week (last week) while he played the Hotel Adelphia (Café Marguery)... Dai says he stopped the show several times and got over very well. Says an English agent caught the act and cabled recommendations to England. Also a scout from Billy Rose's Casa Mañana was there and*

Over The Rainbow

Jeanne's renderings for Vernon's Harlequin costume.

> *possibly it's either England or Billy Rose's. Dai asked me to send the letter on to Paul Fox otherwise I'd send it to you but above is the gist of it. Jeanne is working in the act and doing a good job of it & they've hired a good woman to take care of the kids.*

Holden reported in "New York Notes" in the May 1938 issue of The Linking Ring,

> *Every so often we have a new face in magic that comes in to the front and starts a new craze in magic. This time it is not a new face but the greatest card man in the world. He has built up a most wonderful act of magic that is a sensation and strange to say No Card Tricks. Dai Vernon has produced an act that he has been working on for two years and now has it perfected and opened here at one of the night spots and was immediately booked for Harrisburg and they held him over and now is busy signing contracts with the prospect of the Rainbow Room here in N.Y.C. with European offers, etc.*

Initially, Vernon was interested in traveling to Europe. He had dreamt of performing in England and socializing further with English magicians. He had met several recently who were on tour to magic conventions in the States, and Vernon considered one of them, a greengrocer from Ayr, Scotland named John Ramsay, a master of subtle sleight-of-hand. Vernon had been warned against traveling to Europe, however, by both Chang and Bamberg and elected to follow their advice. Fortunately, Spencer had a contact, John Roy, at the Rainbow Room, and Vernon was invited to be the fourth magician to play the club. The three other magicians were Fred Keating, Miaco (a manipulator in the Cardini-mode) and Russell Swann (a comedy magician). The Rainbow Room, perched on the sixty-fifth floor of Thirty Rockefeller Plaza, the tallest and most prominent building in the Herculean development, symbolized all of the glamour and elegance New York nightlife had to offer.

Even though Vernon had spent two years developing the act—the longest and most intense period he had ever devoted to non-gambling artifice—he was not satisfied with its development. He sought both a more dramatic opening number and a coda to the act. For the opening, he thought a trick described in 1907 by Ellis Stanyon in *Stanyon's Serial Lessons in Conjuring, No. 16* suitable. It had been performed by the English magician Martin Chapender at Egyptian Hall in 1904 and might fit the bill. Chapender entered wearing white gloves. He removed the gloves and tossed them into the air where they morphed into a white dove. For the act's coda, Vernon thought of Compeer. He wanted to toss a coconut, much like the white gloves, into the air and have it transform into Compeer, dressed as a Harlequin.

Unfortunately, Compeer was not as cooperative as the dove. Vernon couldn't train the little monkey. Vernon learned that the few times he inserted the trick into his show that Compeer was more interested in masturbating before the public than he was in following the script. Whether it was the lights or the music, or simply that he was in front of a crowd, Compeer's penis would get hard and red, even when Vernon tried to contain it with a pre-show mustard plaster or tin chastity belt.

Fortunately, magicians had more to gossip about than Vernon producing a monkey in mid-air that would then fondle himself on stage. Max Holden had just reported that *Greater Magic* was now complete, and that magicians could expect this magnum opus to be available in the fall.

Over The Rainbow

Carl Jones, the publishing scion from Minneapolis, spent years piecing the manuscript together. Its original author, John Northern Hilliard, ghostwriter of *The Art of Magic*, had been compiling material for the tome for years but passed away in an Indianapolis hotel room—Hilliard was, at that time, advance agent for the Thurston show—on March 14, 1935. Jones commissioned Jean Hugard in October 1937 to complete the work and retained Harlan Tarbell to illustrate it. Jones and Hugard continued to solicit contributions from both amateur and professional magicians, the goal being to produce the definitive book on modern magic. Vernon was approached but did not want to exert himself writing up material in a form that would do it justice or, given their previous history, communicate the inner workings of his latest discoveries to Hugard.

Vernon did give Jones permission, however, to reprint the tricks and subtleties that had been described years earlier by Ross in *Ten Card Problems* and *Five Close-Up Problems* as well as permission to include An Ace Trick for the Expert, the trick that appeared in *The Sphinx* in 1935. Fritz Braue, a San Francisco-based magic enthusiast, reporter, and part-time columnist for *The Sphinx*, would describe the aforementioned effect in the August 1938 issue as "the most provocative trick of the past decade." Besides, Vernon had his mind focused on the Harlequin Act. The contracts had been signed, and he was set to open at the Rainbow Room in June.

Days before his official opening when Vernon had the opportunity to rehearse the act in the very room, the acerbic *Variety* critic Rober Reinhart, offered him some counsel. He arranged for José Limon, a new and critically acclaimed choreographer, to add grace notes to the act. Vernon had two sessions with Limon, each long enough to shatter his confidence in both his ability and the act. Although Limon was enthusiastic and optimistic, Vernon realized for the first time the enormous challenge that faced him. The Harlequin Act required him to be not just a magician but also an actor and dancer, skills for which he had had no formal training. Vernon described his sessions with Limon.

> *He [Limon] went through the pantomime of these tricks. The beautiful way he held everything; the things he did just sparkled. He did no magic—just the color and the style—months and years of training. Then I felt incomplete; I knew I was only doing 1/100th of what was possible with my act and I lost heart. What really disgusted me was*

The Harlequin enters, removes his cape and performs Osborne's rope trick.

seeing José Limon doing ballet with it and I realized how badly I was doing compared with how it could be done.

Spencer attributed Vernon's lack of confidence to nerves and tried to calm him. Being nervous, Spencer explained, was a sign of a true artist. He added that even Jack Dempsey, the heavyweight champion of the world, would bite his nails and walk around like a caged lion before he got into the ring. Once the bell rang, however, Dempsey was a cool, calculated fighter. Virtuosity, Spencer explained, would always shine through. Vernon, reassured that others felt the same nerves, took comfort in Spencer's remarks and opened as scheduled on Monday, June 20, 1938, accompanied by the Rainbow Room's resident ensemble, Ben Culter and his Orchestra.

The New York critics were effusive. The critic for *Variety* exclaimed, "Dai Vernon, one of the ablest card handlers and close up workers in the prestidigitating field, has arranged a novel floor show routine for the Rainbow Room. Deserting the dress suit formula, Vernon takes a leaf from the pages of magical history and appears in a swell looking Harlequin costume. Booked here by John Roy. It's a natural for smart spots."

Over The Rainbow

Elegance begets elegance; Vernon performs the Ball and Cone and Salt Pour.

Hy Gardner in "Broadway Newsreel" said, "Cardini calls Dai Vernon the only magician he'd take his hat off to. Blackstone says that Vernon is his idea of a real magician. He's a sort of Paul Draper of sleight-of-hand artists, smooth, suave, sleek and yet dazzling." The critic for *New Yorker* quipped, "A sleightly fey atmosphere prevails these nights up in the Rainbow Room where Dai Vernon as "Harlequin" does a sleight of hand act. It's all pantomime, with an elfin musical accompaniment, and the whole thing has a strangely hypnotic effect. Mr. Vernon, as far as I'm concerned, is mammy." Vernon's engagement was extended from one week to *ten*. Paul Fox cabled his congratulations and added, "Big news if it means you have definitely decided to stop side stepping opportunities." He then wrote Ross,

Did you see the A.P. syndicated 3 column write up of Dai — 3 columns with 3 column photo — doing the linking rings in the Rainbow Grill? Swell! Did I get a thrill way out here! It was in the Pueblo paper. They tried to look it up — but had discarded the mat. However they are reprinting without photo with additional comment on his being a summer resident here for several seasons. Just had a letter from Bob Rinehart [sic] — he flew out to Hollywood and he is flying in

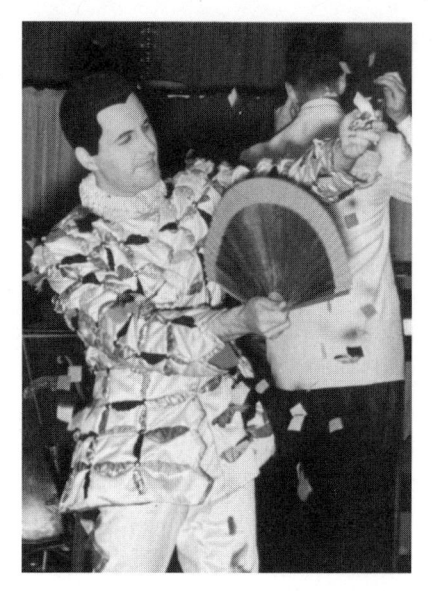

The Linking Rings were followed by a stage-filling performance of Wintertime in China.

here tomorrow arriving at nine o'clock to remain over until Sunday afternoon. Know nothing about his plans. Am looking forward to hearing first hand the details of Dai's "new" act.

Vernon soon discovered that repeating the act stifled his creativity. As Vernon was a composer as much as a performer, and didn't relish taking time away from new work in order to perform old work night after night, he tried to insert new pieces and movements into the act. John Roy, on behalf of the management, reminded him to present the act that had been booked originally. Fortunately, there were incidents, most of which involved the dove, which helped to break up the monotony.

I was using the gloves, changing the gloves into the dove and it happened. I had this little dove, and I threw it. The dove went like a baseball—I thought it was dead—and it landed in a woman's lap. I was scared stiff; I thought the poor little dove had died. Then I heard a tremendous laugh and applause. The little dove had landed in a lady's lap and laid an egg. Listen, I don't think anybody ever did a better trick than that! The audience laughed and applauded.

Over The Rainbow

[Another time] before that, this little dove flew straight out the window, the window was open about six inches, and it just flew out. Well, imagine. My wife is a great lover of pets, and so am I, and we were both so upset about this poor little dove, flying around sixty-six stories up in New York. This was at night—the roaring forties in New York and there are all kinds of pigeons around there, pretty tough pigeons that would coo with an accent, really tough pigeons and we thought of this poor little tame dove, being out there with all these ruffians. We were really heart broken. We thought, "What will happen to the little dove—what will happen to it." So, anyway, we went on home to Brooklyn, and it was about four hours later, and we were in bed—and we heard a little noise—a little pecking.

My wife said, "What is that?"

It kept up—pecking on that window—scratching on the window—so a little later, I opened up the window—and there was that little dove on the windowsill. We were all the way over into Brooklyn—across the East river—at least twelve miles. And this was no homing pigeon—it was just a little white Java dove.

Word of these incidents soon spread, and John Chapman wrote about them in his column "Mainly About Manhattan." They may not have been as exciting as vanishing an elephant but, as Houdini would have said, any publicity was good publicity.

Vernon found, however, other things to complain about. He wanted a new costume. The original was too flamboyant. The satin distracted the eye away from some of the magic and was expensive to clean. Also, it was difficult to coordinate the magic with the music; the Ben Culter Orchestra featured jazz musicians who were unaccustomed to playing a classical score with the precision that the act demanded. The real issue, however, was a familiar one: Vernon had accepted the challenge of creating an act that was both an artistic and commercial success, and now that it was within his grasp, it was time to turn his attention towards another goal.

This did not sit well with Jeanne. For her, the act provided a measure of stability. Not only were they making money, but the class of visitor to their household had improved measurably, now including people whose company she actually enjoyed: Garrick Spencer, Dr. Jacob Daley, Sam Margules and, a newcomer, Francis Finneran, originally from New England, but now of New York. Al Baker, who spied Finneran and his ability with cards when the young man started loitering around his magic shop in Times Square, introduced Finneran to Vernon. Finneran was also, like Larry Gray, an extraordinary mimic and a natural raconteur. His impressions of her husband brought laughter to the household, and for Jeanne laughter had often been her only shield. Now, just when prospects were looking up, her husband contemplated a change of scenery and act. Faucett Ross apprised McLaughlin,

> *Have had quite a few cards from Dai Vernon. Last I heard was that he isn't working now but expects to open at Miami Beach, Fla. shortly. He worked four solid months at the Rainbow Grill and should have saved some $$$ but I don't know. Had a long letter from Francis Finneran recently and said that Dai wants to give up the Harlequin Act and do cards exclusively—a mistake & I've told him so. Confidentially Dai wrote that he and Jeanne were on verge of separation but imagine they've patched things up now.*

As the couple contemplated their next move, the magic community mourned the loss of a master magician: T. Nelson Downs, aged seventy-one, passed away in his sleep in the early morning hours of September 11, 1938. Ross commiserated with McLaughlin and suggested that the best thing they could do was warn Mrs. Downs to be wary of magicians who pry books, apparatus, and ephemera from the widows of famous magicians for resale to hobbyists and collectors. Ross wrote,

> *There's one thing we should do and that is to prevent what has happened so often in similar cases. I mean, see to it that these vulture magicians do not plunder through Tommy's magic things. You may recall that when Houdini died, a horde of self-styled friends ruthlessly stole an incredible number of his prized possessions. Dunninger, I understand, was the worst offender—he really got plenty, I'm told. Mrs. Houdini, of course, didn't realize what was happening until it had happened and then it was too late.*

With the act now in storage, Vernon resumed his late night sessions. At one of them, Ted Annemann, the publisher of *The Jinx*, paid Vernon twenty-five dollars to tip the secret to the mind reading trick he had performed for the past ten years, the one he featured at the Casino De Paree, the Madison Hotel, and private functions around New York. This was the same trick which had been appropriated unceremoniously from Sam Margules by Dunninger, to the general magic community. Vernon also permitted Annemann to write up both a cursory outline of the history of the effect and its technical requirements, in Vernon's voice, as the cover feature of the October 1938 issue of the *Jinx*. Annemann dubbed the trick "The Brain Wave Deck." Professionals and amateurs everywhere embraced it, and soon magic dealers, now knowing not only that the trick used a special deck of cards but also how to construct it, immediately started selling the item. Some, like Max Holden who advertised the trick for one dollar on the back page of the December 1938 *The Linking Ring*, gave Vernon credit. No money, just an acknowledgment that Vernon had created it. Other dealers were less generous. Regardless, the trick soon became a best seller.

Paul Fox lamented the fact that the younger set expected to receive the latest secrets simply because they were, in their own minds, magicians. He wrote Ross,

> *I shudder when I see what is being exposed in literature—Jinx—etc. [Orville] Meyer came to call on me while I was in Denver, and more than ever am impressed how easy it is for these young 'uns to lay their hands on stuff. He gets every new book and subscribes to every magazine and reads them from cover to cover—besides carrying on an extensive correspondence. Was telling me about the long letters he gets from Jean Hugard. Meyer commented, "I don't lay claim to having any ideas but I do like to collect the other fellows stuff and use it." I use him again as an example and I know they are all doing it. The old days are gone forever, eh? It does make one sore though how the stuff gets around and is sold over the counter. It is almost impossible to think anything exclusive the way the new comers are hounding and passing around. They haven't an idea—just swipe the other fellow's ideas and then fight over who got in first—as to priority rights. Don't mention or think that I am singling out Meyer in particular. It just seems to me the new generation is coming by the dope too easily.*

Whatever concerns Fox may have had over the publication of The Brain Wave Deck must have paled in comparison once he read the secrets revealed in the pages of *Greater Magic*. Released in December 1938, *Greater Magic* was heralded by the fraternity as the greatest book ever produced on magic. At 1,030 pages, it was advertised as explaining 715 tricks—with 1,120 illustrations—belonging to 107 magicians: more tricks and more illustrations than Professor Hoffmann's trilogy—*Modern Magic*, *More Magic* and *Later Magic*—combined. Every category of conjuring, including card tricks, coin tricks, magic with silks, balls, cigarettes and cigars, ropes, mind reading, old and new apparatus, stage tricks, and illusions, was represented.

Advertisements indicated that Vernon provided seventeen items to its pages, second only to Al Baker's nineteen. A forty-page "prospectus" distributed to potential purchasers reminded magicians of both Vernon's standing in the community and his contribution to the book:

> *One of the greatest exponents of sleight-of-hand, and many expert judges contend that he is actually the greatest, is Mr. Dai Vernon of New York. His fame as an exponent of the real magic of the hands is*

From left: Horowitz, Margules, Jones, Cardini, and Vernon celebrate the release of Greater Magic *in December, 1938.*

world wide. He has devoted his life to the perfection of the old methods and the invention of new and startling processes in the handling of objects so dear to the heart of the conjurer—playing cards, coins, billiard balls and silks. The result is that his work is the closest approach to absolute perfection that has perhaps ever been attained. Mr. Vernon has confided to the author for inclusion in Greater Magic *seventeen of his greatest tricks, many of them worked out in conjunction with the amateur, S. Leo Horowitz of Jersey City, of whom Hilliard wrote, "Some of the subtlest and cleverest of present day card conjuring feats have emanated from his brain and in his hands they are real masterpieces of deception."*

Vernon's influence, however, on *Greater Magic* extended well beyond seventeen items. The book was a testament to subtle sleight-of-hand, much of which had its origin in card table artifice, the artifice that Vernon mined, catalogued, and disseminated to his extended circle of friends and acquaintances. *Greater Magic* also contained work on 'think a card' tricks but, as Fox had intimated, with little regard for proprietary rights. It describes, for example, Ralph Hull's Mental Discernment as the "best of this kind of trick," oblivious to fact that its genius came from Vernon, not Hull. The introduction to the section on Cups and Balls also illustrated Vernon's influence, again without credit:

This time honored but not time worn trick has enjoyed a new spell of popularity during the last few years. Owing to the demise of vaudeville and the tremendous growth of night club entertaining there is a constantly increasing demand for magicians who can perform close up tricks. For this purpose there is nothing better than a smart routine with the cups and balls. Present day audiences find the mysterious travels of the little balls from cup to cup just as intriguing as did the Egyptians in the days of Tut-Ank-Amen and possibly in the centuries before him.

Jean Hugard, although not particularly on cordial terms with Vernon, did speak of him in glowing words in the chapter titled "Card Stars Of The USA," which listed the ten greatest practitioners of card magic: Theodore Annemann, Al Baker, Cardini, S. Leo Horowitz, Stewart Judah, Nate Leipzig, William H. McCaffrey, Paul Rosini, John Scarne, and Dai Vernon, and provided examples of their skills. Hugard gushed,

> Mr. Vernon is recognized as the most finished card expert in the States. The most modern of moderns, his achievements in card magic are unparalleled. He has an artistry that tingles at his finger tips. Under cover of perfectly natural movements his subtle sleights completely bewilder even the card expert himself.
>
> He has a pride in his craft and one might deduce from his performance the whole theory and practice of artistic conjuring. So, while the art has in too many cases drifted into a vulgar incompetence, the craft is illuminated by many a flash of unexpected talent. The brilliant achievements of a Dai Vernon would relieve the gloom of the darkest era and his masterpieces make atonement for the environing commonplaceness.

As magicians celebrated the release of *Greater Magic,* Sam Margules invited Vernon to perform on a gala show, one he organized annually for B.M.L. Ernst Relief Fund of the Society of American Magicians. The show was scheduled for February 25, 1939 at the Heckscher Theatre. Vernon readily accepted the invitation, as the show was also billed as a "Tribute to Sam Margules" in recognition of the yeoman service Margules had provided to magicians for over two decades. Vernon's performance of the Harlequin Act stopped the show. The assembly awarded him a standing ovation, and John Mulholland wrote in the pages of *The Sphinx* that "the perfect manipulative act of Dai Vernon" was one of the outstanding events of the program.

Magicians were not the only ones bewitched by Vernon. Mark Leddy, Frances Rockefeller King's former assistant, was in attendance that evening and asked Vernon to join his growing stable of performers. Leddy wanted to represent Vernon exclusively and asked him to sign a five-year management contract. Vernon consulted Jeanne and, after being reminded of David Bamberg's experience with the William Morris Agency, declined the invitation. Vernon could see no advantage at this point in his career to being legally represented by just one agent, particularly when that agent could not guarantee work, only representation.

Undeterred, Leddy brokered a marquee engagement for Vernon, a place in a new variety show, *Short Stories,* set to open March 16,

Over The Rainbow

1939 on the world's largest indoor stage, Radio City Music Hall. *Short Stories* was produced by Russell Markert and featured sets by Nat Karson and a variety of performers including Viola Philo, Lida Anchutina, William Dollar, Robert Landrum, The Music Hall Rockettes, Corps de Ballet and Choral Ensemble, and a Symphony Orchestra under the direction of Erno Rapee. (The newspaper advertisements stated that the orchestra would play "The Bolt" by Shostakovich.) The review also included Dale Verner, Vernon's new stage name, one suggested to him by Miss King to capitalize on the popularity of Dale Carnegie, the best selling author and columnist. The contract would be for two weeks, the same run scheduled for the motion picture, *Love Affair*, which *Short Stories* was meant to support.

With prestige comes pressure, and Vernon was understandably nervous for the first of four daily performances. The Harlequin Act was constructed for nightclubs and stages of more modest proportions. There was nothing modest about Radio City Music Hall. Known as the "Showplace of the Nation," the theater was cavernous; it accommodated 6,200 patrons, a size that dwarfed every other venue in New York. The stage was so vast that veteran performers quipped that they did not want to be left alone on it without food or water. Unfortunately, pre-show rehearsals did little to calm Vernon's nerves. Erno Rapee insisted on racing through the music, oblivious to the time Vernon had invested in choreographing every moment of magic to the score. It was particularly difficult on Jeanne, as she had to traverse great distances, transporting props on and off the stage, between numbers.

Leddy addressed Vernon's concerns about the music, advising him not to pay any attention to Rapee. "If he doesn't want to rehearse at your speed," Leddy said, "just go out and do the act. He'll play it right." Unfortunately, Rapee performed as he had practiced, and Vernon was forced to alter the act on the fly at the first show to keep time with the score.

Vernon huddled with Leddy prior to the second show. Leddy offered a new tack. "If Rapee's going to be nasty," he said, "do the same thing to him. If he runs ahead with his music, and you're only three-quarters through the act, just continue. Watch what's going to happen to his orchestra. You'll still be working and his orchestra will look very bad. He'll have to pick up and extend it."

Vernon performed the second show in a slow and languid manner, following the musical score marked indelibly in his mind. He did not panic when, at the salt pour, the orchestra finished playing the furnished score. He continued to perform the act to his internal score and, as Leddy predicted, Rapee, embarrassed, tapped his baton on the music stand and commanded the orchestra to resume play. The third show, although musically sound, would be Vernon's last. The producers terminated his engagement. The act was not suitable for this stage. The props were small, and sometimes, when for example the red billiard ball that Vernon produced at his fingertips blended in with a patch of red on his costume, they disappeared completely from view.

It took a special kind of performer to play that stage, one like David Bamberg who had the ability to diffuse love for his audience. Those performers were few and far between. It would have been difficult for Vernon, whose bible had been *The Expert At The Card Table*, a book for gamblers and cheats in which the author stressed the importance of suppressing emotion over gains and losses. It is hard to diffuse love when your life has been dedicated to concealing regret, anger, and compassion. Colleagues and friends had always chastised him for drifting through life with a pack of cards. Now, the one time he had committed himself emotionally to the goal of standing alone, vulnerable in a spotlight on the world's largest stage, he failed.

Vernon had gambled on the Harlequin Act and lost.

Chapter Ten
Mercury Falling

"It gave me a cold shower when I heard Dai was going to play the Music Hall in view of the size of his effects," wrote Paul Fox in a missive to Faucett Ross. "I always felt the reason Cardini was 'tolerated' in this spot was due to his being a more or less 'name' act—and pursuant to the policy of the Music Hall to give the 'bourgeoisie' an eyeful of what the columnists raved about as high lights in the expensive nightclubs." A connoisseur of both fine jewelry and magic, Fox knew the importance of the proper setting. Unfortunately the Harlequin Act and Radio City Music Hall were a mismatch; the former would have little opportunity to shine.

Vernon's loss, however, was the magic community's gain, giving it the chance to see Vernon perform in the Greater Magic Review, a variety show staged in Philadelphia on March 25, 1939 for Assembly No. 4 of the Society of American Magicians and Ring No. 6 of the International Brotherhood of Magicians. The show, which featured several performers—Al Baker, Leslie Guest, Nate Leipzig and "Dale Verner" among them—who had contributed sleights and tricks to *Greater Magic*, took place in the beautifully appointed 350-seat Delancey Street Theater. Max Holden reported in "New York Notes" in *The Linking Ring* that Vernon, working in Harlequin costume but now using the name Dale Verner, "repeated his success of the Heckscher" and, "as usual, he stopped the show." It would be Vernon's final performance as the Harlequin.

At the urging of others, Vernon took stock of his career and contacts and produced, for the first time, a promotional brochure that extolled the virtues of his work. He had always preferred to let the

Vernon posed for two studio portraits snapped by his school chum Hal Phyfe.

magic speak for itself. Never one for self-promotion, Vernon hated bombast and outlandish claims. He agreed, however, that now more than ever, he had the credentials agents could promote and potential clients would respect.

He started the process by changing his professional name: Dale Verner became Dale Vernon. He then obtained a new promotional photograph, the Harlequin photograph being ill-suited for present purposes. The new image was taken by Hal Phyfe, an old school chum from Ottawa. Phyfe had graduated from Ashbury College in 1910, ventured forth to New York to study art and became, after stints as a magazine illustrator and portrait painter, the preeminent portrait photographer for New York theatricals, fashion shoots, and Hollywood celebrities. In 1939, a Phyfe photograph carried the same weight as a Strobridge lithograph did for stage performers in a previous age or a Hirschfield drawing would do in a later one: it informed both the public and the profession that the subject was top tier.

Phyfe offered Vernon two different looks. The first was a glamour shot—a dapper man manipulating playing cards. The second, and less stereotypical option featured Vernon contemplating a deck of cards, smoke snaking upward from a cigarette in hand. Vernon preferred the latter.

Mercury Falling

The card on the face of the pack which Vernon was contemplating was the ace of clubs, the card that J. Warren Keane imprinted on his mind at their first encounter backstage in Ottawa. Vernon selected the ace of clubs for the photograph as his homage to this great performer. Phyfe's photograph became the cover of Vernon's 8 ½" x 11" brochures. (Mulholland included a full-page rotogravure of the Phyfe photograph in the April issue of *The Sphinx* with the caption: "This skillful and clever magician has originated countless subtle effects which put the magicians of the world in his debt.")

Vernon then turned to another acquaintance, John Lydon, whom he first met at the Algonquin Hotel in the 1920s, to write the copy. Lydon, a staff writer for the *New Yorker*, trumpeted Vernon's encounter with Houdini and then described how Vernon was the most modern of magicians:

Popular stage magic that deals in boxes and barrels, disappearing bird cages and the sawing of women in half holds no interest for Mr. Vernon. Such performers Mr. Vernon recognizes as important in the field of magic. Their popularity, however, he believes, is declining. Modern science with its radios, airplanes, cosmic rays and countless other wonders is outdoing even the most fantastic dreams of the old school of magic.

There are no pistol shots, no cabalistic words, no orchestral crescendos when Mr. Vernon does a trick. What he does is compounded of simple, familiar ingredients. The hands and the voice are the only means utilized—and with these simple instruments he puts on a never ending show. There is nothing prepared beforehand, nothing that cannot be thoroughly examined by a spectator. Despite a certain uncanny quickness about him, his manner is easy and disarming. It induces confidence and promotes illusion. In a perfectly natural way he convinces any audience they are seeing miracles.

Mr. Vernon's work is the product of two factors: skill in manipulation and the psychology of misdirection. Everything is done close at hand and in full view, whereas in "apparatus" magic none of the preliminary preparations are seen—only the final effect. During Mr. Vernon's performance the mind is involved at every stage, being led on step by step to ingeniously defeat its own logic.

To the right of Lydon's copy was a testimonial from Bess Houdini proclaiming Vernon the greatest genius with the cards that she had ever seen, and a montage of press clippings from the Casino De Paree, Madison Hotel, Rainbow Room, and Radio City Music Hall. Vernon then listed on the back page of the brochure (beneath the headline "Dale Vernon Has Entertained the Elite of the World!") a who's who of clientele: President Roosevelt, the Duke of Windsor, President Wilson, Sir Arthur Conan Doyle, D.W. Griffith, Clark Gable, Cary Grant, Irenee Du Pont, William Doubleday, Mrs. A.S. Guggenheimer, Sir Wilfred Laurier, Earl Grey, and Lord Minto. Media quotes anchored the bottom of the page.

One item Vernon could not reproduce, however, was the desire to be before the public. Without desire, there would be no persistence. Successful performers—at least those recognized by the public—need to promote themselves constantly, as Houdini had. Vernon had neither the interest nor the experience in doing this. He preferred the status quo whenever opportunity knocked, regardless of the impact it may have had on his family. He was presented with three opportunities in 1939, all of which he either ignored or rejected.

The first involved his passion for advantage play. Vernon had spent a large part of his life exploring the gambling world and had greater insight into it than perhaps any other figure in America. He not only knew gambits and techniques but had demonstrated them often. It had been his practice, for example, to demonstrate the workings of his prized possession, the silver faro box he had acquired in Miami, at select tables when he performed at the Madison Hotel. America's passion for play resurfaced during the Depression, and the public wanted to know who played square.

It was Michael MacDougall, a former assistant to Horace Goldin, who staked out this terrain after being called in by a friend to opine on the card action in a private club. Shortly thereafter, MacDougall began describing himself as an authority on the subject and submitted articles to major publications like *Cosmopolitan* and *Look* that detailed the modus operandi of cheats. Billed as "The Card Detective" his book *Gamblers Don't Gamble*, written with J.C. Furnas, became a bestseller. Advertisements for the book featured MacDougall performing the butt shuffle, the same shuffle that Vernon had learned from Frank Toby at the World's Fair in Chicago in 1933, the one used by faro dealers, and the one which Vernon had incorporated in his own table work around New York. Though MacDougall was a competent card man, his shameless self-aggrandizement annoyed Vernon the most. In *Gamblers Don't Gamble,* MacDougall wrote,

> *I'm in a crazy racket. It's so crazy that, so far as I know—and I get around a lot—I'm the only living practitioner. Considering how dangerous it is, I'll probably be the only dead practitioner one of these days. But meanwhile it's a living. I'm a card-detective. I ferret out dirty work in all kinds of gambling, whether a chuckaluck game in a low-down honky-tonk or a gentlemen's bridge session in a swanky club. That makes it necessary for me to keep up with all the new answers as well as to know the old ones backward, so I can spot things the moment the man across the table winds up to put over a fast one. Only by knowing as much as all the crooked gamblers put together can I keep up my record of so far—business of knocking on wood—never failing to identify the nigger in the woodpile. In order to show up the nigger after he's found, I also have to be able to match the specialist in dexterity of palming, bottom-dealing, second-dealing, crimping, Greek-bottoming, daubing and marking cards. This may sound like bragging, but it isn't. It's just a part of my business, like an orchestra leader's being able to read scores and play half the instruments in the orchestra. I know only one way to get to be a card-detective—the way I did it myself.*

Vernon, of course, had no desire to be a "Card Detective" and could cite numerous objections to any one who suggested otherwise. He recalled the words of Erdnase: "Excessive vanity proves the undoing of many experts... One single display of dexterity and his usefulness is past in that particular company and the reputation is liable to precede him in many others." What chance would Vernon have of learning new subterfuge if he became known as the public authority on the subject? He believed, and admired, the author of *The Expert at the Card Table* when he wrote that no confidences were betrayed in the writing of his book. Vernon may have been very generous providing information to magicians, but when it came to card table artifice, he parceled out details on a need-to-know basis. Gambling artifice was not meant for everyone. Vernon also recognized, unlike MacDougall, that the best cheats—the Dad Stevens and Allen Kennedys who populated this world—were artists whose skill and creativity were to be admired and not made fodder of for personal gain or reward. Even after *Gamblers Don't Gamble* entered a fourth printing and MacDougall became a celebrity who served the public a steady stream of ancillary publications, Vernon had no regrets about leaving the green baize of the gaming table to another.

Garrick Spencer presented a second option: Dai Vernon, Magic Dealer. Spencer reasoned that Vernon's name carried a great deal of goodwill in the magic community. He had traveled widely and most people in the industry seemed to know and respect him. Vernon could parlay his contacts into a thriving enterprise. The timing was perfect; Vernon had experienced great success as a performer at the Rainbow Room and had been recognized as one of the major contributors to *Greater Magic*. He also started selling his own exclusive line of trickery to magicians, directly from his Flatbush Avenue residence. He advertised Mental Choice in the May 1939 issue of *The Sphinx*, advising potential customers that it and a secondary mystery he would provide to each purchaser were, in his opinion, better than the Brain Wave Deck. Annemann, writing in that month's *Jinx*, stated,

> A current release in super trickery is Vernon's "Mental Choice." Dai is well known as a genial person—but no tricks for magicians. What dug this bit of information out of one of the most talked about of magicdom's planets, we don't know, but what we do know is that the stunt has been, for several years, upsetting the eastern seaboards' most elite.

A Vernon trick—any trick—was always a draw. The main impetus for Spencer making the suggestion, however, was the death of T. Francis Fritz on May 24, 1939. Fritz, known professionally as Frank Ducrot, was the proprietor of Martinka's, the oldest and most prestigious magic shop in America. Vernon could purchase Ducrot's enterprise, and Spencer would see to it that financing would not be an issue.

Vernon, although appreciative of the offer, dismissed the suggestion. It just wasn't in him, he explained, to run a magic shop. He had always championed magic that one *learned* rather than *bought*, and he usually offered it freely rather than for a fee. He was uncomfortable with selling someone a trick just for the sake of making a sale and did not want to deal with complaining customers. Vernon

Mercury Falling

also recounted the time he and Larry Gray subleased space for a magic counter to Jack Davis at their silhouette shop on Broadway. Eventually a screen was erected to prevent magic enthusiasts from bombarding him with questions. Thanks, but no thanks. Vernon let the opportunity pass. (Al Flosso, Vernon's longtime friend from Coney Island, eventually purchased the business, a transaction which *The Sphinx* announced in its October issue.)

The third opportunity was television. Not surprisingly, Vernon did not grasp its significance. Television was a new medium; few understood its underlying technology or its potential, and those magicians who did worried about how it would impact their livelihood. The rule of thumb, from vaudeville, was that a ten-minute act would generate ten-years' worth of income. Who would want to pay for a live act if it could be seen on television for free?

Not all shared this pessimism. Charles Brush, a columnist for *The Sphinx*, suggested almost a year earlier—in August 1938—that magicians should embrace the medium.

> *Slowly but surely television is becoming perfected. It will probably be only a short time until it branches out into a full grown means of entertainment. Here is a new field for magicians. I know that some performers have presented some magic over experimental stations. Magicians who desire to make a hit in this new field should give the subject some thought. Profit by the mistakes of the past, find out all that you can about the technique required, prepare an act suitable and be ready when the time comes. The ones that are prepared will probably step right in and cash in with unbounded popularity.*

Vernon had witnessed demonstrations of this new medium both in Chicago in 1933 and again in this summer of 1939 at the New York World's Fair. He was at the Fair, however, to revisit the past—cutting silhouettes—not to chart his future.

The New York Word's Fair had been under development for four years. The organizing committee had hoped that hosting the international exhibition would help lift the city and the country out of depression. When it finally opened on April 30, 1939, Vernon thought that it might do the same for him. Cutting silhouettes would also give him the opportunity to do what he loved to do most: swap stories and tricks with other magicians. He knew that there would be plenty of magicians both performing at and visiting the Fair. The Society of American Magicians scheduled their national conference for May 27, 28 and 29th to coincide with the Fair.

Vernon was even slated to appear on May 29 at the Gala Show as "Harlequin in Magic," part of a stellar cast that included Dorny, Alladin, Max Holden, The Great Maurice, Al Flosso, Arthur Lloyd, Charles Carrer, Cardini, Nate Leipzig, Kuma, and Hardeen. (Hardeen, known affectionately as "Dash," was the younger brother of Houdini and had once been positioned by Houdini as his competition. Houdini thought that if he was going to have a competitor, better that it be someone from his own family. A faded celebrity in the 1930s, Hardeen was a feature performer in an ode to vaudeville, *Hellz'a'poppin'*, that was packing them in on Broadway.) Vernon failed to perform, however. He had not touched the Harlequin Act in months and was not interested in bringing it back up to speed. The act was like a high performance race car: effective only when all cylinders were firing.

Although 25 million people passed through the gates of the Fair that summer, Vernon's gamble that he could make more money cutting silhouettes than performing magic did not pay off. It was Chicago revisited: people were interested in experiencing the future, not the quaint artistry of the past. The Fair, with its theme "Building the World of Tomorrow," offered much to do and see. Prominent attractions included the Trylon and Perisphere, two white and shimmering art deco buildings that housed a futuristic city, dubbed Democracy. Other attractions included Futurama, sponsored by General Motors, where, once inside, visitors sat in moving chairs and circled a 36,000-square foot model that showed the United States as it would look in the year 1960 (a world of cars, highways, and suburbs). There was also Consolidated Edison's City of Light exhibit, the world's largest diorama, a three-story-tall, block-long model of the New York metropolitan area where in twelve minutes, viewers witnessed a dawn to dusk transition, complete with afternoon thunderstorm. On his best day cutting silhouettes—the fourth of July—Vernon earned a mere seven dollars.

Vernon would certainly have been better off financially if he had performed and sold magic. Professional magicians enjoyed unparalleled opportunities performing in nightclubs around the country, and amateurs feasted on new tricks explained in magazines, sold by magic dealers, or demonstrated and explained at magic conventions. These conferences, outlets where enthusiasts could hobnob with one or more of their celebrated brethren were also an emerging market, out of the public eye, that offered many magicians further employment. Their popularity spread like wildfire.

The Society of American Magicians convention was just one of many. The International Brotherhood of Magicians, which staged the first national conference in 1926, had grown in stature and continued to organize an annual gathering. The Abbott Magic Manufacturing Company, a mail order house controlled by Percy Abbott, sponsored its own get-together in Colon, Michigan that attracted as many as fifteen hundred attendees. These conventions, now held across the country, were reviewed in all of the major magic periodicals, which routinely praised the organizers, attendees and, of course, the talent. As Robert Reinhart indicated in one of his columns, magic would never die as long as it gripped the imagination of amateurs who longed to linger in the fading glow of the golden age of their youth.

Europeans quickly followed suit, staging their own national and international gatherings. John Mulholland proclaimed in the May 1939 issue of *The Sphinx* that "magic was truly an international art." The scope of this international art, however, would experience tremendous change when, on September 1, 1939, Germany invaded Poland and war was declared. (Stewart James, a Canadian magician, garnered international press by predicting both the date and nature of the invasion a year in advance, by sheer coincidence, as part of a publicity stunt for a magic convention.) Europe, as Chang had warned Bamberg and Vernon, was in disarray and although Canada would enter the war in 1939, America was content to sit on the sidelines, surveying the scene.

Any frustrations his close friends may have felt about Vernon's disinterest in the commercial aspects of the profession were tempered by the man's creative output. First, Vernon stated in November 1939 that he was going to create a new act, a more commercial act, one that took the logistical constraints of the Harlequin Act into account. He toyed with the idea of performing in a Chinese mask that Jeanne had sculpted for him years earlier. Second, new routines, sleights and technical refinements, particularly pertaining to playing cards, sprang forth. His close friends were content to gather around his table and follow his lead. Now more than ever, Vernon was exploring new ground.

The time was ripe for a paradigm shift. The pool of virtuoso artists who specialized in sleight-of-hand was evaporating. Magicians like T. Nelson Downs that had inspired Vernon were dying off or, like Arthur Finley, becoming disinterested—some might say disillusioned—in the craft. A recent casualty was Nate Leipzig, aged 66, who passed away on October 13, 1939 after a short battle with cancer. Magicians in America and across the world mourned the loss. It was now Vernon's turn to inspire others. He could be both a link to the past, relaying the tricks and techniques of the many magicians who had inspired him, and a portal to the future.

After his initial grounding in card table artifice, Vernon had explored the coupling of subtle psychological principles with improvisational sleight-of-hand. He then experimented with mechanical aids, trick decks and, to a certain degree, apparatus, resurrecting obscure routines and streamlining classic effects. All of these explorations, however, were performance driven. He developed techniques and routines in order to perform them. His new focus—the paradigm shift—was towards pure composition. Now, instead of collecting fifty-two different string tricks as he had as a boy, Vernon set out to compose, in essence, fifty-two variations of the same trick. This time he would use cards, not string. Cards became notes on his magical scale, and a trick with four aces became the theme he would vary like Bach, the master of counterpoint, did in composing his *Goldberg Variations*.

Although the trick was simple—the magician deals four aces face down on a table and covers each ace with three other cards, the spectator selects a pile and the magician causes the three other aces to congregate by magic into that pile—the handling was convoluted and contrived. Magicians had blindly followed the original approach, attributed to Conus, a French magician who died in 1836, for close to a hundred years after Jean-Nicholas Ponsin, another Frenchman, referred to the effect in his 1853 publication, *Nouvelle Magie Blanche Devoilee* (New White Magic Unveiled).

Prompted by Garrick Spencer's observation that most magic tricks, particularly card tricks, were not interesting because the performer usually took a roundabout way of achieving the effect under the mistaken belief that audiences enjoyed arcane cabalistic machinations, Vernon set out to disembody—compositionally—and then resurrect this venerable card trick into something more mysterious and engaging. His template was the Cups and Balls, the performance of which many considered the true test of a master magician. His solution: make each ace vanish and then reappear in the packet selected by the spectator one at a time so that in each subsequent display, vanish and recovery of an ace became a variation on a theme. He dubbed the trick "Mobilizing the Aces" and described his efforts in *The Sphinx*.

> *Quite recently I thought of the idea of doing the well known Four Ace Trick in a slightly different form. I wished to have the aces pass to the chosen pile one at a time. I worked out at least a dozen methods of getting this result, always bearing in mind the fact that I wished to end the trick with just sixteen cards: to have no extra cards in the packets at the finish of the trick. I talked the effect over with Dr. Jacob Daley and he also worked out numerous original versions. Between us we finally had over thirty different routines. Our object was to arrive at the simplest and most direct presentation.*

Dr. Daley was not Vernon's only student, just his most manic—totally obsessed with magic, even taking the opportunity between meeting patients at his medical practice to pull out from his bureau a typewriter board outfitted with green baize so he could practice shuffle work. Vernon's obsession for detail became his students' obsession too, and each developed his own sensitivity or "touch" with cards as they embraced Vernon's challenge and aesthetic for sleight-of-hand. Sometimes the master would taunt them, dangling an impossibility before them, the secret of which he would not reveal.

Vernon once told Francis Finneran, for example, that although it might sound presumptuous, he had indeed created "the most perfect move in magic." When asked to demonstrate the move, however, Vernon declined. "No one," he said, "was ever going to see it." When asked why he would bother to create such a move if he did not intend to show it to anyone, Vernon replied, in essence, that his goal was to strive towards perfection, the move was irrelevant. Finneran questioned how Vernon could be so confident that it was a perfect move if nobody had actually seen it. Vernon, matter-of-factly, said that he had looked at it quite objectively in the mirror. Finneran knew two things. First, he would probably never get to see the move. Second, it probably was perfect.

Although magicians continued to perform at prominent night spots in and around New York, prompting John Booth to write

Jacob Daley (at right, with cards) entertains at a dinner gathering.

in *The Linking Ring* that magic was a broad and lucrative field, Vernon accepted few engagements, and only when he was in dire straits. He accept, for example, a brief engagement at the Number One on Park Avenue in February 1940. And all the while, other professionals were busy incorporating many of Vernon's routines into their own stage repertoires. Paul Rosini, benefiting from all-night sessions with Vernon, made the Brain Wave Deck a feature of his nightclub performances, and Russell Swann, engaged at the Savoy-Plaza, added the Salt Pour to his set. With his interest focused squarely on composition rather than performance, Vernon seemed content to sit on the sidelines and watch others perform his routines. Max Holden described one such instance in "New York News" in *The Linking Ring* for June 1940:

> After the dinner down to Sam Margules' apartment with Mr. and Mrs. Cardini, Dai Vernon, Dr. Daley, Francis Carlyle [Finneran], Arnold Furst and Mrs. Holden. Four of the cleverest card men in the world here. Dai Vernon's latest and worked by Dr. Daley. The four

aces were removed from the pack and placed on the table face up, one ace was selected by Cardini—Ace of Clubs—this ace was placed to the right. All aces turned face down and on top of each ace three cards dealt on each. Picking up one pile and a riffle the ace has vanished. Picking up the pile to the right it was seen that two aces were there now with a nine of spades and a four of hearts. The second pile now picked up and the ace has vanished. Going back to pile on right, there are three aces now with the nine of spades there. The last pile shows that the ace has vanished, and naturally the four aces are in the pile on the right—sitting right at the table I drew the aces over—but was all wrong—just four ordinary aces. Of all the Ace tricks that I have ever seen, this is the tops.

Not all of Vernon's friends appreciated Vernon's obsessive pursuit of perfection. Paul Fox wrote Faucett Ross,

Thanks for enclosing Dai's letter—am sorry to know that things are as they are re-finances. Too bad—but I still feel Dai failed to follow through on breaks. Maybe not—I don't know. In a way it's sort of sad—Dai still fooling around with new palms while the new comers with a "what of it" attitude steal the spot and cash.

Amateur magicians appreciated, however, people who created new tricks, and magic shops catering to the interests of amateurs thrived. Holden reported that in one day he had seventy-three customers in the front room of his store and another eleven including "such notables as Dave Vernon, Sam Horowitz, George Kaplan, Francis Carlyle [Finneran], Arthur Findlay [Finley], Jean Hugard, Paul Le Paul and others," in a side room. Magic shops were simply hobby stores, the last vestiges of mystery having faded from their façades. Amateurs consumed secrets and then discarded them, searching for the next novelty they could perform after little rehearsal, while still fooling family and friends.

Books and manuscripts that had once cost a fortune were soon sold secondhand for a pittance as amateurs clamored for the latest releases. In the March 1940 issue of *The Sphinx*, for example, the Phenix Publishing Company of Detroit, an outlet that specialized in selling secondhand magic books, offered two limited edition manuscripts, Annemann's *Exclusive Secrets of Annemann's Conception* (1932) and Vernon's *Ten Card Problems* (1932) bound together in one volume—over seventy dollars worth of original material—for the unbelievably low price of $2.50. Amateur magicians also preferred to buy tricks with apparatus or small props on the belief that they could be learned with little effort. Vernon lamented the trend towards "self-working" mechanical magic to John Mulholland, editor of *The Sphinx*. In his August 1940 editorial, Mulholland wrote,

> *Recently Dai Vernon, on a visit to The Sphinx office, was talking about the pleasure a magician gets from the performance of his feats. He pointed out that a person derives a great deal more pleasure from a trick depending upon sleight-of-hand than one in which, for instance, a false bottom box is used. He feels that the reason more magicians do not take up manipulative magic is that they have not learned to read the books and magazines in which sleights and routines are described. He believes that for the study necessary to follow The Expert at the Card Table or Farelli's translation of Hofzinser's book the magician will learn sleights which will give not only him, but his audience, more pleasure than showing another mechanical box.*

In September 1940 Vernon had the opportunity to see one of the most acclaimed magicians in the world, Harry August Jansen, aged 57, make his Broadway debut at the Morosco Theatre on West 45th Street. Jansen, now known professionally as Dante, was a "box magician." Although the show was generally well received and enjoyed an extended run both on Broadway and on a subsequent tour, Vernon considered much of the material and the presentation "old school" when compared to the personality, theatrical style, and presence of David Bamberg.

> *I had an argument with Cardini about Dante because Cardini told me Dante was the greatest magician he had ever seen and I told him Fu Manchu [Bamberg] was the greatest I'd ever seen. So when Dante opened on Broadway, I went with Cardini to see him… Cardini sat with some friends upstairs and I sat downstairs. And right in the middle of the show Dante, when he was doing a trick, one leg disappeared—he went down a trapdoor by mistake and dropped some billiard balls, and he did something else—in other words the show that Dante did was pretty bad that night, and I waved up to the gallery to Cardini as much as to say "This is your Dante, your man who is so good?" I didn't think he was one quarter as good as Fu Manchu, not even an eighth as good.*

Dante produces parasols, costumes and comely assistants from a giant top hat.

Any magician who dared criticize Dante in a magic magazine, however, was pillared by the community. Dante was the master of an old style of performing, presenting large scale illusions and little sleight-of-hand, accompanied by a large cast and, in particular, one stellar assistant with great beauty and grace, Loretta "Moi-Yo" Miller, from Australia. Dante presented the type of magic that attracted many amateurs to the craft, magic with ornately colored boxes and corny patter punctuated with the phrase "Sim Sala Bim." It was the type of magic—boxes and barrels, disappearing bird cages, and sawing women in two—which Vernon's promotional brochure had claimed was made passé by the advances in science and technology. It was the type of magic and presentation, as Mulholland relayed to his readers in the August issue of *The Sphinx*, which Vernon found so unsatisfying to perform. Dante's work held no appeal for Vernon. Vernon was interested in artistry, not in the shenanigans of a showman.

Vernon was interested in the type of magic his friend, Sam Horowitz, presented in the September 1940 issue of *The Sphinx*. Horowitz, influenced perhaps by Vernon's own various name changes, had adopted "Leo Hartz" as his professional name and described in the magazine a staple of his repertoire, Six Coins in Goblet, in which the magician magically plucked six coins from the air, made them vanish one at a time, then caused them to reappear in a stemmed goblet. Vernon provided the illustrations—pen and ink drawings—that accompanied the piece, the first time he illustrated a magic trick of any kind since his hand-colored illustrations graced the manuscripts he produced with Faucett Ross in 1932.

Vernon then decided, because he needed money, to accept William Arenholz's suggestion that he write, illustrate, and publish a new pamphlet of his own secrets. Word of the project traveled fast. William Larsen wrote in his "Genii Speaks" column, "Anent the subject of mighty card men, Dai Vernon... has authored a new book of card tricks. I understand that it will be off the press late this month. I have no idea what the price will be, but whatever it is the volume will be a bargain." He then added, "Meeting Dai Vernon, and watching him work, will satisfy one of my life's ambitions."

The book, *Select Secrets*, would contain few card tricks. (Arenholz had also suggested that Vernon limit the number of card tricks so that the book would appeal to a wide range of magicians.) *Select Secrets* offered twelve items, eight tricks (three with cards plus a variant) and three sleights using a broad range of equipment, including cards, coins, handkerchiefs, and matches. Notable inclusions included Topping the Deck, an "artistic" method of palming a card from the top of the pack that Vernon once described in 1930 in a letter to Sam Horowitz as the Vernon Palm, his most cherished creation. *Select Secrets* also explained two effects performed by T. Nelson Downs, making it the first of many tributes Vernon would pay to the master magicians who had influenced him. The final trick revealed in *Select Secrets* was Vernon's rendition of Snow Storm In China, the very routine he used to close the Harlequin Act. Professional magicians rarely tipped the inner workings of their professional repertoire. As Vernon had no intention of restaging the act, he decided to publish his handling so others could profit from his experience.

Just before release, however, Vernon's booklet was blindsided by the publication on December 10, 1940 of *Expert Card Technique*, another tome produced by Carl Jones, the publisher of *Greater Magic*. *Expert Card Technique* was written by Jean Hugard and Frederick (formerly Fritz) Braue. (Braue was perhaps persuaded to change his first name from Fritz to Frederick just as Nate Leipzig briefly changed his last name to Lincoln decades earlier due to the onset of hostilities in Europe.) As the titled suggested, the book was devoted entirely to card magic. Braue, a writer for the *Oakland Tribune* and frequent contributor to *The Sphinx*, assembled and wrote the lion's share of the material.

Advertised as being two years in preparation and consisting of 470 pages with 341 illustrations, the book explained 341 sleights and tricks and sold at a retail price of five dollars. The book disclosed an "an inventory of the very best work of the master card men of the world including Bert Allerton, Theo Annemann, Cliff Green, Gerald Kaufman, Harold Lloyd, Jack McMillen, Jack Merlin, Paul Rosini, Fred Braue, Dai Vernon, Luis Zingone, Charles Miller, and Jean Hugard." The publisher predicted, "the book will prove to be to the card worker of today what Erdnase's *Expert At The Card Table* was to the generation of 1902" and added, "A special feature is the complete compendium of shakedown sleights employed by gamblers. Erdnase covered this field in his excellent book of thirty years ago but it has never been brought up to date and simplified. Now this has been accomplished in *Expert Card Technique*."

The magic community heralded the book. Tom Bowyer, the reviewer for *The Linking Ring*, wrote in February 1941,

> *Every phase of card chicanery is dealt with, and there are valuable final chapters on misdirection and presentation. The only criticism we can venture is the minor one that further credit for some of the material might have been readily given. This tremendous work is a really marvelous textbook—perhaps the greatest card book ever put out, doing honor not only to its sponsors but to the art as a whole. Explicit but not verbose, erudite without being pedantic, in style as charming as any Hoffmann tome, illustrated by 318 excellent drawings and produced in a manner beyond reproach, it cannot fail to remain a standard reference for many years to come. Read it now and you will be in the "inner circle" among card men, master even part of its contents and (as already intimated) you will be truly expert.*

Bowyer was one of the few critics who flagged the lack of credits. He recognized that many of the items in the book, particularly those pertaining to card table artifice, were Vernon's. Vernon was only credited, however, with two: Two-Six-Four and Dai Vernon's Mental Force. Vernon received a complimentary copy of the book from Jean Hugard and was shocked to learn that much of his work appeared within its pages.

> When this book came out I was absolutely astounded. It almost could have been written by myself. There were many things in it that I felt were my brainchildren. In fact, I checked off dozens of tricks that I knew were my own, a little bit off beat and different. They were my thoughts. I said to Jean [Hugard], "Where did you get the information for this book?" He said, "Mostly from Charlie Miller and Fred Braue." I had shown Charlie Miller most of the tricks in Expert Card Technique—like the things on riffling shuffling and different types of palming, I also recognized a lot of Charlie's original work there, too. But I didn't know who Fred Braue was. I said to Charlie, who was a good friend, "Charlie, you betrayed a lot of confidence. A lot of things in this book are mine. They are not credited to anybody particularly; Braue doesn't say they are his, he doesn't say they are yours." Charlie said, "That is probably my fault: I showed Braue a lot of these tricks but I didn't show him how they were done. He is a good analyst and worked out his own methods." I said, "He came pretty close to my methods." Charlie had a little guilty boy appearance. But he was honest about it.

Like Downs and McGuire before him, Braue was obsessed with secrets, particularly those associated with Vernon. He longed to meet Vernon and see the work first hand. Although Vernon had never set foot in California, Miller had. Miller, who had landed a steady engagement first as an assistant to another magician, S.S. Henry, performing at the Golden Gate Fair in San Francisco and then as a solo performer in a variety review sponsored by the Shell Oil Company, became Braue's conduit to Vernon. The two met at Braue's office where, unbeknownst to Miller and other "contributors" surprised to see some of their work appear in *Expert Card Technique*, Braue recorded the sessions covertly on an office diction device—a wire recorder. Miller was no match for Braue who, like Dunninger in his encounter with Sam Margules years earlier, would readily disregard propriety if it meant obtaining the latest secrets.

Hugard apologized to Vernon. His excuse: he had merely assembled the book from correspondence between Braue, Miller, and himself and, as such, found it difficult to trace the original source of the material. Hugard vowed to provide Vernon, however, with additional credit—no financial compensation, just an acknowledgement—in any reprints or subsequent editions.

From Vernon's perspective, the timing of the release of *Expert Card Technique* could not have been worse. He was now unexpectedly competing against himself. *Expert Card Technique* contained over 300 sleights and tricks and sold for five dollars. *Select Secrets* contained just twelve items and sold for one dollar. Disappointed but undaunted, Vernon placed small advertisements in *The Sphinx*, *The Linking Ring*, and *Genii*, indicating that the pamphlet was only available directly through him. Fortunately, the praise for *Select Secrets* was just as effusive as it had been for *Expert Card Technique*.

Holden wrote, "Seldom does a master of Vernon's caliber break into print. When one does, even more seldom are the secrets revealed of masterpiece status. Here is a 30-page printed booklet that is unique. To be perfectly honest, you will not find any of those highly expertized [sic] sleights for which Dai is famous. On the other hand, the effects described look extremely difficult to the layman...and, for that matter, other magicians, too!"

Kanter, the magic dealer in Philadelphia, endorsing the book in "Kanter's Komments" in the March 1941 issue of *Genii*, wrote "Dai Vernon, the man who gave us the 'Brain Wave Deck' and devised many sleights for which he received no credit, has just issued a gem in *Select Secrets* a 32-page printed book containing ten exclusive effects never released before—cards, coins, matches, cigarettes, silks and paper—fully illustrated." Dr. Raymond Beebe, the reviewer for *Genii*, added, "Here is a book that has 'personality.' Very often the performer who is looking for some extra special effect will find it in a small book of this type rather than a large text-book... If this book is a sample of what Dai Vernon has in store for magicians, let's hope he has his next one well under way, and is gathering material for many more."

Vernon was on a roll. On February 22, 1941, he returned once more to the stage and premiered his new act, one he had been developing intermittently since November 1939, at the Heckscher Theatre at the annual Society of American Magicians Gala. Vernon was not listed in the original advertising or program. Max Holden circulated the rumor, however, that Vernon would be there. Fred Keating, the host for the evening, was replaced for the first half by Roy Benson. Benson, the son of one of the Ford sisters, a famous vaudeville act, was also a protégé of the late Nate Leipzig. Benson had recently returned to New York from Los Angeles, where he had been trying to break into motion pictures, first as a cameraman and then as an actor. Keating arrived, however, in time for the second half and introduced an unscheduled guest, "Dai Yan." Holden described Vernon's new act in "New York News" in the April 1941 issue of *The Linking Ring*.

> *Fred Keating, returning from a theater engagement, now assumed the role of m.c. and introduced the next act, a surprise. And what a surprise! Dai Vernon, in a Chinese costume and wearing a very cleverly made mask, stopped the show with his two effects—the Tenkai card production and the linking rings as they have never before been linked.*

Holden failed to mention that Vernon had a new assistant: his son. Ted, aged fourteen and dressed in an usher's uniform, assisted his father on stage.

Vernon entered the stage in dramatic fashion, through the front curtain, his hands resting in front of him with fingers interlocked. He then performed a piece originally developed by his old acquaintance from Ottawa, Cliff Green, but one that he had retooled over the past two years, adding technical touches he had learned from the great Japanese magician, Tenkai. Vernon rotated the palms of his cupped hands towards the audience, fingers still interlocked, and then back towards his body. He then repeated the motion but this time, a playing card appeared magically in his hands, framed by his interlocked fingers. Vernon let the card tumble to the stage. He repeated this sequence half a dozen times, card after card materializing between his interlocked fingers before fluttering to the boards. The final card seemed to materialize between his outstretched fingertips. Both the technique and the execution were flawless.

Ted then entered, dressed as a page boy, and handed his father a set of six rings, two more than used in the Harlequin Act. These rings were ten inches in diameter, solid, and heavy. Vernon performed the Chinese Linking Rings, but a more elaborate routine, one he created for this particular engagement. The routine, which became known as the Symphony of the Rings, was performed entirely to "Chinese Lullaby," a piece written by Robert Hood Bow-

Vernon as Dai Yan performs with son Ted assisting.

ers for William H. Harris, Jr.'s 1918 Broadway production of *East is West*. (The mask and, theoretically, the character prevented Vernon from speaking directly to the audience.) "Chinese Lullaby" was more accessible to the ear than the "Carillon De Westminster," as it was faintly familiar but not overpowering. Ted assisted his father throughout the routine, taking hold of various rings and displaying formations while his father created others. As Holden indicated, Vernon's poetic performance "stopped the show."

One member of the audience, Chang—David Bamberg's friendly rival who had just returned to New York from Australia to acquire new tricks and routines for his own program—was so enamored with Vernon's performance of the Rings that he asked to learn it. Al Flosso, aware of Vernon precarious financial picture, brokered the lesson. "If you let him take a movie of it, and some notes and give him a lesson for a couple of hours," Flosso informed Vernon, "he'd pay for it. Chang is making plenty of money." Vernon received two hundred and fifty dollars for meeting Chang at his hotel room, walking him through the choreography, and allowing him to shoot a 16 mm motion picture of the routine as a record he could refer to as he set out to master the intricacies of the piece.

With cash now in hand, Vernon abandoned *Select Secrets*. He was tired of processing the orders and dealing with customers and transferred the distribution rights over to Max Holden. Vernon stated,

> *I mailed them out myself; I never got so tired sticking stamps and addressing envelopes by hand and mailing them. I got a deluge of mail saying, "I don't quite understand the second trick." It was virtually impossible for me to answer all these letters so I had a postcard mimeographed which said, "Read it more carefully." Sometimes the questions were very stupid—the explanation was right but they were reading it wrong and not concentrating on it. I may as well have written three more books if I had answered all the letters. I did try to answer those that seemed sensible.*

Holden advertised the transfer in the March 1941 issue of *Genii*: "Frequently magical authors who already have a satisfactory publishing connection will ask us to take the entire charge of putting their books before the magical fraternity...When such a top-notcher as Dai Vernon brings us his 'pets and darlings' for distribution... the House of Holden [is] highly honored." Although Vernon was not one to answer questions by putting pen to paper, he was quite generous with those who approached him in person. Max Holden wrote in "Magic of the East" column in the April 1941 issue of *Genii*,

> *It is interesting to note the personalities of the magicians who call on me. Ever since Dai Vernon's book has appeared Dai has been an almost daily visitor and ever ready to show how the different effects are accomplished. Dick Washington in from St. Paul and Dick asking me how the cigarette switching move was accomplished and Dai taking him in hand and going over every move until Dick had it down pat. Then Dariel Fitzkee asking about the one hand palm and Dai showing just how it was worked and the many many effects possible.*

Vernon slowly warmed to the idea of magic dealers and magazines as an outlet for his creations. He released a flurry of effects including Card of the Gods in the *Jinx No. 105*; The Eight In The

Mercury Falling

Side Pocket in the March 1941 issue of *Genii*; and the Al-N'Dai card trick, manufactured and distributed by Al Baker in which a freely chosen card, put between two deuces, changed places with a card selected by the performer. He also contributed Mobilizing the Aces to the fortieth anniversary issue—published in March 1941—of *The Sphinx*. (Mobilizing the Aces was the first technical explanation of one of his variants of the trick with the four aces and was accompanied by two illustrations, both drawn by Jeanne Verner, of his hands performing requisite sleights.) Trade journal critics and columnists complimented Vernon on his contributions and recommended them highly to their readers.

Vernon's financial plight, however, was worsening. Magicians continued to profit from his creations, performing items from *Expert Card Technique*, *Select Secrets*, and other routines, like the Salt Pour from the Harlequin Act, without any financial remuneration to him. The biggest seller, however, was the Brain Wave Deck, a trick that continued to be pirated, produced, and distributed by many unauthorized dealers. Sam Margules wrote Garrick Spencer on April 24, 1941,

> *In today's mail—I received a magical catalogue from Sterling Magic Co—345 John R. Street, Detroit, Mich.—Harold Sterling—owner.*
>
> *On page 3 of the cat. There is an item...#106—Brain Wave Deck—(Dai Vernon) $1.00. I believe this chap gets these cards from a man by the name of John Snyder Jr., Norwood Ohio.*
>
> *This John Snyder has sold thousands of these decks, selling them to novelty and joke and puzzle stores besides the magical dealers.*
>
> *I don't know a lot about law but it seems to me that to use Dai's name—without any permission at all—of any kind does Dai an injustice.*
>
> *Dai—as you know is badly in need of funds. Do you think an action of some kind would result in a monetary gain for Dai?*

Spencer could offer little legal support. There was little Vernon could do to stop those who profited from his creations. Many argued that those who did were well within their rights. Magic tricks were not subject, they claimed, to copyright and, as John Booth stated so eloquently once before, "the necessity to make a living forces the hand that might otherwise not prostitute the magic we are pleased to call 'art'." Vernon continued to rely on the charity of others. He did not, however, ask for it. Margules, Daley, and Spencer voluntarily addressed the needs of the Vernon family.

When Jeanne mentioned to Garrick Spencer, for example, that her eldest son, Edward, wanted to join the Sea Scouts but could not afford the uniform, Spencer simply provided the money. Spencer also arranged for Vernon to perform at organizations and businesses with which he was affiliated. He always received glowing accounts, however, from the colleagues and acquaintances that retained Vernon's services. Margules, Daley, and Spencer were, in their own way, patrons, and Vernon was their artist. They agreed with Jeanne that her husband was irresponsible but granted him absolution on the basis that he was a "genius." Jeanne acknowledged their argument but reiterated that she had grown tired of hearing it.

Although Vernon was short on funds, when asked, he would often donate his services to worthy causes. Elsa Maxwell, for example, organized a charity gala at the Rainbow Room. The proceeds were directed towards underprivileged children. Vernon accepted the engagement, pleased to be included in a group of artists that included Boris Karloff and Charles Chaplin. Max Holden reported in "New York News" in the May 1941 issue of *The Linking Ring*, "Dai recently followed Charlie Chaplin at an event, and of course he came thru with flying colors." Vernon considered being on the same program as Chaplin as "one of the thrills" of his life.

> *I went on right after Charlie Chaplin. In show business they say it's a bad spot when you follow a star, but this was rather different. Charlie Chaplin at that time didn't really perform. He did his funny little walk and gave a little speech at this party for the underprivileged. He was kind of singing—it was a rather socialistic speech. After he gave his speech and told a few stories, I went on and did some tricks. Yes, this was another thrill. We were sitting at the table, Charlie Chaplin at one end; I was next to Boris Karloff. During the meal I did a few tricks and all Boris Karloff would say was "amazing, absolutely amazing."*

In May 1941, Fred Keating's agent, Carlton Hobb, contacted

Mercury Falling

Vernon. He had a client, The Forbidden City Café, an eastside nightclub near the Madison Hotel, looking for a Chinese magician to augment their staff of strolling musicians. Did Vernon know of any? Vernon did not, but explained that by wearing one of Jeanne's masks, he could create a character so realistic that he could pass as Chinese. Hobb took Vernon to the club to meet the owner. The owner was not Asian, but had hired all Chinese performers. Vernon described the encounter,

> *Sitting off the side I could see the owner was not impressed with Carlton Hobb's build-up of me. So I walked over with my little case and said, "Mr. Hobb, I think I can save a lot of words, just give me two minutes." Then I turned to the owner and said, "I will show you exactly what you will see, if you turn those lights off." So I turned around, put on the gown and mask and you should have seen the expression on this man's face. I did a couple of little passes with a ball. Right away he said, "I'll take it."*

Vernon, engaged as "Dai Yan," performed his set three times each night on a tiny dance floor. It was a difficult space, as the room had not only a balcony but also many mirrored surfaces to expand the look of the room. Balconies and mirrors will crimp any magician's act.

As usual, Vernon experimented with the makeup of the act. He opened with the Production of Cards and performed, of course, the Chinese Linking Rings. He also added several pieces from the Harlequin Act, including the Three to One Rope Trick and the Salt Pour. He occasionally performed his handling of the Horowitz Six Coins in Goblet. His greatest feat, as he learned from one of the Chinese musicians who watched his show night after night, was how he concealed his true identity from both patrons and staff. Vernon learned this, sitting at the bar wearing his dinner jacket, in between shows.

A musician asked Vernon, "Are you one of the bosses?"

Vernon answered, "No" and asked the musician why he was asking.

The musician replied that he was interested in the Chinese magician. "How in the world does he get in and out of here? The boys in the band keep watching. All of a sudden he appears here and then he is gone again. The other night we said we are going to spot him going out or coming in, but I'd be darned. He should know that this is the best trick he does."

Though tempted, Vernon did not tip his identity. He did a few more shows—it took him seconds to get in and out of the costume—and then re-approached the musician. "You still worried about how that fellow gets in? You have been talking to him for ten minutes."

The musician expressed his disbelief. "That's a mask you wear?"

Vernon explained how Jeanne had made the mask and thanked the man for his kind remarks.

Vernon received excellent notices in the New York papers, and few suspected that he was anything other than a real Chinese. He quit, however, after just two weeks. Although he was pleased with the act (it was very different from any other, was easy to set up and perform, and was performed by a character separate and distinct from his off-stage persona), the conditions of the club—the balcony and mirrors—made the venue less than ideal. Unconcerned with money, never driven towards a steady paycheck that could provide stability for his family, Vernon had learned all he could from the act in this setting. It was time to move on, even if moving on meant retreating to the apartment or a late-night coffee shop where he could discuss, explore, practice, and create new magic.

On May 24, 1941, William Larsen, the editor and publisher of *Genii*, arrived in New York, accompanied by his wife Geraldine and young sons, William Jr. and Milton. The family was on a cross-country tour and was about to be feted in New York by the Society of American Magicians. William Larsen expressed the desire to see Vernon perform; Vernon was equally interested in meeting Larsen, having great respect for the man's creative output, particularly when he was a contributor to *The Sphinx*. Vernon was enlisted to perform at the Society of American Magicians' Annual Show and Banquet at the Barbizon Plaza Hotel but failed to appear as scheduled. Larsen was disappointed but learned that he would have a second opportunity, this time in Providence, Rhode Island, where Vernon was engaged to perform, along with Cardini, Horowitz, Baker, and Hugard, at the Society of American Magicians' annual convention. It would be Vernon's first appearance as a feature attraction at a major magic convention.

Vernon appeared in the May 31, 1941 Saturday evening gala show. John Mulholland gave him a glowing review in the June 1941 issue of *The Sphinx*.

> *Dai Vernon (excuse it please, Dai Yan) did his Chinese act which New York newspapers recently have so well liked—and understandably so. He began with a slow motion card production and followed with the salt trick, his own linking ring routine which is beautiful, and winter in China.*

Larsen was equally effusive, writing in *Genii*,

> *Dai Yan, known to magicians everywhere as Dai Vernon, excelled as a Chinese magician, presenting among other things, the salt vanish and wintertime in China. I have often spoken of masters of the linking ring trick and I find pleasure now in adding the name of Dai Vernon to my list of those who are really great. His offering drew thunderous applause.*

Vernon also appeared with Tom Osborne, E.J. Moore, Geraldine Larsen, Bertram Adams, Lu Brent, and Al Baker on the Sunday evening post-banquet show before the Governor of the State of Rhode Island. Wearing a smart dinner jacket, Vernon demonstrated how to cheat at cards by performing a poker deal on a table top that was tilted so all could see. He closed his set with a performance of the Cups and Balls.

The Rhode Island convention staged other events besides formal galas. It included, for example, a show where magic dealers took to the stage to demonstrate some of the tricks they had for sale at their trade booths. Sam Horowitz participated on the dealers' show and demonstrated Mental Control, the card trick Vernon had created and advertised for sale in the pages of *The Sphinx* in May 1939. Vernon and Horowitz also participated in a forum billed as an "Educational Session," where performers such as Tom Osborne, William Larsen, Horowitz, and Vernon lectured about different aspects of magic. The forum was a huge hit and became a regular feature of these types of conferences. These "magic clinics" soon also became separate ticketed events staged independently of the magic conferences. Horowitz, for example, reprised his conference lecture, "Misdirection in Magic," at the Nat Kane Studio, 163 W. 73rd Street, New York City, on June 19, 1941.

After the convention, many of the performers returned to Manhattan where, on June 6, Sigurd and Blanche Nathan held a reception for seventy guests in honor of the Larsens. Vernon attended the party and was cajoled into performing an impromptu program of magic along with Hugard, Cardini, Charles Larson, and several others. Later that month Max Holden published another pamphlet, *More Card Manipulations Number IV,* written by Hugard. Once again Hugard described several techniques and routines that should have been credited to Vernon. (Tom Bowyer, the book reviewer for *The Linking Ring* penciled in, as was his custom, the appropriate credits in his marginal notes in his review copy, one of which stated, "The guy [Vernon] gets no credit again.") One effect, Magnetic Thought, which Hugard attributed to Bert Allerton, had long been associated with Vernon. Vernon had performed this trick (The Challenge) repeatedly for Faucett Ross, among others, a decade earlier. Hugard described the effect,

> *Two cards are placed face downwards upon the table, the magician promising to place his hand upon whichever of the two may be thought of by a spectator. He succeeds in his attempts several times until at last he apparently fails, since he has placed his hand upon the wrong card. Nothing daunted, he flips this wrong card face upwards and shows that it has been magically transformed into the card of which the spectator is thinking.*

The effect and its underlying technique, the subtle shifting of the spectator's points of reference, illustrates how, as John Lydon wrote in Vernon's promotional brochure, Vernon used a combination of skill in manipulation and the psychology of misdirection to lead the spectator's mind step by step to defeat its own logic.

While Vernon was attending magic conventions and toasting visiting magic dignitaries, Jeanne Verner was left at home to attend to the children and make ends meet. By the end of the summer, she had had enough. To no one's real surprise, she separated from her husband and moved with the children into a Brooklyn brownstone with her aunt, Elizabeth Pine.

Faucett Ross wrote Eddie McLaughlin,

> *Last week I got quite a lengthy letter from Dai. He's had domestic & financial issues—broke up his apartment and now has a room at Hotel Clinton on 31st St where Sam Margules lives. Jeanne & the*

boys are living with the prosperous aunt in Brooklyn. Dai claims that he's cut out the stalling around and is now calling on the agents daily. Has four acts—1. His regular old club act. 2. Chinese Act with mask 3. A gambling expose and 4—a kid show. Asked for hints and suggestions on the latter which I gave him. Says he thinks he can make a good living out of magic if he hustles.

Vernon also attempted to eke out a living by selling secrets, in association with Sam Horowitz, to the magic community. In addition to Mental Control, the duo marketed Mind Reading Cards. John Braun, Vernon's longtime acquaintance from Cincinnati, reviewed the trick in the September 1941 issue of *The Linking Ring* and recommended it to his readers "because it is automatic in working, uses questions of the "fortune teller" variety, and sells for the low price of fifty cents."

While Vernon scrambled to make ends meet and, for perhaps the first time, earn the love and respect of his family, the amateur magic community faced its own challenge, the mass exposure of their secrets on television. A television executive, writing in an issue of *The Billboard*, described a forthcoming series. It would consist of fifty-two studio dramatizations (one for each card in the deck) in which magic secrets would be performed and exposed. John Mulholland, writing in the October 1941 issue of *The Sphinx*, chastised amateur magicians on what he perceived would be their response and called for calm.

The type of material he [television executive] tells about exposing seems quite innocuous to the professional magicians who have mentioned the article to me. However there will in all likelihood be a big howl from the amateurs and the sponsors will enjoy the free advertising from such a controversy. When the series begins—which by the way is not the time to attempt to stop it—the entire magic row will begin again. The professional magicians will pay little or no attention to the series and the amateurs will be incensed about disclosing the secrets of magic. As the big organizations of magicians have many more amateur members than professional members the societies also will protest the expose. Whether or not the series will be stopped a great many people will lose their tempers. It seems very strange that amateurs make the rules which prohibit professional magicians from making money by disclosing simple tricks, which

> they, as professional magicians, know will not injure magic, and yet the amateurs do no realize that these very rules permit outsiders from doing limitless exposing. The outsider cares little whom he bothers, as long as he can sell his material for good money, and the better the trick the better the money. The entire subject should be given more thought.

Vernon, of course, was worried more about making his own living and being reunited with his family. He called the agents and sought referrals from friends. With his recent success in the Broadway production of *Hellz'a'poppin'*, Hardeen had set up his own management company, one that recommended acts to various booking agents and presenters. Vernon had known Hardeen a long time, and, although Hardeen was not interested in sleight-of-hand, Vernon considered him a friend. Hardeen had seen "Dai Yan" at the Heckscher Theatre and loved the act, particularly Vernon's dramatic centre stage entrance. All that was missing, he advised Vernon, was a large-scale illusion that could anchor the act. "Put some kind of illusion in it. I can sell this for probably $800 a week. But you got to have one illusion—a disappearing Chinese girl or production of something. Both of us can make money on this." Hardeen then used his substantial network of contacts to arrange for Vernon to appear as "Dr. Chung," yet another character, in a two-week run of a variety show at the Majestic Theatre in Paterson, New Jersey. It would be a place, Hardeen suggested, where he could bring prominent bookers to see Vernon perform the act.

As soon as he signed the contract with the theatre, Vernon was presented with two other conflicting opportunities. The first was to venture to Asheville, North Carolina and cut silhouettes at a function run by the Junior League. It had been quite a few years since he had embarked on a silhouette-cutting tour and, although he had experienced great financial success there in the past, his recent experience cutting silhouettes, particularly at the World's Fair, had not been positive. The second offer, although off the beaten track as far as magicians were concerned, seemed to be the more prudent choice. While visiting Sam Margules—they now lived in the same building—Vernon met a construction contractor working on East River Drive. The contractor was looking for workers who could read blueprints. According to the contractor, the job would pay anywhere from $37.50 to $50 per day and added that the job was easy: Vernon would just have to walk around and look busy from 7:30 am to 3:00 pm. Vernon had studied engineering as a young man. Perhaps it was time to take a real job, earn a steady income, and be reunited with his family. He would still, after all, be able to accept evening engagements. Vernon spoke with Jeanne. Her advice: "You have never worked a day in your life. It's time you did some honest work."

Even though Vernon, aged 47, accepted the job, the first real regular job he had ever had in his life, he still did not want to disappoint Hardeen. He had to figure out how he could still honor the contract with the theatre in Paterson, New Jersey.

The answer: Sam Horowitz. Horowitz could be "Dr. Chung."

Vernon was confident he could teach Horowitz the act so that, with the mask and costume, it would be impossible to tell them apart. They were approximately the same build, and Sam was a gifted sleight-of-hand man. The only part he would have difficulty performing, Vernon surmised, was the production of playing cards in his interlocked hands.

Horowitz was a reluctant participant. "What happens," he asked, "if the manager of the theatre finds out that I am not Dai Vernon?" Vernon danced around this issue. The contract, he advised Horowitz, called for "Dr. Chung"; the theatre manager would get "Dr. Chung." Horowitz, a resident of Jersey City, eventually agreed to the ruse. They would, however, have to act quickly, as "Dr. Chung" was scheduled to appear the following Monday.

That weekend Vernon rented a studio on Broadway and put Horowitz through the paces. All was fine until Horowitz learned that he would have to attend a Monday morning rehearsal with the theatre orchestra. Vernon tried to calm his nerves. "Just hand the orchestra leader the music and tell him how it should be played." Vernon was then surprised to learn that, for a man who had once worked in a piano factory, Horowitz knew absolutely nothing about music. He had never rehearsed with an orchestra before and was sure that he would crack under the pressure.

Vernon said, "All right, I'll solve this for you. I'll call up Roy Benson." Benson, a very charismatic and seasoned performer, agreed to accompany Horowitz as his "manager" that Monday morning and put the orchestra through its paces. When it came time for the first performance, Benson told Horowitz, "Don't get nervous, Sam. When your music plays, just walk out, and do your act. You are behind a mask. If you forget what you are doing, stop and hold your fingers up like a Chinaman. You can wait a full 15-20 seconds while you collect your wits. They don't know what you are doing. Just relax and take your time."

Gradually, as the time got nearer for Sam to go on, he said, "I feel weak in the back; I can hardly stand up."

Benson, suggesting that perhaps a drink or two might calm his nerves, scurried across an alley to a nearby watering hole and returned quickly, cocktails in hand. "Drink this," Benson said, "it will brace you up." Horowitz was not a drinker, but accepted Benson's suggestion. He downed the first, and then the second. Benson was afraid Horowitz might still collapse backstage, however, and tendered another suggestion.

"Listen Sam," Benson said, "in case you get out there and break down—you forget the whole act, or your mind goes blank, or you get in a state where you can't do anything—just look at the audience, bow and waddle off stage. I will instantly put the robe and mask on and I'll go out. I won't have any trouble. I won't do the act but I'll fill out the time. I guarantee."

With plan in hand, Horowitz went out and did the act. It was a little long—eighteen minutes instead of eleven—but he did just as Benson had instructed. Whenever he blanked out, he paused, raised his hands in the air as he collected his thoughts and then continued. Eventually, he made it through and was relieved when, afterwards, the manager said simply, "Great act but too long. You did nearly twenty minutes. Cut some of those tricks out." For the second show he did the reverse. He raced through the act in ten minutes. Benson, acting as "manager," gave him notes on pacing.

Benson, a born actor, played his part to perfection. When the theatre manager attempted to move Vernon's rickety table, a little tray that, if struck, would skid off its three-piece bamboo base, Benson intervened. "Don't touch this table! This is an authentic Chinese piece. It comes from the 4th Dynasty, from generation to generation. Be careful with this table." The manager apologized for his carelessness.

By Wednesday, Horowitz had several performances under his belt, and the manager was satisfied with the act. As far he knew and was concerned, Horowitz was "Dr. Chung." The final performance that evening, however, would be the test. Hardeen would be in the audience with prospective booking agents in tow. The plan was

Mercury Falling

simple enough. Vernon would get off work by 3:30 pm and race to the theatre in Paterson. He would hang out in the dressing room prior to the evening's performance, just in case Hardeen stopped by to wish him well. Horowitz would perform the act as scheduled and then, immediately afterward, disrobe so that Vernon could wear the costume. The assumption was that Hardeen would make a beeline for the dressing room immediately afterward to congratulate Vernon and that they needed to keep up the appearance that it was he who had been onstage. Benson was also in on the plan. His job was to keep an eye on the theatre manager and ensure that he did not enter the dressing room while Vernon was greeting Hardeen. The last thing they needed was for the theatre manager, who knew Hardeen, to blow their cover.

Everything went according to plan. Hardeen visited "Dr. Chung" in his dressing room fifteen minutes prior to the performance, and Vernon was there, robe in hand, pretending to make his final preparations for the evening performance. When Hardeen indicated that he was looking forward to watching the show from backstage, Vernon calmly steered him to the main auditorium, stating that he preferred Hardeen and the agents to experience the show from out front. Horowitz entered the dressing room and slipped on the robe and mask as soon as Hardeen was out of earshot. Vernon watched him perform from the wings, genuinely pleased with the performance. Sam, he thought, did it justice. Vernon returned to the dressing room before Horowitz finished the act, took off his jacket, loosened his shirt and tie, and rumpled his hair. Sam darted back to the dressing as soon as he finished, hung up the mask, and handed Vernon the robe. Relieved, Horowitz lit a cigarette. It wasn't a moment too soon. There was a knock at the door.

"Yes?" Vernon asked, knowing perfectly well that it was Hardeen.

"This is Hardeen—Dash."

"Come in, Theo."

Vernon sat in front of the mirror as if he had just finished the act. Horowitz was there too, coolly smoking the cigarette. Benson, by this time, had also joined them.

Hardeen looked at Horowitz with disdain and asked Vernon, "What's he doing here?"

Vernon said, "You know Sam."

Hardeen replied, "Yes, I know him. What's the idea of having these S.A.M. men hanging around? Get this amateur out of here."

Horowitz recognized the not-so-subtle sign and left. Vernon then looked at Benson.

Hardeen added, "Now, Roy Benson, he's all right. He's a help to you. He's a real trouper and should be here, but why do you have that Horowitz?"

Hardeen then started to critique the act. "Vernon," he said, "this act hadn't the same feeling at all as when I saw you at the Hecksher. There is something about the way you walked, the way you acted; it just simply wasn't you."

Vernon countered, "Well, it is not supposed to be me. I'm a Chinaman."

"I know, but there was something. That beautiful entrance you cut out." Horowitz had entered from the wings rather than through the curtain center stage. "What the hell's the matter with you? The agents are here. I told them about this fantastic entrance and you didn't do it. Furthermore, you didn't do the salt trick the way you did it before. I am not even going to talk to the agents tonight. I am very disappointed. We were going to build an illusion for you, but you let me down. You were nervous. I could tell you weren't yourself."

Vernon had once fooled Houdini with a simple card trick. Now, he had fooled his brother, but just barely. Vernon, however, was not one to gloat. He had genuine affection for Hardeen and did not want to disappoint him. He could not afford, given his current financial and marital strife, to turn down a steady income. The subterfuge worked but, as Vernon would soon discover, at a very high cost.

Vernon returned to work on the construction project the following morning. Although he didn't relish being on site at 7:30 a.m. each day, it was only a short walk to work, and he had few responsibilities once there. His manager told him to take it easy. "If they asked where a tool is direct them to the tool shop, or if you see any workman being lazy on the job, go over and give him a little scare."

Vernon, who was often accused of doing "nothing" as he contemplated the inner meaning of card table artifice, found it particularly hard when hired at the construction site to do just that. He couldn't stand the monotony. Two weeks into the job, he saw a man struggling to carry a pail of mercury up over a wooden plank and up

Mercury Falling

a steel girder. He offered to help. He would lend a hand—both hands—as the pail was surprisingly heavy. Vernon was waddling across the plank with the pail when the plank snapped. He tumbled, bouncing off wood and steel like a rag doll, six stories into the icy cold, oily water below.

The cry from above was loud: "Man overboard!"

He bobbed up and down in the water, slipping in and out of consciousness. He could feel his body being sucked slowly towards a large sewer intake but could do little to stop the drift. The workers tossed him a rope with a noose and screamed for him to take hold of it, unaware that both his arms had been broken in the fall, bone protruding through his skin. He managed, however, to slip one leg into the noose and felt the rope tighten around his leg like a tourniquet as his rescuers pulled the line. He fought for breath, flat on his back, his head surfacing momentarily now and then as the rescuers dragged him towards the pier and hoisted him out of the water. The filth from the East River that spewed from his body was soon replaced by the whisky the workers poured down his throat to numb the pain. He heard sirens. Surely this must be a dream.

The ambulance took him directly to Bellevue Hospital which, at that time, might have been more aptly described as Bedlam Hospital, caring mostly for the down and out, the regular inhabitants of that part of the East side of Manhattan.

When he finally awoke in the hospital, the doctor asked him, "Can you hold a pen?"

Vernon did not understand the question.

"We are very concerned about gangrene, Mr. Verner and, I am sorry to say, we may have to amputate your right arm. We require your authorization."

Where in the world, he thought, *is Dr. Daley?*
I need to see Dr. Daley.

End Notes

Seven years. Actually, it's been over seven years since I embarked on this improbable journey. Fortunately, I had company. Many magicians, historians, archivists, and friends helped along the way. They will be thanked elsewhere. Here I will describe the method to my madness and outline the hierarchy of materials assembled for this work. (I tried to slip in as many references in the main text without being obtrusive. Sources of non-attributed excerpts follow these End Notes.)

I came to the project with much background information, some of which I later discovered was erroneous. Still, I have studied and performed magic for over three decades. My formative years were under the tutelage of Ross Bertram, a confidant of Vernon, Dr. Jacob Daley, and Francis Finneran (Carlyle), and a member of that elite peer group known as the *Stars of Magic*. Bertram also imparted his considerable technical knowledge of *Expert at the Card Table* and *Expert Card Technique* to me.

Being born and raised in Canada also helped me considerably. (Vernon was proud of his Canadian heritage, relinquishing it only in the 1940s so as to enable his son, Edward, to attend Annapolis Naval Academy.)

In the past, I have staged theatrical reconstructions of magic from different eras in an effort to explore the evolution of my craft. *The Conjuror* examined stage magic of the "Golden Age" (1875-1925) and *The Conjuror's Suite,* parlor magic—the precursor of twentieth century sleight-of-hand. I had always planned to track the post-*Conjuror* period and soon recognized that Vernon's life was the thread.

End Notes

Fortunately, two projects motivated me to follow the strand.

The documentary film *Dai Vernon—The Spirit of Magic* for History Television's series *The Canadians: Portraits of a Nation* was the first. Patrick Watson, my esteemed friend and mentor as well as occasional writing partner and director, commissioned the program for the network. Another dear friend, Daniel Zuckerbrot, directed the film. I became Associate Producer and Magic Consultant. All of us were pleased with the results; the film was a commercial and critical success, earning awards from a variety of film festivals. It was through this film that I met Edward and Derek Verner and first entertained the idea of writing a biography of their father.

The second impetus was the funding I received from the Canadian Theatre Museum through the auspices of the Department of Canadian Heritage. I was commissioned to write, with Patrick Watson, a theatrical presentation based on Vernon and develop both a physical and online exhibition articulating his contribution to our craft. (The play has been written; the exhibitions are still in development.)

Once committed, I undertook an exhaustive review of the period and its principle characters as recorded in the pages of magic periodicals. Magicians are fortunate to have extensive public, published records of their craft. The preeminent periodical of the twentieth century was *The Sphinx*, a monthly magazine that ran over fifty consecutive years, commencing in 1902. I acquired a complete file of this magazine from the late Sid Lorraine, complete with many of his penciled-in annotations, and reviewed each issue of the entire run. This I vowed to do only once. I photocopied every entry related to any performer, incident, or trick remotely connected to Vernon and inserted these into a master file. I repeated this process with other key periodicals: *The Linking Ring* (1922-1942), *Jinx* (1934-1941) and *Genii* (1936-1942). Even though digital files now exist for many of these magazines, I enjoyed flipping through each issue page by page, soaking up the history, spotting trends, and connecting dots that might not have been noticeable through a computer-generated search of key words or phrases.

As I worked my way through the various magazines, I acquired pertinent interview transcripts, notebooks, ephemera, and audio and visual support material. Fortunately, many magicians are pack-rats, and others had traveled partway down the same road with respect to Vernon, years before me. Two bear special mention:

Dai Vernon: A Biography

Richard Buffum and Frank Csuri.

Richard Buffum was a Los Angeles area newspaper columnist and amateur magician. He interviewed Vernon over the course of several days in October 1965. The reel to reel tapes of these interviews no longer exist, having deteriorated over time. Bruce Cervon, however, graciously gave me the complete unedited transcripts. I then used an O.C.R. program to convert these hundreds of pages into a digital file. Although much of the information appeared in Bruce Cervon's and Keith Burns' biography *Dai Vernon: The Man Who Fooled Houdini* (L & L Publishing, 1992), I had a much better feel for Vernon after reading the words as they came from his lips. Buffum asked Vernon many of the questions that I also had in mind and I appreciate now, more than ever, Buffum's closing words: "Well, I think that's it; I can't think of anything else." He must have been exhausted.

Amateur magician Frank Csuri also deserves considerable credit. With the support of the principle players, Mr. Csuri compiled and edited seven sets (six copies each) of retyped letters and notes, detailing the tricks, techniques, and repertoire of such master magicians as Dai Vernon, Paul Fox, Charles Miller, and Dr. Jacob Daley. These notebooks—all but two of which remain unpublished—contain a wealth of information. I am grateful to those who provided me with copies of this material.

There is little archival footage of Vernon performing or speaking in his prime. He did record, however, many of his thoughts in the latter part of his life. I reviewed these sources. Notable works include *Revelations*, over twenty hours of Vernon material and anecdotes recorded in Newfoundland in September 1982 by Hans Zahn. These videos are available on DVD through L & L Publishing. (I would like to thank Louis Falanga for giving me first the videos and then the DVDs for this project.) *Dai Vernon An Interview 1974*, conducted and produced by Tony DeLap and released in 1993, is another notable work. (I would also like to thank Tony for generously providing me with a copy of these interviews.) Finally, Pat Page released a raucous 1977 recording of his interview with Vernon, which took place in an English pub, on two audio cassettes entitled *From the End of My Cigar*.

The "Vernon Touch" column, written or dictated by Vernon and appearing monthly between September 1968 and May 1990 in *Genii* magazine, was another primary source. Richard Kaufman, editor

End Notes

and co-publisher of this wonderful magazine, kindly gave me a complete digital file of each column to peruse and use.

I culled additional information from the transcripts of interviews (particularly those with Edward Verner, Derek Verner, Jay Marshall, and Jackie Flosso) that Daniel Zuckerbrot and I conducted for the film *Dai Vernon—The Spirit of Magic*. I also drew on the personal recollections of a host of others including the late Sid Lorraine, Stewart James, and Ozzie Malini as well as Dr. Persi Diaconis and Herb Zarrow.

More primary source materials eventually came into my hands. Derek Verner provided hundreds of silhouettes, scores of photographs, the props used in the Harlequin Act, and his father's personal scrapbook of newspaper clippings, ticket stubs, and advertising materials culled from his silhouette cutting tour in the 1920s and 1930s. Edward Verner supplied additional photographs and, most significantly, a copy of his mother's unpublished manuscript, *I Married Mr. Magic or Laughter Is My Only Shield*, written for but not submitted to a magazine for a contest in the 1940s. I am grateful for being the first person to be granted access to read and quote from this work. It is a treasure trove of insight into Vernon and his family. Derek and Ted were with me every step of the way, willing to answer every question, no matter how difficult or personal, to the best of their abilities.

I was also able to draw on hundreds of letters. These letters came from a variety of sources including the Etienne Lorenceau Collection (Vernon-Horowitz Correspondence); the American Museum of Magic (Dr. William Elliott Correspondence, T. Nelson Downs Correspondence, Eddie McLaughlin Correspondence); the David Sandy Collection (Faucett Ross Correspondence, Eddie McLaughlin Correspondence, Charles Miller Correspondence, Paul Fox Correspondence); and Ken Klosterman Collection (John Braun Correspondence). David Sandy also provided me with dozens of letters from Hugh Hood, Charles Maly, Joe Scott, Earl Violet and others within Faucett Ross' circle in the 1930s and 1940s. John Moering provided me with only one letter—a stunner—in Vernon's hand, describing his audition for Billy Rose at the Casino De Paree. Thank you, John. I am also particularly grateful for the receipt of or access to original correspondence in the collections of Edward Verner and Dr. Gene Matsuura. These gentlemen provided me with copies of Vernon's love letters to Jeanne and correspondence with his father and brother, Napier.

The late Elaine Lund, co-founder of the American Museum of Magic, granted me access to the entire contents of each of the thousands of files that her late husband, Robert Lund, assembled. These files included correspondence, promotional brochures, articles, newspaper accounts, obituaries, and other ephemera essential to piecing together the time frame and characters of the players in this biography.

Other original source documentation used in the preparation of this biography include four of Vernon's personal notebooks (three of which, housed in a private collection, remain unpublished), the obituary of Vernon's grandfather (courtesy of the late Billy McComb via Max Maven), the early history of the Verner family (courtesy of Burke's Peerage), Vernon's father's record of employment and wages from Canadian National Archives, the Ashbury College Headmaster's journal of student records (Courtesy of Ashbury College), Vernon's student record from Royal Military College (Courtesy of Royal Military College), his Notice of Conscription (Courtesy of Bill Bowers) and his World War One medical and military file (Canadian National Archives). For those with an interest in S. W. Erdnase, I should mention that I reviewed (by hand) all entries made to the ledger listing applications for copyright submitted to the Canadian Government between the years 1900 and 1907 at the Copyright office in Ottawa and was able to confirm the entries for both the books by Thurston and Ritter that set various chains in motion for Vernon as a youth.

Finally, it should be noted that the late Irving Desfor, a passionate amateur magician and professional photographer, not only captured Vernon and his contemporaries in scores of photographs in the 1930s and beyond but also had the foresight to date and annotate many of them. The Desfor Collection is now part of the American Museum of Magic and was a wonderful and trustworthy resource in preparing this biography.

The secondary sources are set out in the Bibliography.

Sources

Dai Vernon was a superb raconteur. The majority of first person narrative accounts and the dialogue within the main body of this book written in Vernon's voice were drawn from the transcripts of Vernon's responses to questions posed by Richard Buffum in October 1965. Buffum recorded nineteen reels of tape over the course of one week of interviews with Vernon, and had transcripts made of these recordings. Each reel or tape was numbered. All but one of the subsequent transcripts were then numbered or titled, and then paginated. I know of only two copies of the complete unedited transcripts. The original transcripts are housed in the Bruce Cervon Collection. A copy of these transcripts, which Mr. Cervon provided me, resides in my collection. Additional excerpts, presented in Vernon's voice, were taken from "The Vernon Touch," Vernon's monthly column in *Genii* magazine. An additional source of direct quotations was Jeanne Vernon's unpublished manuscript *I Married Mr. Magic or Laughter Is My Only Shield* (circa 1948). This manuscript, really a collection of various unedited drafts, notes and entries, is owned by her son, Edward Verner.

The entries that follow are formatted in the following manner: page number, "subject," source material.

Chapter 1: Page 25, "Meeting In Carnegie Library," Buffum, Tape 1, Oct. 2, 1965, p. 9.

Chapter 2: 37, "Pool hall practice," Buffum, Tape 5, Oct. 2, 1965, p.

20; 43, "Longing For New York," Buffum, Tape 4, Oct. 2, 1965, p. 20; 55, "Now at this performance," Buffum, Tape 2, Oct. 2, 1965, p. 19; 56, "State's bank," Buffum, Tape 3, Oct. 2, 1965, p. 2; 59, "Crow and the canary," Buffum, Tape 5, Oct. 2, 1965, p. 5; 62, "Enrico Curuso on bandstand," Buffum, Tape 5, Oct. 2, 1965, p. 3.

Chapter 3: 64, Erdnase and John Sprong, "The Vernon Touch," August 1970, p. 518; 65, "The public doesn't know," Buffum, Tape 9, Oct. 4, 1965, p. 15; 71, "Bud was a wiry little ex-cow," Jeanne Verner—*I Married Mr. Magic*; 72, "He knew and hated every cop," Jeanne Verner—*I Married Mr. Magic*; 79, "I'll never forget," Letter to Karl Fulves, February 21, 1977; 85, "I'm not a horseplayer," "The Vernon Touch," July 1969, p. 442; 89, "Once inside, an odor receded," Jeanne Verner—*I Married Mr. Magic*; 90, "Sam had the build of a young," Jeanne Verner—*I Married Mr. Magic*; 90, "From the enthusiastic," Jeanne Verner—*I Married Mr. Magic*; 91, "Each succeeding trick," Jeanne Verner—*I Married Mr. Magic*; 91, "Word got out," Buffum, Tape 7, p.16; 92, "When we did sawing," Buffum, Tape 9, Oct. 4, 1965, p. 5; 92, "It was like a gold mine," Buffum, Tape 3, Oct. 2, 1965, p.18; 93, "In those days you could," Buffum, Tape 9, Oct. 4, 1965, p. 6; 94, "One evening while strolling," Jeanne Verner—*I Married Mr. Magic*; 95, "I made $109 and was just," Buffum, Tape 3, Oct. 2, 1965, p. 15. 96, "He maintained that I was," Jeanne Verner – *I Married Mr. Magic*; 98, "The sum total of our assets," Jeanne Verner – *I Married Mr. Magic*.

Chapter 4: 100, "When we were first married," Buffum, Unmarked (c. Reel 13), p. 1; 101, "It's okay kids, don't let it," Jeanne Verner—*I Married Mr. Magic*; 103, "Well, I brought this fellow in," Buffum, Unmarked (c. Reel 13), p. 3; 112, "Judge Gary had a syndicated," Buffum, Reel 12, p. 80; 114, "The fire chief who evidently," "The Vernon Touch," July 1969, p. 442; 121, "We used to stay together," Buffum, Tape 7, p. 1; 124, "My walls were covered," "The Vernon Touch," November 1989, p. 295; 126, "People were always," Buffum, Reel 12, p. 50; 131, "Dick, you have a beautiful," Buffum, Reel 12, p. 54.

Chapter 5: 132, "As a boy, very early in life," Buffum, Tape 8, Oct.

Sources

4, 1965, p. 13; 144, "I understand you have a," Buffum, Tape 7, p. 19; 154, "Vernon, who recently was," News clipping, Vernon Personal Scrapbook.

Chapter 6: 174, "For a time I was going like," Buffum, Tape 7, p. 17; 174, "Well, for instance—I used to," Buffum, Side 15, p. 18; 181, "Faro dealers, they don't talk," Buffum, Tape 10, Oct. 4, 1965, p. 7; 183, "Now, the old thing, this is not," Buffum, Tape 10, Oct. 4, 1965, p. 7; 184, "Many years ago, at Bayridge," Buffum, Tape 8, Oct. 4, 1965, p. 1; 185, "Paul was an absolute," "The Vernon Touch," February 1977, p. 78; 187, "There's a difference between," Buffum, Reel 11, Oct. 4, 1965, p. 36.

Chapter 7: 197, "Miller was a kind of mother's," Buffum, Tape 9, Oct. 4, 1965, p. 25; 202, "When I arrived in this town," Letter to Miller, April 7, 1932 (Lorenceau collection); 203, "The first thing he did was just," Letter to Miller, April 7, 1932 (Lorenceau collection); 215, "Just before Roosevelt was," Buffum, Tape 8, Oct. 4, 1965, p. 2; 222, "Before long I hope to send," Letter to Horowitz, January 3, 1933 (Lorenceau collection).

Chapter 8: 234, "When my wife was a," Buffum, Tape 10, Oct. 4, 1965, p. 12; 241, "So I started to do regular cups," Buffum, Reel 12, p. 62; 243, "As far as I know, I don't say," Buffum, Tape 9, Oct. 4, 1965, p. 37.

Chapter 9: 266, "He was a young man, a very," Buffum, Reel 11, Oct. 4, 1965, p. 42; 273, "As an audience I have been," Jeanne Verner—*I Married Mr. Magic*; 275, "The baby monkey was named," Jeanne Verner—*I Married Mr. Magic*; 286, "He [Limon] went through the," Buffum, Tape 8, Oct. 4, 1965, p. 17; 289, "I was using the gloves," Buffum, Magic Magic Theories of Dai Vernon, p. 34.

Chapter 10: 311, "I had an argument with," Buffum, Reel 12, p. 48; 315, "When this book came out," Buffum, Tape 18, p. 17; 321, I went on right after, Buffum, Tape 18, p. 22; 322, "Sitting off the side I could," Buffum, Tape 9, p. 13.

Bibliography

In addition to the various sources set out in the previous section, I consulted the following magazines, books, pamphlets, and websites. Please note that the magazines are listed according to the bibliographical data recorded in *A Bibliography of Conjuring Periodicals In English: 1791 -1983* by James B. Alfredson and George L. Daily, Jr. and as augmented by *Magic Magazines of the Second Millennium: A Bibliography of English-language Conjuring Periodicals, August 1791- January 2000* by Father Stephen A. Fernandes.

Magazines

Arcane, Jeff Busby, Oakland, California (1980 -1995).

Broadway Magic News, Al Baker and Martin Sunshine, New York City, New York, July No. 1 (July 1933).

Conjurer's Monthly Magazine, Harry Houdini, New York, New York (1906-1908).

Edwards Monthly, W.G. Edwards, Bridgeburg, Ontario, Canada (1909-1910).

Epilogue, Karl Fulves, Teaneck, New Jersey (1967-1975).

Epoptica, Jeff Busby, Oakland, California (1982-1989).

Felsman's Magical Review, Arthur P. Felsman, Chicago, Illinois (1919-1923).

Gen, Harry Stanley, Jack Hughes and Harry Stanley Studio of

Bibliography

Unique Magic, London, England (1946-1970).

Genii, William W. Larsen, Sr., Los Angeles, California (1936-present).

Ibidem, P. Howard Lyons, Toronto, Canada (1955-1979).

Jinx, Theodore Annemann, Waverly, New York (1934-1941).

Journal of Magic History, Steven Tigner, Toledo, Ohio.

L & L Publishing Presents, Louis Falanga, Tahoma, California, L & L Publishing Co. (1988-present).

Linking Ring, Ernest Schieldge and Gene Gordon, Winnipeg, Canada, International Brotherhood of Magicians (1922-present).

Magic, Ellis Stanyon, London, England (1900-1920).

MAGIC – The Independent Magazine For Magicians, Stan Allen, Lakewood, California (1991-present).

Magic Circular, Nevil Maskelyne, et al., London, England, The Magic Circle (1906-present).

Magic Wand, George McKenzie Munro, et al., London, England (1910-1957).

Magic World, Dr. J.E. Pierce, Philadelphia, Pennsylvania (1917-1924).

Magical Bulletin, Louis Christianer and Floyd Thayer, Los Angeles, California (1914-1925).

Magical World-New Series, Max Sterling (J. MacLachlan), London, England (1913-1914).

Magicol – New Series, Walter Gydesen, et al., Milwaukee, Wisconsin, Magic Collectors' Association (1959-present).

Mahatma, George Little, et al., New York, New York (1895-1906).

N.C.A. Digest, Charles Hagen, New York, New York, National Conjurers' Association (1920-1921).

N.C.A. Recorder, Charles Hagen, New York City, National

Conjurers' Association (1913-n.d.).

New Phoenix, Jay Marshall, et al., New York, New York (1954-1965).

Ollapodrida, Alton Sharpe, Beverley Hills, California (1983-2005).

Pallbearer's Review, Karl Fulves, Teaneck, New Jersey (1965-1975).

Paul Fleming Book Reviews, Paul Fleming (P. Gemmill), Swarthmore, Pennsylvania (1942-n.d.).

S.C.M. Levitator, Wilf Parsons, et al., Scarborough, Ontario, Society of Canadian Magicians (1971-1978).

Seven Circles, Walter Gibson, Three Rivers, Michigan, International Magic Circle (1931-1934).

The Sphinx, William J. Hilliar, et al., Chicago, Illinois (1902-1953).

Thaumaturgist, Jeff Busby, Oakland, California (1988-present).

Tops, Percy Abbott, et al., Colon, Michigan, Abbott's Magic Novelty Co. (1936-1957).

Wizard, P.T. Selbit (P. Tibbles), London, England (1905-1910).

Yankee Magic Collector, Ed Hill and Bob Schoof, Harmony, Rhode Island, New England Magic Collectors Association (1983-present).

Books

Abrams, Max, *Annemann: The Life And Times Of A Legend*, L & L Publishing, Tahoma, California, 1992.

Alfredson, James B., *Jean Hugard*, David Meyer Magic Books, Glenwood, Illinois, 1997.

Annemann, Theodore, *Annemann's Exclusive Secrets*, n.d.

Annemann, Theodore, *Exclusive Secrets of Annemann's Conception*, n.d.

Bibliography

Asbury, Herbert, *Sucker's Progress: An Informal History of Gambling in America*, Dodd, Mead and Company, Inc., New York, New York, 1938.

Atmore, Joseph, *Dunninger's Brain Busters*, H & R Magic Books, Humble, Texas, 2001.

Avadon, David, Joe Berg, and Eric Lewis, *The Berg Book*, Stevens Magic Emporium, Wichita, Kansas, 1983.

Baker, Al, *The Secret Ways Of Al Baker*, edited by Todd Karr, The Miracle Factory, Seattle, 2003.

Bamberg, David, *Illusion Show*, David Meyer Magic Books, Glenwood, Illinois, 1991.

Bayer, Constance Pole, *The Great Wizard Of The North – John Henry Anderson*, Ray Goulet's Magic Art Book Co., Watertown, Massachusetts, 1990.

Bertram, Ross, *Bertram On Sleight Of Hand*, Magic Limited, Oakland, California, 1983.

Bertram, Ross, *Magic and Methods of Ross Bertram*, Magic Limited, Oakland, California, 1978.

Blaine, David, *Mysterious Stranger—A Book of Magic*, Villard, New York, New York, 2002.

Blitz, Antonio, *Fifty Years In The Magic Circle*, by subscription.

Bonville, Frank, *The Little Secrets*, Standard Printing Co., Chicago, Illinois, 1904.

Booth, John, *Extending Magic Beyond Credibility*, L & L Publishing, Tahoma, California, 2001.

Braue, Fred, *Fred Braue on False Deals*, edited by Jeff Busby, Jeff Busby Enterprises, Oakland, California, 1978.

Braue, Fred, *The Fred Braue Notebooks*, Edited by Jeff Busby, Jeff Busby Magic, Inc., Oakland, California, 1985.

Britland, David and Osborne Gary "Gazzo" Macce, *Phantoms of the Card Table*, High Stakes Publishing, United Kingdom, 2003.

Brown, Gary, *The Coney Island Fakir—The Magical Life Of Al Flosso*, L & L Publishing, Taloma, California, 1997.

Burns, Eric and James Sanders, *New York—An Illustrated History*, Alfred A. Knopf, New York, New York, 1999.

Burrows, J.F., *Programmes of Magicians*, L. Davenport & Co., London, England, n.d.

Busby, Jeff, *The Secret of the Palmettos*, Jeff Busby Magic Inc., Wallace, Idaho, 1998.

Cannon, Edward S., *Suppose You Lost Your $100,000 Over Night? The True Story of Tex McGuire*, Lee Jacobs Productions, Pomeroy, Ohio, 1978.

Carlton, Paul, *Magician's Handy Book of Cigarette Tricks*, R. J. Reynolds Tobacco Company, Winston-Salem, North Carolina, 1933. (1992 R.J. Reynolds Tobacco Co. Reprint.)

Caveney, Mike, *Carter The Great*, Mike Caveney's Magic Words, Pasadena, California, 1995.

Caveney, Mike and Miesel, *Kellar's Wonders*, Mike Caveney's Magic Words, Pasadena, California, 2003.

Cervon, Bruce and Keith Burns, *He Fooled Houdini: Dai Vernon A Magical Life*, L & L Publishing, Tahoma, California, 1992.

Charvet, David, *The Bill In Lemon Book featuring The Life and Times of Emil Jarrow*, Charvet Studios, Tigard, Oregon, 1990.

Christopher, Maurine Brooks and George P. Hansen, *The Milbourne Christopher Library II—Magic, Mind Reading, Psychic Research, Spiritualism and the Occult 1901-1996*, Mike Caveney's Magic Words, Pasadena, California, 1998.

Christopher, Milbourne, *The Illustrated History of Magic*, Thomas Y. Crowell Company, New York, New York, 1973.

Christopher, Milbourne, *Panorama of Magic*, Dover Publications, Inc., New York, New York, 1962.

Clark, Hyla M., *The World's Greatest Magic*, Crown Publishers, Inc., New York, New York, 1976.

Clarke, Sidney W., *The Annals of Conjuring*, edited by Edwin A. Dawes and Todd Karr, The Miracle Factory, Seattle, Washington, 2001.

Cremer, W.H., *The Secret Out or, One-Thousand Tricks in Drawing-*

Bibliography

Room or White Magic with An Endless Variety of Entertaining Experiments, John Camden Hotten, Piccadilly, U.K, 1859.

Csuri, Frank F. (compiler), *The Magic of Charles Earle Miller*, unpublished.

Csuri, Frank F. (compiler), *The Magic of Faucett W. Ross*, unpublished.

Csuri, Frank F. (compiler), *The Magic of Paul Fox*, unpublished.

Csuri, Frank F. (compiler), *W. R. (Bill) Woodfield's Gambling and Magic Notes*, unpublished.

Daley, Jacob, *Jacob Daley's Notebooks*, compiled and transcribed by Frank Csuri, The Gutenburg Press, 1975.

Davenport, Anne and John Salisse, *St. George's Hall —Behind The Scenes At England's Home of Mystery*, Mike Caveney's Magic Words, Pasadena, California, 2001.

Desfor, Irving, *Great Magicians in Great Moments—A Photo Album by Irving Desfor*, Lee Jacobs Productions, Pomerory, Ohio, 1983.

Dornfeld, Werner, *Trix and Chatter—A Novelty—Serio-Comic-Magic-ologue*, Arthur P. Felsman, Chicago, Illinois, 1921.

Downs, T. Nelson, *The Art of Magic*, edited by John Northern Hilliard, The Downs-Edwards Company, Buffalo, New York, 1909.

Downs, T. Nelson, *Modern Coin Manipulation*, n.d. (circa 1900).

Dunninger, Joseph, *Dunninger's Monument To Magic*, Lyle Stuart, Inc., Secaucus, New Jersey, 1974.

Dunninger, Joseph, *What's On Your Mind?*, The World Publishing Company, Cleveland, Ohio, 1944.

During, Simon, *Modern Enchantments—The Cultural Power of Secular Magic*, Harvard University Press, Cambridge, Massachusetts, 2002.

Elliott, James William, *Elliott's Last Legacy—Secrets of the King of All Kard Kings*, edited by Houdini, Adams Press Print, New York, New York, 1923.

Erdnase, S.W., *Artifice, Subterfuge & Ruse At The Card Table*, S.W. Erdnase, Chicago, Illinois, 1902.

Ewing, Thomas A., *Conjurors and Cornfields: Magic on the Indianapolis Stage*, Thomas A. Ewing, 1999.

Fabian, Ann, *Card Sharps and Bucket Shops—Gambling in Nineteenth-Century America*, Routledge, New York, New York, 1999.

Farelli, Victor, *Nate Leipzig's Card Stab*, Penshaw Press, London, England,1952.

Farelli, Victor, *Thanks to Leipzig!*, George Armstrong, London, England, 1948.

Fechner, Christian, *The Magic of Robert-Houdin "An Artist's Life"*, translated from the French by Stacey Dagron, Editions F.C.F., Boulogne, France, 2002.

Findlay, J.B. and Thomas A. Sawyer, *Professor Hoffmann: A Study*, Thomas A. Sawyer, Tustin, California, 1977.

Fischer, Ottokar, *J. N. Hofzinser's Card Conjuring*, edited by S. H. Sharpe, George Johnson, London, England, 1931.

Fisher, John, *Paul Daniels and the Story of Magic*, Jonathan Cape Ltd., London, England, 1987.

Fitzkee, Dariel, *Rings In Your Fingers*, Magic Limited, Oakland, California, 1977.

Flosso, Jack, *The World's Oldest Magic Shop*, as told to Ben Robinson, Flosso Hornmann Magic, New York, New York, n.d.

Fulves, Karl, *A History Of The Brainwave Principle*, Karl Fulves, Teaneck, New Jersey, 1983.

Ganson, Lewis, *The Dai Vernon Cups And Balls*, n.d.

Ganson, Lewis, *Dai Vernon's Symphony of The Rings*, Harry Stanley, n.d.

Ganson, Lewis, *Dai Vernon's Tribute to Nate Leipzig*, Harry Stanley, London, England, n.d.

Ganson, Lewis, *Dai Vernon's Further Inner Secrets of Card Magic*,

Bibliography

Harry Stanley, London, England, n.d.

Ganson, Lewis, *Dai Vernon's Inner Secrets of Card Magic – Part One*, Harry Stanley, London, England, n.d.

Ganson, Lewis, *Dai Vernon's More Inner Secrets of Card Magic*, Harry Stanley, London, England, n.d.

Ganson, Lewis, *Dai Vernon's Ultimate Secrets of Card Magic*, Harry Stanley, London, England, n.d.

Ganson, Lewis, *Magic With Faucett Ross*, The Supreme Magic Company, Bideford, England, n.d.

Ganson, Lewis, *The Dai Vernon Book of Magic*, Harry Stanley, London, England n.d.

Gaultier, Camille, *Magic Without Apparatus*, Translated by Jean Hugard, Fleming Book Company, Berkeley Heights, New Jersey, 1945.

German, Tony, *A Character of its Own: Ashbury College 1891-1991*, Creative Bound Inc., Carp, Ontario, 1991.

Gilbert, Douglas, *American Vaudeville—Its Life and Times*, Whittlesey House, York, Pennsylvania, 1940.

Goldin, Horace, *It's Fun To Be Fooled*, Stanley Paul & Co. Ltd., London, England, n.d.

Gordon, Mel, *Lazzi—The Comic Routines of the Commedia dell'Arte*, Performing Arts Journal Publications, New York, New York, 1983.

Grantham, Barry, *Playing Commedia—A Training Guide to Commedia Techniques*, Nick Hern Books, London, England, 2000.

Green, Abel and Joe Laurie, *Show Biz from Vaude to Video*, Henry Holt and Company, New York, New York, 1951.

Green, Cliff, *Professional Card Magic*, Louis Tannen, New York, New York, 1961.

Green, Jonathan H., *Gambling Exposed*, T. B. Peterson, Philadelphia, Pennsylvania 1857.

Hofzinser, Johann Nepomuk, *The Magic of Johann Nepomuk*

Hofzinser, compiled by Ottokar Fischer, translated by Richard Hatch, Modern Litho, Omaha, Nebraska, 1985.

Hahne, Nelson C., and Joe Berg, *Here's Magic*, Joe Berg, Chicago, Illinois, 1930.

Hardison, Theo, *Poker*, Hardison Publishing Co., St. Louis, Missouri, 1914. (Gamblers Book Club Reprint)

Hatton, Henry and Adrian Plate, *Magicians' Tricks and How They Are Done*, The Century Co., New York, New York, 1910.

Henning, Doug and Charles Reynolds, *Houdini: His Legend and His Magic*, Warner Books, New York, New York, 1977.

Holden, Max, *Programmes of Famous Magicians*, Max Holden, New York, New York, 1937.

Hilliard, John Northern, *Greater Magic*, Kaufman and Greenberg Edition, Kaufman and Greenberg, Washington, D.C., 1994.

Hilliard, John Northern, *The Lost Notebooks of John Northern Hilliard*, The Genii Corporation, Washington, D.C., 2001.

Hoffmann, Professor, *Modern Magic—A Practical Treatise on the Art of Conjuring*, David McKay Company, Philadelphia, Pennsylvania, n.d.

Houdini, Harry and Patrick Culliton, *Houdini Unlocked*, Kieran Press, 1997.

Hugard, Jean, *Card Manipulations No. 1 and 2*, Max Holden, New York, New York, n.d.

Hugard, Jean (ed), *Encyclopedia of Card Tricks*, Max Holden, New York, New York, 1937.

Hugard, Jean and Frederick Braue, *Expert Card Technique*, Carl Waring Jones, Minneapolis, Minnesota, 1940.

Hugard, Jean, *More Card Manipulations Number IV*, Max Holden, New York, New York, 1941.

Hull, Burling, *Expert Billiard Ball Manipulation—Part 1*, 3rd Edition, American Magic Corporation, New York, New York, 1914.

Hull, Ralph W., *Hull's Mental Discernment*, Ralph Hull,

Bibliography

Crooksville, Ohio, n.d.

Immerso, Michael, *Coney Island—The People's Playground*, Rutgers University Press, New Jersey, 2002.

James, Stewart, *Stewart James In Print: The First Fifty Years*, Jogestja Ltd., Toronto, Canada, 1989.

Jarrett, Guy E., and Jim Steinmeyer, *The Complete Jarrett*, Hahne, Burbank, California, 2001.

Jay, Ricky, *Learned Pigs & Fireproof Women*, Villard Books, New York, New York, 1986.

Jay, Ricky, *Many Mysteries Unraveled—Conjuring Literature in America 1786-1874*, American Antiquarian Society, Worcester, Massachusetts, 1990.

Jayne, Caroline Furness, *String Figures And How To Make Them—A Study of Cat's Cradle in Many Lands*, Dover Publications, New York, New York, 1962. (Reprint of Charles Scribner's Sons 1906 title String Figures.)

Johnson, Karl, *The Magician and the Cardsharp – The Search For American's Greatest Sleight-Of-Hand Artist*, Henry Holt and Company, New York, New York, 2005.

Jordan, Charles T., *Collected Tricks*, edited by Karl Fulves, Karl Fulves, Teaneck, New Jersey, 1975.

Joyal, Martin, *The Joyal Index—V as in Vernon*, Martin Joyal, Canada, 2004.

Judah, Stewart, *The Magic World of Stewart Judah*, edited by John Braun, Magic, Inc. Chicago, Illinois, 1966.

Koval, Frank, *The Illustrated Houdini Research Diary, Part 5: 1916 to 1920 and Part 6: 1920 to 1926*, Frank Koval Publications, Oldham, England, 1994.

Lewis, Eric and Peter Warlock, *P.T. Selbit—Magical Innovator*, Magical Publications, Pasadena, California, 1989.

MacDougall, Michael, *Don't Be A Sucker!*, Malba Books, New York, New York, 1945.

MacDougall, Michael and J.C. Furnas, *Gamblers Don't Gamble*, Garden City Publishing Co., Inc, New York, New York, 1939.

McCosker, Susan, *Representative Performances of Stage Magic, 1650-1900*, New York University PhD., 1982, University Microfilms International, Ann Arbor, Michigan, 1982.

McGuire, Eddie, *The Phantom of the Card Table*, Gambler's Book Club Edition, Las Vegas, Nevada, 1976.

Meyer, David (compiler), *Howard Thurston's Card Tricks—An Illustrated and Descriptive Checklist of Various Editions Covering a 50 Year Period*, David Meyer Magic Books, Glenwood, Illinois, 1991.

Meyer, Joseph, *Protection—The Sealed Book*, (1911) Tenth Edition, Mead Publishing Company, Las Vegas, Nevada, 1999.

Minch, Stephen, *From Witchcraft To Card Tricks—Notes Toward an History of Western Close-up Magic (1584-1897)*, Hermetic Press, Seattle, Washington, 1991.

Minch, Stephen, *Dai Vernon The Lost Inner Secrets—A Tribute By Bruce Cervon and Larry Jennings*, L & L Publishing, Tahoma, California, 1987.

Minch, Stephen, *Dai Vernon More Lost Inner Secrets—A Tribute To A Master*, L & L Publishing, Tahoma, California, 1988.

Minch, Stephen, *Dai Vernon Further Lost Inner Secrets—A Tribute To A Master*, L & L Publishing, Tahoma, California, 1989.

Moulton, H.J., *Houdini's History Of Magic In Boston 1792-1915*, Meyerbooks, Glenwood, Illinois, 1983.

Murray, Joan, *The Last Buffalo—The Work of Frederick Arthur Verner, Painter of the Northwest*, Pagurian Press, Toronto, Canada, 1984.

Neil, C. Lang, *The Modern Conjurer And Drawing-Room Entertainer*, C. Arthur Pearson Ltd., London, England, 1903.

Novak, Bob, *Jack Miller's Famous Linking Ring Routine*, Louis Tannen, New York, New York, 1945.

Parrish, Robert, *An Evening With Charlie Miller*, Ireland Magic Company, Chicago, Illinois, 1961.

Ortiz, Darwin, *The Annotated Erdnase*, A Magical Publication, Pasadena, California, 1991.

Bibliography

Osborne, Tom, *Cups and Balls Magic*, Kanter's Magic Shop, Philadelphia, Pennsylvania, 1937.

Osborne, Tom, *Tom Osborne's 3 to 1 Rope Trick*, Kanter's Magic Shop, Philadelphia, Pennsylvania, 1938.

Pickard, Frank, *28 Card Secrets*, Frank's Magic Shop, Miami, Florida, n.d.

Pietropaolo, Domenico (ed.), *The Science of Buffoonery: Theory and History of the Commedia dell-Arte*, University of Toronto Italian Studies, Doverhouse Editions, Toronto, Canada, 1989.

Price, David, *Magic—A Pictorial History of Conjurers in the Theater*, Cornwall Books, Cranbury, New Jersey, 1985.

Quinn, John Philip, *Gambling And Gambling Devices*, Publication No. 48: Patterson Smith Reprint Series In Criminology, Law Enforcement, And Social Problems, Patterson Smith, Montclair, New Jersey, 1969.

Romano, Charles, *The Art Of Deception—The Affinity Between Conjuring & Art*, Charles J. Romano, South Elgin, Illinois, 1997.

Romano, Charles, *The House of Cards—The Life & Magic of Paul Rosini*, Charles J. Romano, South Elgin, Illinois, 1999.

Roterberg, Augustus, *New Era Card Tricks*, (1897) Magico, New York, New York, 2004.

Sawyer, Thomas A., *S. W. Erdnase: Another View*, Second Edition, Thomas A. Sawyer, Tustin, California, 1997.

Sachs, Edwin T., *Sleight Of Hand*, edited by Paul Fleming, Fleming Book Company, Berkeley Heights, New Jersey, 1946.

Scarne, John, *The Amazing Worlds of John Scarne—A Personal History*, Crown Publishers, Inc., New York, New York, 1956.

Scarne, John, *The Odd Against Me—The Autobiography of John Scarne*, Simon and Schuster, New York, New York, 1966.

Sharpe, S. H. (trans.), *Ponsin On Conjuring*, George Johnson, London, England, 1937.

Slaight, Allan, *The James File*, Hermetic Press, Inc., Toronto, Canada, 2000.

Silverman, Kenneth, *HOUDINI!!! The Career of Ehrich Weiss*, HarperCollins, New York, New York, 1996.

Stanyon, Ellis, *Stanyon's Serial Lessons in Conjuring*, Kaufman and Greenberg, Washington, D.C., 1996.

Steele, W. F., *Paul Rosini's Magical Gems—A Memorial*, Edited by Robert Parrish, W.F. Steele, Chicago, Illinois, 1950.

Steinmeyer, Jim, *The Glorious Deception—The Double Life of William Robinson, aka Chung Ling Soo the "Marvelous Chinese Conjuror,"* Carroll & Graf Publishers, New York, New York, 2005.

Tarbell, Harlan, *Magic*, Tarbell System, Incorporated, Chicago, Illinois, 1926.

Temple, Phil, *Dante—The Devil Himself*, Phil Temple, 1991.

Thurston, Howard, *Howard Thurston's Card Tricks*, L. Upcott Gill, London, England, 1901.

Thurston, Howard, *Howard Thurston's Illusion Show Work Book*, Edited by Maurine Christopher, Additional material by Jim Steinmeyer, Magical Publications, Pasadena, California, 1991.

Thurston, Howard, Jane Thurston Shepard, *Our Magic Life*, A Phil Temple Publication, California, 1989.

Toole Stott, Raymond, *A Bibliography of English Conjuring 1581-1876*, Harpur & Sons of Derby Limited, Bristol, England, 1976.

Vernon, Dai, *Early Vernon—The Magic of Dai Vernon in 1932*, edited by Faucett W. Ross, Ireland Magic Co., Chicago, Illinois, 1962.

Vernon, Dai, *Five Close-Up Problems*, n.d.

Vernon, Dai, *Malini And His Magic*, edited by Lewis Ganson, Harry Stanley, London, England, 1962.

Vernon, Dai and Sam Horowitz, *Mind Control*, n.d.

Vernon, Dai, *Revelations*, A Magical Publication, Pasadena, California, 1984.

Vernon, Dai, *Select Secrets*, Dai Vernon, Brooklyn, New York, 1941.

Bibliography

Vernon, Dai, *Ten Card Problems*, edited by F.W. Ross, n.d.

Walker, Stanley, *The Night Club Era*, The Johns Hopkins University Press, Baltimore, Maryland, 1933.

Waller, Charles, *Magical Nights At The Theatre*, Gerald Taylor, Melbourne, Australia, 1980.

Waters, T.A., *The Encyclopedia of Magic and Magicians*, Facts On File Publications, New York, New York, 1988.

Whaley, Bart and Martin Gardner and Jeff Busby, *The Man Who Was Erdnase*, Jeff Busby Magic, Inc., Oakland, California, 1991.

Whaley, Bart, *Bart Whaley's Encyclopedic Dictionary of Magic 1584-1988*, Volumes One and Two, Jeff Busby Magic, Inc., Oakland, California, 1989.

Whaley, Bart, *Who's Who In Magic—An International Biographical Guide From Past To Present*, Jeff Busby Magic, Inc., Oakland, California, 1990.

Willmarth, Philip Reed, *The Magic of Matt Schulien*, Ireland Magic Co., Chicago, Illinois, 1959.

Websites

I perused a variety of websites for information related to William Gibson, the Art Students League, the Chicago World's Fair, Jascha Heifetz, Louis Vierne, the Rainbow Room, Radio City Music Hall, the New York World's Fair, and the Chinese Lullaby.

Acknowledgements

So many people to thank!

Edward Verner and Derek Verner for permitting me to write the biography of their father, for answering all of my questions, and for providing unfettered access to their family archives.

Bruce Cervon, David Sandy, the late Elaine Lund, and Etienne Lorenceau. I will never forget Mr. Lorenceau's gracious response to my request for information when he said, "I would consider it an honor to be a pebble on the alleyway that is Dai Vernon." The contributions of Bruce Cervon, David Sandy, Elaine Lund, and Etienne Lorcenceau represent not pebbles but the very foundation for this work.

Richard Kaufman, the editor and co-publisher of *Genii*, for the information and support; Karl Johnson for his unwavering enthusiasm, friendship, sharing of resources, wise counsel, and high standards; Mike Caveney for setting the bar for historical publications and inspiring me to try and jump over it; and Jamy Ian Swiss for being a sounding board that resonates so much good information and advice.

To the late Ross Bertram, Jackie Flosso, Stewart James, Sid Lorraine, Ozzie Malini, and Jay Marshall for their candid recollections of Vernon and his contemporaries.

To Derek Verner, Dr. Persi Diaconis, Dr. Gene Matsuura, Patrick Watson, and Herb Zarrow for reviewing the manuscript and offering me their comments and suggestions.

To Stephanie Gray for editing the manuscript and Kevin McGroarty for designing the cover.

Acknowledgements

To the many magicians, historians, archivists, and friends that provided information, research, and suggestions over the many years I was assembling this work including David Alexander, Bill Bowers, John Carney, Michael Claxton, Conjuring Arts Research Center, Dr. Edwin Dawes, George Daily, Julie Eng, Robert Farmer, Suleyman Fattah, John Fisher, Ann Marie Fleming, Mgsr. Vincent Foy, Steve Freeman, Jake Friedman, Karl Fulves, Ray Goulet, John A. Greget, Richard Hatch, Sam Hiyate, Jonathan Howells, Ricky Jay, William Kalush, Bert Kish, Ken Klosterman, Ken Krenzel, Peter Lane, David Lavin, Noah Levine, Pat Lyons, William McComb, William McIlhany, Joshua Malinsky, Margaret Fox Mandel, Ray Massecar, Max Maven, David Meyer, William Miesel, Stephen Minch, John Mintz, Mark Mitton, John Moehring, David Peck, Sal Perrotta, David Pigott, Jeff Pinsky, Dr. Ed Prendergast, Sidney Radner, Charlie Randall, Tom Ransom, Robert Rastorp, Heather Reisman, Charles Reynolds, David Rinaldo, Harry Riser, Jim Riser, Gerald Schwartz, Howie Schwarzman, Allan Slaight, Teller, John Thiessen, John Thompson, Ron Wohl, and Donna and Daniel Zuckerbrot.

To Professor Robert Kennedy and the Pleasant Hill Historical Society for the photograph of Allen Kennedy, and to Jack Wally for permission to include his candid and covert photograph of a Kansas City gambling den.

To Vicky Wilgress, Director of Stewardship and Gift Planning at Ashbury College for allowing me to dig through the archives; to the Canadian Theatre Museum and the Department of Canadian Heritage for funding the development of a physical and online exhibition related to Dai Vernon; to the Ontario Trillium Foundation for supporting Magicana and to the Board of Directors and my colleagues at Magicana for their support and encouragement.

To Gabe Fajuri for his friendship, enthusiasm, and care and consideration as publisher.

To Jan Howlett and, in particular, my sons Courtney and Harrison: I love you both very deeply and hope that even though you are now young men, you still believe in miracles.

All photographs are from the author's collection, except the following: David Sandy Collection: frontispiece; American Museum of Magic: 137, 193, 288-290, 294, 310; Fajuri Collection: 9, 18, 27, 45, 50, 89, 123, 242, 267, 300 (left), 313; Margaret Fox Mandel: 188; Dr. Gene Matsuura Collection: 42, 219; David Meyer Collection: 81, 105; Pleasant Hill Historical Society: 204; Jack Wally: 200.

Index

A
Abbott, Percy, 307
Abbott Magic Manufacturing Company, 307
Academy of the Art of Magic, 268
Ackerman, Eddy, 73
Adams, Bertram 325
Al Baker's First Book, 236
Albee, Edward, 12
Allerton, Bert, 315, 326
An Ace Trick for the Expert, 256, 287
Annemann, Ted (Theodore Squires Annemann), 134, 148, 161, 162, 169, 169, 191, 245, 266, 273, 292, 293, 295, 304, 315
Art of Magic, The, 32, 227, 246, 262, 282, 287
Art Students League, 43, 44, 58
Ashbury College, 34, 35, 39, 40, 60

B
Baker, Al, 130, 132, 134, 148, 150, 157, 158, 159, 164-167, 171, 179, 183, 184, 186, 236, 250, 262, 268, 274, 292, 294, 295, 299, 321, 325
Baker, Walter, 120
Bamberg, David, 266, 267, 268, 270, 283, 286, 296, 298, 312, 319
Beck, Martin, 12, 32
Benson, Roy, 317, 318, 329, 330-332
Berg, Joe, 168
Billboard, The. 76
Blackstone, Harry, 208, 257
Bland's Magical & Conjuring Repository, 7
Blitz, Signor, 5
Bowyer, Tom, 190, 315, 326
Brain Wave Deck, The, 293, 304, 310, 319, 321
Braue, Fritz (Fred), 287, 314, 315, 316
Booth, J.R., 17
Booth, John 263, 309, 322
Braun, John 78
Brown, Edward (Vernon pseudonym), 115
Brown, Judson, 151, 192, 253
Bridges, Milton, 223
Burgess, Clinton, 127

Index

Butterfly and Fan, 283

C

Cagliostro, 21
Campbell, Loring, 214
Canadian National Exhibition, 279
Cardini (Richard Pitchford), 126, 127, 128, 129, 131, 132, 148, 149, 157, 158, 159, 165, 170, 171, 175, 182, 184, 186, 188, 189, 231, 232, 238-240, 242, 243, 251, 255, 258, 259, 261, 262, 299, 306, 310, 311, 312, 324, 326
Cardini, Richard, 132
Cardini, Swan, 128, 129
Card Manipulations No. 2, 246
Card Stars Of The USA, 295
Cards Up The Sleeve (trick), 108, 115
Carillon de Westminster, 280, 319
Carlton, Paul (magician), 44, 225
Carnegie, Andrew, 112
Carrer, Charles, 306
Carter, Charles, 234
Caruso, Enrico, 62
Casey, Pat (theater manager), 115
Casino de Paree 237, 238, 268, 293
Cat's Cradle, 13
Center deal (sleight) 196, 203, 206, 212, 215, 217, 222, 224, 227
Cervantes Theatre, 266
Chang, 270, 286, 307, 319
Chapender, Martin, 286
Chaplin, Charlie, 217, 322
Chicago World's Fair, 231, 232, 234-238
Ching Ling Foo, 47
Christ, Henry, 51, 170

Chung Ling Soo, 279
Clark, Keith, 232
Clyde W. Powers (magic shop), 44, 45
Cole, Judson, 119, 130, 131
Combined Treatise on Advantage Card Playing and Draw Poker, 22
Comedia Dell'Arte, 278
Compeer (monkey), 275, 276, 286
Coney Island, 51, 52, 54-56, 58, 60, 72, 74, 75, 78, 85, 87-91, 95, 100, 101, 103, 108, 110, 119, 235, 245, 264, 305
Conus (magician), 308
Crawford, T.J., 223
Crow and the Canary (fable), 59
Cups and Balls Magic, 278

D

Dai Yan, 318, 319, 323, 325, 328
Daley, Dr. Jacob, 249, 250, 291, 309, 310, 333
Dallas Davenport (Dai Vernon), 91
Dante (Harry A. Jansen), 312, 313
Davis, John (magic dealer), 97
Davenport Brothers, 47
Davenports (magic shop), 14
de Kolta, Bautier, 240
Dempsey, Jack, 288
Desfor, Irving, 257
Deviltry, 278
De Vega, 278
Dickens, Charles, 7
Dime and Penny (trick), 177
Dr. Chung, 2, 328, 329, 330, 331
Donahue (waiter), 55, 57
Downs, T. Nelson, 19, 32, 41, 115, 130, 134, 135-139, 146, 147, 156, 157, 158, 159, 166, 167,

168, 172, 175, 177, 188-191, 193, 196, 207-209, 211, 212-215, 217, 218, 221, 223-233, 243, 308, 314, 316
Downs-Edwards Company, 32
Dreamland Circus Sideshow, 52, 107
Dunninger, Joseph, 49, 110, 147, 240, 245, 292, 293, 316
Duo Flight (trick), 217
Durbin, W.W. 135, 146, 225, 226
Durcrot, Frank 103, 148, 304
Duval, Ade, 257

E

East Indian Needle Trick, 240
Eastman, George, 113
Egg Bag (trick), 177
Egyptian Hall, 26, 286
Elliott, Dr. James William, 11, 47, 49, 50, 75, 116, 256
Elliott's Last Legacy, 107, 127
Encyclopedia of Card Tricks, The, 274
England, Harlan "Bud", 71
Erdnase, S.W., 23, 32, 33, 49, 63-65, 67-69, 79, 84, 125, 233, 255, 303, 315
Erskine, Helen E. (Mrs. James Verner), 9, 20, 21
Ervin, Dr. E.G., 190
Evans, H.C. (magic supply house), 168
Exclusive Secrets of Annemann's Conception, 169, 311
Expert At The Card Table, The, 23, 47, 49, 53, 64, 67, 84, 108, 180, 186, 255, 298, 303, 312
Expert Billiard Ball Manipulation, 278

Expert Card Technique, 314-317, 321

F

Faro (game), 56, 57, 151, 152
Faro box 201, 206, 302
Fifty Years In The Magic Circle, 5
Finley, Arthur, 76-78, 97, 102, 103, 110, 114, 116, 120-124, 130, 132, 144, 157, 158, 164-166, 184, 211, 212, 217, 221, 243, 308, 311
Finneran, Francis (Francis Carlyle), 291, 292, 309
Fish, Eddie (second dealer), 171
Fish Bowl Production (trick), 177
Fitzkee, Dariel, 320
Five Close-Up Problems, 223, 233, 287
Florsheim, Sam, 105, 106
Flosso, Al (Albert Levinson), 52, 107, 305, 306, 319
Fools of Fortune, 36
Forbidden City Café, 323
Ford's Theatre, 32
Fox Sisters, 47
Fox, Paul (Paul Fuchs) 183-187, 189, 213-216, 231, 232, 243, 245, 262, 268, 270, 277, 281-283, 285, 289, 293, 295, 299, 311
Frederick J. Drake & Co., 64
Furst, Arnold, 311

G

Gamble, Keller, 35
Gamblers Don't Gamble, 302-304
Gary, Judge, 112
Gavin, Henry. *See* Arthur Finley
Genii, 272

Index

Gibson, Charles Dana, 58
Goldie (carny), 53, 54
Goldin, Horace, 87, 89, 91, 94, 95, 264
Gordien, Henry, 282
Gray, Larry, 55, 119, 122, 125, 127, 128, 129, 130, 214, 292, 305
Great Northern Hotel, 79
Greater Magic, 286, 294-296, 299, 304, 314
Green, Cliff, 38, 46, 51, 315, 318
Guest, Leslie, 148, 299

H

Hahne, Nelson, 168
Hamley, W. & F., 7
Hardeen (Theodore Weiss), 306, 328-332
Hardin, Henry, 144
Harlequin Act, (Chapter 9)
Hart, Bill, 52
Heckscher Theatre 296, 299, 317, 328
Hellz'a'poppin' (show), 306, 328
Here's Magic, 168
Herrmann, Alexander 10, 11, 132, 256, 258, 279
Herrmann, Leon, 17
Hilliar, William J., 9, 19, 279, 287
Hilliard, John Northern, 32, 227
Hobb, Carlton 322, 323
Hoffmann, Professor, 7, 32, 39
Hofzinser, Johann Nepomuk, 6, 118, 187, 215
Holden, Max 103, 116, 118, 122, 123, 129, 130, 132, 133-137, 145, 146, 147, 149-151, 155, 157-159, 166-169, 175, 179, 182, 191, 218, 235, 246, 266, 285, 286, 293, 299, 306, 310, 311, 317-320, 322, 326
Horn, Chet, 216
Horowitz, Sam (S. Leo Horowitz), 51, 102, 132, 135-139, 146, 147, 155-159, 161, 162, 164, 165, 167-170, 173, 175, 177, 178, 182-185, 187, 190-193, 205, 212, 217, 221, 223, 224, 227, 268, 270, 294, 295, 311, 313, 314, 323-325, 327, 329-332
Hotel Adelphia, 284
Hotel McAlpin, 107
Houdini, Beatrice (Bess), 80, 83, 84, 85, 140
Houdini, Harry, 12, 32, 47, 64, 76, 79, 80, 81, 82, 83, 84, 85, 91, 106, 107, 116, 117, 124, 125, 129, 130, 234, 240, 243, 255, 256, 258, 259, 301, 302, 306, 332
Howard Thurston's Card Tricks, 17
Hugard, Jean, 75, 273, 287, 293, 295, 296, 311, 314-316
Hull, Burling, 278
Hull, R.W., 169, 221, 295
Hull's Mental Discernment, 169, 221
Hunt's (gambling supply house), 70
Hunter, G.W., 262

I

Illusion Show, 268
Impey, Eric F., 149, 150
Innes Department Store, 201, 206
International Brotherhood of Magicians 106, 136, 208, 225, 235, 282, 299, 307

361

International Magic Circle, 208
It's Fun To Be Fooled... But It's
    More Fun To Know, 225, 264

J
James, Stewart, 307
Jarrow, Emil, 32, 282
Jinx, The, 245, 266, 273, 292, 293,
    304, 320
Jones, Carl, 287
Jordan, Charles, 138, 139, 144, 196,
    227
Judah, Stewart, 78, 124, 169, 283,
    295

K
Kansas City Card Company, 198,
    199, 201
Kanter's Magic Shop, 278, 281
Karloff, Boris, 322
Keane, J. Warren, 27-28, 32, 48, 51,
    142, 152, 223, 269, 281, 301
Keating, Fred, 188, 240, 244, 257,
    259, 286, 317, 318, 322
Keefer, Allan, 39, 40
Keefer, Tom, 39
Keith, B.F., 12, 109
Kellar, Harry, 11, 31, 32, 47, 48, 132,
    186, 256, 258, 261
Kennedy, Allen, 201, 203-207, 224,
    303
King, Frances Rockefeller, 108-114,
    118, 132, 133, 140, 147, 239,
    240, 247, 251, 273, 274, 297
Kit Kat Club, 257
Krieger, Pop, 243
Kreisler, Fritz, 111, 186
Kuma (magician), 306

L
Lane, Frank, 217
Langworthy, "Red," 198, 199, 201
Larsen, Milton, 324
Larsen, William, 134, 314, 324, 325
Larson, Charles, 326
Later Magic, 294
Lazia, John, 198, 199
Leddy, Mark, 296-298
Lee, Garnet, 101
Lee, Old Man, 201
Leipzig, Nate, 32, 50, 61, 124, 130-
    132, 155, 170, 211, 227, 246,
    250, 255, 257, 262, 268, 295,
    299, 306, 308, 314, 318
LePaul, Paul, 232, 311
Levitation of Princess Karnac, 26,
    47
Lewis, Mary Carlile (wife of
    Arthur Finley), 78
Limon, José, 287, 288
Linking Ring, The (periodical), 235,
    263, 266, 285, 290, 293, 299,
    310, 315, 317, 318, 322, 326,
    327
Linking Rings (trick), 269, 279, 280,
    282, 290, 318, 323
Little Blue Bookshop, 99, 102, 107,
    108, 274
Little Church Around the Corner,
    98
Lorraine, Sid, 190
Louie, Gooey, 101, 274
Lydon, John, 301, 326
Lyman, Ellsworth, 144, 145, 147,
    154, 156, 162, 176, 183

M
MacDougall, Michael, 302-304

Index

Mackenzie, William Lyon, 6
Madison Hotel, 247, 249-251, 268, 293, 302, 323
Magicians Club of New York, 51
Magicians' Tricks And How They Are Done, 283
Mahatma, 11
Majestic Theatre, 2, 328
Malini, Max, 32, 39, 103, 104, 105, 106, 112, 113, 138, 147, 161, 164, 176, 177, 178, 182, 189, 237, 242, 244, 250, 253, 254, 255, 262, 277, 279
Maly, Charles 167, 170, 171, 190, 191
"Man from Beyond, The" (film), 80
Margules, Sam, 3, 51-53, 72, 73, 79, 80, 81, 85, 87-95, 107, 245, 264, 270, 291, 293, 294, 296, 310, 316, 321, 322, 326, 328
Martinka & Co., 8, 43, 44, 49, 75, 304
Maskelyne, John Nevil, 26, 165
Masqué, l'Homme, 21
McCaffrey, William H., 295
McGill University, 39, 44, 60, 130
McGuire, Eddie, 116, 117, 134, 135, 136, 137, 138, 139, 146, 147, 156, 157, 158, 161, 164, 165, 166, 167, 171, 175, 176, 190, 193, 205, 207, 224, 316
McLaughlin, Edward, 117, 130, 134, 135, 136, 137, 138, 139, 146, 147, 156, 158, 166, 167, 170, 171, 175, 188, 189, 193, 196, 207-209, 211, 213, 218, 221, 224, 227-230, 232, 233, 269, 284, 292, 326
McMillen, Jack, 315

Mental Choice, 304
Merlin, Jack, 315
Miaco, 286
Miller, Charles Earle, 134, 152, 190, 192, 196-200, 203, 206, 212, 217, 252-254, 262, 273, 283, 315
Miller, Moi-Yo, 313
Modern Coin Manipulation, 19
Modern Conjuror, The, 22
Modern Magic, 8, 32, 39, 294
Moore, E.J., 325
More Card Manipulations Number IV, 326
More Magic, 294
Morey, Bert, 107, 116, 138, 234
Morosco Theatre, 312
Mulholland, John, 225, 266, 270, 296, 301, 307, 312, 313, 324, 327

N

National Conjurors' Association, 75
New Era Card Tricks, 16
New York World's Fair, 305
Nightingale (gambler), 33
Nouvelle Magie Blanche Devoilee, 308

O

Office Act, 115
Original Card Mysteries, 149
Orloff, Count, 274
Osborne, Tom, 278, 281
Otto, George, 115
Out of Sight, Out of Mind (trick), 136

P

Palace Theatre, 109, 117, 182

Palmer House, 255
Peck, Dr. Gordon Caldwell, 104
Perry (silhouette artist), 56, 57
Phenix Publishing Company, 311
Phyfe, Hal, 300
Pike's Peak, 185
Ping Pong (gambler), 69, 70, 172, 173, 175, 182
Ping Pong shift (sleight), 175, 182
Plate, Adrian, 50
Ponsin, Jean-Nicholas, 308
Powers, Clyde, 44, 45, 175
Prince of Wales, 110, 267
Punch (gambling device), 165, 172

Q
Quinn, John Phillip, 36

R
R.J. Reynolds Tobacco Company, 225, 264
Radio City Music Hall, 297, 299, 302
Rainbow Room, 285-289, 302, 304, 322
Ramsay, John, 286
Rapee, Enro, 297, 298
Reinhart, Robert, 258, 265, 307
Rideau Club, 33, 36, 103
Riffle cull, 68, 69
Ritter, F.R., 22
Robert-Houdin, Jean Eugène, 6
Rondo Capriccioso in A minor, Opus 28, 284
Rose, Billy, 237-241, 247, 284, 285
Roosevelt, Franklin Delano, 215, 216
Rosini, Paul (Paul Vucic), 148, 254, 266, 295, 310, 315

Ross, Faucett, 134, 135, 136, 137, 138, 139, 146, 147, 156, 166, 167, 170, 171, 175, 188-193, 196, 207-215, 218, 220-225, 227-229, 231-233, 238, 243, 244, 246, 251-255, 262, 269, 270, 272, 277, 279, 282, 284, 287, 289, 292, 293, 299, 311, 314, 326
Roterberg's (magic shop), 14, 64
Royal Military College, 3, 39, 40, 41, 44, 60
Russell Hotel, 37, 38
Russell Theatre, 17

S
S.S. Adams Company, 248
Sachs, Edwin, 12
Saint George's Hall, 87
Salon Hofzinser, 7
Salt Pour, 310, 321, 323
Sawing A Woman In Half, 87, 89, 90, 94
Scarne, John, 103, 155, 158, 159, 165, 166, 175, 295
Schwab, Charles M., 111
Scott, Walter, 139, 156, 157, 158, 159, 161, 163-167, 170, 171, 178, 190, 192, 224
Secret Out, The, 16
Secrets (booklet), 97, 170, 171, 179, 180
Selbit, P.T. (Percy Thomas Tibbles), 87
Select Secrets, 314, 317, 320, 321
Shaw, Allan, 36, 130
Shelby tubing, 281
Sherman, Robert (magic dealer), 97, 126

Index

Shock (gambler), 171, 172, 173, 182, 194, 199
Shockley, Marjorie, 221, 223, 236
Silent Mora (William Louis McCord), 39, 124
Slip the Jit Harry, 101
Slow Motion Card Vanish, 233
Snyder, John, 321
Society of American Magicians, 78, 79, 106, 107, 149, 276, 296, 299, 306, 307, 317, 324
Soper, Warren, 15
Spencer, Garrick, 244, 261, 262, 266, 268, 277-280, 282, 284, 286, 288, 291, 304, 308, 321, 322
Sphinx, The (periodical), 48, 51, 75, 76, 80, 103, 118, 120, 122, 124, 133-135, 147, 148, 150, 151, 155, 156, 159, 167-169, 182, 191, 193, 222, 223, 225, 244, 256, 266, 278, 279, 287, 298, 301, 304, 305, 307, 309, 311-313, 315, 317, 321, 324, 325, 327
Sprong, John C., 64, 195, 217
Stanyon, Ellis, 16
Stanyon's Serial Lessons in Conjuring, 286
Sterling Magic Co., 321
Stevens, Dad, 65, 66, 69, 70, 162, 163, 164, 174, 194, 206, 303
Stock, George W., 78
Strobridge Lithography Co., 25
Superman (variety performer), 93
Swann, Russell, 286

T

Tarbell, Harlan, 120, 128, 186, 283, 287
Tarbell Course in Magic, 135, 186, 283
Tenkai (Tenkai Ishida), 318
Ten Card Problems, 233, 237, 273, 287, 311
Texas Guinan (nightclub), 250
Thayer, Floyd, 278
Thirds (dealing), 68
Three to One Rope Trick, 281, 323
Thurston, Howard, 12, 31, 32, 36, 47, 48, 49, 83, 230, 240, 255, 256, 258, 259, 261, 266, 287
Toby, Frank, 235, 236, 302
Trinity College, 5
Twenty Dollar Manuscript, 219

U

Union League Club, 112, 113
Usher, Harry, 73, 74

V

Valadon, Paul, 25, 31, 32
Van Hoven, Frank, 117
Variety, 237, 238, 265, 287, 288
Verner, Arthur Cole, 4, 5, 6, 8, 9
Verner, Charles Napier, 19, 42, 43, 60, 62, 63, 64, 277
Verner, David Derek, 214, 215, 275
Verner, Edward "Ted", 140, 318, 319
Verner, Frederick, 3
Verner, James, 3, 4, 9, 10, 13, 16, 19, 20, 22, 33, 34, 37, 39, 40, 43, 51, 60, 63
Verner, Jeanne (Eugenia Hayes), 87, 88, 89, 90, 91, 94, 95, 96, 97, 9899, 100, 101, 102, 107, 108, 109, 113, 119, 120, 129, 132, 140, 141, 173, 174, 178-

180, 183, 189, 206, 207, 209-213, 215, 224, 233, 235-237, 250-252, 257, 263, 266, 269, 271, 274, 275, 276, 279, 281, 284, 285, 291, 292, 296, 297, 307, 321, 322, 324, 326, 329

Verner, William, 4

Vernon, Dai (David Frederick Wingfield Verner),
    Arrested in Chicago, 70
    Birth, 10
    Bridge accident, 1, 2,
    Buys *The Expert at the Card Table*, 22-24
    At Coney Island, 51-54, 60, 72-75, 91
    Dr. Chung act, 2
    Engaged by Ms. King, 108-115
    Family history, (Chapter 1)
    First interest in magic, 3, 4, 12-15
    Fools Dr. Elliott, 49
    Fools Houdini, (Chapter 3)
    Harlequin Act, (Chapter 9)
    In Cuba, 92-94
    Joins military, 62
    Long sleep stunt, 209-211
    Marriage, 98
    Meets J. Warren Keane, 27
    Meets Jeanne (wife), 90
    Meets Malini, 104
    Move to New York, 43
    Schooling, (Chapter 2)
    Silhouette cutting, 55, 57, 58, 62, 92, 95-97, 99

Vernerville, 6

Villasenor, Amador, 193, 194

Violet, Earle, 190

Volstead Act, 118

W

Waiters' Club, 66, 69, 157

Welworth Magic Co., 191

White, Frances, 111

Whitley, Jim (Faro dealer), 179-181, 201

Wilson, Dr. A. M., 80

Wintertime In China, 283

Z

Zancig, Julius, 148, 266

Zingone, Louis, 155, 159, 164, 167, 238, 315